Humo[r ...]

An [An]thol[ogy]

Humor in America
An Anthology

Edited by Enid Veron
University of Virginia

Harcourt Brace Jovanovich, Inc.
New York • *Chicago* • *San Francisco* • *Atlanta*

ISBN: 0-15-540475-X

Library of Congress Catalog Card Number: 76-1416

Printed in the United States of America

Cover drawing by Chas. Addams; © 1950
The New Yorker Magazine, Inc.

For permission to use the selections reprinted in this book, the editor is grateful
to the following publishers and copyright holders:

THE BOBBS-MERRILL COMPANY, INC., for "The American Sense of Humor" from *Company
Manners*, copyright 1951, 1953, 1954 by Louis Kronenberger, reprinted by permission of
the publisher, the Bobbs-Merrill Company, Inc.

THE DIAL PRESS for "Anon Visits the Home of Heroes," excerpted from *Anon and Various
Time Machine Poems* by Dick Allen, copyright © 1971 by Dick Allen, reprinted by
permission of Delacorte Press. For "Tom Edison's Shaggy Dog," copyright © 1953 by Kurt
Vonnegut, Jr., which originally appeared in *Collier's*, and is reprinted from *Welcome to
the Monkey House* by Kurt Vonnegut, Jr., with the permission of Delacorte Press/
Seymour Lawrence.

DODD, MEAD & COMPANY, INC., for "The Ferrari in the Bedroom," reprinted by permission of
Dodd, Mead & Company, Inc., from *The Ferrari in the Bedroom* by Jean Shepherd,
copyright © 1970, 1971, 1972 by Jean Shepherd.

DOUBLEDAY & COMPANY, INC., for "archy and mehitabel," from *archy and mehitabel* by Don
Marquis, copyright 1927 by Doubleday & Company, Inc., reprinted by permission of the
publisher. For "TV Situation Comedies" from *TV: The Most Popular Art*, copyright ©
1974 by Horace Newcomb, reprinted by permission of Doubleday & Company, Inc.

FARRAR, STRAUS & GIROUX, INC., for "The Policemen's Ball," reprinted with the permission of
Farrar, Straus & Giroux, Inc., from *City Life* by Donald Barthelme, copyright © 1968, 1970
by Donald Barthelme; "The Policemen's Ball" originally appeared in *The New Yorker*. For
"The Jewbird" from *Idiots First* by Bernard Malamud, copyright © 1963 by Bernard
Malamud.

GROSSET & DUNLAP, INC., for "Comedy's Greatest Era" from *Agee on Film* by James Agee,
copyright © 1946, 1948, 1958 by The James Agee Trust, used by permission of Grosset &
Dunlap, Inc.

*Acknowledgments continue on pages 349–350, which are regarded as part of the
copyright page.*

For my father

"How many two-cent stamps in a dozen?"

Preface

Humor in America is a unique anthology of some of the most meaningful, as well as some of the most mirthful, American writing. It is intended to serve not only as a text in its own right or a refreshing "change-of-pace" reader, but also as an anthology adaptable to the teaching of rhetoric and composition. All the selections, in addition to being included in the thematic table of contents, are listed according to rhetorical mode at the beginning of the book. The suggested topics for themes at the end of the book and the critical commentary in the concluding section of the text invite students to write their own analyses and ventures in American humor in its many forms.

Humor has played, and continues to play, a crucial role in our literature; as critic Constance Rourke points out, American humor "has moved into literature not merely as an occasional touch, but as a force determining large patterns and intentions." These large patterns and intentions are precisely what this text explores. The word "humor" has been used here in its broadest sense, to include many comic styles; for the variety of our humor reflects the variety of our national experience. Thus, the first group of selections in the book constitutes an overview of contemporary comedy that attempts to answer two questions: What does it mean to be an American today? What strains of humor do Americans use to deal with that reality?

The next three parts trace the growth of our comic heritage by focusing on its three basic types of symbolic characters—the wise fool, the storyteller, and the little soul. The wise fool, or cracker-box philosopher, has continued to engage America's comic imagination since Ben Franklin first gave us Poor Richard. It is as storyteller, though, that the American humorist is probably best known. In fact, the master yarn-spinner of them all, Mark Twain, believed that the humorous tale was a uniquely American form. Twain's own fictions drew brilliantly on two native sources—the conventions of the frontier anecdote and the style of the so-called literary comedian—until, with him, American humor reached its first full flowering. When it blossomed again, as in the work of James Thurber, we see that the emphasis has been vastly altered.

Rural settings have become urban; obstacles petty to the point of embarrassment seem insurmountable; most important, the narrator has put on a distinctly twentieth-century guise and is incredibly diminished. The day of the little soul has arrived.

In Part 5 a variety of critical commentary is presented, with the aim of indicating the primary impulses in our humor, rather than offering pat definitions. Louis D. Rubin, Jr., and Louis Kronenberger probe the heart of American humor. The other essayists deal with some of its highlights: Constance Rourke, the tall tale; James Agee, the great silent-film comedians; Arthur Asa Berger, the comic strip; Horace Newcomb, TV situation comedy; and Ihab Hassan, the dark comedy that dominates modern fiction.

The aim throughout is to encourage students to think perceptively and imaginatively. The introductions to the five parts, the headnotes and questions accompanying the individual selections, and the Suggested Topics for Writing and Discussion at the back of the book can be starting points for class analysis or for independent research projects. The Glossary of Critical Terms and the Brief History of Humor in American Literature provide background information. Reading lists, a filmography, and a list of comedy on records have also been appended, as guides to both instructor and student in supplementing the readings in the text. Finally, a few examples of cartoon and vaudeville humor have been included, to point the way toward related areas of study. The anthology, in short, has been carefully constructed to foster an interdisciplinary approach to its subject.

Above all, *Humor in America* is meant to be savored and enjoyed. The selections are genuinely fun to read and have been chosen to demonstrate humor's primary role in the American literary tradition. Many of the authors have had the most powerful imaginations in American literature; others, less well known, are here because they have succeeded in capturing something of the American wit and joy in living. As life grows more complex and bewildering, as our country spins from one crisis to another and the voices of our doomsday prophets grow louder, students urgently need a firm grasp of the comic perspective that is so essential a part of our national heritage. I hope this text will satisfy that need.

It is, of course, a pleasure to write acknowledgments. First and foremost, I wish to thank William A. Pullin, Senior Editor, Harcourt Brace Jovanovich, whose generous encouragement and appreciation of keen wit made the book possible. To the students in my American humor classes at the University of Bridgeport and the University of Virginia, who shared with me their love of learning and of laughter, I owe a special debt, for together we formulated the contents and format of the text. The ground-breaking research of scholars like Constance Rourke, Walter Blair, Norris W. Yates, Hamlin Hill, and many others has of course contributed very greatly. I am grateful also to Professors David Thorburn of Yale University, M. Thomas Inge of Virginia Commonwealth University, John R. Clark of the University of South Florida, and James F. Light of Herbert H. Lehman College, who made helpful suggestions during the preparation of the manuscript. My editors, Claire T. Rubin and Catherine Fauver, have provided invaluable help throughout. Finally, thanks are due to Lori and Dick Allen, who not only advised me during the writing of the book but provided me with continual inspiration and encouragement.

Enid Veron

Contents

part 3 The Storyteller 107

part 4 The Little Soul 201

part 5 Theories and Criticism 251

Rhetorical Table of Contents

Humor in America

An Anthology

Introduction

In one of the best American tall tales, T. B. Thorpe's "The Big Bear of Arkansas," the boastful hunter Jim Doggett tells of his attempts to capture a mysterious huge bear. When the animal finally came within shooting range—after emerging miraculously from the woods—the hapless Jim attempted to give chase, only to be tripped up, as he says, by his "inexpressibles." The hero, victim of an old joke, had been caught with his britches down. No matter; in the midst of the confusion the bear simply keeled over and died.

The scene is classically American, a splendid realization of the tension that informs our national life and pervades our humor. Jim's experience makes clear that the hero, "swelled up considerable" by his previous success as a hunter, is human, like the rest of us, quite physical, quite fallible after all. For comedy is the great democratic leveler. It punctures pretensions, pokes at the privileged, undercuts the powerful. When it has done its job, everyone—the educated as well as the illiterate, the rich and the poor, the backwoodsman and the city dweller—is seen to be pretty much the same. As the American comic sense has intuited, humor can diminish more than people. It reduces entire political and social systems and makes vast stretches of landscape seem smaller. It domesticates the unknown and, often, the unknowable, beating down what we most fear cannot be beaten. The demonic threat represented by Jim's bear is in great measure defeated by buffoonery.

Jim Doggett's encounter with the bear, marked by visual and verbal pratfalls, is a set piece of low comedy, but at the same time it is animated by the spirit of high comedy. If low comedy deflates, high comedy exalts, creating large comic heroes, who bounce back from calamities that would crush their tragic counterparts. American history is the story of such people, affirming life, suggesting possibilities of rebirth, renewal, harmony. Critics have often written that the American temper fails to nourish tragic heroes. Melville's Captain Ahab, in his relentless pursuit of the embodiment of evil—the white whale Moby Dick—is an exception; our literature has few Ahabs valorously but vainly defying the forces of the universe. We have many Ishmaels, ordinary seamen who serve as lackeys to the Captain. When Ahab, like all tragic heroes, is humbled and vanquished, destroyed with his ship by the whale, the comic Ishmael,

1

clinging ridiculously in mid-ocean to a floating coffin, survives. As does Jim Doggett. Clumsily gathering up his trousers and stumbling after the bear, Jim knows "that that bar was an *unhuntable bar, and died when his time come.*" In admitting he never will understand the unusual bear hunt, Jim recognizes that there are mysteries in the universe that are best left unprobed. In compromise, in acceptance, lies the triumph of the comic hero.

Significantly, both strains of comedy—the high and the low—seem vital to the American tradition. The consequence has been a humor at once realistic, critical of our national life, and romantic, insistent on its potentialities. Our comic vision is multiple: in part an anodyne for the pain of the democratic adventure; in part an antiseptic for national ills; in part an affirmation of the American will for survival. The humorists mirror the worst and the best in our culture—pettifoggery, sordidness, and downright stupidity, as well as our highest ideals and hopes. We laugh at ourselves, but in laughter we also celebrate the largeness of our vision. Our comedy is marked by paradox, but, then, we are a paradoxical people.

In giving shape to this broad humor, Americans run a wide gamut of comic styles, ranging from gentle lampoon and low-keyed satire to the ferocity of a darker comedy. Often we bubble into whimsy or collapse into pure nonsense. And we need only recall Fitzgerald and Wharton and James to be assured that we have our comedy of manners, too. Indeed, the diverse elements of the American character seem reflected in our comic strategies: the taciturn Yankee in our tactic of understatement, in our epigrams and quips; the exuberant westerner in the puffery of our tall tales. As critic Max Eastman sums up the richness of our comic spirit: "It is in the humorists that imagination in its full vigor has flourished among us. That is what has made these humorists something of a sensation in the world."

The strength of imagination that distinguishes our humor is brilliantly crystallized in the major character types that American comedy has brought to life: the wise fool, the storyteller, and the little soul. In assuming these roles, our comedians have both captured and created a native mythology. Not that these larger types are exclusively or even indigenously American. All have analogues throughout Western literature. Still, if we have borrowed the prototypes, we have generally invested them with details that are particularly American. Our grass-roots philosophers speak with an irreverence that is especially democratic; our most famous raconteurs weave tales charged with the energy of a young nation; our small souls, citizens struggling to stay sane in the twentieth century, bring into focus the quotidian details of American life. At their best, our comic figures exhibit a vitality of language that is remarkably American. Our humor, celebrating the generative power of the American spirit, celebrates as well the generative power of the American language.

To suspend reality and re-create his bear hunt imaginatively, Jim Doggett relies on the colorful vernacular of the backwoods. Ultimately, it is only through their guises that our funmakers succeed at all. Laughter, as Northrop Frye explains, is in part a reflex that can be conditioned by a repeated pattern. The pattern is a cue for laughter, but it also works in another, perhaps more important way. Comedy depends on a delicate balance of familiarity and aesthetic distance between audience and subject. If the audience does not identify with what is happening, it will find no occasion for laughter; on the other hand, the joke is doomed if the identification is too close. The humorous masks of the writer are conventions much like the painted faces of a clown; they give us exaggerated images of ourselves to allow us emotional room for laughter. There is a tendency among critics to say that emotion is the enemy of laughter. This is not altogether true. The greatest comedy always stirs our emotions. Jim Doggett's tale is fraught with tragic overtones: the inexplicable death of the bear, whom Jim regards as a "brother," is a slapstick farce cast in somber metaphysical shadows. Consider Charlie Chaplin, whose comedy verges on the maudlin: poor little tramp, with his mustache too small and his pants too big, trying desperately to cling to the emblems of his dignity—his cane and hat. He captures the imagination of millions because we share his predicament. Yet we can laugh because none of us is quite so pathetic, quite so stupid—at least, so we think.

part 1

The Comic American

When the United States was still in its infancy, the Scottish novelist Sir Walter Scott offered an American disciple this crucial advice: to learn the character of a nation, look at its ordinary people. Significantly, the younger writer, Washington Irving, became one of his country's first humorists. Irving knew that, unlike tragedy, which concerns the extraordinary, comedy represents the prosaic world of plain people. In comedy lies the quintessence of a nation's character.

The comic American has many faces—rural and urban faces, the faces of northerners and southerners, of the young and the old. If we discern, in the contemporary portraits that follow, the image of a nuclear

American, it is the image of a dreamer who believes in perfectibility and success. Americans, raised on the great national myths of Lincoln moving from log cabin to White House, Vanderbilt earning his fortune, Edison inventing the light bulb, are self-improvers. "Each time I read through the latest bulletin of extension courses, I make immediate plans to drop everything and return to school," confesses Woody Allen in "Spring Bulletin," a survey of adult-education programs. For twenty summers Sally Poker Sash, the heroine of Flannery O'Connor's story "A Late Encounter with the Enemy," has been going to the state teachers' college to earn her degree. Advertisements offer products guaranteed to enrich our lives. In "The Ferrari in the Bedroom," Jean Shepherd tells how his interest is caught by a four-color double-page ad promising "VARROOOOMMM! New excitement in the bedroom!"

But the desire to improve sours to disenchantment; the dream, a fraud, degenerates to a joke. Despite extension courses, Woody Allen remains, as he says, an "unextended adult." Instead of finding *"FORTY-NINE NEW EXCITING ORGASMS!"* Jean Shepherd is abandoned by his girl friend, left with his masterwork of "Slob Art"—a bed that is an "authentic copy" of a Ferrari racing car. "We've got this thing about making stuff to look like other things," Shepherd realizes, adding, "Some psychologist could do a hell of a paper on this subtle undercurrent in American life." For Flannery O'Connor, the falsity of our chromium culture is blazoned forth by the floodlights of the Hollywood premiere; for the Marx Brothers, it is announced by the rigmarole in business contracts. The light bulb, explains Kurt Vonnegut, Jr., was invented not by Tom Edison but by his dog. We have been hoodwinked by the American Dream, lured to goals that are always unattainable, often unworthy. Like Bernard Malamud's sadly comic Jewbird, many Americans ask for so little and suffer so much. For them, the dream has become nightmare. Donald Barthelme's "The Policemen's Ball," a story about "fine men, the finest," concludes:

> The horrors had moved outside Horace's apartment. Not even policemen and their ladies are safe, the horrors thought. No one is safe. Safety does not exist. Ha ha ha ha ha ha ha ha ha ha!

Increasingly, a sense of nightmare has enveloped our sense of fun. The modern American imagination sees itself the butt not merely of a national joke but of a cosmic hoax, taken in by the belief that the universe has rational order and human life, nobility and purpose. So-called black humor, born of the grim realization that life is absurd, is macabre indeed in its choice of terror and pain as subjects. In conventional comedy we are always assured that, no matter how bad things are, they will be resolved happily, that boy and girl will go off hand in hand into the sunset. Not so in black humor. Despite the burlesque routine in Joseph Heller's novel *Catch-22*, Snowden is really dead; Yossarian will soon be splattered by his guts. Heller's definition of "Catch-22" expresses the modern American's dilemma: his feeling of impotence while struggling against forces that seem both inscrutable and invincible. It is the dilemma of those who write for advice to Nathanael West's *Miss Lonelyhearts*, those crippled, anguished human beings who want to make life better in a brutally cruel world and who sign their letters with such names as "Desperate" and "Sick-of-it-all." Caught between dream and nightmare, affirmation and anomie, the comic American embodies our sense of crisis.

Groucho and Chico Make a Deal

George S. Kaufman and Morrie Ryskind

The popularity of the Marx Brothers is perennial. Their films continue to be revived and their records continue to sell. They evoked belly laughs with every performance, but in their best work this celebrated zaniness was not gratuitous. It was a strategy that allowed them to take sharp jabs at American institutions and values. In a large sense, Groucho's song from their film Horse Feathers *sums up their attitude: "Whatever It Is I'm Against It." In that film, their target is the university; in* Monkey Business, *high society; in* Duck Soup, *democratic government. This scene from MGM's* A Night at the Opera *is a classic illustration not only of their comic method but also of their portrayal of the comic American: Groucho as the fast-talking wheeler-dealer, Chico as the seemingly naive immigrant. As their verbal tomfoolery dissolves the scene into comic anarchy, American business sense is reduced to total nonsense.*

GROUCHO: Two beers, bartender.

CHICO: I'll take two beers, too.

GROUCHO *(drifting right into that barroom conversation):* Well, things seem to be getting better around the country.

CHICO: I don't know—I'm a stranger here myself.

GROUCHO *(looking at him curiously):* Stranger? Aren't you an Italian?

CHICO: No, no. I just look that way because my mother and father are Italian.

GROUCHO: I just remembered—I came back here looking for somebody. You don't know who it is, do you?

CHICO: Funny—it just slipped my mind.

GROUCHO *(snapping his fingers):* I remember now, the greatest tenor in the world! That's what I'm after!

CHICO: That's funny. I am his manager.

GROUCHO: Whose manager?

CHICO: The greatest tenor in the world.

GROUCHO: The fellow that sings at the opera here?

CHICO: Sure!

GROUCHO: What's his name?

CHICO: What do you care? Some Italian name—I can't pronounce it. What you want with him?

9

GROUCHO: Well, I'd like to offer him a job. Would he be interested?
CHICO: I don't know, but *I'm* interested. That's the main thing. What sort of job?
GROUCHO: With the New York Opera. America is waiting to hear him sing.
CHICO: Well, he can sing loud, but he can't sing that loud.
GROUCHO: Well, I think we can get America to meet him halfway. The main thing is, can he sail tomorrow night?
CHICO: If you pay him enough money, he can sail *last* night. How much you pay him?
GROUCHO *(aside)*: Let's see—a thousand dollars a night. I'm entitled to a little profit. *(To* CHICO*)* How about ten dollars a night?
  CHICO *laughs scornfully.*
CHICO: Ten dollars! . . . *(A quick change of mood)* All right. I'll take it.
GROUCHO: That's fine. Of course, I want a ten-per-cent commission for putting the deal over.
CHICO: And I get ten per cent as his manager.
GROUCHO: Well, that leaves eight dollars. Say he sings once a week— that's eight dollars a week clear profit for him.
CHICO *(considering a week)*: He sends five dollars home to his mother.
GROUCHO: Well, that still leaves him three dollars.
CHICO: Three dollars. Can he live in New York on that?
GROUCHO: Like a prince—of course, he won't be able to eat but he can live like a prince. Oh, I forgot to tell you. He'll have to pay income tax on that three dollars.
CHICO: Income tax?
GROUCHO: Yes, there's a federal tax and the state tax and there may be a city tax. And, naturally, a sales tax.
CHICO: How much does that all come to?
GROUCHO: Well, I figure if he doesn't sing too often, he can break even.
CHICO: All right. We'll take it.
GROUCHO: Fine! *(He pulls out two contracts)* Now just his name there and you sign on the bottom. You don't have to read yours because it's a duplicate.
CHICO: What?
GROUCHO: A duplicate. (CHICO *looks at him)* Don't you know what duplicates are?
CHICO: Oh, sure! Those five kids up in Canada.
GROUCHO: Well, I wouldn't know about that. I haven't been in Canada for years.
CHICO: Wait a minute. Before I sign anything, what does it say?
GROUCHO: Go ahead and read it.
CHICO *(a little reluctantly)*: Well—er—you read it. I don't like to read anything unless I know what it says.
GROUCHO *(catching on)*: I see. All right, *I'll* read it to you. Can you hear?

CHICO: I haven't heard anything yet. Did you say anything?

GROUCHO: Well, I haven't said anything worth hearing.

CHICO: I guess that's why I didn't hear anything.

GROUCHO *(having the last word)*: Well, that's why I didn't say anything. *(He scans the contract, holding it near him and then far away.* CHICO *watches him suspiciously)*

CHICO: Wait a minute. Can *you* read?

GROUCHO *(holding contract farther and farther away)*: I can read, but I can't see it. If my arms were a little longer, I could read it. . . . Ah, here we are. Now pay attention to this first clause. *(Reads)* "The party of the first part shall be known in this contract as the party of the first part." How do you like that. Pretty neat, eh?

CHICO: No, that'sa no good.

GROUCHO *(indignantly)*: What's the matter with it?

CHICO *(conciliatorily)*: I don't know—let's hear it again.

GROUCHO: "The party of the first part shall be known in this contract as the party of the first part."

CHICO: It sounds a little better this time.

GROUCHO: Well, it grows on you. Want to hear it once more?

CHICO: Only the first part.

GROUCHO: The *party* of the first part?

CHICO: No. The *first part* of the party of the first part.

GROUCHO: Well, it says "The first part of the party of the first part shall be known in this contract"—look! Why should we quarrel about a thing like that? *(He tears off the offending clause)* We'll take it right out.

CHICO *(tearing the same clause out of his contract)*: Sure, it's too long anyhow. Now what have we got left?

GROUCHO: Well, I've got about a foot and a half. . . . Now, then: "The party of the second part shall be known in this contract as the party of the second part."

CHICO: Well, I don't know. I don't like the second party, either.

GROUCHO: You should have come to the first party. We didn't get home till around four in the morning. *(Slight pause)* I was blind for three days.

CHICO: Look, couldn't the first part of the second party be the second part of the first party? Then we got something.

GROUCHO: Look! Rather than go through all that again, what do you say? *(He indicates a willingness to tear further)*

CHICO: Fine. *(They both tear off another piece)*

GROUCHO: Now, I've got something here you're *bound* to like. You'll be crazy about it.

CHICO: No, I don't like it.

GROUCHO: You don't like what?

CHICO: Whatever it is.

GROUCHO: All right. Why should we break up an old friendship over a thing like this? Ready?

CHICO: Okay. *(They both tear)* Now, the next part I don't think *you're* going to like.

GROUCHO: All right—your word's good enough for me. *(They both tear)* Now then, is *my* word good enough for *you?*

CHICO: I should say not.

GROUCHO: All right—let's go. *(They both tear.* GROUCHO *looking at the contract)* The party of the eighth part—

CHICO: No. *(They tear)*

GROUCHO: The party of the ninth part—

CHICO: No. *(They tear)* Say, how is it I got a skinnier contract than you?

GROUCHO: I don't know. You must have been out on a tear last night. Anyhow, now we're all set. Now sign right here. *(He produces a fountain pen)*

CHICO: I forgot to tell you. I can't write.

GROUCHO: That's all right. There's no ink in the pen, anyway. But, listen, it's a bargain, isn't it? We've got a contract, no matter how small it is.

CHICO *(extending hand.* GROUCHO *clasps it):* You betcha! Only one thing I want to know: what does this say? *(Showing last piece of contract left)*

GROUCHO: Oh, that's nothing. That's the usual clause in every contract. It says if any of the parties participating in the contract are shown not to be in their right mind, the contract is nullified.

CHICO: What do you call it?

GROUCHO: That's what they call a sanity clause.

CHICO: You can't fool me. There ain't no sanity clause!

QUESTIONS

1. Describe the comic roles assumed by Groucho and Chico. What character traits do they poke fun at?

2. The essence of satire is criticism. How is this skit critical of American values? If it is satiric, does it aim to reform our vices and follies?

3. The Marx Brothers are noted for their verbal humor. What are some of the puns used here? Which is your favorite?

4. Much of their humor is sheer nonsense. Explain how the contract is shortened. How can the tenor "break even"? When does Groucho want him to begin work?

5. The effectiveness of this brand of humor depends on rapid-fire delivery. Try reading the scene aloud with a friend, concentrating on the timing.

Spring Bulletin

Woody Allen

Thomas Jefferson hoped American education would produce an intellectual aristocracy for our Republic. But in this description of college courses Woody Allen belittles the intellectual and moral values of universities today. He punctures academic bombast, as the Marx Brothers did with legalese, to expose the nonsense at its core. In films like Sleeper, *in books like* Getting Even *and* Without Feathers, *and in stand-up comedy routines, Allen has made famous his image of the modern American. He confesses, "I am desperately inept at everything." Even his tape recorder talks to him sympathetically, saying "I know. I know."*

The number of college bulletins and adult-education come-ons that keep turning up in my mailbox convinces me that I must be on a special mailing list for dropouts. Not that I'm complaining; there is something about a list of extension courses that piques my interest with a fascination hitherto reserved for a catalogue of Hong Kong honeymoon accessories, sent to me once by mistake. Each time I read through the latest bulletin of extension courses, I make immediate plans to drop everything and return to school. (I was ejected from college many years ago, the victim of unproved accusations not unlike those once attached to Yellow Kid Weil.) So far, however, I am still an uneducated, unextended adult, and I have fallen into the habit of browsing through an imaginary, handsomely printed course bulletin that is more or less typical of them all:

Summer Session

Economic Theory: A systematic application and critical evaluation of the basic analytic concepts of economic theory, with an emphasis on money and why it's good. Fixed coefficient production functions, cost and supply curves, and nonconvexity comprise the first semester, with the second semester concentrating on spending, making change, and keeping a neat wallet. The Federal Reserve System is analyzed, and advanced students are coached in the proper method of filling out a deposit slip.

Other topics include: Inflation and Depression—how to dress for each. Loans, interest, welching.

History of European Civilization: Ever since the discovery of a fossilized eohippus in the men's washroom at Siddon's Cafeteria in East Rutherford, New Jersey, it has been suspected that at one time Europe and America were connected by a strip of land that later sank or became East Rutherford, New Jersey, or both. This throws a new perspective on the formation of European society and enables historians to conjecture about why it sprang up in an area that would have made a much better Asia. Also studied in the course is the decision to hold the Renaissance in Italy.

Introduction to Psychology: The theory of human behavior. Why some men are called "lovely individuals" and why there are others you just want to pinch. Is there a split between mind and body, and, if so, which is better to have? Aggression and rebellion are discussed. (Students particularly interested in these aspects of psychology are advised to take one of these Winter Term courses: Introduction to Hostility; Intermediate Hostility; Advanced Hatred; Theoretical Foundations of Loathing.) Special consideration is given to a study of consciousness as opposed to unconsciousness, with many helpful hints on how to remain conscious.

Psychopathology: Aimed at understanding obsessions and phobias, including the fear of being suddenly captured and stuffed with crabmeat, reluctance to return a volleyball serve, and the inability to say the word "mackinaw" in the presence of women. The compulsion to seek out the company of beavers is analyzed.

Philosophy I: Everyone from Plato to Camus is read, and the following topics are covered:
   Ethics: The categorical imperative, and six ways to make it work for you.
   Aesthetics: Is art the mirror of life, or what?
   Metaphysics: What happens to the soul after death? How does it manage?
   Epistemology: Is knowledge knowable? If not, how do we know this?
   The Absurd: Why existence is often considered silly, particularly for men who wear brown-and-white shoes. Manyness and oneness are studied as they relate to otherness. (Students achieving oneness will move ahead to twoness.)

Philosophy XXIX-B: Introduction to God. Confrontation with the Creator of the universe through informal lectures and field trips.

The New Mathematics: Standard mathematics has recently been rendered obsolete by the discovery that for years we have been writing the numeral five backward. This has led to a reëvaluation of counting as a method of getting from one to ten. Students are taught advanced concepts of Boolean Algebra, and formerly unsolvable equations are dealt with by threats of reprisals.

Fundamental Astronomy: A detailed study of the universe and its care and cleaning. The sun, which is made of gas, can explode at any moment, sending our entire planetary system hurtling to destruction; students are advised what the average citizen can do in such a case. They are also taught to identify various constellations, such as the Big Dipper, Cygnus the Swan, Sagittarius the Archer, and the twelve stars that form Lumides the Pants Salesman.

Modern Biology: How the body functions, and where it can usually be found. Blood is analyzed, and it is learned why it is the best possible thing to have coursing through one's veins. A frog is dissected by students and its digestive tract is compared with man's, with the frog giving a good account of itself except on curries.

Rapid Reading: This course will increase reading speed a little each day until the end of the term, by which time the student will be required to read *The Brothers Karamazov* in fifteen minutes. The method is to scan the page and eliminate everything except pronouns from one's field of vision. Soon the pronouns are eliminated. Gradually the student is encouraged to nap. A frog is dissected. Spring comes. People marry and die. Pinkerton does not return.

Musicology III: The Recorder. The student is taught how to play "Yankee Doodle" on this end-blown wooden flute, and progresses rapidly to the Brandenburg. Concertos. Then slowly back to "Yankee Doodle."

Music Appreciation: In order to "hear" a great piece of music correctly, one must: (1) know the birthplace of the composer, (2) be able to tell a rondo from a scherzo, and back it up with action. Attitude is important. Smiling is bad form unless the composer has intended the music to be funny, as in *Till Eulenspiegel*, which abounds in musical jokes (although the trombone has the best lines). The ear, too, must be trained, for it is our most easily deceived organ and can be made to think it is a nose by bad placement of stereo speakers. Other topics include: The four-bar rest and its potential as a political weapon. The Gregorian Chant: Which monks kept the beat.

Writing for the Stage: All drama is conflict. Character development is also very important. Also what they say. Students learn that long, dull speeches are not so effective, while short, "funny" ones seem to go over well. Simplified audience psychology is explored: Why is a play about a lovable old character named Gramps often not as interesting in the theatre as staring at the back of someone's head and trying to make him turn around? Interesting aspects of stage history are also examined. For example, before the invention of italics, stage directions were often mistaken for dialogue, and great actors frequently found themselves saying, "John rises, crosses left." This naturally led to embarrassment and, on some occasions, dreadful notices. The phenomenon is analyzed in detail, and students are guided in avoiding mistakes. Required text: A. F. Shulte's *Shakespeare: Was He Four Women?*

Introduction to Social Work: A course designed to instruct the social worker who is interested in going out "in the field." Topics covered include: how to organize street gangs into basketball teams, and vice versa; playgrounds as a means of preventing juvenile crime, and how to get potentially homicidal cases to try the sliding pond; discrimination; the broken home; what to do if you are hit with a bicycle chain.

Yeats and Hygiene, A Comparative Study: The poetry of William Butler Yeats is analyzed against a background of proper dental care. (Course open to a limited number of students.)

QUESTIONS

1. What do Woody Allen's course descriptions reveal about our educational system? How does this burlesque of college catalogues have wider implications as social satire?

2. What kind of person is the narrator? Compare his attitude toward education with the Marx Brothers' attitude toward business.

3. What makes these descriptions humorous? To what extent does Woody Allen rely on nonsense humor?

The Ferrari in the Bedroom

Jean Shepherd

A popular television and radio raconteur, Jean Shepherd here spins a yarn about the American of the not-too-distant future. Parodying the language of commercials and the themes of pulp fiction—romance and success—Shepherd shows where the pursuit of kitsch is leading the Distraught Citizen: to the ultimate in "Slob Art." As he heroically prepares to meet the dentist, expecting the worst to happen, Shepherd symbolically assumes the posture of the modern American. His most recent book is In God We Trust.

Slowly and mechanically, without really seeing anything, I leafed through the pages of a big fat silky ladymag. My mind was barely ticking over, receiving no inputs, producing no output. (Have you noticed these days that minds don't have ideas; they have *concepts*; they don't have stimuli; they have *outputs*. Jesus, if we work hard enough and fool with the language enough we may be able to *will* ourselves into becoming foolproof transistorized computers capable of beating those IBM monsters at their own game.)

I leafed on, one small corner of my inner being carrying on its continual battle with the imps of hell which keep raging down there, begging me to get started on my true career as a firebomb terrorist or a graffiti-scrawler. Now I'm not the kind who spends much time looking over gurleymags of the *Cosmo* stripe, although I find their banner headlines on the cover page more than slightly great:

FORTY-NINE NEW EXCITING ORGASMS, A Smashing Color Feature!

Or:

FIFTY-THREE FAMOUS WOMEN REVEAL THEIR TOP SE-CRETS FOR SENSUALITY!

Sensuality, I thought listlessly, that's the new big *Cosmo* word. Last year the big word was "Fun." The year before it was "wild." Everything was "wild." Too bad they don't have good old sexy women any more. Sensuality is in; sexy is out. Or, a real chiller, from the same issue, blunt and to the point:

WHAT TO DO WHEN HE WON'T MARRY YOU

Holy Gloria Steinem, I breathed, hurrying faster through the steaming

pages filled with quivering, Jello-y gurleyprose. I skimmed through
WHAT YOU CAN LEARN FROM FRENCH GIRLS, which was a
hell of a letdown since it yammered on about how to dress, when
actually the best thing anyone can learn from French girls is how to
*un*dress with style. *THE COMPLETE GUIDE TO ENCOUNTER
GROUPS* held me for a second or two. Complete Guide, I thought,
what the hell is a Complete Guide? Some of the best encounter groups
I've ever known in my life happened like spontaneous combustion in the
back seat of a Pontiac, and you sure as hell won't find them listed in the
Complete Guide. Oh well.

My mind takes these evil turns when I'm squatting nervously in my
dentist's waiting room, which is where I infrequently have my torrid
encounters with the world of Rona Jaffe and Helen Gurley Brown. The
dog-eared *National Geographics* had long since palled and I find *The
Orthodontist Quarterly* curiously unrefreshing. In the next room,
the arena, I heard muffled moans and occasional subdued thumpings.
Some other poor devil was on the rack and it soon would be my turn. My
dentist is an odd duck, as most of them are. He paints water colors and
smiles enigmatically as he scans the X-Rays. A man who has peered into
the gaping maws of caries-ridden humanity has few illusions. The thin
whistling whirr of the highspeed drill mingled with the soft tones of
Muzak as I tried to concentrate on *FORTY-NINE NEW EXCITING
ORGASMS*. I flipped another page.

Without warning it got me full between the eyes—ZONK!

> VARROOOOMMM! New excitement in the bedroom! The *now* look
> in groovy exciting varooomm-y beddy-time Fun! Made of high-impact
> top grade vinyl, this authentic copy of a real racing Ferrari will add the
> excitement and speed of Monte Carlo, Sebring and Le Mans to your
> nocturnal hours. Available in Italian Racing Red, British Racing Green
> and Chaparral White. At better stores everywhere.

The quivering copy undulated across a spectacular four-color double-
page spread. It showed a bedroom displaying obvious signs of being
inhabited by someone exceedingly well-heeled and spectacularly hedo-
nistic. The decor was conventional, standard Department Store Mod
except for that varoom-y exception. There in this haven of rest, in the
spot where the bed used to be in the good old days, was what looked like,
at first glance, a brilliant blood-red Ferrari roadster.

Mamma Mia! I muttered as I so often do these days after being
forever influenced by an Alka-Seltzer commercial. I convulsively crossed
myself, which is somewhat surprising since I am not Catholic, but since
I've seen plenty of ballplayers and wrestlers do it on the boob tube I
figure what the hell, you can't lose anything by trying. *Mamma Mia*, a
Ferrari in the bedroom!

For a crazy instant I thought, what a great title for a Sophia Loren pizza-opera co-starring Marcello Mastroianni as the aging world-weary Italian architect who one day meets this girl on the train for Sorrento and. . . . Cut it out! That gets you nowhere.

I examined the ad closely. Sure enough, there it was. It was not a vagrant hallucination. A bed shaped almost exactly like a Ferrari. It even had vinyl wheels with vinyl knockoffhubs; STP and CASTROL decals plastered all over it. I instantly knew what I was seeing. (I have this way of instantly knowing these things.) I was looking at a true masterwork of Slob Art, fully worthy to stand beside the concrete Mexicans, the Seven Dwarf lawn sprinklers and the Praying Hands day-glo reading lamp in the pantheon of true Slob Art.

I was interrupted by a sudden ringing shout of pain from the next room as my fellow victim became forcibly aware that he had a nervous system and it was sensitive as hell.

Jesus! We've got this thing about making stuff to look like other things. Second-rate restaurants disguised as derbies; radios disguised as Brunswick three-hole bowling balls, ballpoint pens sneakily passing as cigars. Some psychologist could do a hell of a paper on this subtle undercurrent in American life. But—the Ferrari in the bedroom: Now *dat'sa* spicy meat-a-ball-a!

Immediately my monster intelligence, which was influenced in infancy by William Inge and Smoky Stover, conjured up a scene. The dentist's waiting room with its forty-nine new exciting orgasms and its limp water colors faded and I found myself magically peering into an analyst's inner sanctum of the Future:

A distraught citizen lies writhing on the couch. The analyst of the future, his hair hanging in great waves to the floor, wearing blue isinglass shades, squats like Buddha behind his mother-of-pearl desk.

The dialogue begins:

Analyst: (hereafter referred to as A) "Come, come, Witherspoon, you've been here every day at three for seven years and I, for one, am getting damn tired of it."

Distraught Patient: (hereafter referred to as DP) "I know, Doctor, but . . . but . . . but. . . ." (He hurls himself to the floor where he lies kicking off his shoes in a muffled tantrum.)

A: "Look, Witherspoon, I know it is unprofessional of me to tell you to get on the stick, but for God sakes, man, if I can use the expression, I didn't spend fifteen years in training to listen to you snivel and whine. There must be some reason why you have a blind, insensate, totally destructive hate and fear of all Italian cars."

DP: "I know, Doctor, but. . . ." (rising to his feet, his eyes hollow, staring.)

A: "No buts. Let's can the crap. What's bugging you, Jack?" (It is obvious that A is a practicing representative of the emerging school of Guts Psychiatry which has recently discovered that a kick in the ass is worth ten thousand logged hours on the soft down of the couch.)

DP: "All right, dammit! I've got to get it out sometime!" (He screams incoherently, beating his fists on the wall.)

A: "Watch it, Witherspoon." (A squirts DP with a plastic fire-extinguisher) "You've been seeing too many Jules Feiffer movies, Jack. Now cool it."

DP: (his voice low, tremulous, breast heaving) "All right. I'll tell you what's eating at my very soul."

A: "It's about time, Witherspoon. You can't go around forever chopping up Fiats and Maseratis on the streets with a fire axe and escape the booby hatch."

DP: "I know, I know! I try to control myself, but just the sight of one of those red devils with all them STP stickers all over 'em drives me out of my mind. Everything goes black and I . . . I. . . ."

A: "You don't have to tell me what you do. I had to bail you out three times last month alone. And those guys from Allstate Insurance are starting to get nasty."

DP: "Doc, do you remember Clara?"

A: (caught off guard) "Clara? What's she got to do with Maseratis?"

DP: "Plenty!"

A: (affably lighting up a joint) "Aha! So, just as I thought. I knew sex was behind it somewhere. Go on. Spill it."

DP: "You remember me telling you about how much I loved her, how from the first time I saw her that afternoon in the rain at the Orange Julius stand eating a brownie, that I had to have her? You remember me telling you about that? Do you?"

A: "Of course. I have it in my notes. You never did tell me how that all came out."

DP: (stifling a sob) "That's just it, Doctor. I haven't been able to face it till now. Clara is the only girl I've ever loved. Her eyes! Her skin! The way she smiled in that mysterious way, like the girl in the Unscented Arid commercial on TV. My God, she's a goddess, a real goddess! I plotted night and day to get near her, to caress her, to fondle her, to whisper sweet nothings into her alabaster ear, to lay my life down for her, . . . to . . . ." (He breaks off, choked with emotion.)

A: "There, there, Witherspoon. Here, have a drag on my joint."

DP: (unhearing, lost in his own world) "Six months went by and then it finally happened. All my dreams were about to come true. I had wined her and dined her, taken her to every rotten musical for miles around, and then, one night with the moon shining in her eyes I asked her to come up to my pad. She had never been there before. I was afraid to ask her. She said in that beautiful deep voice, like Candy Bergen's: 'Why, yes, Virgil.' "

A: (leaning forward, savoring the story) "That must have made you feel good, eh, Witherspoon? What happened then?"

DP: "I bought wine, flowers; burned incense. Got the pre-amp on my stereo fixed. And then, that night after dinner—which I had prepared from my *Julia Child TV Cookbook*—I swept her off her feet in the candle-light and carried her into my bedroom. I could feel her lithe pulsing body underneath the shimmering gossamer she wore that night."

A: "Yes, yes. Go on, man!"

DP: "I slipped out of my H.I.S. bells. I saw a brief flash of alabaster flesh in the faint shimmering moonlight, and then, and then everything blew up in my face. All that I had hoped for, dreamed for exploded before me."

A: (breathing heavily in excitement) "What happened?"

DP: "She laughed. . . . *Laughed!!* My God, it was terrible. Have you ever had a girl laugh at you in your own bedroom? It was terrible. At first I couldn't believe my ears. That insane laughter in the dark. I asked her 'What's wrong? Why are you laughing?' and then . . . then . . . she said it!" (His voice trails off in sobs.)

A: "Said *what?*"

DP: "She said, 'What the hell's that cockamamie thing?' I answered, 'It's my Varrooommmm Ferrari Bed. It adds new zest and exhilaration to beddy-by time.' And . . . *she* said, 'A plastic Ferrari? With pillows? And STP stickers? Jeez! I seen some nutty scenes in my time . . . I been with plenty of kooky johns that go for bullwhips and track shoes. But lemme out of here! I don't want nothin' to do with any plastic kiddy-cars. What kinda freak do you think I am?' And then, Doctor, she hit me in the mouth with my Yogi Bear FM radio and ran out. I never saw her again. And ever since that night I have this uncontrollable urge, every time I see an Italian car, to. . . ."

A: "That's enough, Witherspoon. I've heard enough! I've listened to sick stories in my time myself, and you're damn lucky I don't have you tied up right here and carted off. Don't bother to come back. We don't need your sort around here."

DP: "I understand, Doctor. Please forgive me."

A: "Get out of here, you bum! If there's anything I can't stand it's your kind of Sickies. And anyway, your 55 minutes are up." (The scene ends with DP skulking out into the night, carrying an axe, hunting for a helpless Fiat 850 fastback.)

For a long moment I sat watching in the fetid, chewing-gum-laden theater of my mind the scurrying departure of DP as A took a final drag on his roach and prepared to greet his next patient.

"You're next. And how's that little old wisdom tooth this week?"

"Varroommm!" I blurted out involuntarily.

"What was that?" My dentist, a hardened customer thickly calloused by the tartar of Life, eyed me narrowly.

"Uh . . . bruummmf! I was just clearing my throat."

"I thought you said 'Varroom.' "

"Why no, Doctor, that's silly. Why would I say varroom?"

"Search me, pal. Now let's get down to that wisdom tooth." I bravely marched into the torture chamber, ready to take the worst he could give me.

QUESTIONS

1. What is "Slob Art"? What does it reveal about our culture? What examples of this art form are cited in the essay? What others would you add?

2. Compare the narrator of "The Ferrari in the Bedroom" with the narrator in Woody Allen's "Spring Bulletin." How are they like or unlike people you know?

3. Discuss Shepherd's method of humor. Consider his use of exaggeration, parody, and incongruity.

4. How does Clara's laughter affect Virgil? Explain why the psychiatrist becomes so angry with Virgil.

Tom Edison's Shaggy Dog

Kurt Vonnegut, Jr.

If Jean Shepherd looks into the future to lampoon our vulgarity, Kurt Vonnegut, Jr., contrasts the present with the past. "Tom Edison's Shaggy Dog," one of the stories from his popular collection Welcome to the Monkey House, *is a modern tall tale. Traditionally an exaggerated account of an adventure designed to glorify a frontier hero, the tall story is turned topsy-turvy by Vonnegut to demythologize Edison's achievement. The setting is not the Wild West, but a retirement community in Florida; the American appears now as the old businessman Bullard; the tone is one of gentle cynicism. Bullard's faith in American ingenuity and skill is made to seem ludicrously outdated. In his other best-selling books—*God Bless You, Mr. Rosewater, Slaughterhouse-Five, The Sirens of Titan, Breakfast of Champions—*Vonnegut also satirizes the failure of the Great American Dream.*

Two old men sat on a park bench one morning in the sunshine of Tampa, Florida—one trying doggedly to read a book he was plainly enjoying while the other, Harold K. Bullard, told him the story of his life in the full, round, head tones of a public address system. At their feet lay Bullard's Labrador retriever, who further tormented the aged listener by probing his ankles with a large, wet nose.

Bullard, who had been, before he retired, successful in many fields, enjoyed reviewing his important past. But he faced the problem that complicates the lives of cannibals—namely: that a single victim cannot be used over and over. Anyone who had passed the time of day with him and his dog refused to share a bench with them again.

So Bullard and his dog set out through the park each day in quest of new faces. They had had good luck this morning, for they had found this stranger right away, clearly a new arrival in Florida, still buttoned up tight in heavy serge, stiff collar and necktie, and with nothing better to do than read.

"Yes," said Bullard, rounding out the first hour of his lecture, "made and lost five fortunes in my time."

"So you said," said the stranger, whose name Bullard had neglected to ask. "Easy, boy. No, no, no, boy," he said to the dog, who was growing more aggressive toward his ankles.

"Oh? Already told you that, did I?" said Bullard.

"Twice."

"Two in real estate, one in scrap iron, and one in oil and one in trucking."

"So you said."

"I did? Yes, guess I did. Two in real estate, one in scrap iron, one in oil, and one in trucking. Wouldn't take back a day of it."

"No, I suppose not," said the stranger. "Pardon me, but do you suppose you could move your dog somewhere else? He keeps—"

"Him?" said Bullard, heartily. "Friendliest dog in the world. Don't need to be afraid of him."

"I'm not afraid of him. It's just that he drives me crazy, sniffing at my ankles."

"Plastic," said Bullard, chuckling.

"What?"

"Plastic. Must be something plastic on your garters. By golly, I'll bet it's those little buttons. Sure as we're sitting here, those buttons must be plastic. That dog is nuts about plastic. Don't know why that is, but he'll sniff it out and find it if there's a speck around. Must be a deficiency in his diet, though, by gosh, he eats better than I do. Once he chewed up a whole plastic humidor. Can you beat it? *That's* the business I'd go into now, by glory, if the pill rollers hadn't told me to let up, to give the old ticker a rest."

"You could tie the dog to that tree over there," said the stranger.

"I get so darn' sore at all the youngsters these days!" said Bullard. "All of 'em mooning around about no frontiers any more. There never have been so many frontiers as there are today. You know what Horace Greeley would say today?"

"His nose is wet," said the stranger, and he pulled his ankles away, but the dog humped forward in patient pursuit. "Stop it, boy!"

"His wet nose shows he's healthy," said Bullard. " 'Go plastic, young man!' That's what Greeley'd say. 'Go atom, young man!' "

The dog had definitely located the plastic buttons on the stranger's garters and was cocking his head one way and another, thinking out ways of bringing his teeth to bear on those delicacies.

"Scat!" said the stranger.

" 'Go electronic, young man!' " said Bullard. "Don't talk to me about no opportunity any more. Opportunity's knocking down every door in the country, trying to get in. When I was young, a man had to go out and find opportunity and drag it home by the ears. Nowadays—"

"Sorry," said the stranger, evenly. He slammed his book shut, stood and jerked his ankle away from the dog. "I've got to be on my way. So good day, sir."

He stalked across the park, found another bench, sat down with a sigh and began to read. His respiration had just returned to normal, when he felt the wet sponge of the dog's nose on his ankles again.

"Oh—it's you!" said Bullard, sitting down beside him. "He was tracking you. He was on the scent of something, and I just let him have his head. What'd I tell you about plastic?" He looked about contentedly. "Don't blame you for moving on. It was stuffy back there. No shade to speak of and not a sign of a breeze."

"Would the dog go away if I bought him a humidor?" said the stranger.

"Pretty good joke, pretty good joke," said Bullard, amiably. Suddenly he clapped the stranger on his knee. "Sa-ay, you aren't in plastics, are you? Here I've been blowing off about plastics, and for all I know that's your line."

"My line?" said the stranger crisply, laying down his book. "Sorry— I've never had a line. I've been a drifter since the age of nine, since Edison set up his laboratory next to my home, and showed me the intelligence analyzer."

"Edison?" said Bullard. "Thomas Edison, the inventor?"

"If you want to call him that, go ahead," said the stranger.

"If I *want* to call him that?"—Bullard guffawed—"I guess I just will! Father of the light bulb and I don't know what all."

"If you want to think he invented the light bulb, go ahead. No harm in it." The stranger resumed his reading.

"Say, what is this?" said Bullard, suspiciously. "You pulling my leg? What's this about an intelligence analyzer? I never heard of that."

"Of course you haven't," said the stranger. "Mr. Edison and I promised to keep it a secret. I've never told anyone. Mr. Edison broke his promise and told Henry Ford, but Ford made him promise not to tell anybody else—for the good of humanity."

Bullard was entranced. "Uh, this intelligence analyzer," he said, "it analyzed intelligence, did it?"

"It was an electric butter churn," said the stranger.

"Seriously now," Bullard coaxed.

"Maybe it *would* be better to talk it over with someone," said the stranger. "It's a terrible thing to keep bottled up inside me, year in and year out. But how can I be sure that it won't go any further?"

"My word as a gentleman," Bullard assured him.

"I don't suppose I could find a stronger guarantee than that, could I?" said the stranger, judiciously.

"There is no stronger guarantee," said Bullard, proudly. "Cross my heart and hope to die!"

"Very well." The stranger leaned back and closed his eyes, seeming to travel backward through time. He was silent for a full minute, during which Bullard watched with respect.

"It was back in the fall of eighteen seventy-nine," said the stranger at last, softly. "Back in the village of Menlo Park, New Jersey. I was a boy of nine. A young man we all thought was a wizard had set up a laboratory next door to my home, and there were flashes and crashes inside, and all sorts of scary goings on. The neighborhood children were warned to keep away, not to make any noise that would bother the wizard.

"I didn't get to know Edison right off, but his dog Sparky and I got to be steady pals. A dog a whole lot like yours, Sparky was, and we used to wrestle all over the neighborhood. Yes, sir, your dog is the image of Sparky."

"Is that so?" said Bullard, flattered.

"Gospel," replied the stranger. "Well, one day Sparky and I were wrestling around, and we wrestled right up to the door of Edison's laboratory. The next thing I knew, Sparky had pushed me in through the door, and bam! I was sitting on the laboratory floor, looking up at Mr. Edison himself."

"Bet he was sore," said Bullard, delighted.

"You can bet I was scared," said the stranger. "*I* thought I was face to face with Satan himself. Edison had wires hooked to his ears and running down to a little black box in his lap! I started to scoot, but he caught me by my collar and made me sit down.

" 'Boy,' said Edison, 'it's always darkest before the dawn. I want you to remember that.'

" 'Yes, sir,' I said.

" 'For over a year, my boy,' Edison said to me, 'I've been trying to find a filament that will last in an incandescent lamp. Hair, string, splinters— nothing works. So while I was trying to think of something else to try, I started tinkering with another idea of mine, just letting off steam. I put this together,' he said, showing me the little black box. 'I thought maybe intelligence was just a certain kind of electricity, so I made this intelligence analyzer here. It works! You're the first one to know about it, my boy. But I don't know why you shouldn't be. It will be your generation that will grow up in the glorious new era when people will be as easily graded as oranges.' "

"I don't believe it!" said Bullard.

"May I be struck by lightning this very instant!" said the stranger. "And it did work, too. Edison had tried out the analyzer on the men in his shop, without telling them what he was up to. The smarter a man was, by gosh, the farther the needle on the indicator in the little black box swung to the right. I let him try it on me, and the needle just lay where it was and trembled. But dumb as I was, then is when I made my one and only contribution to the world. As I say, I haven't lifted a finger since."

"Whadja do?" said Bullard, eagerly.

"I said, 'Mr. Edison, sir, let's try it on the dog.' And I wish you could have seen the show that dog put on when I said it! Old Sparky barked and howled and scratched to get out. When he saw we meant business, that he wasn't going to get out, he made a beeline right for the intelligence analyzer and knocked it out of Edison's hands. But we cornered him, and Edison held him down while I touched the wires to his ears. And would you believe it, that needle sailed clear across the dial, way past a little red pencil marker on the dial face!"

"The dog busted it," said Bullard.

" 'Mr. Edison, sir,' I said, 'what's the red mark mean?'

" 'My boy,' said Edison, 'it means that the instrument is broken, because that red mark is me.' "

"I'll say it was broken," said Bullard.

The stranger said gravely, "But it wasn't broken. No, sir. Edison checked the whole thing, and it was in apple-pie order. When Edison told me that, it was then that Sparky, crazy to get out, gave himself away."

"How?" said Bullard, suspiciously.

"We really had him locked in, see? There were three locks on the door—a hook and eye, a bolt, and a regular knob and latch. That dog stood up, unhooked the hook, pushed the bolt back and had the knob in his teeth when Edison stopped him."

"No!" said Bullard.

"Yes!" said the stranger, his eyes shining. "And then is when Edison showed me what a great scientist he was. He was willing to face the truth, no matter how unpleasant it might be.

" 'So!' said Edison to Sparky. 'Man's best friend, huh? Dumb animal, huh?'

"That Sparky was a caution. He pretended not to hear. He scratched himself and bit fleas and went around growling at ratholes—anything to get out of looking Edison in the eye.

" 'Pretty soft, isn't it, Sparky?' said Edison. 'Let somebody else worry about getting food, building shelters and keeping warm, while you sleep in front of a fire or go chasing after the girls or raise hell with the boys. No mortgages, no politics, no war, no work, no worry. Just wag the old tail or lick a hand, and you're all taken care of.'

" 'Mr. Edison,' I said, 'do you mean to tell me that dogs are smarter than people?'

" 'Smarter?' said Edison. 'I'll tell the world! And what have I been doing for the past year? Slaving to work out a light bulb so dogs can play at night!'

" 'Look, Mr. Edison,' said Sparky, 'why not—' "

"Hold on!" roared Bullard.

"Silence!" shouted the stranger, triumphantly. " 'Look, Mr. Edison,' said Sparky, 'why not keep quiet about this? It's been working out to everybody's satisfaction for hundreds of thousands of years. Let sleeping dogs lie. You forget all about it, destroy the intelligence analyzer, and I'll tell you what to use for a lamp filament.'"

"Hogwash!" said Bullard, his face purple.

The stranger stood. "You have my solemn word as a gentleman. That dog rewarded *me* for my silence with a stock-market tip that made me independently wealthy for the rest of my days. And the last words that Sparky ever spoke were to Thomas Edison. 'Try a piece of carbonized cotton thread,' he said. Later, he was torn to bits by a pack of dogs that had gathered outside the door, listening."

The stranger removed his garters and handed them to Bullard's dog. "A small token of esteem, sir, for an ancestor of yours who talked himself to death. Good day." He tucked his book under his arm and walked away.

QUESTIONS

1. In many American tall tales the listener is collared by the storyteller and forced to hear a story of exaggerated exploits. In Vonnegut's modernization, how does the "victim" turn the tables on the storyteller? In what way is Vonnegut's tale a parody or imitation of the tall tale?

2. Describe Bullard. Why is his name appropriate? What American character traits does he satirize? Consider his remarks about Horace Greeley and plastics.

3. What is a "shaggy dog story"? How is the title a joke?

4. Humorists often tell about animals with human characteristics. Why? How does Sparky help Edison? What happens to Sparky? What other humanlike animals are well known in our comic lore? You may want to refer to Arthur Asa Berger's article, "Peanuts: The Americanization of Augustine," on page 298.

5. Why does the stranger give his garters to Bullard's dog? Explain the moral of Vonnegut's parable.

A Late Encounter with the Enemy

Flannery O'Connor

Like Kurt Vonnegut, Jr., Flannery O'Connor uses the degeneration of our heroes as an emblem of the corrosion of the national character. Comparing the moral decadence of three generations of Americans, she gives us a story remarkably rich in satiric contrasts—the narrow-minded teacher who will not learn, the impotent old soldier who lusts after pretty girls, the selfish Boy Scout who finds the American Dream fulfilled in the Coke machine. One of America's most acclaimed contemporary writers, Flannery O'Connor has also written Wise Blood, A Good Man Is Hard to Find, *and* Everything That Rises Must Converge.

General Sash was a hundred and four years old. He lived with his granddaughter, Sally Poker Sash, who was sixty-two years old and who prayed every night on her knees that he would live until her graduation from college. The General didn't give two slaps for her graduation but he never doubted he would live for it. Living had got to be such a habit with him that he couldn't conceive of any other condition. A graduation exercise was not exactly his idea of a good time, even if, as she said, he would be expected to sit on the stage in his uniform. She said there would be a long procession of teachers and students in their robes but that there wouldn't be anything to equal *him* in his uniform. He knew this well enough without her telling him, and as for the damn procession, it could march to hell and back and not cause him a quiver. He liked parades with floats full of Miss Americas and Miss Daytona Beaches and Miss Queen Cotton Products. He didn't have any use for processions and a procession full of schoolteachers was about as deadly as the River Styx to his way of thinking. However, he was willing to sit on the stage in his uniform so that they could see him.

Sally Poker was not as sure as he was that he would live until her graduation. There had not been any perceptible change in him for the last five years, but she had the sense that she might be cheated out of her triumph because she so often was. She had been going to summer school every year for the past twenty because when she started teaching, there were no such things as degrees. In those times, she said, everything was normal but nothing had been normal since she was sixteen, and for the

29

past twenty summers, when she should have been resting, she had had to take a trunk in the burning heat to the state teachers' college; and though when she returned in the fall, she always taught in the exact way she had been taught not to teach, this was a mild revenge that didn't satisfy her sense of justice. She wanted the General at her graduation because she wanted to show what she stood for, or, as she said, "what all was behind her," and was not behind them. This *them* was not anybody in particular. It was just all the upstarts who had turned the world on its head and unsettled the ways of decent living.

She meant to stand on that platform in August with the General sitting in his wheel chair on the stage behind her and she meant to hold her head very high as if she were saying, "See him! See him! My kin, all you upstarts! Glorious upright old man standing for the old traditions! Dignity! Honor! Courage! See him!" One night in her sleep she screamed, "See him! See him!" and turned her head and found him sitting in his wheel chair behind her with a terrible expression on his face and with all his clothes off except the general's hat and she had waked up and had not dared to go back to sleep again that night.

For his part, the General would not have consented even to attend her graduation if she had not promised to see to it that he sit on the stage. He liked to sit on any stage. He considered that he was still a very handsome man. When he had been able to stand up, he had measured five feet four inches of pure game cock. He had white hair that reached to his shoulders behind and he would not wear teeth because he thought his profile was more striking without them. When he put on his full-dress general's uniform, he knew well enough that there was nothing to match him anywhere.

This was not the same uniform he had worn in the War between the States. He had not actually been a general in that war. He had probably been a foot soldier; he didn't remember what he had been; in fact, he didn't remember that war at all. It was like his feet, which hung down now shriveled at the very end of him, without feeling, covered with a blue-gray afghan that Sally Poker had crocheted when she was a little girl. He didn't remember the Spanish-American War in which he had lost a son; he didn't even remember the son. He didn't have any use for history because he never expected to meet it again. To his mind, history was connected with processions and life with parades and he liked parades. People were always asking him if he remembered this or that—a dreary black procession of questions about the past. There was only one event in the past that had any significance for him and that he cared to talk about: that was twelve years ago when he had received the general's uniform and had been in the premiere.

"I was in that preemy they had in Atlanta," he would tell visitors sitting on his front porch. "Surrounded by beautiful guls. It wasn't a thing local about it. It was nothing local about it. Listen here. It was a nashnul event and they had me in it—up onto the stage. There was no bob-tails at it. Every person at it had paid ten dollars to get in and had to wear his tuxseeder. I was in this uniform. A beautiful gul presented me with it that afternoon in a hotel room."

"It was in a suite in the hotel and I was in it too, Papa," Sally Poker would say, winking at the visitors. "You weren't alone with any young lady in a hotel room."

"Was, I'd a known what to do," the old General would say with a sharp look and the visitors would scream with laughter. "This was a Hollywood, California, gul," he'd continue. "She was from Hollywood, California, and didn't have any part in the pitcher. Out there they have so many beautiful guls that they don't need that they call them a extra and they don't use them for nothing but presenting people with things and having their pitchers taken. They took my pitcher with her. No, it was two of them. One on either side and me in the middle with my arms around each of them's waist and their waist ain't any bigger than a half a dollar."

Sally Poker would interrupt again. "It was Mr. Govisky that gave you the uniform, Papa, and he gave me the most exquisite corsage. Really, I wish you could have seen it. It was made with gladiola petals taken off and painted gold and put back together to look like a rose. It was exquisite. I wish you could have seen it, it was . . ."

"It was as big as her head," the General would snarl. "I was tellin it. They gimme this uniform and they gimme this soward and they say, 'Now General, we don't want you to start a war on us. All we want you to do is march right up on that stage when you're innerduced tonight and answer a few questions. Think you can do that?' 'Think I can do it!' I say. 'Listen here. I was doing things before you were born,' and they hollered."

"He was the hit of the show," Sally Poker would say, but she didn't much like to remember the premiere on account of what had happened to her feet at it. She had bought a new dress for the occasion—a long black crepe dinner dress with a rhinestone buckle and a bolero—and a pair of silver slippers to wear with it, because she was supposed to go up on the stage with him to keep him from falling. Everything was arranged for them. A real limousine came at ten minutes to eight and took them to the theater. It drew up under the marquee at exactly the right time, after the big stars and the director and the author and the governor and the mayor and some less important stars. The police kept traffic from jamming and there were ropes to keep the people off who couldn't go. All the people who couldn't go watched them step out of the limousine into the lights. Then they walked down the red and gold foyer and an usherette in a Confederate cap and little short skirt conducted them to their special seats. The audience was already there and a group of UDC members began to clap when they saw the General in his uniform and that started everybody to clap. A few more celebrities came after them and then the doors closed and the lights went down.

A young man with blond wavy hair who said he represented the motion-picture industry came out and began to introduce everybody and each one who was introduced walked up on the stage and said how really happy he was to be here for this great event. The General and his granddaughter were introduced sixteenth on the program. He was introduced as General Tennessee Flintrock Sash of the Confederacy, though Sally Poker had told Mr. Govisky that his name was George Poker Sash and that he had only been a major. She helped him up from his seat but her heart was beating so fast she didn't know whether she'd make it herself.

The old man walked up the aisle slowly with his fierce white head high and his hat held over his heart. The orchestra began to play the Confederate Battle Hymn very softly and the UDC members rose as a group and did not sit down again until the General was on the stage. When he reached the center of the stage with Sally Poker just behind him guiding his elbow, the orchestra burst out in a loud rendition of the Battle Hymn and the old man, with real stage presence, gave a vigorous trembling salute and stood at attention until the last blast had died away. Two of the usherettes in Confederate caps and short skirts held a Confederate and a Union flag crossed behind them.

The General stood in the exact center of the spotlight and it caught a weird moon-shaped slice of Sally Poker—the corsage, the rhinestone buckle and one hand clenched around a white glove and handkerchief. The young man with the blond wavy hair inserted himself into the circle of light and said he was *really* happy to have here tonight for this great event, one, he said, who had fought and bled in the battles they would soon see daringly re-acted on the screen, and "Tell me, General," he asked, "how old are you?"

"Niiiiiinnttty-two!" the General screamed.

The young man looked as if this were just about the most impressive thing that had been said all evening. "Ladies and gentlemen," he said, "let's give the General the biggest hand we've got!" and there was applause immediately and the young man indicated to Sally Poker with a motion of his thumb that she could take the old man back to his seat now so that the next person could be introduced; but the General had not finished. He stood immovable in the exact center of the spotlight, his neck thrust forward, his mouth slightly open, and his voracious gray eyes drinking in the glare and the applause. He elbowed his granddaughter roughly away. "How I keep so young," he screeched, "I kiss all the pretty guls!"

This was met with a great din of spontaneous applause and it was at just that instant that Sally Poker looked down at her feet and discovered that in the excitement of getting ready she had forgotten to change her shoes: two brown Girl Scout oxfords protruded from the bottom of her dress. She gave the General a yank and almost ran with him off the stage. He was very angry that he had not got to say how glad he was to be here for this event and on the way back to his seat, he kept saying as loud as he could, "I'm glad to be here at this preemy with all these beautiful guls!" but there was another celebrity going up the other aisle and nobody paid any attention to him. He slept through the picture, muttering fiercely every now and then in his sleep.

Since then, his life had not been very interesting. His feet were completely dead now, his knees worked like old hinges, his kidneys functioned when they would, but his heart persisted doggedly to beat. The past and the future were the same thing to him, one forgotten and the other not remembered; he had no more notion of dying than a cat. Every year on Confederate Memorial Day, he was bundled up and lent to the Capitol City Museum where he was displayed from one to four in a musty room full of old photographs, old uniforms, old artillery, and historic documents. All these were carefully preserved in glass cases so that children would not put their hands on them. He wore his general's uniform from the premiere and sat, with a fixed scowl, inside a small roped area. There was nothing about him to indicate that he was alive except an occasional movement in his milky gray eyes, but once when a bold child touched his sword, his arm shot forward and slapped the hand off in an instant. In the spring when the old homes were opened for pilgrimages, he was invited to wear his uniform and sit in some conspicuous spot and lend atmosphere to the scene. Some of these times he only snarled at the visitors but sometimes he told about the premiere and the beautiful girls.

If he had died before Sally Poker's graduation, she thought she would have died herself. At the beginning of the summer term, even before she knew if she would pass, she told the Dean that her grandfather, General Tennessee Flintrock Sash of the Confederacy, would attend her graduation and that he was a hundred and four years old and that his mind was still clear as a bell. Distinguished visitors were always welcome and could sit on the stage and be introduced. She made arrangements with her nephew, John Wesley Poker Sash, a Boy Scout, to come wheel the General's chair. She thought how sweet it would be to see the old man in his courageous gray and the young boy in his clean khaki—the old and the new, she thought appropriately—they would be behind her on the stage when she received her degree.

Everything went almost exactly as she had planned. In the summer while she was away at school, the General stayed with other relatives and they brought him and John Wesley, the Boy Scout, down to the graduation. A reporter came to the hotel where they stayed and took the General's picture with Sally Poker on one side of him and John Wesley on the other. The General, who had had his picture taken with beautiful girls, didn't think much of this. He had forgotten precisely what kind of event this was he was going to attend but he remembered that he was to wear his uniform and carry the sword.

On the morning of the graduation, Sally Poker had to line up in the academic procession with the B.S.'s in Elementary Education and she couldn't see to getting him on the stage herself—but John Wesley, a fat blond boy of ten with an executive expression, guaranteed to take care of everything. She came in her academic gown to the hotel and dressed the old man in his uniform. He was as frail as a dried spider. "Aren't you just thrilled, Papa?" she asked. "I'm just thrilled to death!"

"Put the soward acrost my lap, damm you," the old man said, "where it'll shine."

She put it there and then stood back looking at him. "You look just grand," she said.

"God damm it," the old man said in a slow monotonous certain tone as if he were saying it to the beating of his heart. "God damm every goddam thing to hell."

"Now, now," she said and left happily to join the procession.

The graduates were lined up behind the Science building and she found her place just as the line started to move. She had not slept much the night before and when she had, she had dreamed of the exercises, murmuring, "See him, see him?" in her sleep but waking up every time just before she turned her head to look at him behind her. The graduates had to walk three blocks in the hot sun in their black wool robes and as she plodded stolidly along she thought that if anyone considered this academic procession something impressive to behold, they need only wait until they saw that old General in his courageous gray and that clean young Boy Scout stoutly wheeling his chair across the stage with the sunlight catching the sword. She imagined that John Wesley had the old man ready now behind the stage.

The black procession wound its way up the two blocks and started on the main walk leading to the auditorium. The visitors stood on the grass, picking out their graduates. Men were pushing back their hats and wiping their foreheads and women were lifting their dresses slightly from the shoulders to keep them from sticking to their backs. The graduates in their heavy robes looked as if the last beads of ignorance were being sweated out of them. The sun blazed off the fenders of automobiles and beat from the columns of the buildings and pulled the eye from one spot of glare to another. It pulled Sally Poker's toward the big red Coca-Cola machine that had been set up by the side of the auditorium. Here she saw the General parked, scowling and hatless in his chair in the blazing sun while John Wesley, his blouse loose behind, his hip and cheek pressed to the red machine, was drinking a Coca-Cola. She broke from the line and galloped to them and snatched the bottle away. She shook the boy and thrust in his blouse and put the hat on the old man's head.

"Now get him in there!" she said, pointing one rigid finger t
door of the building.

For his part the General felt as if there were a little hole beginning to
widen in the top of his head. The boy wheeled him rapidly down a walk
and up a ramp and into a building and bumped him over the stage
entrance and into position where he had been told and the General
glared in front of him at heads that all seemed to flow together and eyes
that moved from one face to another. Several figures in black robes came
and picked up his hand and shook it. A black procession was flowing up
each aisle and forming to stately music in a pool in front of him. The
music seemed to be entering his head through the little hole and he
thought for a second that the procession would try to enter it too.

He didn't know what procession this was but there was something
familiar about it. It must be familiar to him since it had come to meet
him, but he didn't like a black procession. Any procession that came to
meet him, he thought irritably, ought to have floats with beautiful guls
on them like the floats before the preemy. It must be something
connected with history like they were always having. He had no use for
any of it. What happened then wasn't anything to a man living now and
he was living now.

When all the procession had flowed into the black pool, a black figure
began orating in front of it. The figure was telling something about
history and the General made up his mind he wouldn't listen, but the
words kept seeping in through the little hole in his head. He heard his
own name mentioned and his chair was shuttled forward roughly and the
Boy Scout took a big bow. They called his name and the fat brat bowed.
Goddam you, the old man tried to say, get out of my way, I can stand
up!—but he was jerked back again before he could get up and take the
bow. He supposed the noise they made was for him. If he was over, he
didn't intend to listen to any more of it. If it hadn't been for the little
hole in the top of his head, none of the words would have got to him. He
thought of putting his finger up there into the hole to block them but
the hole was a little wider than his finger and it felt as if it were getting
deeper.

Another black robe had taken the place of the first one and was talking
now and he heard his name mentioned again but they were not talking
about him, they were still talking about history. "If we forget our past,"
the speaker was saying, "we won't remember our future and it will be as
well for we won't have one." The General heard some of these words
gradually. He had forgotten history and he didn't intend to remember it
again. He had forgotten the name and face of his wife and the names
and faces of his children or even if he had a wife and children, and he
had forgotten the names of places and the places themselves and what
had happened at them.

He was considerably irked by the hole in his head. He had not expected to have a hole in his head at this event. It was the slow black music that had put it there and though most of the music had stopped outside, there was still a little of it in the hole, going deeper and moving around in his thoughts, letting the words he heard into the dark places of his brain. He heard the words, Chickamauga, Shiloh, Johnston, Lee, and he knew he was inspiring all these words that meant nothing to him. He wondered if he had been a general at Chickamauga or at Lee. Then he tried to see himself and the horse mounted in the middle of a float full of beautiful girls, being driven slowly through downtown Atlanta. Instead, the old words began to stir in his head as if they were trying to wrench themselves out of place and come to life.

The speaker was through with that war and had gone on to the next one and now he was approaching another and all his words, like the black procession, were vaguely familiar and irritating. There was a long finger of music in the General's head, probing various spots that were words, letting in a little light on the words and helping them to live. The words began to come toward him and he said, Dammit! I ain't going to have it! and he started edging backwards to get out of the way. Then he saw the figure in the black robe sit down and there was a noise and the black pool in front of him began to rumble and to flow toward him from either side to the black slow music, and he said, Stop dammit! I can't do but one thing at a time! He couldn't protect himself from the words and attend to the procession too and the words were coming at him fast. He felt that he was running backwards and the words were coming at him like musket fire, just escaping him but getting nearer and nearer. He turned around and began to run as fast as he could but he found himself running toward the words. He was running into a regular volley of them and meeting them with quick curses. As the music swelled toward him, the entire past opened up on him out of nowhere and he felt his body riddled in a hundred places with sharp stabs of pain and he fell down, returning a curse for every hit. He saw his wife's narrow face looking at him critically through her round gold-rimmed glasses; he saw one of his squinting bald-headed sons; and his mother ran toward him with an anxious look; then a succession of places—Chickamauga, Shiloh, Marthasville—rushed at him as if the past were the only future now and he had to endure it. Then suddenly he saw that the black procession was almost on him. He recognized it, for it had been dogging all his days. He made such a desperate effort to see over it and find out what comes after the past that his hand clenched the sword until the blade touched bone.

The graduates were crossing the stage in a long file to receive their scrolls and shake the president's hand. As Sally Poker, who was near the end, crossed, she glanced at the General and saw him sitting fixed and fierce, his eyes wide open, and she turned her head forward again and held it a perceptible degree higher and received her scroll. Once it was all over and she was out of the auditorium in the sun again, she located her kin and they waited together on a bench in the shade for John Wesley to wheel the old man out. That crafty scout had bumped him out the back way and rolled him at high speed down a flagstone path and was waiting now, with the corpse, in the long line at the Coca-Cola machine.

QUESTIONS

1. What statement does O'Connor make about American values? Explain the significance of the dream Sally has. Who or what is the enemy in the story?

2. A traditional comic design is to have the old replaced by the young. In one sense, this is the pattern of "A Late Encounter with the Enemy." But how is Sally's graduation a travesty of rebirth or renewal? Why does she want the General to attend? How does she regard her education?

3. How do the images in the story work as devices for satire? Comment on Sally's corsage, the afghan, the Coke machine, the procession of graduates, the Boy Scout, and, of course, the General's full-dress uniform and sword.

4. Describe the premiere. What did the General like best? How does his account of this event differ from his granddaughter's? Why had she rushed him from the stage?

5. O'Connor's characters are frequently called "grotesques." Is that an appropriate description for General Sash and Sally Poker Sash? Explain. You may find it useful to refer to Ihab Hassan's analysis of Flannery O'Connor on page 319.

6. Discuss O'Connor's strategies for humor. How does she use dialect? Reversal? Exaggeration?

Miss Lonelyhearts, Help me, Help Me

Nathanael West

When modern men and women are opposed not just by a berserk and indifferent society but by a crazed and malevolent universe, the pressure is intolerable. Few American writers have understood this struggle so poignantly or portrayed it so brilliantly as Nathanael West, whose novels Miss Lonelyhearts *and* The Day of the Locust *helped set the literary trend toward black humor, that form of comedy in which the ludicrous and the grim coalesce. These cries for help, burlesques of letters sent to a newspaper advice columnist, fuse anguish with comic naiveté and funny misspelling. West's "particular kind of joking," as it has been called, expresses his vision of the modern American—living in a moral wasteland, he or she suffers grotesquely, without hope and without reason, for religion and art, the forms that traditionally give meaning to life, have become little more than obscene jokes.*

The Miss Lonelyhearts of the New York *Post-Dispatch* (Are you in trouble?—Do-you-need-advice?—Write-to-Miss-Lonelyhearts-and-she-will-help-you) sat at his desk and stared at a piece of white cardboard. On it a prayer had been printed by Shrike, the feature editor.

> "Soul of Miss L, glorify me.
> Body of Miss L, nourish me.
> Blood of Miss L, intoxicate me.
> Tears of Miss L, wash me.
> Oh good Miss L, excuse my plea,
> And hide me in your heart,
> And defend me from mine enemies.
> Help me, Miss L, help me, help me.
> In sæcula sæculorum. Amen."

Although the deadline was less than a quarter of an hour away, he was still working on his leader. He had gone as far as: "Life *is* worth while, for it is full of dreams and peace, gentleness and ecstasy, and faith that burns like a clear white flame on a grim dark altar." But he found it impossible to continue. The letters were no longer funny. He could not go on finding the same joke funny thirty times a day for months on end. And on most days he received more than thirty letters, all of them alike, stamped from the dough of suffering with a heart-shaped cookie knife. On his desk were piled those he had received this morning. He started through them again, searching for some clue to a sincere answer.

Dear Miss Lonelyhearts—

> I am in such pain I dont know what to do sometimes I think I will kill myself my kidneys hurt so much. My husband thinks no woman can be a good catholic and not have children irregardless of the pain. I was married honorable from our church but I never knew what married life meant as I never was told about man and wife. My grandmother never told me and she was the only mother I had but made a big mistake by not telling me as it dont pay to be inocent and is only a big disapointment. I have 7 children in 12 yrs and ever since the last 2 I have been so sick. I was operated on twice and my husband promised no more children on the doctors advice as he said I might die but when I got back from the hospital he broke his promise and now I am going to have a baby and I don't think I can stand it my kidneys hurts so much. I am so sick and scared because I cant have an abortion on account of being a catholic and my husband so religious. I cry all the time it hurts so much and I dont know what to do.

> *Yours respectfully*
> *Sick-of-it-all*

Miss Lonelyhearts threw the letter into an open drawer and lit a cigarette.

Dear Miss Lonelyhearts—

> I am sixteen years old now and I dont know what to do and would appreciate it if you could tell me what to do. When I was a little girl it was not so bad because I got used to the kids on the block makeing fun of me, but now I would like to have boy friends like the other girls and go out on Saturday nites, but no boy will take me beeause I was born without a nose—although I am a good dancer and have a nice shape and my father buys me pretty clothes.
> I sit and look at myself all day and cry. I have a big hole in the middle of my face that scares people even myself so I cant blame the boys for not wanting to take me out. My mother loves me, but she crys terrible when she looks at me.
> What did I do to deserve such a terrible bad fate? Even if I did do some bad things I didnt do any before I was a year old and I was born this way. I asked Papa and he says he doesnt know, but that maybe I did something in the other world before I was born or that maybe I was being punished for his sins. I dont believe that because he is a very nice man. Ought I commit suicide?

> *Sincerely yours,*
> *Desperate*

The cigarette was imperfect and refused to draw. Miss Lonelyhearts took it out of his mouth and stared at it furiously. He fought himself quiet, then lit another one.

Dear Miss Lonelyhearts—

I am writing to you for my little sister Gracie because something awfull hapened to her and I am afraid to tell mother about it. I am 15 years old and Gracie is 13 and we live in Brooklyn. Gracie is deaf and dumb and biger than me but not very smart on account of being deaf and dumb. She plays on the roof of our house and dont go to school except to deaf and dumb school twice a week on tuesdays and thursdays. Mother makes her play on the roof because we dont want her to get run over as she aint very smart. Last week a man came on the roof and did something dirty to her. She told me about it and I dont know what to do as I am afraid to tell mother on account of her being lible to beat Gracie up. I am afraid that Gracie is going to have a baby and I listened to her stomack last night for a long time to see if I could hear the baby but I couldn't. If I tell mother she will beat Gracie up awfull because I am the only one who loves her and last time when she tore her dress they loked her in the closet for 2 days and if the boys on the blok hear about it they will say dirty things like they did on Peewee Conors sister the time she got caught in the lots. So please what would you do if the same hapened in your family.

Yours truly,
Harold S.

He stopped reading. Christ was the answer, but, if he did not want to get sick, he had to stay away from the Christ business. Besides, Christ was Shrike's particular joke. "Soul of Miss L, glorify me. Body of Miss L, save me. Blood of . . ." He turned to his typewriter.

Although his cheap clothes had too much style, he still looked like the son of a Baptist minister. A beard would become him, would accent his Old-Testament look. But even without a beard no one could fail to recognize the New England puritan. His forehead was high and narrow. His nose was long and fleshless. His bony chin was shaped and cleft like a hoof. On seeing him for the first time, Shrike had smiled and said, "The Susan Chesters, the Beatrice Fairfaxes and the Miss Lonelyhearts are the priests of twentieth-century America."

A copy boy came up to tell him that Shrike wanted to know if the stuff was ready. He bent over the typewriter and began pounding its keys.

But before he had written a dozen words, Shrike leaned over his shoulder. "The same old stuff," Shrike said. "Why don't you give them something new and hopeful? Tell them about art. Here, I'll dictate:

"*Art Is a Way Out.*

"Do not let life overwhelm you. When the old paths are choked with the débris of failure, look for newer and fresher paths. Art is just such a

path. Art is distilled from suffering. As Mr. Polnikoff exclaimed through his fine Russian beard, when, at the age of eighty-six, he gave up his business to learn Chinese, 'We are, as yet, only at the beginning. . . .'
"Art Is One of Life's Richest Offerings.
"For those who have not the talent to create, there is appreciation. For those . . .
"Go on from there."

QUESTIONS

1. Describe the letters Miss Lonelyhearts receives. How are they signed? Why does Miss Lonelyhearts have difficulty answering them? Do you find them funny? Explain.

2. Discuss Shrike's statement that the Miss Lonelyhearts are the priests of twentieth-century America. How does West connect Lonelyhearts with an older American tradition? What advice columns do you, your family, or your friends read?

3. What American attitudes does the editor represent? Explain the significance of his name. How does he feel about religion? Art?

4. Why do you think critics describe West as a "black humorist"? You may want to refer to the introduction to this section. How do you account for the popularity of black humor? What insights does it provide on contemporary American life?

5. How does West use parody or imitation as a device for satire? In what way is the name Miss Lonelyhearts one of the central jokes of the story?

The Policemen's Ball

Donald Barthelme

Donald Barthelme uses policemen as a metaphor for Americans—not for the weak and maimed who write to Miss Lonelyhearts, but for the strong, for those "on the force" in America. Part of the grotesque joke of the story, made into a pun by the hero's name, is that the powerful who should protect us have, instead, become identified with the horrors that threaten society. The juxtaposition of the Pendragon's pompous rhetoric and the officer's banal thought— "Would Margot 'put out' tonight?"—is a strategy of social satire, but the crazed laughter with which the story concludes is the sound of black humor. As Margot symbolically becomes a Game Hen ready for the oven, the greatest joke of all is shown to be life itself. Works by Donald Barthelme include City Life; Unspeakable Practices, Unnatural Acts; Snow White; *and his most recent,* The Dead Father.

Horace, a policeman, was making Rock Cornish Game Hens for a special supper. The Game Hens are frozen solid, Horace thought. He was wearing his blue uniform pants.

Inside the Game Hens were the giblets in a plastic bag. Using his needlenose pliers Horace extracted the frozen giblets from the interior of the birds. Tonight is the night of the Policemen's Ball, Horace thought. We will dance the night away. But first, these Game Hens must go into a three-hundred-and-fifty-degree oven.

Horace shined his black dress shoes. Would Margot "put out" tonight? On this night of nights? Well, if she didn't—Horace regarded the necks of the birds which had been torn asunder by the pliers. No, he reflected, that is not a proper thought. Because I am a member of the force. I must try to keep my hatred under control. I must try to be an example for the rest of the people. Because if they can't trust us . . . the blue men . . .

In the dark, outside the Policemen's Ball, the horrors waited for Horace and Margot.

Margot was alone. Her roommates were in Provincetown for the weekend. She put pearl-colored lacquer on her nails to match the pearl of her new-bought gown. Police colonels and generals will be there, she thought. The Pendragon of Police himself. Whirling past the dais, I will glance upward. The pearl of my eyes meeting the steel gray of high rank.

Margot got into a cab and went over to Horace's place. The cabdriver was thinking: A nice-looking piece. I could love her.

Horace removed the birds from the oven. He slipped little gold frills, which had been included in the package, over the ends of the drumsticks. Then he uncorked the wine, thinking: This is a town without pity, this town. For those whose voices lack the crack of authority. Luckily the uniform . . . Why won't she surrender her person? Does she think she can resist the force? The force of the force?

"These birds are delicious."

Driving Horace and Margot smoothly to the Armory, the new cabdriver thought about basketball.

Why do they always applaud the man who makes the shot?

Why don't they applaud the ball?

It is the ball that actually goes into the net.

The man doesn't go into the net.

Never have I seen a man going into the net.

Twenty thousand policemen of all grades attended the annual fete. The scene was Camelot, with gay colors and burgees. The interior of the Armory had been roofed with lavish tenting. Police colonels and generals looked down on the dark uniforms, white gloves, silvery ball gowns.

"Tonight?"

"Horace, not now. This scene is so brilliant. I want to remember it."

Horace thought: It? Not me?

The Pendragon spoke. "I ask you to be reasonable with the citizens. They pay our salaries after all. I know that they are difficult sometimes, obtuse sometimes, even criminal sometimes, as we often run across in our line of work. But I ask you despite all to be reasonable. I know it is hard. I know it is not easy. I know that for instance when you see a big car, a '70 Biscayne hardtop, cutting around a corner at a pretty fair clip, with three in the front and three in the back, and they are all mixed up, ages and sexes and colors, your natural impulse is to—I know your first thought is, All those people! Together! And your second thought is, Force! But I must ask you in the name of force itself to be restrained. For force, that great principle, is most honored in the breach and the observance. And that is where you men are, in the breach. You are fine men, the finest. You are Americans. So for the sake of America, be careful. Be reasonable. Be slow. In the name of the Father and of the Son and of the Holy Ghost. And now I would like to introduce Vercingetorix, leader of the firemen, who brings us a few words of congratulation from that fine body of men."

Waves of applause for the Pendragon filled the tented area.

"He is a handsome older man," Margot said.

"He was born in a Western state and advanced to his present position through raw merit," Horace told her.

The government of Czechoslovakia sent observers to the Policemen's Ball. "Our police are not enough happy," Colonel-General Čepicky explained. "We seek ways to improve them. This is a way. It may not be the best way of all possible ways, but . . . Also I like to drink the official whiskey! It makes me gay!"

A bartender thought: Who is that yellow-haired girl in the pearl costume? She is stacked.

The mood of the Ball changed. The dancing was more serious now. Margot's eyes sparkled from the jorums of champagne she had drunk. She felt Horace's delicately Game Hen-flavored breath on her cheek. I will give him what he wants, she decided. Tonight. His heroism deserves it. He stands between us and them. He represents what is best in the society: decency, order, safety, strength, sirens, smoke. No, he does not represent smoke. Firemen represent smoke. Great billowing oily black clouds. That Vercingetorix has a noble look. With whom is Vercingetorix dancing, at present?

The horrors waited outside patiently. Even policemen, the horrors thought. We get even policemen, in the end.

In Horace's apartment, a gold frill was placed on a pearl toe.

The horrors had moved outside Horace's apartment. Not even policemen and their ladies are safe, the horrors thought. No one is safe. Safety does not exist. Ha ha ha ha ha ha ha ha ha ha!

QUESTIONS

1. This story is rich in word play, like the pun on "Horace" and "horrors." What other puns do you find? How do they express the theme of the story?

2. A caricature is an exaggeration that is distorted. In what way is Horace a caricature? Margot? Colonel-General Čepicky?

3. Discuss the tone of Barthelme's humor. Which elements in the story are funny? Which are frightening? What effect does the author achieve by mingling the two?

4. Explain what happens at the conclusion. What is the significance of the Game Hens? What are the "horrors"?

The Jewbird

Bernard Malamud

The American as victim of Donald Barthelme's "horrors" is symbolized in much recent fiction by the schlemiel, that stock character of Jewish humor who is plagued by bad luck. To add to the comedy in this parable, Malamud makes the schlemiel a talking bird with a taste for jarred herring. But comedy spills into pathos as the bird is tormented by an Americanized Jew—a frozen-foods salesman hoping to get his son into an Ivy League college—who incarnates the icy materialism of modern urban America. Winner of the Pulitzer Prize and twice winner of the National Book Award, Malamud has written the novels A New Life, The Assistant, *and* The Fixer, *and two collections of short stories,* Idiots First *and* The Magic Barrel.

The window was open so the skinny bird flew in. Flappity-flap with its frazzled black wings. That's how it goes. It's open, you're in. Closed, you're out and that's your fate. The bird wearily flapped through the open kitchen window of Harry Cohen's top-floor apartment on First Avenue near the lower East River. On a rod on the wall hung an escaped canary cage, its door wide open, but this black-type longbeaked bird—its ruffled head and small dull eyes, crossed a little, making it look like a dissipated crow—landed if not smack on Cohen's thick lamb chop, at least on the table, close by. The frozen foods salesman was sitting at supper with his wife and young son on a hot August evening a year ago. Cohen, a heavy man with hairy chest and beefy shorts; Edie, in skinny yellow shorts and red halter; and their ten-year-old Morris (after her father)—Maurie, they called him, a nice kid though not overly bright—were all in the city after two weeks out, because Cohen's mother was dying. They had been enjoying Kingston, New York, but drove back when Mama got sick in her flat in the Bronx.

"Right on the table," said Cohen, putting down his beer glass and swatting at the bird. "Son of a bitch."

"Harry, take care with your language," Edie said, looking at Maurie, who watched every move.

The bird cawed hoarsely and with a flap of its bedraggled wings—feathers tufted this way and that—rose heavily to the top of the open kitchen door, where it perched staring down.

"Gevalt, a pogrom!"

"It's a talking bird," said Edie in astonishment.

"In Jewish," said Maurie.

"Wise guy," muttered Cohen. He gnawed on his chop, then put down the bone. "So if you can talk, say what's your business. What do you want here?"

"If you can't spare a lamb chop," said the bird, "I'll settle for a piece of herring with a crust of bread. You can't live on your nerve forever."

"This ain't a restaurant," Cohen replied. "All I'm asking is what brings you to this address?"

"The window was open," the bird sighed; adding after a moment, "I'm running. I'm flying but I'm also running."

"From whom?" asked Edie with interest.

"Anti-Semeets."

"Anti-Semites?" they all said.

"That's from who."

"What kind of anti-Semites bother a bird?" Edie asked.

"Any kind," said the bird, "also including eagles, vultures, and hawks. And once in a while some crows will take your eyes out."

"But aren't you a crow?"

"Me? I'm a Jewbird."

Cohen laughed heartily. "What do you mean by that?"

The bird began dovening. He prayed without Book or tallith, but with passion. Edie bowed her head though not Cohen. And Maurie rocked back and forth with the prayer, looking up with one wide-open eye.

When the prayer was done Cohen remarked, "No hat, no phylacteries?"

"I'm an old radical."

"You're sure you're not some kind of a ghost or dybbuk?"

"Not a dybbuk," answered the bird, "though one of my relatives had such an experience once. It's all over now, thanks God. They freed her from a former lover, a crazy jealous man. She's now the mother of two wonderful children."

"Birds?" Cohen asked slyly.

"Why not?"

"What kind of birds?"

"Like me. Jewbirds."

Cohen tipped back in his chair and guffawed. "That's a big laugh. I've heard of a Jewfish but not a Jewbird."

"We're once removed." The bird rested on one skinny leg, then on the other. "Please, could you spare maybe a piece of herring with a small crust of bread?"

Edie got up from the table.

"What are you doing?" Cohen asked her.

"I'll clear the dishes."

Cohen turned to the bird. "So what's your name, if you don't mind saying?"

"Call me Schwartz."

"He might be an old Jew changed into a bird by somebody," said Edie, removing a plate.

"Are you?" asked Harry, lighting a cigar.

"Who knows?" answered Schwartz. "Does God tell us everything?"

Maurie got up on his chair. "What kind of herring?" he asked the bird in excitement.

"Get down, Maurie, or you'll fall," ordered Cohen.

"If you haven't got matjes, I'll take schmaltz," said Schwartz.

"All we have is marinated, with slices of onion—in a jar," said Edie.

"If you'll open for me the jar I'll eat marinated. Do you have also, if you don't mind, a piece of rye bread—the spitz?"

Edie thought she had.

"Feed him out on the balcony," Cohen said. He spoke to the bird. "After that take off."

Schwartz closed both bird eyes. "I'm tired and it's a long way."

"Which direction are you headed, north or south?"

Schwartz, barely lifting his wings, shrugged.

"You don't know where you're going?"

"Where there's charity I'll go."

"Let him stay, papa," said Maurie. "He's only a bird."

"So stay the night," Cohen said, "but no longer."

In the morning Cohen ordered the bird out of the house but Maurie cried, so Schwartz stayed for a while. Maurie was still on vacation from school and his friends were away. He was lonely and Edie enjoyed the fun he had, playing with the bird.

"He's no trouble at all," she told Cohen, "and besides his appetite is very small."

"What'll you do when he makes dirty?"

"He flies across the street in a tree when he makes dirty, and if nobody passes below, who notices?"

"So all right," said Cohen, "but I'm dead set against it. I warn you he ain't gonna stay here long."

"What have you got against the poor bird?"

"Poor bird, my ass. He's a foxy bastard. He thinks he's a Jew."

"What difference does it make what he thinks?"

"A Jewbird, what a chuzpah. One false move and he's out on his drumsticks."

At Cohen's insistence Schwartz lived out on the balcony in a new wooden birdhouse Edie had bought him.

"With many thanks," said Schwartz, "though I would rather have a human roof over my head. You know how it is at my age. I like the warm, the windows, the smell of cooking. I would also be glad to see

once in a while the *Jewish Morning Journal* and have now and then a
schnapps because it helps my breathing, thanks God. But whatever you
give me, you won't hear complaints."

However, when Cohen brought home a bird feeder full of dried corn,
Schwartz said, "Impossible."

Cohen was annoyed. "What's the matter, crosseyes, is your life getting
too good for you? Are you forgetting what it means to be migratory? I'll
bet a helluva lot of crows you happen to be acquainted with, Jews or
otherwise, would give their eyeteeth to eat this corn."

Schwartz did not answer. What can you say to a grubber yung?

"Not for my digestion," he later explained to Edie. "Cramps. Herring
is better even if it makes you thirsty. At least rainwater don't cost
anything." He laughed sadly in breathy caws.

And herring, thanks to Edie, who knew where to shop, was what
Schwartz got, with an occasional piece of potato pancake, and even a bit
of soupmeat when Cohen wasn't looking.

When school began in September, before Cohen would once again
suggest giving the bird the boot, Edie prevailed on him to wait a little
while until Maurie adjusted.

"To deprive him right now might hurt his school work, and you know
what trouble we had last year."

"So okay, but sooner or later the bird goes. That I promise you."

Schwartz, though nobody had asked him, took on full responsibility
for Maurie's performance in school. In return for favors granted, when
he was let in for an hour or two at night, he spent most of his time
overseeing the boy's lessons. He sat on top of the dresser near Maurie's
desk as he laboriously wrote out his homework. Maurie was a restless
type and Schwartz gently kept him to his studies. He also listened to him
practice his screechy violin, taking a few minutes off now and then to rest
his ears in the bathroom. And they afterwards played dominoes. The boy
was an indifferent checker player and it was impossible to teach him
chess. When he was sick, Schwartz read him comic books though he
personally disliked them. But Maurie's work improved in school and
even his violin teacher admitted his playing was better. Edie gave
Schwartz credit for these improvements though the bird pooh-poohed
them.

Yet he was proud there was nothing lower than C minuses on Maurie's
report card, and on Edie's insistence celebrated with a little schnapps.

"If he keeps up like this," Cohen said, "I'll get him in an Ivy League
college for sure."

"Oh I hope so," sighed Edie.

But Schwartz shook his head. "He's a good boy—you don't have to
worry. He won't be a shicker or a wifebeater, God forbid, but a scholar
he'll never be, if you know what I mean, although maybe a good
mechanic. It's no disgrace in these times."

"If I were you," Cohen said, angered, "I'd keep my big snoot out of other people's private business."

"Harry, please," said Edie.

"My goddamn patience is wearing out. That crosseyes butts into everything."

Though he wasn't exactly a welcome guest in the house, Schwartz gained a few ounces although he did not improve in appearance. He looked bedraggled as ever, his feathers unkempt, as though he had just flown out of a snowstorm. He spent, he admitted, little time taking care of himself. Too much to think about. "Also outside plumbing," he told Edie. Still there was more glow to his eyes so that though Cohen went on calling him crosseyes he said it less emphatically.

Liking his situation, Schwartz tried tactfully to stay out of Cohen's way, but one night when Edie was at the movies and Maurie was taking a hot shower, the frozen foods salesman began a quarrel with the bird.

"For Christ sake, why don't you wash yourself sometimes? Why must you always stink like a dead fish?"

"Mr. Cohen, if you'll pardon me, if somebody eats garlic he will smell from garlic. I eat herring three times a day. Feed me flowers and I will smell like flowers."

"Who's obligated to feed you anything at all? You're lucky to get herring."

"Excuse me, I'm not complaining," said the bird. "You're complaining."

"What's more," said Cohen, "even from out on the balcony I can hear you snoring away like a pig. It keeps me awake at night."

"Snoring," said Schwartz, "isn't a crime, thanks God."

"All in all you are a goddamn pest and free loader. Next thing you'll want to sleep in bed next to my wife."

"Mr. Cohen," said Schwartz, "on this rest assured. A bird is a bird."

"So you say, but how do I know you're a bird and not some kind of a goddamn devil?"

"If I was a devil you would know already. And I don't mean because your son's good marks."

"Shut up, you bastard bird," shouted Cohen.

"Grubber yung," cawed Schwartz, rising to the tips of his talons, his long wings outstretched.

Cohen was about to lunge for the bird's scrawny neck but Maurie came out of the bathroom, and for the rest of the evening until Schwartz's bedtime on the balcony, there was pretended peace.

But the quarrel had deeply disturbed Schwartz and he slept badly. His snoring woke him, and awake, he was fearful of what would become of him. Wanting to stay out of Cohen's way, he kept to the birdhouse as much as possible. Cramped by it, he paced back and forth on the balcony ledge, or sat on the birdhouse roof, staring into space. In the evenings, while overseeing Maurie's lessons, he often fell asleep. Awakening, he nervously hopped around exploring the four corners of the room. He spent much time in Maurie's closet, and carefully examined his bureau drawers when they were left open. And once when he found a large paper bag on the floor, Schwartz poked his way into it to investigate what possibilities were. The boy was amused to see the bird in the paper bag.

"He wants to build a nest," he said to his mother.

Edie, sensing Schwartz's unhappiness, spoke to him quietly.

"Maybe if you did some of the things my husband wants you, you would get along better with him."

"Give me a for instance," Schwartz said.

"Like take a bath, for instance."

"I'm too old for baths," said the bird. "My feathers fall out without baths."

"He says you have a bad smell."

"Everybody smells. Some people smell because of their thoughts or because who they are. My bad smell comes from the food I eat. What does his come from?"

"I better not ask him or it might make him mad," said Edie.

In late November Schwartz froze on the balcony in the fog and cold, and especially on rainy days he woke with stiff joints and could barely move his wings. Already he felt twinges of rheumatism. He would have liked to spend more time in the warm house, particularly when Maurie was in school and Cohen at work. But though Edie was good-hearted and might have sneaked him in in the morning, just to thaw out, he was afraid to ask her. In the meantime Cohen, who had been reading articles about the migration of birds, came out on the balcony one night after work when Edie was in the kitchen preparing pot roast, and peeking into the birdhouse, warned Schwartz to be on his way soon if he knew what was good for him. "Time to hit the flyways."

"Mr. Cohen, why do you hate me so much?" asked the bird. "What did I do to you?"

"Because you're an A-number-one trouble maker, that's why. What's more, whoever heard of a Jewbird? Now scat or it's open war."

But Schwartz stubbornly refused to depart so Cohen embarked on a campaign of harassing him, meanwhile hiding it from Edie and Maurie. Maurie hated violence and Cohen didn't want to leave a bad impression. He thought maybe if he played dirty tricks on the bird he would fly off without being physically kicked out. The vacation was over, let him make his easy living off the fat of somebody else's land. Cohen worried about the effect of the bird's departure on Maurie's schooling but decided to take the chance, first, because the boy now seemed to have the knack of studying—give the black bird-bastard credit—and second, because Schwartz was driving him bats by being there always, even in his dreams.

The frozen foods salesman began his campaign against the bird by mixing watery cat food with the herring slices in Schwartz's dish. He also blew up and popped numerous paper bags outside the birdhouse as the bird slept, and when he had got Schwartz good and nervous, though not enough to leave, he brought a full-grown cat into the house, supposedly a gift for little Maurie, who had always wanted a pussy. The cat never stopped springing up at Schwartz whenever he saw him, one day managing to claw out several of his tailfeathers. And even at lesson time, when the cat was usually excluded from Maurie's room, though somehow or other he quickly found his way in at the end of the lesson, Schwartz was desperately fearful of his life and flew from pinnacle to pinnacle—light fixture to clothes-tree to door-top—in order to elude the beast's wet jaws.

Once when the bird complained to Edie how hazardous his existence was, she said, "Be patient, Mr. Schwartz. When the cat gets to know you better he won't try to catch you any more."

"When he stops trying we will both be in Paradise," Schwartz answered. "Do me a favor and get rid of him. He makes my whole life worry. I'm losing feathers like a tree loses leaves."

"I'm awfully sorry but Maurie likes the pussy and sleeps with it."

What could Schwartz do? He worried but came to no decision, being afraid to leave. So he ate the herring garnished with cat food, tried hard not to hear the paper bags bursting like fire crackers outside the birdhouse at night, and lived terror-stricken closer to the ceiling than the floor, as the cat, his tail flicking, endlessly watched him.

Weeks went by. Then on the day after Cohen's mother had died in her flat in the Bronx, when Maurie came home with a zero on an arithmetic test, Cohen, enraged, waited until Edie had taken the boy to his violin lesson, then openly attacked the bird. He chased him with a broom on the balcony and Schwartz frantically flew back and forth, finally escaping into his birdhouse. Cohen triumphantly reached in, and grabbing both skinny legs, dragged the bird out, cawing loudly, his wings wildly beating. He whirled the bird around and around his head. But Schwartz, as he moved in circles, managed to swoop down and catch Cohen's nose in his beak, and hung on for dear life. Cohen cried out in great pain, punched the bird with his fist, and tugging at its legs with all his might, pulled his nose free. Again he swung the yawking Schwartz around until the bird grew dizzy, then with a furious heave, flung him into the night. Schwartz sank like stone into the street. Cohen then tossed the birdhouse and feeder after him, listening at the ledge until they crashed on the sidewalk below. For a full hour, broom in hand, his heart palpitating and nose throbbing with pain, Cohen waited for Schwartz to return but the brokenhearted bird didn't.

That's the end of that dirty bastard, the salesman thought and went in. Edie and Maurie had come home.

"Look," said Cohen, pointing to his bloody nose swollen three times its normal size, "what that sonofabitchy bird did. It's a permanent scar."

"Where is he now?" Edie asked, frightened.

"I threw him out and he flew away. Good riddance."

Nobody said no, though Edie touched a handkerchief to her eyes and Maurie rapidly tried the nine times table and found he knew approximately half.

In the spring when the winter's snow had melted, the boy, moved by a memory, wandered in the neighborhood, looking for Schwartz. He found a dead black bird in a small lot near the river, his two wings broken, neck twisted, and both bird-eyes plucked clean.

"Who did it to you, Mr. Schwartz?" Maurie wept.

"Anti-Semeets," Edie said later.

QUESTIONS

1. Describe Schwartz. What comic qualities does he have? What reasons does he offer for his poor appearance? How does he help Maurie with his schoolwork?

2. Why does Cohen dislike the bird? How does he torment Schwartz? How does he finally get rid of him?

3. "The Jewbird" is a mixture of realism and fantasy. What serious statement does it make about love and compassion in a modern American city? How does anti-Semitism function as a metaphor in the story? Explain the significance of Cohen's occupation.

4. Compare Schwartz with Vonnegut's Sparky. What do they have in common? In what ways is Schwartz an emblem of the Wandering Jew?

5. How is dialect used in the story to create humor? How do the last words in the story—Edie's mispronounced "anti-Semeets"—intensify the irony?

Catch-22: The Great American Trap

Joseph Heller

Joseph Heller's novel Catch-22, *on its way to becoming a classic, says much about our age—about the military bureaucracy that governs America's politics and the military logic that governs its thinking, a logic epitomized in the obscure regulation known as Catch-22 that Heller defines here. Masking unreason behind a semblance of reason, Catch-22 not only protects those in power but institutionalizes their power as well. In a style reminiscent of the Marx Brothers', Yossarian's dialogue substitutes sound for sense, suggesting the absurdity and chaos of life in America, where Chief Halfoat is an illiterate intelligence officer and Aarfy a B-25 navigator who cannot find his way. But Yossarian's will to live testifies to the fact that the comic spirit is alive, if not quite well, in America. Other works by Joseph Heller include* We Bombed in New Haven *and* Something Happened.

Chief White Halfoat was a handsome, swarthy Indian from Oklahoma with a heavy, hard-boned face and tousled black hair, a half-blooded Creek from Enid who, for occult reasons of his own, had made up his mind to die of pneumonia. He was a glowering, vengeful, disillusioned Indian who hated foreigners with names like Cathcart, Korn, Black and Havermeyer and wished they'd all go back to where their lousy ancestors had come from.

"You wouldn't believe it, Yossarian," he ruminated, raising his voice deliberately to bait Doc Daneeka, "but this used to be a pretty good country to live in before they loused it up with their goddam piety."

Chief White Halfoat was out to revenge himself upon the white man. He could barely read or write and had been assigned to Captain Black as assistant intelligence officer.

"How could I learn to read or write?" Chief White Halfoat demanded with simulated belligerence, raising his voice again so that Doc Daneeka would hear. "Every place we pitched our tent, they sank an oil well. Every time they sank a well, they hit oil. And every time they hit oil, they made us pack up our tent and go someplace else. We were human divining rods. Our whole family had a natural affinity for petroleum deposits, and soon every oil company in the world had technicians chasing us around. We were always on the move. It was one hell of a way to bring a child up, I can tell you. I don't think I ever spent more than a week in one place."

His earliest memory was of a geologist.

"Every time another White Halfoat was born," he continued, "the stock market turned bullish. Soon whole drilling crews were following us around with all their equipment just to get the jump on each other. Companies began to merge just so they could cut down on the number of people they had to assign to us. But the crowd in back of us kept growing. We never got a good night's sleep. When we stopped, they stopped. When we moved, they moved, chuckwagons, bulldozers, derricks, generators. We were a walking business boom, and we began to receive invitations from some of the best hotels just for the amount of business we would drag into town with us. Some of those invitations were mighty generous, but we couldn't accept any because we were Indians and all the best hotels that were inviting us wouldn't accept Indians as guests. Racial prejudice is a terrible thing, Yossarian. It really is. It's a terrible thing to treat a decent, loyal Indian like a nigger, kike, wop or spic." Chief White Halfoat nodded slowly with conviction.

"Then, Yossarian, it finally happened—the beginning of the end. They began to follow us around from in front. They would try to guess where we were going to stop next and would begin drilling before we even got there, so we couldn't even stop. As soon as we'd begin to unroll our blankets, they would kick us off. They had confidence in us. They wouldn't even wait to strike oil before they kicked us off. We were so tired we almost didn't care the day our time ran out. One morning we found ourselves completely surrounded by oilmen waiting for us to come their way so they could kick us off. Everywhere you looked there was an oilman on a ridge, waiting there like Indians getting ready to attack. It was the end. We couldn't stay where we were because we had just been kicked off. And there was no place left for us to go. Only the Army saved me. Luckily, the war broke out just in the nick of time, and a draft board picked me right up out of the middle and put me down safely in Lowery Field, Colorado. I was the only survivor."

Yossarian knew he was lying, but did not interrupt as Chief White Halfoat went on to claim that he had never heard from his parents again. That didn't bother him too much, though, for he had only their word for it that they were his parents, and since they had lied to him about so many other things, they could just as well have been lying to him about that too. He was much better acquainted with the fate of a tribe of first cousins who had wandered away north in a diversionary movement and pushed inadvertently into Canada. When they tried to return, they were stopped at the border by American immigration authorities who would not let them back into the country. They could not come back in because they were red.

It was a horrible joke, but Doc Daneeka didn't laugh until Yossarian came to him one mission later and pleaded again, without any real expectation of success, to be grounded. Doc Daneeka snickered once and was soon immersed in problems of his own, which included Chief White Halfoat, who had been challenging him all that morning to Indian wrestle, and Yossarian, who decided right then and there to go crazy.

"You're wasting your time," Doc Daneeka was forced to tell him.

"Can't you ground someone who's crazy?"

"Oh, sure. I have to. There's a rule saying I have to ground anyone who's crazy."

"Then why don't you ground me? I'm crazy. Ask Clevinger."

"Clevinger? Where is Clevinger? You find Clevinger and I'll ask him."

"Then ask any of the others. They'll tell you how crazy I am."

"They're crazy."

"Then why don't you ground them?"

"Why don't they ask me to ground them?"

"Because they're crazy, that's why."

"Of course they're crazy," Doc Daneeka replied. "I just told you they're crazy, didn't I? And you can't let crazy people decide whether you're crazy or not, can you?"

Yossarian looked at him soberly and tried another approach. "Is Orr crazy?"

"He sure is," Doc Daneeka said.

"Can you ground him?"

"I sure can. But first he has to ask me to. That's part of the rule."

"Then why doesn't he ask you to?"

"Because he's crazy," Doc Daneeka said. "He has to be crazy to keep flying combat missions after all the close calls he's had. Sure, I can ground Orr. But first he has to ask me to."

"That's all he has to do to be grounded?"

"That's all. Let him ask me."

"And then you can ground him?" Yossarian asked.

"No. Then I can't ground him."

"You mean there's a catch?"

"Sure there's a catch," Doc Daneeka replied. "Catch-22. Anyone who wants to get out of combat duty isn't really crazy."

There was only one catch and that was Catch-22, which specified that a concern for one's own safety in the face of dangers that were real and immediate was the process of a rational mind. Orr was crazy and could be grounded. All he had to do was ask; and as soon as he did, he would no longer be crazy and would have to fly more missions. Orr would be crazy to fly more missions and sane if he didn't, but if he was sane he had to fly them. If he flew them he was crazy and didn't have to; but if he didn't want to he was sane and had to. Yossarian was moved very deeply by the absolute simplicity of this clause of Catch-22 and let out a respectful whistle.

"That's some catch, that Catch-22," he observed.

"It's the best there is," Doc Daneeka agreed.

Yossarian saw it clearly in all its spinning reasonableness. There was an elliptical precision about its perfect pairs of parts that was graceful and shocking, like good modern art, and at times Yossarian wasn't quite sure that he saw it all, just the way he was never quite sure about good modern art or about the flies Orr saw in Appleby's eyes. He had Orr's word to take for the flies in Appleby's eyes.

"Oh, they're there, all right," Orr had assured him about the flies in Appleby's eyes after Yossarian's fist fight with Appleby in the officers' club, "although he probably doesn't even know it. That's why he can't see things as they really are."

"How come he doesn't know it?" inquired Yossarian.

"Because he's got flies in his eyes," Orr explained with exaggerated patience. "How can he see he's got flies in his eyes if he's got flies in his eyes?"

It made as much sense as anything else, and Yossarian was willing to give Orr the benefit of the doubt because Orr was from the wilderness outside New York City and knew so much more about wild-life than Yossarian did, and because Orr, unlike Yossarian's mother, father, sister, brother, aunt, uncle, in-law, teacher, spiritual leader, legislator, neighbor and newspaper, had never lied to him about anything crucial before. Yossarian had mulled his newfound knowledge about Appleby over in private for a day or two and then decided, as a good deed, to pass the word along to Appleby himself.

"Appleby, you've got flies in your eyes," he whispered helpfully as they passed by each other in the doorway of the parachute tent on the day of the weekly milk run to Parma.

"What?" Appleby responded sharply, thrown into confusion by the fact that Yossarian had spoken to him at all.

"You've got flies in your eyes," Yossarian repeated. "That's probably why you can't see them."

Appleby retreated from Yossarian with a look of loathing bewilderment and sulked in silence until he was in the jeep with Havermeyer riding down the long, straight road to the briefing room, where Major Danby, the fidgeting group operations officer, was waiting to conduct the preliminary briefing with all the lead pilots, bombardiers and navigators. Appleby spoke in a soft voice so that he would not be heard by the driver or by Captain Black, who was stretched out with his eyes closed in the front seat of the jeep.

"Havermeyer," he asked hesitantly. "Have I got flies in my eyes?"
Havermeyer blinked quizzically. "Sties?" he asked.
"No, flies," he was told.
Havermeyer blinked again. "Flies?"
"In my eyes."
"You must be crazy," Havermeyer said.
"No, I'm not crazy. Yossarian's crazy. Just tell me if I've got flies in my eyes or not. Go ahead. I can take it."
Havermeyer popped another piece of peanut brittle into his mouth and peered very closely into Appleby's eyes.
"I don't see any," he announced.
Appleby heaved an immense sigh of relief. Havermeyer had tiny bits of peanut brittle adhering to his lips, chin and cheeks.
"You've got peanut brittle crumbs on your face," Appleby remarked to him.
"I'd rather have peanut brittle crumbs on my face than flies in my eyes," Havermeyer retorted.

The officers of the other five planes in each flight arrived in trucks for the general briefing that took place thirty minutes later. The three enlisted men in each crew were not briefed at all, but were carried directly out on the airfield to the separate planes in which they were scheduled to fly that day, where they waited around with the ground crew until the officers with whom they had been scheduled to fly swung off the rattling tailgates of the trucks delivering them and it was time to climb aboard and start up. Engines rolled over disgruntedly on lollipop-shaped hardstands, resisting first, then idling smoothly awhile, and then the planes lumbered around and nosed forward lamely over the pebbled ground like sightless, stupid, crippled things until they taxied into the line at the foot of the landing strip and took off swiftly, one behind the other, in a zooming, rising roar, banking slowly into formation over mottled treetops, and circling the field at even speed until all the flights of six had been formed and then setting course over cerulean water on the first leg of the journey to the target in northern Italy or France. The planes gained altitude steadily and were above nine thousand feet by the time they crossed into enemy territory. One of the surprising things always was the sense of calm and utter silence, broken only by the test rounds fired from the machine guns, by an occasional toneless, terse remark over the intercom, and, at last, by the sobering pronouncement of the bombardier in each plane that they were at the I.P. and about to turn toward the target. There was always sunshine, always a tiny sticking in the throat from the rarefied air.

The B-25s they flew in were stable, dependable, dull-green ships with twin rudders and engines and wide wings. Their single fault, from where Yossarian sat as a bombardier, was the tight crawlway separating the bombardier's compartment in the plexiglass nose from the nearest escape hatch. The crawlway was a narrow, square, cold tunnel hollowed out beneath the flight controls, and a large man like Yossarian could squeeze through only with difficulty. A chubby, moon-faced navigator with little reptilian eyes and a pipe like Aarfy's had trouble, too, and Yossarian used to chase him back from the nose as they turned toward the target, now minutes away. There was a time of tension then, a time of waiting with nothing to hear and nothing to see and nothing to do but wait as the antiaircraft guns below took aim and made ready to knock them all sprawling into infinite sleep if they could.

The crawlway was Yossarian's lifeline to outside from a plane about to fall, but Yossarian swore at it with seething antagonism, reviled it as an obstacle put there by providence as part of the plot that would destroy him. There was room for an additional escape hatch right there in the nose of a B-25, but there was no escape hatch. Instead there was the crawlway, and since the mess on the mission over Avignon he had learned to detest every mammoth inch of it, for it slung him seconds and seconds away from his parachute, which was too bulky to be taken up front with him, and seconds and seconds more after that away from the escape hatch on the floor between the rear of the elevated flight deck and the feet of the faceless top turret gunner mounted high above. Yossarian longed to be where Aarfy could be once Yossarian had chased him back from the nose; Yossarian longed to sit on the floor in a huddled ball right on top of the escape hatch inside a sheltering igloo of extra flak suits that he would have been happy to carry along with him, his parachute already hooked to his harness where it belonged, one fist clenching the red-handled rip cord, one fist gripping the emergency hatch release that would spill him earthward into air at the first dreadful squeal of destruction. That was where he wanted to be if he had to be there at all, instead of hung out there in front like some goddam cantilevered goldfish in some goddam cantilevered goldfish bowl while the goddam foul black tiers of flak were bursting and booming and billowing all around and above and below him in a climbing, cracking, staggered, banging, phantasmagorical, cosmological wickedness that jarred and tossed and shivered, clattered and pierced, and threatened to annihilate them all in one splinter of a second in one vast flash of fire.

Aarfy had been no use to Yossarian as a navigator or as anything else, and Yossarian drove him back from the nose vehemently each time so that they would not clutter up each other's way if they had to scramble suddenly for safety. Once Yossarian had driven him back from the nose, Aarfy was free to cower on the floor where Yossarian longed to cower, but he stood bolt upright instead with his stumpy arms resting comfortably on the backs of the pilot's and co-pilot's seats, pipe in hand, making affable small talk to McWatt and whoever happened to be co-pilot and pointing out amusing trivia in the sky to the two men, who were too busy to be interested. McWatt was too busy responding at the controls to Yossarian's strident instructions as Yossarian slipped the plane in on the bomb run and then whipped them all away violently around the ravenous pillars of exploding shells with curt, shrill, obscene commands to McWatt that were much like the anguished, entreating nightmare yelpings of Hungry Joe in the dark. Aarfy would puff reflectively on his pipe throughout the whole chaotic clash, gazing with unruffled curiosity at the war through McWatt's window as though it were a remote disturbance that could not affect him. Aarfy was a dedicated fraternity man who loved cheerleading and class reunions and did not have brains enough to be afraid. Yossarian did have brains enough and was, and the only thing that stopped him from abandoning his post under fire and scurrying back through the crawlway like a yellow-bellied rat was his unwillingness to entrust the evasive action out of the target area to anybody else. There was nobody else in the world he would honor with so great a responsibility. There was nobody else he knew who was as big a coward. Yossarian was the best man in the group at evasive action, but had no idea why.

There was no established procedure for evasive action. All you needed was fear, and Yossarian had plenty of that, more fear than Orr or Hungry Joe, more fear even than Dunbar, who had resigned himself submissively to the idea that he must die someday. Yossarian had not resigned himself to that idea, and he bolted for his life wildly on each mission the instant his bombs were away, hollering, *"Hard, hard, hard, hard, you bastard, hard!"* at McWatt and hating McWatt viciously all the time as though McWatt were to blame for their being up there at all to be rubbed out by strangers, and everybody else in the plane kept off the intercom, except for the pitiful time of the mess on the mission to Avignon when Dobbs went crazy in mid-air and began weeping pathetically for help.

"Help him, help him," Dobbs sobbed. "Help him, help him."

"Help who? Help who?" called back Yossarian, once he had plugged his headset back into the intercom system, after it had been jerked out when Dobbs wrested the controls away from Huple and hurled them all down suddenly into the deafening, paralyzing, horrifying dive which had plastered Yossarian helplessly to the ceiling of the plane by the top of his head and from which Huple had rescued them just in time by seizing the controls back from Dobbs and leveling the ship out almost as suddenly right back in the middle of the buffeting layer of cacophonous flak from which they had escaped successfully only a moment before. *Oh, God! Oh, God, oh, God,* Yossarian had been pleading wordlessly as he dangled from the ceiling of the nose of the ship by the top of his head, unable to move.

"The bombardier, the bombardier," Dobbs answered in a cry when

Yossarian spoke. "He doesn't answer, he doesn't answer. Help the bombardier, help the bombardier."

"I'm the bombardier," Yossarian cried back at him. "I'm the bombardier. I'm all right. I'm all right."

"Then help him, help him," Dobbs begged. "Help him, help him."

And Snowden lay dying in back.

QUESTIONS

1. Discuss Catch-22. How does it keep Orr from being grounded? Do you agree with Doc Daneeka that it's the best catch there is?

2. Explain how Catch-22 applies to other selections in Part 1 of this book. For example, how does it explain the plight of those who write to Miss Lonelyhearts? Of Malamud's Jewbird?

3. What image does Heller present of the modern American? Examine Yossarian as a comic hero. Why is he the best man at evasive action?

4. Describe the other characters in the story. How do they expose American faults? What does Chief White Halfoat tell us about bigotry? Why does Yossarian believe what Orr tells him?

5. In what ways is this an example of black humor? What issues does Heller deal with that seem beyond satire? Explain.

A Group of Vultures Waiting for the Storm to "Blow Over."—"Let Us *Prey*."

The wise fool, representative of the average American citizen, has typically been concerned with politics. Often, his satiric humor has helped to defeat political corruption, as with this cartoon drawn more than a century ago by Thomas Nast. Nast's target was the venal Tweed Ring in New York; his weapons, the comic strategies of exaggeration, distortion, and animalism. The caricature is one of a series Nast drew for Harper's Weekly. *Tweed himself, eventually jailed, paid tribute to the power of the comic artist: "I don't care a straw for your newspaper articles, my constituents don't know how to read, but they can't help seeing them damned pictures." (Cartoon courtesy of the Library of Congress)*

part 2

The Wise Fool

The wise fool, the earliest sharply defined type in our comic folklore, embodies those traits that Americans traditionally hold most dear. In a democracy, where equality is a national shibboleth, guaranteed by the Constitution and ritualized in the voting process, the pronouncements of the man in the street are to be respected if not reverenced. The wise fool speaks with authority on subjects that concern the ordinary citizen—politics, religion, war, marriage, the young. Often, despite poor education and low social status, he presumes to be the counselor and colleague of men of affairs; Bill Nye, resigning as Postmaster of Laramie, cautions the President to break the news carefully to foreign diplomats.

A fusion, in varying degrees, of common sense and folly, the fool-savant is likely to be a complex character. Sometimes, to present their messages more subtly, comic writers use the fool ironically, so that we cannot take him seriously. He may be a hypocrite, like the speaker in Oliver Wendell Holmes's poem "Contentment," an arrant scoundrel, like James Russell Lowell's Birdofredum Sawin, or an unprincipled coward, like Petroleum Vesuvius Nasby, who hopes his dandruff will keep him from being drafted. Benjamin Franklin's "Poor Richard," one of the first oracles of native wisdom, seems, in fact, to change character; in the earlier almanacs he is a dunderhead given to foolish statements, but he grows considerably wiser. The ironic fool continues to be a popular comic figure, as shown by the contemporary columnist Art Buchwald, who, tongue in cheek, explains his nonsensical suggestions for prison reform.

Often it is the language of the naive wit that identifies him as "just folks." In the mid-nineteenth century, America's favorite comedians, dubbed the "misspellers" or "phunny phellows," relied on deformed English as a stock comic device. As the sage who could not spell, for instance, Artemus Ward delivered moral lectures on such timely topics as Free Love, lampooning both his own characterization of the ignorant, hypocritical conservative and various radical social movements. Influenced by Ward, Mark Twain slipped into the role of the plain-talking, untutored literary critic in his classic satire of the early American novelist James Fenimore Cooper. The language of the fool may announce his regional or ethnic background as well. The broad dialect and homely metaphors of New England pepper the speech of Jack Downing, the fictional yokel created in 1830 by Maine editor Seba Smith. But Jack and his Yankee cousins have been succeeded by a variety of wise-fool personages: Hoosier backwoodsmen and westerners, immigrants and members of minority groups. The twentieth-century Will Rogers, twirling his lariat and boasting that he knows only what he reads in the papers, achieves spectacular success as the cowboy philosopher. With Finley Peter Dunne's Mr. Dooley and Langston Hughes's Jesse Semple, the intonations are those of the Irish and the blacks, but the cracker-box traits are still clearly visible. The bartender Dooley speaks of "me frind Willum J. O'Brien," and Semple, whose letters on national affairs recall those of Jack Downing, reads the *New York Times* only when he chances to "pick up a copy blowing around in the subway."

Although the idiom and environment have been refashioned by succeeding generations, the essential characteristics of the uncouth wit remain unchanged today. In *Crackerbox Philosophers in American Humor and Satire*, Jennette Tandy reminds us, "Consciously or unconsciously, our lives are shaped by those real or imaginary homely critics, the unlettered philosophers." Witness the wide popularity of TV's Archie Bunker, a 1970 avatar of the fool character. When Archie bellowed about intellectual "meatheads" and female "dingbats," were audiences laughing with him or at him? Or were they, like the audiences of Artemus Ward a century before, doing a bit of both? Having exchanged his straw hat for a union card, the cracker-barrel thinker has grown with America to remain an emblem of the national character.

The Wisdom of Poor Richard

Benjamin Franklin

Benjamin Franklin is generally regarded as the father of American humor. Although Franklin wrote numerous political satires and an autobiography, the work he is remembered best for today is the famous series of almanacs, begun in 1732, that featured jokes, light verse, satiric comments on everyday life, and comic predictions. When Franklin, in the almanac for 1733, pretended to foretell the death of his rival, Titan Leeds, Philadelphia laughed heartily at Leeds's indignant reply. But Franklin's most notable contribution to American humor was the creation of Poor Richard, the fool character who represented the typical American. The wit and wisdom of Poor Richard have become legendary. In the maxims used to fill empty spaces on the pages of his almanac, Richard persuaded readers to be industrious and frugal. While the proverbs were borrowed from the stored wisdom of all nations and ages, the utilitarian philosophy known as "Poor Richardism" expressed the values of the young American republic.

Courteous Reader,

I might in this place attempt to gain thy favour by declaring that I write Almanacks with no other view than that of the publick good, but in this I should not be sincere; and men are now a-days too wise to be deceiv'd by pretences, how specious soever. The plain truth of the matter is, I am excessive poor, and my wife, good woman, is, I tell her, excessive proud; she cannot bear, she says, to sit spinning in her shift of tow, while I do nothing but gaze at the stars; and has threatened more than once to burn all my books and rattling-traps, (as she calls my instruments,) if I do not make some profitable use of them for the good of my family. The printer has offer'd me some considerable share of the profits, and I have thus began to comply with my dame's desire.

Indeed, this motive would have had force enough to have made me publish an Almanack many years since, had it not been overpowered by my regard for my good friend and fellow-student, Mr. *Titan Leeds*, whose interest I was extreamly unwilling to hurt. But this obstacle (I am far from speaking it with pleasure,) is soon to be removed, since inexorable death, who was never known to respect merit, has already prepared the mortal dart, the fatal sister has already extended her destroying shears, and that ingenious man must soon be taken from us. He dies, by my calculation, made at his request, on Oct. 17, 1733, 3 ho., 29 m., P.M., at the very instant of the ♂ of ☉ and ☿. By his own calculation he will survive till the 26th of the same month. This small difference between us we have disputed whenever we have met these nine years past; but at length he is inclinable to agree with my judgment. Which of us is most exact, a little time will now determine. As, therefore, these Provinces may not longer expect to see any of his performances after this year I think myself free to take up the task, and request a share of publick encouragement, which I am the more apt to hope for on this account, that the buyer of my Almanack may consider himself not only as purchasing an useful utensil, but as performing an act of charity to his poor

Friend and servant,
R. SAUNDERS.

More nice than wise

Old batchelor would have a wife that's wise,
  Fair, rich, and young, a maiden for his bed;
Not proud, nor churlish, but of faultless size,
  A country housewife in the city bred.
    He's a nice fool, and long in vain hath staid;
    He should bespeak her, there's none ready made.

Never spare the parson's wine, nor the baker's pudding.

A house without woman and firelight, is like a body without soul or sprite.

Kings and bears often worry their keepers.

He's a fool that makes his doctor his heir.

Ne'er take a wife till thou hast a house (and a fire) to put her in.

He's gone, and forgot nothing but to say farewell to his creditors.

Hunger never saw bad bread.

Kind Katherine to her husband kiss'd these words,
  "Mine own sweet Will, how dearly I love thee!"
If true (quoth Will) the world no such affords.
  And that its true I durst his warrant be:
    For ne'er heard I of woman good or ill,
    But always loved best, her own sweet Will.

Great talkers, little doers.

A rich rogue is like a fat hog, who never does good till as dead as a log.

Relation without friendship, friendship without power, power without will, will without effect, effect without profit, and profit without virtue, are not worth a farto.

Mirth pleaseth some, to others 't is offence,
Some commend plain conceit, some profound sense;
Some wish a witty jest, some dislike that,
And most would have themselves they know not what.
Then he that would please all, and himself too,
Takes more in hand than he is like to do.

The favour of the great is no inheritance.

Fools make feasts, and wise men eat them.

Beware of the young doctor and the old barber.

Eat to live, and not live to eat.

After three days men grow weary of a wench, a guest, and weather rainy.

To lengthen thy life, lessen thy meals.

The proof of gold is fire; the proof of woman, gold; the proof of man, a woman.

Many estates are spent in the getting,
Since women for tea forsook spinning and knitting.

He that lieth down with dogs, shall rise up with fleas.

Tongue double, brings trouble.

Take counsel in wine, but resolve afterwards in water.

A taught horse, and a woman to teach, and teachers practising what they preach.

He is ill clothed that is bare of virtue.

Men and melons are hard to know.

He's the best physician that knows the worthlessness of the most medicines.

The heart of the fool is in his mouth, but the mouth of the wise man is in his heart.

Time was my spouse and I could not agree,
Striving about superiority:
The text which saith that man and wife are one,
Was the chief argument we stood upon:
She held, they both one woman should become;
I held they should be man, and both but one.
Thus we contended daily, but the strife
Could not be ended, till both were one wife.

Cheese and salt meat should be sparingly eat.

Doors and walls are fools paper.

Anoint a villain and he'll stab you, stab him, and he'll anoint you.

Keep your mouth wet, feet dry.

My neighbour H———y by his pleasing tongue,
Hath won a girl that's rich, wise, fair, and young;
The match (he saith) is half concluded, he
Indeed is wondrous willing; but not she,
And reason good, for he has run thro' all
Almost the story of the prodigal;
Yet swears he never with the hogs did dine;
That's true, for none would trust him with their swine.

Where bread is wanting, all's to be sold.

Snowy winter, a plentiful harvest.

Nothing more like a fool, than a drunken man.

She that will eat her breakfast in her bed,
And spend the morn in dressing of her head,
And sit at dinner like a maiden bride,
And talk of nothing all day but of pride;
God in his mercy may do much to save her,
But what a case is he that shall have her.

God works wonders now and then;
Behold! a lawyer, an honest man.

He that lives carnally, won't live eternally.

Time eateth all things, could old poets say,
The times are chang'd, our times *drink* all away.

THE BENEFIT OF GOING TO LAW

Dedicated to the Countess of K———t and H-n-r-d-n

Two beggars travelling along,
    One blind, the other lame.
Pick'd up an oyster on the way,
    To which they both laid claim:
The matter rose so high, that they
    Resolv'd to go to law,
As often richer fools have done,
    Who quarrel for a straw.
A lawyer took it straight in hand,
    Who knew his business was
To mind nor one nor t'other side,
    But make the best o' th' cause,
As always in the law's the case;
    So he his judgment gave,
And lawyer-like he thus resolv'd
    What each of them should have;
        Blind plaintif, lame defendant, share
        The friendly laws impartial care,
        A shell for him, a shell for thee,
        The middle is the *lawyer's fee.*

QUESTIONS

1. Explain the joke Franklin played on Titan Leeds. What was its purpose? Describe similar hoaxes played by other comic writers.

2. In "Tom Edison's Shaggy Dog" (see p. 23), Kurt Vonnegut, Jr., satirizes the American dream. What is Franklin's attitude toward the dream? How do you account for the change?

3. Women are a frequent butt for Franklin's humor. Why? To what extent have Americans maintained a comic vision of women?

4. Which of Poor Richard's maxims do you like best? Which have you heard before? What lesson does "The Benefit of Going to Law" teach?

To Cousin Ephraim Downing, Up in Downingville

Seba Smith

American literary humor is commonly said to have begun in 1830 when the letters and "other dockyments" of Jack Downing began to appear. Jack was the creation and pseudonym of Seba Smith, a Maine editor, who shrewdly saw the rustic fool as a means of increasing the circulation of his paper. This description of the political ties in the legislature, like other letters collected in My Thirty Years Out of the Senate, *makes comic capital out of Jack's New England dialect and naively wise comments. Downing became so popular that voters even nominated him in real political campaigns. Eventually his political interests became national, and he "footed it" to Washington, where he became an invaluable member of Andrew Jackson's Kitchen Cabinet. On one occasion, when the President was too tired to shake hands, Jack stood behind him, reached his arms under the President's, and shook hands for him.*

Portland, Monday, Jan. 18, 1830.

Dear Cousin Ephraim:

I now take my pen in hand to let you know that I am well, hoping these few lines will find you enjoying the same blessing. When I come down to Portland I didn't think o' staying more than three or four days, if I could sell my load of ax handles, and mother's cheese, and cousin Nabby's bundle of footings; but when I got here I found Uncle Nat was gone a freighting down to Quoddy, and Aunt Sally said as how I shouldn't stir a step home till he come back agin, which won't be this month. So here I am, loitering about this great town, as lazy as an ox. Ax handles don't fetch nothing; I couldn't hardly give 'em away. Tell Cousin Nabby I sold her footings for nine-pence a pair, and took it all in cotton cloth. Mother's cheese come to seven-and-sixpence; I got her half a pound of shushon, and two ounces of snuff, and the rest in sugar. When Uncle Nat comes home I shall put my ax handles aboard of him, and let him take 'em to Boston next time he goes; I saw a feller tother day, that told me they'd fetch a good price there. I've been here now a whole fortnight, and if I could tell ye one half I've seen, I guess you'd stare worse than if you'd seen a catamount. I've been to meeting, and to the museum, and to both Legislaters, the one they call the House, and the one they call the Sinnet. I spose Uncle Joshua is in a great hurry to hear something about these Legislaters; for you know he's always reading newspapers and talking politics, when he can get anybody to talk with him. I've seen him when he had five tons of hay in the field well made, and a heavy shower coming up, stand two hours disputing with Squire W. about Adams and Jackson—one calling Adams a tory and a fed, and the other saying Jackson was a murderer and a fool; so they kept it up, till the rain began to pour down, and about spoilt all his hay.

Uncle Joshua may set his heart at rest about the bushel of corn that he bet 'long with the postmaster, that Mr. Ruggles would be Speaker of that Legislater they call the House; for he's lost it, slick as a whistle. As I hadn't much to do, I've been there every day since they've been a setting. A Mr. White, of Monmouth, was the Speaker the first two days; and I can't see why they didn't keep him in all the time; for he seemed to be a very clever, good-natured sort of man, and he had such a smooth, pleasant way with him, that I couldn't help feeling sorry when they turned him out and put in another. But some said he wasn't put in hardly fair; and I don't know as he was, for the first day, when they were all coming in and crowding round, there was a large, fat man, with a round, full, jolly sort of a face, I suppose he was the captain, for he got up and commanded them to come to order, and then he told this Mr. White to whip into the chair quicker than you could say Jack Robinson. Some of 'em scolded about it, and I heard some, in a little room they called the lobby, say 'twas a mean trick; but I couldn't see why, for I thought Mr. White made a capital Speaker, and when *our* company turns out, the cap'n always has a right to do as he's a mind to.

They kept disputing most all the time the first two days about a poor Mr. Roberts, from Waterborough. Some said he shouldn't have a seat because he adjourned the town meeting and wasn't fairly elected. Others said it was no such thing, and that he was elected as fairly as any of 'em. And Mr. Roberts himself said he was, and said he could bring men that would swear to it, and good men too. But, notwithstanding all this, when they came to vote, they got three or four majority that he shouldn't have a seat. And I thought it a needless piece of cruelty, for they wan't crowded, and there was a number of seats empty. But they would have it so, and the poor man had to go and stand up in the lobby.

Then they disputed awhile about a Mr. Fowler's having a seat. Some said he shouldn't have a seat, because when he was elected some of his votes were given for his father. But they were more kind to him than they were to Mr. Roberts, for they voted that he *should* have a seat; and I suppose it was because they thought he had a lawful right to inherit whatever was his father's. They all declared there was no party politics about it, and I don't think there was; for I noticed that all who voted that Mr. Roberts *should* have a seat, voted that Mr. Fowler should *not;* and all who voted that Mr. Roberts should *not* have a seat, voted that Mr. Fowler *should.* So, as they all voted *both* ways, they must have been conscientious, and I don't see how there could be any party about it.

It's a pity they couldn't be allowed to have two Speakers, for they seemed to be very anxious to choose Mr. Ruggles and Mr. Goodenow. They two had every vote except one, and if they had had *that,* I believe they would both have been chosen; as it was, however, they both came within a hum-bird's eye of it. Whether it was Mr. Ruggles voted for Mr. Goodenow, or Mr. Goodenow for Mr. Ruggles, I can't exactly tell; but I rather guess it was Mr. Ruggles voted for Mr. Goodenow, for he appeared to be very glad to see Mr. Goodenow in the chair, and shook hands with him as good-natured as could be. I would have given half my load of ax handles, if they could both have been elected and set up there together, they would have been so happy. But as they can't have but one Speaker at a time, and as Mr. Goodenow appears to understand the business very well, it is not likely Mr. Ruggles will be Speaker any this winter. So Uncle Joshua will have to shell out his bushel of corn, and I hope it will learn him better than to bet about politics again. Before I came from home, some of the papers said how there was a majority of ten or fifteen *National Republicans* [Whigs] in the Legislater, and the other party said there was a pretty clever little majority of *Democratic Republicans* [Democrats]. Well, now everybody says it has turned out jest as that queer little paper, called the Daily Courier, said 'twould. That paper said it was such a close rub it couldn't hardly tell which side would beat. And it's jest so, for they've been here now most a fortnight acting jest like two boys playin see-saw on a rail. First one goes up, and then 'tother; but I reckon one of the boys is rather heaviest, for once in a while he comes down chuck, and throws the other up into the air as though he would pitch him head over heels. Your loving cousin till death.

JACK DOWNING.

QUESTIONS

1. Describe Jack Downing. Why is he loitering in Portland? Why is he writing to Cousin Ephraim?

2. Discuss Jack's understanding of political events. Why does he feel sorry for Mr. White? Mr. Roberts? Why does he think Mr. Ruggles voted for Mr. Goodenow? Who is being satirized? Jack? The legislators? Both?

3. The legislature is well balanced between Whigs and Democrats. What image does Jack use to describe this state of affairs? What impression does it give us of the government? What other comic descriptions does Jack use?

Contentment

Oliver Wendell Holmes

A more cultivated exponent of Yankee good sense was the monologuist created by Oliver Wendell Holmes. As The Autocrat of the Breakfast-Table *(1857–1858) and as a professor and a poet in the later* Breakfast-Table *sketches, he displayed Dr. Holmes's vast erudition, praised his favorite ideas, and arraigned human follies. In this character vignette, regarded by many critics as a tiny masterpiece, a self-exposed hypocrite describes what he needs to be content. So successful is the hedonist's pretense of austerity that he seems to have fooled even himself.*

"Man wants but little here below."

Little I ask; my wants are few;—
   I only wish a hut of stone,
(A *very plain* brown stone will do,)
   That I may call my own;—
And close at hand is such a one,
In yonder street that fronts the sun.

Plain food is quite enough for me;
   Three courses are as good as ten;—
If Nature can subsist on three,
   Thank Heaven for three. Amen!
I always thought cold victual nice;—
My *choice* would be vanilla-ice.

I care not much for gold or land;—
   Give me a mortgage here and there,—
Some good bank-stock,—some note of hand,
   Or trifling railroad share;—
I only ask that Fortune send
A *little* more than I shall spend.

Honors are silly toys, I know,
    And titles are but empty names;—
I would, *perhaps*, be Plenipo,—
        But only near St. James;—
I'm very sure I should not care
To fill our Gubernator's chair.

Jewels are baubles; 't is a sin
    To care for such unfruitful things;—
One good-sized diamond in a pin,—
        Some, *not so large*, in rings,—
A ruby and a pearl, or so,
Will do for me;—I laugh at show.

My dame should dress in cheap attire;
    (Good, heavy silks are never dear;)—
I own perhaps I *might* desire
        Some shawls of true cashmere,—
Some marrowy crapes of China silk,
Like wrinkled skins on scalded milk.

I would not have the horse I drive
    So fast that folks must stop and stare:
An easy gait—two, forty-five—
        Suits me; I do not care;—
Perhaps, for just a *single spurt*,
Some seconds less would do no hurt.

Of pictures, I should like to own
    Titians and Raphaels three or four.—
I love so much their style and tone,—
        One Turner, and no more,—
(A landscape,—foreground golden dirt,—
The sunshine painted with a squirt.)—

Of books but few,—some fifty score
    For daily use, and bound for wear;
The rest upon an upper floor;—
        Some *little* luxury *there*
Of red morocco's gilded gleam,
And vellum rich as country cream.

Busts, cameos, gems,—such things as these,
    Which others often show for pride,
I value for their power to please,
    And selfish churls deride;—
One Stradivarius, I confess,
Two Meerschaums, I would fain possess.

Wealth's wasteful tricks I will not learn,
    Nor ape the glittering upstart fool;—
Shall not carved tables serve my turn,
    But *all* must be of buhl?
Give grasping pomp its double share,—
I ask but *one* recumbent chair.

Thus humble let me live and die,
    Nor long for Midas' golden touch,
If Heaven more generous gifts deny,
    I shall not miss them *much*,—
Too grateful for the blessing lent
Of simple tastes and mind content!

QUESTIONS

1. The humor in the poem is largely generated by irony. What does the speaker think of himself? What do we know about him? Do you think he is a hypocrite? Explain.

2. What tone of voice is the speaker using? Try reading the poem aloud, giving special stress to the words in italics.

3. What pattern do most stanzas of the poem follow? How does the speaker continually undercut himself?

4. Consider the lines "I only ask that Fortune send / A *little* more than I shall spend." Do they express your own desires? Those of your friends?

The Complaint of B. Sawin, Esq.

James Russell Lowell

Even James Russell Lowell, a member of one of America's most distinguished literary families, assumed the guise of a wise fool to reach a wide audience. In 1846, using the name Hosea Biglow, Lowell began publishing letters and poetry in broad Yankee dialect. One of the most memorable American types created by Lowell was Hosea's young flag-waver friend, Birdofredum Sawin ("bird of freedom soaring"), who is cruelly disillusioned by the Mexican War. In this macabre "Complaint," an excerpt from his second letter, the numskull Sawin casually takes stock of the losses he has suffered as an enlisted man. Lowell uses this physical breakdown to indicate Sawin's moral decay as the patriot becomes a parasite on the society that has betrayed him.

I spose you wonder ware I be; I can't tell, fer the soul o' me,
Exactly ware I be myself,—meanin' by thet the holl o' me.
Wen I left hom, I hed two legs, an' they worn't bad ones neither,
(The scaliest trick they ever played wuz bringin' on me hither,)
Now one on 'em's I dunno ware;—they thought I wuz adyin',
An' sawed it off because they said 't wuz kin' o' mortifyin';
I'm willin' to believe it wuz, an' yit I don't see, nuther,
Wy one should take to feelin' cheap a minnit sooner 'n t' other,
Sence both wuz equilly to blame; but things is ez they be;
It took on so they took it off, an' thet's enough fer me:
There's one good thing, though, to be said about my wooden new one,—
The liquor can't get into it ez 't used to in the true one;
So it saves drink; an' then, besides, a feller could n't beg
A gretter blessin' then to hev one ollers sober peg;
It's true a chap's in want o' two fer follerin' a drum,
But all the march I'm up to now is jest to Kingdom Come.

I've lost one eye, but thet's a loss it's easy to supply
Out o' the glory that I've got, fer thet is all my eye;
An' one is big enough, I guess, by diligently usin' it,
To see all I shall ever git by way o' pay fer losin' it;

Off'cers I notice, who git paid fer all our thumps an' kickins,
Do wel by keepin' single afta the fattest pickins;
So, ez the eye's put fairly out, I'll larn to go without it,
An' not allow *myself* to be no gret put out about it.
Now, le' me see, thet is n't all; I used, 'fore leavin Jaalam,
To count things on my finger-eends, but sumthin' seems to ail 'em:
Ware's my left hand? O, darn it, yes, I recollect wut 's come on 't;
I haint no left arm but my right, an' thet 's got jest a thumb on 't;
It aint so hendy ez it wuz to cal'late a sum on 't.
I've hed some ribs broke,—six (I b'lieve),—I haint kep' no account on
    'em;
Wen pensions git to be the talk, I'll settle the amount on 'em.
An' now I'm speakin' about ribs, it kin' o' brings to mind
One thet I could n't never break,—the one I lef' behind;
Ef you should see her, jest clear out the spout o' your invention
An' pour the longest sweetnin' in about an annooal pension,
An' kin' o' hint (in case, you know, the critter should refuse to be
Consoled) I aint so 'xpensive now to keep ez wut I used to be;
There's one arm less, ditto one eye, an' then the leg thet's wooden
Can be took off an' sot away wenever ther 's a puddin'.

QUESTIONS

1. Compare Birdofredum Sawin with Jack Downing in the previous selection. In what ways are they similar? How are they different?

2. What injuries does Sawin sustain in the war? How does he console himself for each injury? What do we learn about him from his various consolations?

3. Which rib has Sawin left behind? What message does he send to the rib he "could n't never break"?

Nasby Shows Why He Should Not Be Drafted

Petroleum Vesuvius Nasby

For comic rascality, Petroleum V. Nasby stands almost without equal in American literature. Unlike Lowell's Sawin, Nasby cannot degenerate; morally he is at rock bottom from the outset. His sins, ranging from bigotry and bigamy on the one hand to loafing and lying on the other, made him an ideal ironic mouthpiece for his creator, David Ross Locke. Locke, a Union supporter during the Civil War, made Nasby a Southern sympathizer living in Ohio. As Nasby attempts to convince us that he is unfit for the draft, Locke subtly persuades us that the Confederacy is unworthy of our support. Abraham Lincoln commented that he would gladly give up his office for the genius to write the Nasby letters.

August 6, 1862

I see in the papers last nite that the Government hez institooted a draft, and that in a few weeks sum hundreds uv thousands uv peeceable citizens will be dragged to the tented field.[1] I know not wat uthers may do, but ez for me, I cant go. Upon a rigid eggsaminashun uv my fizzleckle man, I find it wood be wus nor madnis for me to undertake a campane, to-wit:—

1. I'm bald-headid, and hev bin obliged to wear a wig these 22 years.

2. I hev dandruff in wat scanty hair still hangs around my venerable temples.

3. I hev a kronic katarr.

4. I hev lost, sence Stanton's order to draft, the use uv wun eye entirely, and hev kronic inflammashen in the other.

5. My teeth is all unsound, my palit aint eggsactly rite, and I hev hed bronkeetis 31 yeres last Joon. At present I hev a koff, the paroxisms uv wich is friteful to behold.

6. I'm holler-chestid, am short-winded, and hev alluz hed pains in my back and side.

7. I am afflictid with kronic diarrear and kostivniss. The money I hev

---

[1] One of the most surprising results of the conscription was the amount of disease disclosed among men between "eighteen and forty-five," in districts where quotas could not be raised by volunteering.—Locke's note.

paid (or promist to pay), for Jayneses karminnytiv balsam and pills wood astonish almost enny body.

8. I am rupchered in nine places, and am entirely enveloped with trusses.

9. I hev verrykose vanes, hev a white-swellin on wun leg and a fever sore on the uther; also wun leg is shorter than tother, though I handle it so expert that nobody never noticed it.

10. I hev korns and bunyons on both feet, wich wood prevent me from marchin.

I don't suppose that my political opinions, wich are aginst the prossekooshn uv this unconstooshnel war, wood hev any wate, with a draftin orfiser; but the above reesons why I cant go, will, I make no doubt, be suffishent.

QUESTIONS

1. What kind of person is Nasby? When did he lose the use of an eye? Discuss such statements as "the money I hev paid (or promist to pay)" and "though I handle it so expert that nobody never noticed it."

2. How do we know Nasby is an ironic spokesman? Do you think there is a danger of some readers taking him seriously? Do you find his reasons humorous? Why?

3. What does Locke say in his note? How relevant are his words today? Explain.

4. Compare Nasby's words, "I know not wat uthers may do, but ez for me, I cant go," with the words of John F. Kennedy, "Ask not what your country can do for you—ask what you can do for your country." Why is Nasby's line an example of anticlimax?

Among the Free Lovers

Artemus Ward

Although President Lincoln was a great fan of the Nasby letters, it was a comic story by Artemus Ward that he read to his Cabinet before presenting the Emancipation Proclamation. For, in the guise of the thoughtful rogue Artemus Ward, Charles Farrar Browne combined the character traits of Yankee and backwoodsman to burlesque the typical American. This account of Ward's supposed visit to the Free Love Colony at Berlin Heights, Ohio, reveals his typical ridicule of high-flown language and radical ideas. One of the most successful and influential of the so-called literary comedians—comic writers and lecturers popular during the second half of the nineteenth century—Ward relied heavily on such devices of humor as poor spelling, invented words, and distorted grammar.

AMONG THE FREE LOVERS.*

Some years ago I pitched my tent and onfurled my banner to the breeze, in Berlin Hites, Ohio. I had hearn that Berlin Hites was ockepied by a extensive seck called Free Lovers, who beleeved in affinertys and sich, goin back on their domestic ties without no hesitation whatsomever. They was likewise spirit rappers and high presher reformers on gineral principles. If I can improve these 'ere misgided peple by showin them my onparalleld show at the usual low price of admitants, methunk, I shall not hav lived in vane! But bitterly did I cuss the day I ever sot foot in the retchid place. I sot up my tent in a field near the Love Cure, as they called it, and bimeby the free lovers begun for to congregate around the door. A ornreer set I have never sawn. The men's faces was all covered with hare and they lookt half-starved to deth. They didn't wear no weskuts for the purpuss (as they sed) of allowin the free air of hevun to blow onto their boozums. Their pockets was filled with tracks and pamplits and they was bare-footed. They sed the Postles didn't wear boots, & why should they? That was their stile of argyment.

---

* Some queer people, calling themselves "Free Lovers," and possessing very original ideas about life and morality, established themselves at Berlin Heights, in Ohio, a few years since. Public opinion was resistlessly against them, however, and the association was soon disbanded.

The wimin was wuss than the men. They wore trowsis, short gownds, straw hats with green ribbins, and all carried bloo cotton umbrellers.

Presently a perfeckly orful lookin female presented herself at the door. Her gownd was skanderlusly short and her trowsis was shameful to behold.

She eyed me over very sharp, and then startin back she sed, in a wild voice:

"Ah, can it be?"

"Which?" sed I.

"Yes, 'tis troo, O 'tis troo!"

"15 cents, marm," I anserd.

She bust out a cryin & sed:

"And so I hav found you at larst—at larst, O at larst!"

"Yes," I anserd, "you have found me at larst, and you would have found me at fust, if you had cum sooner."

She grabd me vilently by the coat collar, and brandishin her umbreller wildly round, exclaimed:

"Air you a man?"

Sez I, "I think I air, bit if you doubt it, you can address Mrs. A. Ward, Baldinsville, Injianny, postage pade, & she will probly giv you the desired informashun."

"Then thou ist what the cold world calls marrid?"

"Madam, I istest!"

The exsentric female then clutched me franticly by the arm and hollerd:

"Your air mine, O you air mine!"

"Scacely," I sed, endeverin to git loose from her. But she clung to me and sed:

"You air my Affinerty!"

"What upon arth is that?" I shouted.

"Dost thou not know?"

"No, I dostent!"

"Listin man, & I'll tell ye!" sed the strange female; "for years I hav yearned for thee. I knowd thou wast in the world, sumwhares, tho I didn't know whare. My hart sed he would cum and I took courage. He *has* cum—he's here—you air him—you air my Affinerty! O 'tis too mutch! too mutch!" and she sobbed agin.

"Yes," I anserd, "I think it is a darn site too mutch!"

"Hast thou not yearned for me?" she yelled, ringin her hands like a female play acter.

"Not a yearn!" I bellerd at the top of my voice, throwin her away from me.

The free lovers who was standin round obsarvin the scene commenst for to holler "shame!" "beast," etsettery, etsettery.

I was very mutch riled, and fortifyin myself with a spare tent stake, I addrest them as follers: "You pussylanermus critters, go way from me and take this retchid woman with you. I'm a law-abidin man, and bleeve in good, old-fashioned institutions. I am marrid & my orfsprings resemble me if I am a showman! I think your Affinity bizniss is cussed noncents, besides bein outrajusly wicked. Why don't you behave desunt like other folks? Go to work and earn a honist livin and not stay round here in this lazy, shiftless way, pizenin the moral atmosphere with your pestifrous idees! You wimin folks go back to your lawful husbands if you've got any, and take orf them skanderlous gownds and trowsis, and dress respectful like other wimin. You men folks, cut orf them pirattercal whiskers, burn up them infurnel pamplits, put sum weskuts on, go to work choppin wood, splittin fence rales, or tillin the sile." I pored 4th my indignashun in this way till I got out of breth, when I stopt. I shant go to Berlin Hites agin, not if I live to be as old as Methooseler.

QUESTIONS

1. Give examples of Ward's humorous misspellings. Which words does he seem to invent? How do the misspellings and poor grammar affect our image of the speaker?

2. Discuss such remarks as "If I can improve these 'ere misgided peple by showin them my onparalleld show at the usual low price of admitants, methunk, I shall not hav lived in vane!" What do they reveal about the narrator?

3. Describe the "female" Ward meets. What are his complaints about the Free Lovers?

Fenimore Cooper's Limitations

Mark Twain

In 1863, the year he met Artemus Ward, young Samuel Clemens adopted that famous pen name, the river boatman's cry meaning that the water was two fathoms deep—Mark Twain. By common consent, Twain holds the first rank in American humor, perhaps in American letters. American literature begins, Ernest Hemingway claimed, with Huckleberry Finn. One of the great triumphs of Twain's novel is its fusion of the two strains in the American temper—romanticism and realism. In this excerpt from "Fenimore Cooper's Literary Offenses," a satire of the early-nineteenth-century American novelist James Fenimore Cooper, Twain argues against the extreme romanticism that characterized much early American fiction. Using common sense as a touchstone, he exposes the absurdity of Cooper's exaggerations and the shortsightedness of the educated critics who praised them.

Cooper's gift in the way of invention was not a rich endowment; but such as it was he liked to work it, he was pleased with the effects, and indeed he did some quite sweet things with it. In his little box of stage-properties he kept six or eight cunning devices, tricks, artifices for his savages and woodsmen to deceive and circumvent each other with, and he was never so happy as when he was working these innocent things and seeing them go. A favorite one was to make a moccasined person tread in the tracks of the moccasined enemy, and thus hide his own trail. Cooper wore out barrels and barrels of moccasins in working that trick. Another stage-property that he pulled out of his box pretty frequently was his broken twig. He prized his broken twig above all the rest of his effects, and worked it the hardest. It is a restful chapter in any book of his when somebody doesn't step on a dry twig and alarm all the reds and whites for two hundred yards around. Every time a Cooper person is in peril, and absolute silence is worth four dollars a minute, he is sure to step on a dry twig. There may be a hundred handier things to step on, but that wouldn't satisfy Cooper. Cooper requires him to turn out and find a dry twig; and if he can't do it, go and borrow one. In fact, the Leatherstocking Series ought to have been called the Broken Twig Series.

I am sorry there is not room to put in a few dozen instances of the delicate art of the forest, as practised by Natty Bumppo and some of the other Cooperian experts. Perhaps we may venture two or three samples. Cooper was a sailor—a naval officer; yet he gravely tells us how a vessel, driving toward a lee shore in a gale, is steered for a particular spot by her skipper because he knows of an *undertow* there which will hold her back against the gale and save her. For just pure woodcraft, or sailorcraft, or whatever it is, isn't that neat? For several years Cooper was daily in the society of artillery, and he ought to have noticed that when a cannon-ball strikes the ground it either buries itself or skips a hundred feet or so; skips again a hundred feet or so—and so on, till finally it gets tired and rolls. Now in one place he loses some "females"—as he always calls women—in the edge of a wood near a plain at night in a fog, on purpose to give Bumppo a chance to show off the delicate art of the forest before the reader. These mislaid people are hunting for a fort. They hear a cannon-blast, and a cannon-ball presently comes rolling into the wood and stops at their feet. To the females this suggests nothing. The case is very different with the admirable Bumppo. I wish I may never know peace again if he doesn't strike out promptly and *follow the track* of that cannon-ball across the plain through the dense fog and find the fort. Isn't it a daisy? If Cooper had any real knowledge of Nature's ways of doing things, he had a most delicate art in concealing the fact. For instance: one of his acute Indian experts, Chingachgook (pronounced Chicago, I think), has lost the trail of a person he is tracking through the forest. Apparently that trail is hopelessly lost. Neither you nor I could ever have guessed out the way to find it. It was very different with Chicago. Chicago was not stumped for long. He turned a running stream out of its course, and there, in the slush in its old bed, were that person's moccasin tracks. The current did not wash them away, as it would have done in all other like cases—no, even the eternal laws of Nature have to vacate when Cooper wants to put up a delicate job of woodcraft on the reader.

We must be a little wary when Brander Matthews tells us that Cooper's books "reveal an extraordinary fullness of invention." As a rule, I am quite willing to accept Brander Matthews's literary judgments and applaud his lucid and graceful phrasing of them; but that particular statement needs to be taken with a few tons of salt. Bless your heart, Cooper hadn't any more invention than a horse; and I don't mean a high-class horse, either; I mean a clothes-horse. It would be very difficult to find a really clever "situation" in Cooper's books, and still more difficult to find one of any kind which he has failed to render absurd by his handling of it. Look at the episodes of "the caves"; and at the celebrated scuffle between Magua and those others on the table-land a few days later; and at Hurry Harry's queer water-transit from the castle to the ark; and at Deerslayer's half-hour with his first corpse; and at the quarrel between Hurry Harry and Deerslayer later; and at—but choose for yourself; you can't go amiss.

If Cooper had been an observer his inventive faculty would have worked better; not more interestingly, but more rationally, more plausibly. Cooper's proudest creations in the way of "situations" suffer noticeably from the absence of the observer's protecting gift. Cooper's eye was splendidly inaccurate. Cooper seldom saw anything correctly. He saw nearly all things as through a glass eye, darkly. Of course a man who cannot see the commonest little every-day matters accurately is working at a disadvantage when he is constructing a "situation." In the *Deerslayer* tale Cooper has a stream which is fifty feet wide where it flows out of a lake; it presently narrows to twenty as it meanders along for no given reason, and yet when a stream acts like that it ought to be required to explain itself. Fourteen pages later the width of the brook's outlet from the lake has suddenly shrunk thirty feet, and become "the narrowest part of the stream." This shrinkage is not accounted for. The stream has bends in it, a sure indication that it has alluvial banks and cuts them; yet these bends are only thirty and fifty feet long. If Cooper had been a nice and punctilious observer he would have noticed that the bends were oftener nine hundred feet long than short of it.

Cooper made the exit of that stream fifty feet wide, in the first place, for no particular reason; in the second place, he narrowed it to less than twenty to accommodate some Indians. He bends a "sapling" to the form of an arch over this narrow passage, and conceals six Indians in its foliage. They are "laying" for a settler's scow or ark which is coming up the stream on its way to the lake; it is being hauled against the stiff current by a rope whose stationary end is anchored in the lake; its rate of progress cannot be more than a mile an hour. Cooper describes the ark, but pretty obscurely. In the matter of dimensions "it was little more than a modern canal-boat." Let us guess, then, that it was about one hundred and forty feet long. It was of "greater breadth than common." Let us guess, then, that it was about sixteen feet wide. This leviathan had been prowling down bends which were but a third as long as itself, and scraping between banks where it had only two feet of space to spare on each side. We cannot too much admire this miracle. A low-roofed log dwelling occupies "two-thirds of the ark's length"—a dwelling ninety feet long and sixteen feet wide, let us say—a kind of vestibule train. The dwelling has two rooms—each forty-five feet long and sixteen feet wide, let us guess. One of them is the bedroom of the Hutter girls, Judith and Hetty; the other is the parlor in the daytime, at night it is papa's bedchamber. The ark is arriving at the stream's exit now, whose width has been reduced to less than twenty feet to accommodate the Indians—say to eighteen. There is a foot to spare on each side of the boat. Did the Indians notice that there was going to be a tight squeeze there? Did they notice that they could make money by climbing down out of that arched sapling and just stepping aboard when the ark scraped by? No, other Indians would have noticed these things, but Cooper's

Indians never notice anything. Cooper thinks they are marvelous creatures for noticing, but he was almost always in error about his Indians. There was seldom a sane one among them.

The ark is one hundred and forty-feet long; the dwelling is ninety feet long. The idea of the Indians is to drop softly and secretly from the arched sapling to the dwelling as the ark creeps along under it at the rate of a mile an hour, and butcher the family. It will take the ark a minute and a half to pass under. It will take the ninety-foot dwelling a minute to pass under. Now, then, what did the six Indians do? It would take you thirty years to guess, and even then you would have to give it up, I believe. Therefore, I will tell you what the Indians did. Their chief, a person of quite extraordinary intellect for a Cooper Indian, warily watched the canal-boat as it squeezed along under him, and when he had got his calculations fined down to exactly the right shade, as he judged, he let go and dropped. And *missed the house!* That is actually what he did. He missed the house, and landed in the stern of the scow. It was not much of a fall, yet it knocked him silly. He lay there unconscious. If the house had been ninety-seven feet long he would have made the trip. The fault was Cooper's not his. The error lay in the construction of the house. Cooper was no architect.

There still remained in the roost five Indians. The boat has passed under and is now out of their reach. Let me explain what the five did—you would not be able to reason it out for yourself. No. 1 jumped for the boat, but fell in the water astern of it. Then No. 2 jumped for the boat, but fell in the water still farther astern of it. Then No. 3 jumped for the boat, and fell a good way astern of it. Then No. 4 jumped for the boat, and fell in the water *away* astern. Then even No. 5 made a jump for the boat—for he was a Cooper Indian. In the matter of intellect, the difference between a Cooper Indian and the Indian that stands in front of a cigar-shop is not spacious. The scow episode is really a sublime burst of invention; but it does not thrill, because the inaccuracy of the details throws a sort of air of factitiousness and general improbability over it. This comes of Cooper's inadequacy as an observer.

QUESTIONS

1. Why does Twain think the Leatherstocking series should have been called the Broken Twig Series? What does this indicate about Cooper's ability as a writer?

2. How does Twain pronounce "Chingachgook"? What effect does this have on our image of the Indian? What does Chingachgook do that violates natural laws?

3. Describe the cannonball incident. Why does it upset Twain?

4. Tell what happens when the Indians try to board the ark. Why does Twain conclude that Cooper's Indians were seldom sane?

5. How is Twain's language comic? What image does his narrator present? How close does his satire come to pure invective or name-calling? For example, what kind of horse does he associate with Cooper?

The Laramie Postoffice

Bill Nye

The comic potential of the wise fool was used to its fullest by Edgar Wilson Nye. As Bill Nye, the average American, he made a joke out of democracy in his "Boomerang History of the United States." Among the last of the literary comedians to gain fame after the Civil War, Nye uses in these sketches their favorite humorous devices—misspelling and mispronunciation. Most of all, however, his humor depends on characterization, as in this example of the nitwit who explains to the President how to run the Laramie Postoffice.

ACCEPTING THE LARAMIE POSTOFFICE

Office of Daily Boomerang, Laramie City, Wy.
August 9, 1882.

My dear General:

I have received by telegraph the news of my nomination by the President and my confirmation by the Senate, as postmaster at Laramie, and wish to extend my thanks for the same.

I have ordered an entirely new set of boxes and post-office outfit, including new corrugated cuspidors for the lady clerks.

I look upon the appointment as a great triumph of eternal truth over error and wrong. It is one of the epochs, I may say, in the Nation's onward march toward political purity and perfection. I do not know when I have noticed any stride in the affairs of state, which so thoroughly impressed me with its wisdom.

Now that we are co-workers in the same department, I trust that you will not feel shy or backward in consulting me at any time relative to matters concerning postoffice affairs. Be perfectly frank with me, and feel free to bring anything of that kind right to me. Do not feel reluctant because I may at times appear haughty and indifferent, cold or reserved. Perhaps you do not think I know the difference between a general delivery window and a three-em quad, but that is a mistake.

My general information is far beyond my years.
With profoundest regard, and a hearty endorsement of the policy of
the President and the Senate, whatever it may be,

> *I remain, sincerely yours,*
> BILL NYE, P.M.

A RESIGN

Postoffice Divan, Laramie City, W.T.,
Ct. 1, 1883

To the President of the United States:

Sir: I beg leave at this time officially to tender my resignation as
postmaster at this place, and in due form to deliver the great seal and the
key to the front door of the office. The safe combination is set on the
numbers 33, 66 and 99, though I do not remember at this moment which
comes first, or how many times you revolve the knob, or in which
direction you should turn it first to make it operate.

There is some mining stock in my private drawer in the safe, which I
have not yet removed. It is a luxury, but you may have it. I have decided
to keep a horse instead of this mining stock. The horse may not be so
pretty, but it will cost less to keep him.

You will find the postal cards that have not been used under the
distributing table, and the coal down in the cellar. If the stove draws too
hard, close the damper in the pipe and shut the general delivery window.

Looking over my stormy and eventful administration as postmaster
here, I find abundant cause for thanksgiving. At the time I entered upon
the duties of my office the department was not yet on a paying basis. It
was not even self-sustaining. Since that time, with the active coöperation
of the chief executive and the heads of the department, I have been able
to make our postal system a paying one, and on top of that I am now
able to reduce the tariff on average-sized letters from three cents to two.
I might add that this is rather too too, but I will not say anything that
might seem undignified in an official resignation which is to become a
matter of history.

Acting under the advice of Gen. Hatton, a year ago, I removed the
feather bed with which my predecessor, Deacon Hayford, had bolstered
up his administration by stuffing the window, and substituted glass.
Finding nothing in the book of instructions to postmasters which made
the feather bed a part of my official duties, I filed it away in an obscure
place and burned it in effigy, also in the gloaming.

It was not long after I had taken my official oath before an era of
unexampled prosperity opened for the American people. The price of

beef rose to a remarkable altitude, and other vegetables commanded a good figure and a ready market. We then began to make active preparations for the introduction of the strawberry-roan two-cent stamps and the black-and-tan postal note. One reform has crowded upon the heels of another, until the country is to-day upon the foam-crested wave of permanent prosperity.

Mr. President, I cannot close this letter without thanking yourself and the heads of departments at Washington for your active, cheery and prompt coöperation in these matters. You may do as you see fit, of course, about incorporating this idea into your Thanksgiving proclamation, but rest assured it would not be ill-timed or inopportune. It is not alone a credit to myself. It reflects credit upon the administration also.

I need not say that I herewith transmit my resignation with great sorrow and genuine regret. We have toiled on together month after month, asking for no reward except the innate consciousness of rectitude and the salary as fixed by law. Now we are to separate. Here the roads seem to fork, as it were, and you and I, and the cabinet, must leave each other at this point.

You will find the key under the door-mat, and you had better turn the cat out at night when you close the office. If she does not go readily, you can make it clearer to her mind by throwing the cancelling stamp at her.

If Deacon Hayford does not pay up his box-rent, you might as well put his mail in the general delivery, and when Bob Head gets drunk and insists on a letter from one of his wives every day in the week, you can salute him through the box delivery with an old Queen Anne tomahawk, which you will find near the Etruscan water-pail. This will not in any manner surprise either of these parties.

Tears are unavailing! I once more become a private citizen, clothed only with the right to read such postal cards as may be addressed to me, and to curse the inefficiency of the postoffice department. I believe the voting class to be divided into two parties; viz., those who are in the postal service, and those who are mad because they cannot receive a registered letter every fifteen minutes of each day, including Sunday.

Mr. President, as an official of this Government I now retire. My term of office would not expire until 1886. I must, therefore, beg pardon for my eccentricity in resigning. It will be best, perhaps, to keep the heart-breaking news from the ears of European powers until the dangers of a financial panic are fully past. Then hurl it broadcast with a sickening thud.

QUESTIONS

1. Discuss Nye's persona as wise fool. How is it revealed when he endorses the policy of the President and Senate? When he gives the combination of the safe? When he describes categories of voters?

2. When he becomes postmaster, what is the first change Nye makes? What other changes follow?

3. When he resigns, what instructions does he give the President concerning Deacon Hayford? Bob Head? The stove? The cat? What procedure does he think the President should follow in breaking the news to the European powers?

4. How had Deacon Hayford used the feather bed? What does Nye do with it? Why?

5. Nye uses several devices common to the literary comedians. What examples do you find of exaggeration? Mixed metaphor? Pun? Anticlimax?

Mr. Dooley on Reform Candidates

Finley Peter Dunne

In his first book on Mr. Dooley, Finley Peter Dunne described the Chicago bartender who was to become a popular national figure during the Spanish-American War: "He read the newspapers with solemn care, heartily hated them, and accepted all they printed. . . . From the cool heights of life in the Archey Road, uninterrupted by the jarring noises of crickets and cows, he observed the passing show and meditated thereon." His meditations, expressed in Irish dialect, touched a broad range of topics, affording us such sharp insights on the American character as this: "There's only one thing that would make me allow mesilf to be a hero of the American people, and that is it don't last long." In the following explanation of the electoral process, Dunne's satire grows out of the disparity between democratic ideals and political reality.

"That frind iv ye'ers, Dugan, is an intilligent man," said Mr. Dooley. "All he needs is an index an' a few illusthrations to make him a bicyclopedja iv useless information."

"Well," said Mr. Hennessy, judiciously, "he ain't no Soc-rates an' he ain't no answers-to-questions colum; but he's a good man that goes to his jooty, an' as handy with a pick as some people are with a cocktail spoon. What's he been doin' again ye?"

"Nawthin'," said Mr. Dooley, "but he was in here Choosday. 'Did ye vote?' says I. 'I did,' says he. 'Which wan iv th' distinguished bunko steerers got ye'er invalu'ble suffrage?' says I. 'I didn't have none with me,' says he, 'but I voted f'r Charter Haitch,' says he. 'I've been with him in six ilictions,' says he, 'an' he's a good man,' he says. 'D'ye think ye're votin' f'r th' best?' says I. 'Why, man alive,' I says, 'Charter Haitch was assassinated three years ago,' I says. 'Was he?' says Dugan. 'Ah, well, he's lived that down be this time. He was a good man,' he says.

"Ye see, that's what thim rayform lads wint up again. If I liked rayformers, Hinnissy, an' wanted f'r to see thim win out wanst in their lifetime, I'd buy thim each a suit iv chilled steel, ar-rm thim with raypeatin' rifles, an' take thim east iv State Sthreet an' south iv Jackson Bullyvard. At prisint th' opinion that pre-vails in th' ranks iv th' gloryous ar-rmy iv ray-form is that there ain't annything worth seein' in this lar-rge an' commodyous desert but th' pest-house an' the bridewell. Me frind

Willum J. O'Brien is no rayformer. But Willum J. undherstands that there's a few hundherds iv thousands iv people livin' in a part iv th' town that looks like nawthin' but smoke fr'm th' roof iv th' Onion League Club that have on'y two pleasures in life, to wur-ruk an' to vote, both iv which they do at th' uniform rate iv wan dollar an' a half a day. That's why Willum J. O'Brien is now a sinitor an' will be an aldherman afther next Thursdah, an' it's why other people are sinding him flowers.

"This is th' way a rayform candydate is ilicted. Th' boys down town has heerd that things ain't goin' r-right somehow. Franchises is bein' handed out to none iv thim; an' wanst in a while a mimber iv th' club, comin' home a little late an' thryin' to riconcile a pair iv r-round feet with an embroidered sidewalk, meets a sthrong ar-rm boy that pushes in his face an' takes away all his marbles. It begins to be talked that th' time has come f'r good citizens f'r to brace up an' do somethin', an' they agree to nomynate a candydate f'r aldherman. 'Who'll we put up?' says they. 'How's Clarence Doolittle?' says wan. 'He's laid up with a coupon thumb, an' can't r-run.' 'An' how about Arthur Doheny?' 'I swore an oath whin I came out iv colledge I'd niver vote f'r a man that wore a made tie.' 'Well, thin, let's thry Willie Boye.' 'Good,' says th' comity. 'He's jus' th' man f'r our money.' An' Willie Boye, after thinkin' it over, goes to his tailor an' ordhers three dozen pairs iv pants, an' decides f'r to be th' sthandard-bearer iv th' people. Musin' over his fried eyesthers an' asparagus an' his champagne, he bets a polo pony again a box of golf-balls he'll be ilicted unanimous; an' all th' good citizens make a vow f'r to set th' alar-rm clock f'r half-past three on th' afthernoon iv iliction day, so's to be up in time to vote f'r th' riprisintitive iv pure gover'mint.

" 'Tis some time befure they comprehind that there ar-re other candydates in th' field. But th' other candydates know it. Th' sthrongest iv thim—his name is Flannigan, an' he's a re-tail dealer in wines an' liquors, an' he lives over his establishment. Flannigan was nomynated enthusyastically at a prim'ry held in his bar-rn; an' befure Willie Boye had picked out pants that wud match th' color iv th' Austhreelyan ballot this here Flannigan had put a man on th' day watch, tol' him to speak gently to anny raygistered voter that wint to sleep behind th' sthove, an' was out that night visitin' his frinds. Who was it judged th' cake walk? Flannigan. Who was it carrid th' pall? Flannigan. Who was it sthud up at th' christening? Flannigan. Whose ca-ards did th' grievin' widow, th' blushin' bridegroom, or th' happy father find in th' hack? Flannigan's. Yet bet ye'er life. Ye see Flannigan wasn't out f'r th' good iv th' community. Flannigan was out f'r Flannigan an' th' stuff.

"Well, iliction day come around; an' all th' imminent frinds iv good gover'mint had special wires sthrung into th' club, an' waited f'r th' returns. Th' first precin't showed 28 votes f'r Willie Boye to 14 f'r Flannigan. 'That's my precin't,' says Willie. 'I wondher who voted thim fourteen?' 'Coachmen,' says Clarence Doolittle. 'There are thirty-five precin'ts in this ward,' says th' leader iv th' rayform ilimint. 'At this rate, I'm sure iv 440 meejority. Gossoon,' he says, 'put a keg iv sherry wine on th' ice,' he says. 'Well,' he says, 'at last th' community is relieved fr'm misrule,' he says. 'To-morrah I will start in arrangin' amindmints to th' tariff schedool an' th' ar-bitration threety,' he says. 'We must be up an' doin',' he says. 'Hol' on there,' says wan iv th' comity. 'There must be some mistake in this fr'm th' sixth precin't,' he says. 'Where's the sixth precin't?' says Clarence. 'Over be th' dumps,' says Willie. 'I told me futman to see to that. He lives at th' cor-ner iv Desplaines an' Bloo Island Av'noo on Goose's Island,' he says. 'What does it show?' 'Flannigan, three hundherd an' eighty-five; Hansen, forty-eight; Schwartz, twinty; O'Malley, sivinteen; Casey, ten; O'Day, eight; Larsen, five; O'Rourke, three; Mulcahy, two; Schmitt, two; Moloney, two; Riordon, two; O'Malley, two; Willie Boye, wan.' 'Gintlemin,' says Willie Boye, arisin' with a stern look in his eyes, 'th' rascal has bethrayed me. Waither, take th' sherry wine off th' ice. They'se no hope f'r sound financial legislation this year. I'm goin' home.'

"An', as he goes down th' sthreet, he hears a band play an' sees a procission headed be a calceem light; an', in a carredge, with his plug hat in his hand an' his di'mond makin' th' calceem look like a piece iv punk in a smokehouse, is Flannigan, payin' his first visit this side iv th' thracks."

QUESTIONS

1. What political insights does Dooley share with us? How widespread is corruption among the voters? How does Flannigan win the election? Why doesn't Dooley like the reform candidate? What was unusual about the candidate Dugan voted for?

2. Comic characters often have "sidekicks," as Mr. Dooley has Hennessy. What function does Hennessy serve?

3. Discuss Dooley's humorous mangling of the English language. How does he describe Dugan?

Reports of a Self-made Diplomat to His President

Will Rogers

Like Finley Peter Dunne, Will Rogers often joked about American politics. The Ziegfeld Follies star became a self-made ambassador because, as he put it, the President needed a "diplomat that could really go in and dip." Rogers's naive explanations, written in a folksy western vernacular spiced with misspellings, satirize political situations by reducing them to domestic problems. In the tradition of the earlier Jack Downing, Rogers was often nominated for political office. When Rogers died in a plane accident in 1935, the Senate majority leader described him as "probably the most widely known citizen in the United States and certainly the best beloved."

White House, Washington. D.C.

Mr. Calvin Coolidge:

Certain news is so urgent that it is nessary for me to cable you, so from time to time you may get something "Collect." I hope there is an appropriation to cover this, look under the heading "Ways and Means."

WILLROG (diplomatic code name).

London, May 18, '26.

My Dear Mr. President:

England has the best Statesmen and the Rottenest coffee of any country in the World. I just hate to see morning come, because I have to get up and drink this Coffee. Is there nothing can be done about this? What does Kellogg say? He was over here and had to drink it. Or did Mrs. Kellogg build his for him every morning? I tell you it's the thing that is keeping these Countries apart more than anything I know of. Personally, I will be perfectly willing to sign over my share in the debt settlement for just one good cup of Coffee. Dam it, we give 'em good tea, and all we demand is reciprocity. Look into this, will you? Next to Farmers' relief, it's one of the big problems that is confronting us today. For every Fool American is coming over this summer, and it's the fool vote that we have got to watch for. I would even drink New Orleans Coffee if I had it now.

Best wishes from your Coffee Hound Servant.

W.R.

P. S. How is Pinchot and Pepper making out? I just toured that State and told them that they better look out for this fellow Vare. They all said to me, "Oh, no, Will! The better element are all against him." Well, I knew that, but I also knew Pennsylvania. There are very few of the better element in Pennsylvania. I don't know offhand of a State, according to its population, that has fewer better element. Of course I hope that nothing disastrous turns out, but I warned them three months ago to procure more Better Element.

W.R.

QUESTIONS

1. How does Rogers create the image of cowboy philosopher? What impresses him most about England? What do you think of his choice of code name? To what extent does he rely on poor grammar and misspelling?

2. Rogers achieves humor by reducing large issues to the personal level. For example, what does he say about international reciprocity? Ways and Means?

3. Though these letters seem so foolish, they touch on important issues. How does Rogers characterize his fellow Americans? What political points does he make?

4. Like Bill Nye, Will Rogers offers counsel to the President of the United States. In what way is this brand of comedy "democratic"?

Upping Prison Requirements

Art Buchwald

The genial brand of humor practiced by Will Rogers is similar to the humor of Art Buchwald. A widely syndicated newspaper humorist, Buchwald in his columns pokes fun at the contemporary American scene. But, as more than one critic has complained, his satire lacks real bite. That harmlessness may explain why his books—Getting High in Government Circles, Have I Ever Lied to You, and I Never Danced at the White House—have proved so popular. In this explanation of how we can achieve prison reform, Buchwald carries to nonsensical extremes the traditional American faith in rational categorizing and self-improvement—values implanted in the American psyche as far back as Ben Franklin.

I know you're not going to believe this, but Governor Lester Maddox of Georgia told a news conference recently, in answer to criticism about Georgia prison reform: "We're doing the best we can, and before we do much better, we're going to have to get a better grade of prisoner."

Once again, Governor Maddox hit the ax handle on the head. While penologists, sociologists, parole officers, and prison commissions all have been at odds about how to rehabilitate prisoners, Maddox has come up with the simplest and, without doubt, most sensible solution.

It has been known for years that prisons have been accepting a very low-class type of inmate, some without any education, others who are unstable, and some who are just plain antisocial.

No effort has been made to attract a better grade of prisoner, who would not only improve the caliber of our rehabilitation programs, but would also make society treat prisoners with the respect they deserve. For too long now we've been taking our prisoners for granted, and the standard for convicted felons has declined to a point where almost anyone can get into prison without his qualifications being questioned.

This trend must be reversed if we ever hope to rehabilitate our prisoners. The first thing to do would be to set up a recruiting drive in high schools and colleges to get a better class of inmate. This would have to be coupled with higher pay for prisoners, so being behind bars would become worthwhile.

Intelligence tests have to be set up at prisons to weed out those unfit to be imprisoned. Then personal interviews would be given to the prospective convicts to see if they've got what it takes to be rehabilitated. If they can't cut the mustard, then the prison should have the right to reject them.

Besides the tests and the interviews, the admissions board would demand references from the candidates to see that the convicted were of high moral character. It's also possible, in the case of federal prisons, that each Congressman and Senator could recommend two candidates for each penitentiary, as they do to West Point and Annapolis. In the case of state prisons, the governor could select the ones he believed had the most on the ball.

After making the application, taking his tests, submitting to a personal interview, and writing a composition telling why he believes he would make a good prisoner, the candidate would be sent home and told he would be notified by the FBI about whether he made it or not. If he failed to get in, the candidate could reapply again—after he robbed another bank.

Many people say that by being selective, we would be making too many demands on our prisoners; but the taxpayers are paying for them, and we should have the right to have the best convicts that money can buy.

I'm sure that Governor Maddox will be ridiculed for his ideas on prison reform, but he is the first person to come along and point out what is wrong with the penal system in this country. It isn't the courts, nor is it the physical facilities holding us back, but the fact that we have not concentrated on improving the quality of the people we take in.

Anyone who has ever visited a prison in this country knows that Governor Maddox is right. For years we have been scraping the bottom of the barrel for inmates, and it's no wonder they don't live up to our expectations.

It is only by raising the requirements for admission and paying a decent wage that we're going to get the grade of prisoner that Governor Maddox and the rest of us can be proud of.

QUESTIONS

1. Why does Buchwald suggest we raise prison requirements? How does he think we should go about this?

2. Compare Buchwald's advice with Will Rogers's suggestion that Pennsylvania "procure more Better Element." What qualities of the American ethos do both humorists ridicule?

3. The narrator in this essay seems to be serious. Why do his recommendations sound reasonable? What is he parodying? How can we be sure he is joking?

Dear Dr. Butts

Langston Hughes

Paradoxically, though our Republic has relied strongly on education to create an informed citizenry, Americans have characteristically regarded book learning as inferior to native horse sense. Jesse Semple, a modern version of the cracker-box philosopher, brings hard reality and practical shrewdness to bear in his argument against the abstract theorizing of Dr. Butts. While the names of the characters—Semple and Butts—make a joke of their viewpoints, the issues are complex and cogent. As Hughes himself has said, "Humor is what you wish in your secret heart were not funny, but it is, and you must laugh. Humor is your own unconscious therapy." In addition to his series of books about Jesse Semple, Langston Hughes has published Not Without Laughter, Tambourines to Glory, *and collections of black poetry and folklore.*

Harlem, U.S.A.
One Cold February Day

Dear Dr. Butts,

I seen last week in the colored papers where you have writ an article for *The New York Times* in which you say America is the greatest country in the world for the Negro race and Democracy the greatest kind of government for all, *but* it would be better if there was equal education for colored folks in the South, and if everybody could vote, and if there were not Jim Crow in the army, also if the churches was not divided up into white churches and colored churches, and if Negroes did not have to ride on the back seats of busses South of Washington.

Now, all this later part of your article is hanging onto your *but.* You start off talking about how great American democracy is, then you *but* it all over the place. In fact, the *but* end of your see-saw is so far down on the ground I do not believe the other end can ever pull it up. So me myself, I would not write no article for no *New York Times* if I had to put in so many *buts.* I reckon maybe you come by it naturally, though, that being your name, dear Dr. Butts.

I hear tell that you are a race leader, but I do not know who you lead because I have not heard tell of you before and I have not laid eyes on you. But if you are leading me, *make me know it,* because I do not read the *New York Times* very often, less I happen to pick up a copy blowing around in the subway, so I did not know you were my leader. But since you are my leader, lead on, and see if I will follow behind your *but*—because there is more behind that *but* than there is in front of it.

Dr. Butts, I am glad to read that you writ an article in *The New York Times,* but also *sometime* I wish you would write one in the colored papers and let me know how to get out from behind all these *buts* that are staring me in the face. I know America is a great country *but*—and it is that *but* that has been keeping me where I is all these years. I can't get over it, I can't get under it, and I can't get around it, so what am I supposed to do? If you are leading me, lemme see. Because we have too many colored leaders now that nobody knows until they get from the white papers to the colored papers and from the colored papers to me who has never seen hair nor hide of you. Dear Dr. Butts, are you hiding from me—and *leading* me, too?

From the way you write, a man would think my race problem was made out of nothing but *buts.* But this, *but* that, and, yes, there is Jim Crow in Georgia *but*—. America admits they bomb folks in Florida— *but* Hitler gassed the Jews. Mississippi is bad—*but* Russia is worse. Detroit slums are awful—*but* compared to the slums in India, Detroit's Paradise Valley is Paradise.

Dear Dr. Butts, Hitler is dead. I don't live in Russia. India is across the Pacific Ocean. And I do not hope to see Paradise no time soon. I am nowhere near some of them foreign countries you are talking about being so bad. *I am here!* And you know as well as I do, Mississippi is hell. There ain't no *but* in the world can make it out different. They tell me when Nazis gas you, you die slow. But when they put a bomb under you like in Florida, you don't have time to say your prayers. As for Detroit, there is as much difference between Paradise Valley and Paradise as there is between heaven and Harlem. I don't know nothing about India, but I been in Washington, D.C. If you think there ain't slums there, just take your *but* up Seventh Street late some night, and see if you still got it by the time you get to Howard University.

I should not have to be telling you these things. You are colored just like me. To put a *but* after all this Jim Crow fly-papering around our feet is just like telling a hungry man, "*But* Mr. Rockefeller has got plenty to eat." It's just like telling a joker with no overcoat in the winter time, "*But* you will be hot next summer." The fellow is liable to haul off and say, "I am hot now!" And bop you over your head.

Are you in your right mind, dear Dr. Butts? Or are you just writing? Do you really think a new day is dawning? Do you really think Christians are having a change of heart? I can see you now taking your pen in hand to write, "*But* just last year the Southern Denominations of Hell-Fired

Salvation resolved to work toward Brotherhood." In fact, that is what you already writ. Do you think Brotherhood means *colored* to them Southerners?

Do you reckon they will recognize you for a brother, Dr. Butts, since you done had your picture taken in the Grand Ballroom of the Waldorf-Astoria shaking hands at some kind of meeting with five hundred white big-shots and *five* Negroes, all *five of them Negro leaders,* so it said underneath the picture? I did not know any of them Negro leaders by sight, neither by name, but since it says in the white papers that they are leaders, I reckon they are. Anyhow, I take my pen in hand to write you this letter to ask you to make yourself clear to me. When you answer me, do not write no "so-and-so-and-so *but*—." I will not take *but* for an answer. Negroes have been looking at Democracy's *but* too long. What we want to know is how to get rid of that *but.*

Do you dig me, dear Dr. Butts?

Sincerely very truly,
JESSE B. SEMPLE

QUESTIONS

1. Discuss Semple as a representative of America's blue-collar workers. What does his name suggest about him? Although he has not had much formal schooling, in what ways is he presented as an admirable character?

2. What are Semple's complaints about democracy? How does he answer Dr. Butts's defense of America?

3. What is the meaning of the name "Butts"? How is it a pun?

4. Why hasn't Semple heard of Dr. Butts before? What does he suggest Butts do? Do you agree with Semple?

The fantastic imagination of our comic storytellers ani-
mates George Herriman's "Krazy Kat," generally acclaimed a
comic-strip classic. The basic plot is at once simple and immensely
complex. Krazy, of ambiguous gender, is in love with Ignatz Mouse,
though Ignatz's greatest pleasure is to "krease that Kat's bean with
a brick." The Mouse does not understand that Krazy regards the
brick as a token of love. Nor is this irony understood by Offisa B.
Pupp, who adores the Kat and continues to jail the Mouse. For
more than thirty years, until his death in 1944, Herriman wove
stories around his bizarre love triangle. His surrealistic settings and
poetic language enriched the comic dramas that grew out of
conflicts between destiny and the individual, illusion and reality,
love and hate—the raw materials of all our comic storytellers.
(© King Features Syndicate 1969.)

part 3
The Storyteller

A soldier whose leg has been lost in battle is being carried to safety by a comrade. Meanwhile, the wounded man's head is also shot off. Unaware of this, the Good Samaritan trudges on, until he is stopped finally by an officer who asks where he is going with that headless carcass. Examining his burden, the soldier exclaims indignantly, "But he TOLD me IT WAS HIS LEG!!!!!" In "How to Tell a Story," Mark Twain cited this tale as comical; that is, the contradiction is so obvious that "a machine" could tell the story. However, if the raconteur imitates a dull-witted farmer, then the characterization makes the story humorous—and much funnier. "To string incongruities and absurdities together in a wandering and sometimes purposeless way, and seem innocently unaware that they are absurdities, is the basis of . . . the Art." And the art of telling humorous stories, Twain insisted, is peculiarly American.

Whether or not we agree with Twain's distinction between the comical and the humorous, surely oral storytelling is an American tradition. Nurtured in frontier outposts and desolate mining camps, polished by lawyers and reporters on the judicial circuits, the habit of oral narrative became deeply ingrained in the American character. The written literature everywhere bears the indelible stamp of this folk art, often in the form of anecdotes that, like those collected by Joel Chandler Harris in his *Uncle Remus* books, began as oral tales and later were given to print. Stories not actually culled from the oral tradition reflect its impact in their emphasis on a speaking voice, like the stories told by our vaudeville comedians. Even such a literate piece as Alexander Woollcott's "Our Mrs. Parker" focuses attention on the subject's own words.

Many yarns retain their oral flavor in an effort to portray American life realistically. Of his *Georgia Scenes*, the first collection of southwestern humorous tales, A. B. Longstreet asserted that "there is scarcely one word from the beginning to the end of the book which is not strictly *Georgian*." So we hear, in Longstreet's "Georgia Theatrics":

> "You kin, kin you?"
> "Yes, I kin, and am able to do it! Boo-oo-oo! Oh, wake snakes, and walk your chalks! Brimstone and—fire! Don't hold me, Nick Stoval! The fight's made up, and let's go at it—My soul if I don't jump down his throat, and gallop every chitterling out of him before you can say 'quit'!"

Such realistic portrayals also show the violence and cruelty that frequently mark the American brand of humor. Freud perceived that laughter was an outlet for aggression: when we smile, we bare our teeth. As the comedian W. C. Fields puts it: "If it causes pain, it's funny; if it doesn't, it isn't." In American stories, comic pain is often caused by a trickster. George W. Harris's Sut Lovingood and William Faulkner's auctioneer inflict mental and physical anguish, Sut by sending lizards up the parson's pants during a sermon, the auctioneer by conning a group of Mississippi farmers into buying a herd of wild horses.

The trickster, a character of peculiar fascination for American storytellers, appears in many versions—Down East peddler, frontier rogue, sophisticated swindler. At their worst, like those that appear in the definitions and fables of Ambrose Bierce, tricksters represent the shoddiness and phoniness of our culture. Before beginning a grisly amputation, Herman Melville's Dr. Cuticle, a heartless hypocrite, removes his wig, false teeth, and glass eye. Frequently, however, as in the popular movie *The Sting*, the trickster is an ambivalent hero. George Ade's preacher, who spouts nonsense to win the admiration of his congregation, and Edgar Allan Poe's diddlers, who have made an art if not a science of their confidence schemes, inspire our contempt, but perhaps a degree of admiration as well. A familiar folk motif—the trickster tricked—is used by Paul Laurence Dunbar in his poem about jealousy and by Joel Chandler Harris in his tale about Brer Rabbit. Our fabulists themselves often assume the role of prankster. Washington Irving, in "Adventure of the German Student," and Mark Twain, in "A Medieval Romance," play jokes on the reader. Maybe it is the confusion caused by trickery that appeals so strongly. In James Thurber's "The Day the Dam Broke," based on a real incident in Columbus, Ohio, two thousand people are deceived—no one is sure how—into fleeing from imaginary flood waters.

Though many American tales are rooted in reality, the most famous flower in fantasy. They are the "whoppers," tall stories colored by the exaggeration of the hero legends. Such larger-than-life figures as Davy Crockett and Mike Fink, prototypes of the "gamecock of the wilderness," ranted of their supernatural strength and unbeatable prowess. They were, they said, half horse, half alligator, and they could lick anything. Jim Doggett, the hero of T. B. Thorpe's "The Big Bear of Arkansas," boasts that he is "reckoned a buster, and allowed to be decidedly the best bar hunter." The "ring-tailed roarer"—an American version of the *alazones* or braggarts of classical comedy—continues to be a stock figure in our comic lore. But if our humorists have aggrandized our heroes, they have miniaturized them as well, as in David Ossman's playlet "The Adventures of Mark Time, Star Detective of the Circum-Solar Federation." From the tension between these two impulses—on one hand to enlarge our self-image, on the other to reduce it—American storytellers have created some of the world's most remarkable comic fantasies.

Adventure of the German Student

Washington Irving

Washington Irving, the first distinguished American fabulist, was also a satirist who wore a number of masks: Jonathan Oldstyle, Diedrich Knicker-bocker, the bachelor Salmagundi. But it is probably as storyteller that he has influenced American literature the most. His fiction lives on a substratum of myth; his characters are comic types who endure in the American imagination. One of these, Rip Van Winkle, incarnation of our impulse to retreat from reality, has been reborn in a host of characters, from Twain's Huck Finn to Joseph Heller's Yossarian. Another, the German student in love with an ideal woman, symbolizes the American's mythic flight to a dream world. However, the bizarre joke at the conclusion, as well as the sustained exaggeration throughout the story, gently mocks our faith in the supernatural and the romantic.

On a stormy night, in the tempestuous times of the French revolution, a young German was returning to his lodgings, at a late hour, across the old part of Paris. The lightning gleamed, and the loud claps of thunder rattled through the lofty narrow streets—but I should first tell you something about this young German.

Gottfried Wolfgang was a young man of good family. He had studied for some time at Göttingen, but being of a visionary and enthusiastic character, he had wandered into those wild and speculative doctrines which have so often bewildered German students. His secluded life, his intense application, and the singular nature of his studies, had an effect on both mind and body. His health was impaired; his imagination diseased. He had been indulging in fanciful speculations on spiritual essences, until, like Swedenborg, he had an ideal world of his own around him. He took up a notion, I do not know from what cause, that there was an evil influence hanging over him; an evil genius or spirit seeking to ensnare him and ensure his perdition. Such an idea working on his melancholy temperament, produced the most gloomy effects. He became haggard and desponding. His friends discovered the mental malady preying upon him, and determined that the best cure was a change of scene; he was sent, therefore, to finish his studies amidst the splendors and gayeties of Paris.

Wolfgang arrived at Paris at the breaking out of the revolution. The popular delirium at first caught his enthusiastic mind, and he was captivated by the political and philosophical theories of the day: but the scenes of blood which followed shocked his sensitive nature, disgusted him with society and the world, and made him more than ever a recluse. He shut himself up in a solitary apartment in the *Pays Latin*, the quarter of students. There, in a gloomy street not far from the monastic walls of the Sorbonne, he pursued his favorite speculations. Sometimes he spent hours together in the great libraries of Paris, those catacombs of departed authors, rummaging among their hoards of dusty and obsolete works in quest of food for his unhealthy appetite. He was, in a manner, a literary ghoul, feeding in the charnel-house of decayed literature.

Wolfgang, though solitary and recluse, was of an ardent temperament, but for a time it operated merely upon his imagination. He was too shy and ignorant of the world to make any advances to the fair, but he was a passionate admirer of female beauty, and in his lonely chamber would often lose himself in reveries on forms and faces which he had seen, and his fancy would deck out images of loveliness far surpassing the reality.

While his mind was in this excited and sublimated state, a dream produced an extraordinary effect upon him. It was of a female face of transcendent beauty. So strong was the impression made, that he dreamt of it again and again. It haunted his thoughts by day, his slumbers by night; in fine, he became passionately enamoured of this shadow of a dream. This lasted so long that it became one of those fixed ideas which haunt the minds of melancholy men, and are at times mistaken for madness.

Such was Gottfried Wolfgang, and such his situation at the time I mentioned. He was returning home late one stormy night, through some of the old and gloomy streets of the *Marais*, the ancient part of Paris. The loud claps of thunder rattled among the high houses of the narrow streets. He came to the Place de Grève, the square where public executions are performed. The lightning quivered about the pinnacles of the ancient Hôtel de Ville, and shed flickering gleams over the open space in front. As Wolfgang was crossing the square, he shrank back with horror at finding himself close by the guillotine. It was the height of the reign of terror, when this dreadful instrument of death stood ever ready, and its scaffold was continually running with the blood of the virtuous and the brave. It had that very day been actively employed in the work of carnage, and there it stood in grim array, amidst a silent and sleeping city, waiting for fresh victims.

Wolfgang's heart sickened within him, and he was turning shuddering from the horrible engine, when he beheld a shadowy form, cowering as it were at the foot of the steps which led up to the scaffold. A succession of vivid flashes of lightning revealed it more distinctly. It was a female figure, dressed in black. She was seated on one of the lower steps of the scaffold, leaning forward, her face hid in her lap; and her long dishevelled tresses hanging to the ground, streaming with the rain which fell in torrents. Wolfgang paused. There was something awful in this solitary monument of woe. The female had the appearance of being above the common order. He knew the times to be full of vicissitude, and that many a fair head, which had once been pillowed on down, now wandered houseless. Perhaps this was some poor mourner whom the dreadful axe had rendered desolate, and who sat here heart-broken on the strand of existence, from which all that was dear to her had been launched into eternity.

He approached, and addressed her in the accents of sympathy. She raised her head and gazed wildly at him. What was his astonishment at beholding, by the bright glare of the lightning, the very face which had haunted him in his dreams. It was pale and disconsolate, but ravishingly beautiful.

Trembling with violent and conflicting emotions, Wolfgang again accosted her. He spoke something of her being exposed at such an hour of the night, and to the fury of such a storm, and offered to conduct her to her friends. She pointed to the guillotine with a gesture of dreadful signification.

"I have no friend on earth!" said she.

"But you have a home," said Wolfgang.

"Yes—in the grave!"

The heart of the student melted at the words.

"If a stranger dare make an offer," said he, "without danger of being misunderstood, I would offer my humble dwelling as a shelter; myself as a devoted friend. I am friendless myself in Paris, and a stranger in the land; but if my life could be of service, it is at your disposal, and should be sacrificed before harm or indignity should come to you."

There was an honest earnestness in the young man's manner that had its effect. His foreign accent, too, was in his favor; it showed him not to be a hackneyed inhabitant of Paris. Indeed, there is an eloquence in true enthusiasm that is not to be doubted. The homeless stranger confided herself implicitly to the protection of the student.

He supported her faltering steps across the Pont Neuf, and by the place where the statue of Henry the Fourth had been overthrown by the populace. The storm had abated, and the thunder rumbled at a distance. All Paris was quiet; that great volcano of human passion slumbered for a while, to gather fresh strength for the next day's eruption. The student conducted his charge through the ancient streets of the *Pays Latin*, and by the dusky walls of the Sorbonne, to the great dingy hotel which he inhabited. The old portress who admitted them stared with surprise at the unusual sight of the melancholy Wolfgang with a female companion.

On entering his apartment, the student, for the first time, blushed at the scantiness and indifference of his dwelling. He had but one chamber—an old-fashioned saloon—heavily carved, and fantastically furnished with the remains of former magnificence, for it was one of those hotels in the quarter of the Luxembourg palace, which had once belonged to nobility. It was lumbered with books and papers, and all the usual apparatus of a student, and his bed stood in a recess at one end.

When lights were brought, and Wolfgang had a better opportunity of contemplating the stranger, he was more than ever intoxicated by her beauty. Her face was pale, but of a dazzling fairness, set off by a profusion of raven hair that hung clustering about it. Her eyes were large and brilliant, with a singular expression approaching almost to wildness. As far as her black dress permitted her shape to be seen, it was of perfect symmetry. Her whole appearance was highly striking, though she was dressed in the simplest style. The only thing approaching to an ornament which she wore, was a broad black band round her neck, clasped by diamonds.

The perplexity now commenced with the student how to dispose of the helpless being thus thrown upon his protection. He thought of abandoning his chamber to her, and seeking shelter for himself elsewhere. Still he was so fascinated by her charms, there seemed to be such a spell upon his thoughts and senses, that he could not tear himself from her presence. Her manner, too, was singular and unaccountable. She spoke no more of the guillotine. Her grief had abated. The attentions of the student had first won her confidence, and then, apparently, her heart. She was evidently an enthusiast like himself, and enthusiasts soon understand each other.

In the infatuation of the moment, Wolfgang avowed his passion for her. He told her the story of his mysterious dream, and how she had possessed his heart before he had even seen her. She was strangely affected by his recital, and acknowledged to have felt an impulse towards him equally unaccountable. It was the time for wild theory and wild actions. Old prejudices and superstitions were done away; everything was under sway of the "Goddess of Reason." Among the rubbish of the old times, the forms and ceremonies of marriage began to be considered superfluous bonds for honorable minds. Social compacts were the vogue. Wolfgang was too much of a theorist not to be tainted by the liberal doctrines of the day.

"Why should we separate?" said he: "our hearts are united; in the eye of reason and honor we are as one. What need is there of sordid forms to bind high souls together?"

The stranger listened with emotion: she had evidently received illumination at the same school.

"You have no home nor family," continued he; "let me be everything to you, or rather let us be everything to one another. If form is necessary, form shall be observed—there is my hand. I pledge myself to you forever."

"Forever?" said the stranger, solemnly.

"Forever!" repeated Wolfgang.

The stranger clasped the hand extended to her: "Then I am yours," murmured she, and sank upon his bosom.

The next morning the student left his bride sleeping, and sallied forth at an early hour to seek more spacious apartments suitable to the change in his situation. When he returned, he found the stranger lying with her head hanging over the bed and one arm thrown over it. He spoke to her, but received no reply. He advanced to awaken her from her uneasy posture. On taking her hand, it was cold—there was no pulsation—her face was pallid and ghastly. In a word, she was a corpse.

Horrified and frantic, he alarmed the house. A scene of confusion ensued. The police was summoned. As the officer of police entered the room, he started back on beholding the corpse.

"Great heaven!" cried he, "how did this woman come here?"

"Do you know anything about her?" said Wolfgang eagerly.

"Do I?" exclaimed the officer: "she was guillotined yesterday."

He stepped forward; undid the black collar round the neck of the corpse, and the head rolled on the floor!

The student burst into a frenzy. "The fiend! the fiend has gained possession of me!" shrieked he: "I am lost forever."

They tried to soothe him, but in vain. He was possessed with the frightful belief that an evil spirit had reanimated the dead body to ensnare him. He went distracted, and died in a mad-house.

Here the old gentleman with the haunted head finished his narrative.

"And is this really a fact?" said the inquisitive gentleman.

"A fact not to be doubted," replied the other. "I had it from the best authority. The student told it me himself. I saw him in a mad-house in Paris."

QUESTIONS

1. Why did Gottfried Wolfgang come to Paris? Describe the dream that haunts him.

2. How does Irving set the scene for his story? What kind of hotel does Wolfgang live in? What is happening in Paris at the time?

3. Why is the student shocked when he meets the woman? Describe her appearance. What does she say to him?

4. What happens the next morning? What does Wolfgang learn about her? How does he explain the incident?

5. How does the "punch line" turn the story into a burlesque? In what ways does this story anticipate modern black humor?

Georgia Theatrics

A. B. Longstreet

A. B. Longstreet, who penned the first and most influential collection of southwestern humorous tales, also plays a joke on the reader in this episode from Georgia Scenes. Though his aim was to give a realistic account of life in Georgia, Longstreet seemed both attracted and repelled by the savagery of his fellow Georgians. Caught between fidelity to fact and an inclination to moralize, he deals in "Georgia Theatrics" most ingeniously with the violent contest, the most common plot in southwestern humor, by substituting the ritual brag for the battle itself.

If my memory fail me not, the 10th of June, 1809, found me, at about eleven o'clock in the forenoon, ascending a long and gentle slope in what was called "The Dark Corner" of Lincoln. I believe it took its name from the moral darkness which reigned over that portion of the county at the time of which I am speaking. If in this point of view it was but a shade darker than the rest of the county, it was inconceivably dark. If any man can name a trick or sin which had not been committed at the time of which I am speaking, in the very focus of all the county's illumination (Lincolnton), he must himself be the most inventive of the tricky and the very Judas of sinners. Since that time, however (all humor aside), Lincoln has become a living proof "that light shineth in darkness." Could I venture to mingle the solemn with the ludicrous, even for the purposes of honorable contrast, I could adduce from this county instances of the most numerous and wonderful transitions from vice and folly to virtue and holiness which have ever, perhaps, been witnessed since the days of the apostolic ministry. So much, lest it should be thought by some that what I am about to relate is characteristic of the county in which it occurred.

Whatever may be said of the moral condition of the Dark Corner at the time just mentioned, its natural condition was anything but dark. It smiled in all the charms of spring; and spring borrowed a new charm from its undulating grounds, its luxuriant woodlands, its sportive streams, its vocal birds, and its blushing flowers.

Rapt with the enchantment of the season and the scenery around me, I was slowly rising the slope, when I was startled by loud, profane, and

boisterous voices, which seemed to proceed from a thick covert of undergrowth about two hundred yards in the advance of me and about one hundred to the right of my road.

"You kin, kin you?"

"Yes, I kin, and am able to do it! Boo-oo-oo! Oh, wake snakes, and walk your chalks! Brimstone and—fire! Don't hold me, Nick Stoval! The fight's made up, and let's go at it—My soul if I don't jump down his throat, and gallop every chitterling out of him before you can say 'quit'!"

"Now, Nick, don't hold him! Jist let the wild-cat come, and I'll tame him. Ned'll see me a fair fight! Won't you, Ned?"

"Oh yes; I'll see you a fair fight, blast my old shoes if I don't!"

"That's sufficient, as Tom Haynes said when he saw the elephant. Now let him come!"

Thus they went on, with countless oaths interspersed which I dare not even hint at, and with much that I could not distinctly hear.

In mercy's name! thought I, what band of ruffians has selected this holy season and this heavenly retreat for such pandemoniac riots! I quickened my gait, and had come nearly opposite to the thick grove whence the noise proceeded, when my eye caught, indistinctly and at intervals, through the foliage of the dwarf-oaks and hickories which intervened, glimpses of a man, or men, who seemed to be in a violent struggle; and I could occasionally catch those deep-drawn, emphatic oaths which men in conflict utter when they deal blows. I dismounted, and hurried to the spot with all speed. I had overcome about half the space which separated it from me, when I saw the combatants come to the ground, and, after a short struggle, I saw the uppermost one (for I could not see the other) make a heavy plunge with both his thumbs, and at the same instant I heard a cry in the accent of keenest torture, "Enough! My eye's out!"

I was so completely horror-struck that I stood transfixed for a moment to the spot where the cry met me. The accomplices in the hellish deed which had been perpetuated had all fled at my approach—at least, I supposed so, for they were not to be seen.

"Now, blast your corn-shucking soul!" said the victor (a youth about eighteen years old) as he rose from the ground—"come cutt'n' your shines 'bout me agin, next time I come to the court-house, will you? Get your owl eye in agin if you can!"

At this moment he saw me for the first time. He looked excessively embarrassed, and was moving off, when I called to him, in a tone emboldened by the sacredness of my office and the iniquity of his crime, "Come back, you brute, and assist me in relieving your fellow-mortal, whom you have ruined forever!"

My rudeness subdued his embarrassment in an instant; and, with a taunting curl of the nose, he replied, "You needn't kick before you're spurr'd. There a'n't nobody there, nor ha'n't been nother. I was jist seein' how I could 'a' fout." So saying, he bounded to his plough, which stood in the corner of the fence about fifty yards beyond the battle-ground.

And, would you believe it, gentle reader? his report was true. All that I had heard and seen was nothing more nor less than a Lincoln rehearsal, in which the youth who had just left me had played all the parts of all the characters in a court-house fight.

I went to the ground from which he had risen, and there were the prints of his two thumbs, plunged up to the balls in the mellow earth, about the distance of a man's eyes apart; and the ground around was broken up as if two stags had been engaged upon it.

QUESTIONS

1. How did this portion of Lincoln get its name? Why does this brief sketch have such an elaborate introduction?

2. What irony is there in Longstreet's reference to his reader as "gentle reader"? What other reversals provide cause for humor?

3. How are the narrator and the youth different? How are these differences made clear to us through the language they use?

The Big Bear of Arkansas

T. B. Thorpe

In "The Big Bear of Arkansas," the humor of the southwestern storyteller reaches a new height. Thorpe's tale-within-a-tale is similar to Longstreet's; an urbane narrator introduces the backwoods raconteur, so that comedy derives from the incongruities between language modes and character types. The greatest incongruity, however, is that between fantasy and reality. The rustic, a braggart, uses his fertile imagination in an effort at self-aggrandizement, but his boasts of prowess are undercut by actual events. If the joke is on him, it is also on the reader, for the expected climax in this tale of violence does not occur. The emphasis on nature, on creation, and on mystery lends "Big Bear" the aura of myth, making it a triumph of the tall-tale form. Thorpe's stories are collected in The Mysteries of the Backwoods *and* The Hive of the Bee-Hunter.

A steamboat on the Mississippi frequently, in making her regular trips, carries between places varying from one to two thousand miles apart; and as these boats advertise to land passengers and freight at "all intermediate landings," the heterogeneous character of the passengers of one of these up-country boats can scarcely be imagined by one who has never seen it with his own eyes. Starting from New Orleans in one of these boats, you will find yourself associated with men from every state in the Union, and from every portion of the globe; and a man of observation need not lack for amusement or instruction in such a crowd, if he will take the trouble to read the great book of character so favourably opened before him. Here may be seen jostling together the wealthy Southern planter, and the pedlar of tin-ware from New England—the Northern merchant, and the Southern jockey—a venerable bishop, and a desperate gambler—the land speculator, and the honest farmer—professional men of all creeds and characters—Wolvereens, Suckers, Hoosiers, Buckeyes, and Corn-crackers, beside a "plentiful sprinkling" of the half-horse and half-alligator species of men, who are peculiar to "old Mississippi," and who appear to gain a livelihood simply by going up and down the river. In the pursuit of pleasure or business, I have frequently found myself in such a crowd.

On one occasion, when in New Orleans, I had occasion to take a trip of a few miles up the Mississippi, and I hurried on board the well-known "high-pressure-and-beat-every-thing" steamboat *Invincible,* just as the last note of the last bell was sounding; and when the confusion and bustle that is natural to a boat's getting under way had subsided, I discovered that I was associated in as heterogeneous a crowd as was ever got together. As my trip was to be of a few hours' duration only, I made no endeavours to become acquainted with my fellow passengers, most of whom would be together many days. Instead of this, I took out of my pocket the "latest paper," and more critically than usual examined its contents; my fellow passengers at the same time disposed themselves in little groups. While I was thus busily employed in reading, and my companions were more busily employed in discussing such subjects as suited their humours best, we were startled most unexpectedly by a loud Indian whoop, uttered in the "social hall," that part of the cabin fitted off for a bar; then was to be heard a loud crowing, which would not have continued to have interested us—such sounds being quite common in that place of spirits—had not the hero of these windy accomplishments stuck his head into the cabin and hallooed out, "Hurra for the Big Bar of Arkansaw!" and then might be heard a confused hum of voices, unintelligible, save in such broken sentences as "horse," "screamer," "lightning is slow," &c. As might have been expected, this continued interruption attracted the attention of every one in the cabin; all conversation dropped, and in the midst of this surprise the "Big Bar" walked into the cabin, took a chair, put his feet on the stove, and looking back over his shoulder, passed the general and familiar salute of "Strangers, how are you?" He then expressed himself as much at home as if he had been at "the Forks of Cypress," and "perhaps a little more so." Some of the company at this familiarity looked a little angry, and some astonished; but in a moment every face was wreathed in a smile. There was something about the intruder that won the heart on sight. He appeared to be a man enjoying perfect health and contentment: his eyes were as sparkling as diamonds, and good-natured to simplicity. Then his perfect confidence in himself was irresistibly droll. "Perhaps," said he, "gentlemen," running on without a person speaking, "perhaps you have been to New Orleans often; I never made *the first visit before,* and I don't intend to make another in a crow's life. I am thrown away in that ar place, and useless, that ar a fact. Some of the gentlemen thar called me *green*—well, perhaps I am, said I, *but I arn't so at home;* and if I ain't off my trail much, the heads of them perlite chaps themselves weren't much the hardest; for according to my notion, they were real *know-nothings,* green as a pumpkin vine—couldn't, in farming, I'll bet, raise a crop of turnips: and as for shooting, they'd miss a barn if the door was swinging, and that, too, with the best rifle in the country. And then they talked to me 'bout hunting, and laughed at my calling the principal game in Arkansaw poker, and high-low-jack. 'Perhaps,' said I, 'you prefer chickens and rolette'; at this they laughed harder than ever, and asked me if I lived in the woods, and didn't know what *game* was? At this I rather think I laughed. 'Yes,' I roared, and says, 'Strangers, if you'd asked me *how we got our meat* in Arkansaw, I'd a told you at once, and given you a list of varmints that would make a caravan, beginning with the bar, and ending off with the cat; that's *meat* though, not game.' Game, indeed that's what city folks call it; and with them it means chippen-birds and shite-pokes; maybe such trash live in my diggins, but I arn't noticed them yet: a bird any way is too trifling. I never did shoot at but one, and I'd never forgiven myself for that, had it weighed less than forty pounds. I wouldn't draw a rifle on any thing less than that; and when I meet with another wild turkey of the same weight I will drap him."

"A wild turkey weighing forty pounds!" exclaimed twenty voices in the cabin at once.

"Yes, strangers, and wasn't it a whopper? You see, the thing was so fat that it couldn't fly far; and when he fell out of the tree, after I shot him, on striking the ground he bust open behind, and the way the pound gobs of tallow rolled out of the opening was perfectly beautiful."

"Where did all that happen?" asked a cynical-looking Hoosier.

"Happen! happened in Arkansaw: where else could it have happened, but in the creation state, the finishing-up country—a state where the *sile* runs down to the centre of the 'arth, and government gives you a title to every inch of it? Then its airs—just breathe them, and they will make you snort like a horse. It's a state without a fault, it is."

"Excepting mosquitoes," cried the Hoosier.

"Well, stranger, except them; for it ar a fact that they are rather *enormous*, and do push themselves in somewhat troublesome. But, stranger, they never stick twice in the same place; and give them a fair chance for a few months, and you will get as much above noticing them as an alligator. They can't hurt my feelings, for they lay under the skin; and I never knew but one case of injury resulting from them, and that was to a Yankee: and they take worse to foreigners, any how, than they do to natives. But the way they used that fellow up! first they punched him until he swelled up and busted; then he su-per-a-ted, as the doctor called it, until he was as raw as beef; then he took the ager, owing to the warm weather, and finally he took a steamboat and left the country. He was the only man that ever took mosquitoes to heart that I know of. But mosquitoes is natur, and I never find fault with her. If they ar large, Arkansaw is large, her varmints ar large, her trees ar large, her rivers ar large, and a small mosquito would be of no more use in Arkansaw than preaching in a canebrake."

This knock-down argument in favour of big mosquitoes used the Hoosier up, and the logician started on a new track, to explain how numerous bear were in his "diggins," where he represented them to be "about as plenty as blackberries, and a little plentifuler."

Upon the utterance of this assertion, a timid little man near me inquired if the bear in Arkansaw ever attacked the settlers in numbers.

"No," said our hero, warming with the subject, "no, stranger, for you see it ain't the natur of bar to go in droves; but the way they squander about in pairs and single ones is edifying. And the way I hunt them the old black rascals know the crack of my gun as well as they know a pig's squealing. They grow thin in our parts, it frightens them so, and they do take the noise dreadfully, poor things. That gun of mine is perfect *epidemic among bar;* if not watched closely, it will go off as quick on a warm scent as my dog Bowie-knife will: and then that dog—whew! why the fellow thinks that the world is full of bar, he finds them so easy. It's lucky he don't talk as well as think; for with his natural modesty, if he should suddenly learn how much he is acknowledged to be ahead of all other dogs in the universe, he would be astonished to death in two minutes. Strangers, the dog knows a bar's way as well as a horse-jockey knows a woman's: he always barks at the right time, bites at the exact place, and whips without getting a scratch. I never could tell whether he was made expressly to hunt bar, or whether bar was made expressly for him to hunt: any way, I believe they were ordained to go together as naturally as Squire Jones says a man and woman is, when he moralizes in marrying a couple. In fact, Jones once said, said he, 'Marriage according to law is a civil contract of divine origin; it's common to all countries as well as Arkansaw, and people take to it as naturally as Jim Doggett's Bowie-knife takes to bar.' "

"What season of the year do your hunts take place?" inquired a gentlemanly foreigner, who, from some peculiarities of his baggage, I suspected to be an Englishman, on some hunting expedition, probably at the foot of the Rocky Mountains.

"The season for bar hunting, stranger," said the man of Arkansaw, "is generally all the year round, and the hunts take place about as regular. I read in history that varmints have their fat season, and their lean season. That is not the case in Arkansaw, feeding as they do upon the *spontenacious* productions of the sile, they have one continued fat season the year round: though in winter things in this way is rather more greasy than in summer, I must admit. For that reason bar with us run in warm weather, but in winter, they only waddle. Fat, fat! it's an enemy to speed; it tames everything that has plenty of it. I have seen wild turkeys, from its influence, as gentle as chickens. Run a bar in this fat condition, and the way it improves the critter for eating is amazing; it sort of mixes the ile up with the meat, until you can't tell t'other from which. I've done this often. I recollect one perty morning in particular, of putting an old fellow on the stretch, and considering the weight he carried, he run well. But the dogs soon tired him down, and when I came up with him wasn't he in a beautiful sweat—I might say fever; and then to see his tongue sticking out of his mouth a feet, and his sides sinking and opening like a bellows, and his cheeks so fat he couldn't look cross. In this fix I blazed at him, and pitch me naked into a briar patch if the steam didn't come out of the bullet-hole ten foot in a straight line. The fellow, I reckon was made on the high-pressure system, and the lead sort of bust his biler."

"That column of steam was rather curious, or else the bear must have been *warm*," observed the foreigner, with a laugh.

"Stranger, as you observe, that bar was WARM, and the blowing off of the steam show'd it, and also how hard the varmint had been run. I have no doubt if he had kept on two miles farther his insides would have been stewed; and I expect to meet with a varmint yet of extra bottom, who will run himself into a skinfull of bar's grease: it is possible, much onlikelier things have happened."

"Whereabouts are these bears so abundant?" inquired the foreigner, with increasing interest.

"Why, stranger, they inhabit the neighbourhood of my settlement, one of the prettiest places on old Mississippi—a perfect location, and no mistake; a place that had some defects until the river made the 'cut-off' at 'Shirt-tail bend,' and that remedied the evil, as it brought my cabin on the edge of the river—a great advantage in wet weather, I assure you, as you can now roll a barrel of whiskey into my yard in high water from a boat, as easy as falling off a log. It's a great improvement, as toting it by land in a jug, as I used to do, *evaporated* it too fast, and it became expensive. Just stop with me, stranger, a month or two, or a year if you like, and you will appreciate my place. I can give you plenty to eat; for beside hog and hominy, you can have bar-ham, and bar sausages, and a mattrass of bar-skins to sleep on, and a wildcat-skin, pulled off hull, stuffed with corn-shucks, for a pillow. That bed would put you to sleep if you had rheumatics in every joint in your body. I call that ar bed a *quietus.* Then look at my land—the government ain' got another such a piece to dispose of. Such timber, and such bottom land, why you can't preserve any thing natural you plant in it unless you pick it young, things thar will grow out of shape so quick. I once planted in those diggins a few potatoes and beets: they took a fine start, and after that an ox team couldn't have kept them from growing. About that time I went off to old Kentuck on bisiness, and did not hear from them things in three months, when I accidentally stumbled on a fellow who had stopped at my place, with an idea of buying me out. 'How did you like things?' said I. 'Pretty well,' said he; 'the cabin is convenient, and the timber land is good; but that bottom land ain't worth the first red cent.' 'Why?' said I. ' 'Cause,' said he. ' 'Cause what?' said I. ' 'Cause it's full of cedar stumps and Indian mounds,' said he, *'and it can't be cleared.'* 'Lord,' said I, 'them ar "cedar stumps" is beets, and them ar "Indian mounds" ar tater hills.' As I expected, the crop was overgrown and useless: the sile is too rich, *and planting in Arkansaw is dangerous.* I had a good-sized sow killed in that same bottom land. The old thief stole an ear of corn, and took it down where she slept at night to eat. Well, she left a grain or two on the ground, and lay down on them: before morning the corn shot up, and the percussion killed her dead. I don't plant any more; natur intended Arkansaw for a hunting ground, and I go according to natur."

The questioner who thus elicited the description of our hero's settlement, seemed to be perfectly satisfied, and said no more; but the "Big Bar of Arkansaw" rambled on from one thing to another with a volubility perfectly astonishing, occasionally disputing with those around him, particularly with a "live Sucker" from Illinois, who had the daring to say that our Arkansaw friend's stories "smelt rather tall."

In this manner the evening was spent; but conscious that my own association with so singular a personage would probably end before morning, I asked him if he would not give me a description of some particular bear hunt; adding that I took great interest in such things, though I was no sportsman. The desire seemed to please him, and he squared himself round towards me, saying, that he could give me an idea of a bar hunt that was never beat in this world, or in any other. His manner was so singular, that half of his story consisted in his excellent way of telling it, the great peculiarity of which was, the happy manner he had of emphasizing the prominent parts of his conversation. As near as I can recollect, I have italicized them, and given the story in his own words.

"Stranger," said he, "in bar hunts *I am numerous*, and which particular one, as you say, I shall tell, puzzles me. There was the old she devil I shot at the Hurricane last fall—then there was the old hog thief I popped over at the Bloody Crossing, and then—Yes, I have it! I will give you an idea of a hunt, in which the greatest bar was killed that ever lived, *none excepted*; about an old fellow that I hunted, more or less, for two or three years; and if that ain't a particular bar hunt, I ain't got one to tell. But in the first place, stranger, let me say, I am pleased with you, because you ain't ashamed to gain information by asking, and listening, and that's what I say to Countess's pups every day when I'm home; and I have got great hopes of them ar pups, because they are continually *nosing* about; and though they stick it sometimes in the wrong place, they gain experience any how, and may learn something useful to boot. Well, as I was saying about this big bar, you see when I and some more first settled in our region, we were drivin to hunting naturally; we soon liked it, and after that we found it an easy matter to make the thing our business. One old chap who had pioneered 'afore us, gave us to understand that we had settled in the right place. He dwelt upon its merits until it was affecting, and showed us, to prove his assertions, more marks on the sassafras trees than I ever saw on a tavern door 'lection time. 'Who keeps that ar reckoning?' said I. 'The bar,' said he. 'What for?' said I. 'Can't tell,' said he; 'but so it is: the bar bite the bark and wood too, at the highest point from the ground they can reach, and you can tell, by the marks,' said he, 'the length of the bar to an inch.' 'Enough,' said I; 'I've learned something here a'ready, and I'll put it in practice.'

"Well, stranger, just one month from that time I killed a bar, and told its exact length before I measured it, by those very marks; and when I did that, I swelled up considerable—I've been a prouder man ever since. So I went on, larning something every day, until I was reckoned a buster, and allowed to be decidedly the best bar hunter in my district; and that is a reputation as much harder to earn than to be reckoned first man in Congress, as an iron ramrod is harder than a toadstool. Did the varmints grow over-cunning by being fooled with by green-horn hunters, and by this means get troublesome, they send for me as a matter of course; and thus I do my own hunting, and most of my neighbours'. I walk into the varmints though, and it has become about as much the same to me as drinking. It is told in two sentences—a bar is started, and he is killed. The thing is somewhat monotonous now—I know just how much they will run, where they will tire, how much they will growl, and what a thundering time I will have in getting them home. I could give you this history of the chase with all particulars at the commencement, I know the signs so well—*Stranger, I'm certain*. Once I met a match though, and I will tell you about it; for a common hunt would not be worth relating.

"On a fine fall day, long time ago, I was trailing about for bar, and what should I see but fresh marks on the sassafras trees, about eight inches above any in the forests that I knew of. Says I, 'them marks is a hoax, or it indicates the d————t bar that was ever grown.' In fact, stranger, I couldn't believe it was real, and I went on. Again I saw the same marks, at the same height, and *I knew the thing lived*. That conviction came home to my soul like an earthquake. Says I, 'here is something a-purpose for me; that bar is mine, or I give up the hunting business.' The very next morning what should I see but a number of buzzards hovering over my cornfield. 'The rascal has been there,' said I, 'for that sign is certain': and, sure enough, on examining, I found the bones of what had been as beautiful a hog the day before, as was ever raised by a Buckeye. Then I tracked the critter out of the field to the woods, and all the marks he left behind, showed me that he was *the bar*.

"Well, stranger, the first fair chase I ever had with that big critter, I saw him no less than three distinct times at a distance: the dogs run him over eighteen miles and broke down, my horse gave out, and I was as nearly used up as a man can be, made on *my* principle, *which is patent*. Before this adventure, such things were unknown to me as possible; but, strange as it was, that bar got me used to it before I was done with him; for he got so at last, that he would leave me on a long chase *quite easy*. How he did it, I never could understand. That a bar runs at all, is puzzling; but how this one could tire down and bust up a pack of hounds and a horse, that were used to overhauling everything they started after in no time, was past my understanding. Well, stranger, that bar finally got so sassy, that he used to help himself to a hog off my premises whenever he wanted one; the buzzards followed after what he left, and so between the *bar and buzzard*, I rather think I was *out of pork*.

"Well, missing that bar so often took hold of my vitals, and I wasted away. The thing had been carried too far, and it reduced me in flesh faster than an ager. I would see that bar in every thing I did: *he hunted me*, and that, too, like a devil, which I began to think he was. While in this fix, I made preparations to give him a last brush, and be done with it. Having completed every thing to my satisfaction, I started at sunrise, and to my great joy, I discovered from the way the dogs run, that they were near him; finding his trail was nothing, for that had become as plain to the pack as a turnpike road. On we went, and coming to an open country, what should I see but the bar very leisurely ascending a hill, and the dogs close at his heels, either a match for him in speed, or else he did not care to get out of their way—I don't know which. But wasn't he a beauty, though? I loved him like a brother.

"On he went, until he came to a tree, the limbs of which formed a crotch about six feet from the ground. Into this crotch he got and seated himself, the dogs yelling all around it; and there he sat eyeing them as quiet as a pond in low water. A green-horn friend of mine, in company, reached shooting distance before me, and blazed away, hitting the critter in the centre of his forehead. The bar shook his head as the ball struck it, and then walked down from that tree as gently as a lady would from a carriage. 'Twas a beautiful sight to see him do that—he was in such a rage that he seemed to be as little afraid of the dogs as if they had been sucking pigs; and the dogs warn't slow in making a ring around him at a respectful distance, I tell you; even Bowie-knife, himself, stood off. Then the way his eyes flashed—why the fire of them would have singed a cat's hair; in fact that bar was *wrath all over*. Only one pup came near him, and he was brushed out so totally with the bar's left paw, that he entirely disappeared; and that made the old dogs more cautious still. In the mean time, I came up, and taking deliberate aim as a man should do, at his side, just back of his foreleg, *if my gun did not snap*, call me a coward, and I won't take it personal. Yes, stranger, *it snapped*, and I could not find a cap about my person. While in this predicament, I turned round to my fool friend—says I, 'Bill,' says I, 'you're an ass—you're a fool—you might as well have tried to kill that bar by barking the tree under his belly, as to have done it by hitting him in the head. Your shot has made a tiger of him, and blast me, if a dog gets killed or wounded when they come to blows, I will stick my knife into your liver, I will—' my wrath was up. I had lost my caps, my gun had snapped, the fellow with me had fired at the bar's head, and I expected every moment to see him close in with the dogs, and kill a dozen of them at least. In this thing I was mistaken, for the bar leaped over the ring formed by the dogs, and giving a fierce growl, was off—the pack, of course, in full cry after him. The run this time was short, for coming to the edge of a lake the varmint jumped in, and swam to a little island in the lake, which it reached just a moment before the dogs. 'I'll have him now,' said I, for I had found my caps in the *lining of my coat*—so, rolling a log into the lake, I paddled myself across to the island, just as the dogs had cornered the bar in a thicket. I rushed up and fired—at the same time the critter leaped over the dogs and came within three feet of me, running like mad; he jumped into the lake, and tried to mount the log I had just deserted, but every time he got half his body on it, it would roll over and send him under; the dogs, too, got around him, and pulled him about, and finally Bowie-knife clenched with him, and they sunk into the lake together. Stranger, about this time, I was excited, and I stripped off my coat, drew my knife, and intended to have taken a part with Bowie-knife myself, when the bar rose to the surface. But the varmint staid under—Bowie-knife came up alone, more dead than alive, and with the pack came ashore. 'Thank God,' said I, 'the old villain has got his deserts at last.' Determined to have the body, I cut a grape-vine for a rope, and dove down where I could see the bar in the water, fastened my queer rope to his leg, and fished him, with great difficulty, ashore. Stranger, may I be chawed to death by young alligators, if the thing I looked at wasn't a *she bar, and not the old critter after all.* The way matters got mixed on that island was onaccountably curious, and thinking of it made me more than ever convinced that I was hunting the devil himself. I went home that night and took to my bed—the thing was killing me. The entire team of Arkansaw in bar-hunting, acknowledged himself used up, and the fact sunk into my feelings like a snagged boat will in the Mississippi. I grew as cross as a bar with two cubs and a sore tail. The thing got out 'mong my neighbours, and I was asked how come on that individu-al that never lost a bar when once started? and if that same individu-al didn't wear telescopes when he turned a she bar, of ordinary size, into an old he one, a little larger than a horse? 'Perhaps,' said I, 'friends'—getting wrathy—'perhaps you want to call somebody a liar.' 'Oh, no,' said they, 'we only heard such things as being *rather common* of late, but we don't believe one word of it; oh, no,'—and then they would ride off and laugh like so many hyenas over a dead nigger. It was too much, and I determined to catch that bar, go to Texas, or die,—and I made my preparations accordin'. I had the pack shut up and rested. I took my rifle to pieces and iled it. I put caps in every pocket about my person, *for fear of the lining.* I then told my neighbours, that on Monday morning—naming the day—I would start THAT BAR, and bring him home with me, or they might divide my settlement among them, the owner having disappeared. Well, stranger, on the morning previous to the great day of my hunting expedition, I went into the woods near my house, taking my gun and Bowie-knife along, just *from habit*, and there sitting down also from habit, what should I see, getting over my fence, but *the bar!* Yes, the old varmint was within a hundred yards of me, and the way he walked *over that fence*—stranger, he loomed up like a *black mist,* he seemed so large, and he walked right towards me. I raised myself, took deliberate aim, and fired. Instantly the varmint wheeled, gave a yell, and *walked through the fence* like a falling tree would through a cobweb. I started after, but was tripped up by my inexpressibles, which either from habit, or the excitement of the moment, were about my heels, and before I had really gathered myself up, I heard the old varmint groaning in a thicket near by, like a thousand sinners, and by the time I reached him he was a corpse. Stranger, it took five niggers and myself to put that carcase on a mule's back and old long-ears waddled under the load, as if he was foundered in every leg of his body, and with a common whopper of a bar, he would have trotted off, and enjoyed himself. 'Twould astonish you to know how big he was: I made a *bed-spread of his skin,* and the way it used to cover my bar mattress, and leave several feet on each side to tuck up, would have delighted you. It was in fact a creation bar, and if it had lived in Samson's time, and had met him, in a fair fight, it would have licked him in the twinkling of a dice-box. But, strangers, I never like the way I hunted, and *missed him.* There is something curious about it, I could never understand,—and I never was satisfied at his giving in so easy at last. Perhaps, he had heard of my preparations to hunt him the next day, so he jist come in, like Capt. Scott's coon, to save his wind to grunt with in dying; but that ain't likely. My private opinion is, that that bar was an *unhuntable bar, and died when his time come.*"

When the story was ended, our hero sat some minutes with his auditors in a grave silence; I saw there was a mystery connected with the bear whose death he had just related, that had evidently made a strong impression on his mind. It was also evident that there was some superstitious awe connected with the affair,—a feeling common with all "children of the wood," when they meet with any thing out of their everyday experience. He was the first one, however, to break the silence, and jumping up, he asked all present to "liquor" before going to bed,—a thing which he did, with a number of companions, evidently to his heart's content.

Long before day, I was put ashore at my place of destination, and I can only follow with the reader, in imagination, our Arkansas friend, in his adventures at the "Forks of Cypress" on the Mississippi.

QUESTIONS

1. Like many tall tales, this is a "frame" story, that is, a story framed within another. Here Jim Doggett's tale is framed by the narrator's tale of taking a steamboat ride. How does the frame device serve to heighten the story's humor?

2. For all his boasting, Doggett appears as a somewhat foolish hero. Explain.

3. Though the story is full of crude violence in many ways, a major joke of the story is passed over delicately. What is Jim doing when the bear walks in? How do you account for Thorpe's treatment of this episode?

4. Discuss Doggett's language. How appropriate is it for his subject matter? Which words does he invent? What comic similes does he use?

5. Describe the big bear. How does Thorpe succeed in raising him to the realm of myth?

How Mr. Rabbit Was Too Sharp for Mr. Fox

Joel Chandler Harris

The Uncle Remus *tales also have their beginnings in folklore, in the southern slaves' lore that Joel Chandler Harris heard so much of as a child. After the Civil War he collected these tales, hoping to preserve for the New South the fantasies that had appealed so strongly to his own sensitive nature. In the preface to his first book, he wrote, "It needs no scientific investigation to show why [the black] selects as his hero the weakest and most harmless of all animals, and brings him out victorious in contest with the bear, the wolf, and the fox." The forerunner of wily creatures like Bugs Bunny, the triumphant rabbit of* Uncle Remus *remains one of our most beloved comic characters.*

"Uncle Remus," said the little boy one evening, when he had found the old man with little or nothing to do, "did the fox kill and eat the rabbit when he caught him with the Tar-Baby?"

"Law, honey, ain't I tell you 'bout dat?" replied the old darkey, chuckling slyly. "I 'clar ter grashus I ought er tole you dat, but ole man Nod wuz ridin' on my eyeleds 'twel a lettle mo'n I'd a dis'member'd my own name, en den on to dat here come yo' mammy hollerin' atter you.

"W'at I tell you w'en I fus' begin? I tole you Brer Rabbit wuz a monstus soon beas'; leas'ways dat's w'at I laid out fer ter tell you. Well, den, honey, don't you go en make no udder kalkalashuns, kaze in dem days Brer Rabbit en his fambly wuz at de head er de gang w'en enny racket wuz on han', en dar dey stayed. 'Fo' you begins fer ter wipe yo' eyes 'bout Brer Rabbit, you wait en see whar'bouts Brer Rabbit gwineter fetch up at. But dat's needer yer ner dar.

"W'en Brer Fox fine Brer Rabbit mixt up wid de Tar-Baby, he feel mighty good, en he roll on de groun' en laff. Bimeby he up'n say, sezee:—

" 'Well, I speck I got you dis time, Brer Rabbit,' sezee: 'maybe I ain't, but I speck I is. You been runnin' roun' here sassin' atter me a mighty long time, but I speck you done come ter de een' er de row. You bin cuttin' up yo' capers en bouncin' 'roun' in dis naberhood ontwel you come ter b'leeve yo'se'f de boss er de whole gang. En den youer allers some'rs whar you got no bizness,' sez Brer Fox, sezee. 'Who ax you fer ter come en strike up a 'quaintence wid dish yer Tar-Baby? En who stuck you up dar whar you iz? Nobody in de roun' worril. You des tuck en jam yo'se'f on dat Tar-Baby widout waitin' fer enny invite,' sez Brer Fox, sezee, 'en dar you is, en dar you'll stay twel I fixes up a bresh-pile and fires her up, kaze I'm gwineter bobbycue you dis day, sho,' sez Brer Fox, sezee.

"Den Brer Rabbit talk mighty 'umble.

" 'I don't keer w'at you do wid me, Brer Fox,' sezee, 'so you don't fling me in dat brier-patch. Roas' me, Brer Fox,' sezee, 'but don't fling me in dat brier-patch,' sezee.

" 'Hit's so much trouble fer ter kindle a fier,' sez Brer Fox, sezee, 'dat I speck I'll hatter hang you,' sezee.

" 'Hang me des ez high as you please, Brer Fox,' sez Brer Rabbit, sezee, 'but do fer de Lord's sake don't fling me in dat brier-patch,' sezee.

" 'I ain't got no string,' sez Brer Fox, sezee, 'en now I speck I'll hatter drown you,' sezee.

" 'Drown me des ez deep ez you please, Brer Fox,' sez Brer Rabbit, sezee, 'but don't fling me in dat brier-patch,' sezee.

" 'Dey ain't no water nigh,' sez Brer Fox, sezee, 'en now I speck I'll hatter skin you,' sezee.

" 'Skin me, Brer Fox,' sez Brer Rabbit, sezee, 'snatch out my eyeballs, t'ar out my years by de roots, en cut off my legs,' sezee, 'but do please, Brer Fox, don't fling me in dat brier-patch,' sezee.

"Co'se Brer Fox wanter hurt Brer Rabbit bad ez he kin, so he cotch 'im by de behime legs en slung 'im right in de middle er de brier-patch. Dar wuz a considerbul flutter whar Brer Rabbit struck de bushes, en Brer Fox sorter hang 'roun' fer ter see w'at wuz gwineter happen. Bimeby he hear somebody call 'im, en way up de hill he see Brer Rabbit settin' cross-legged on a chinkapin log koamin' de pitch outen his har wid a chip. Den Brer Fox know dat he bin swop off mighty bad. Brer Rabbit wuz bleedzed fer ter fling back some er his sass, en he holler out:

" 'Bred en bawn in a brier-patch, Brer Fox—bred en bawn in a brier-patch!' en wid dat he skip out des ez lively ez a cricket in de embers."

QUESTIONS

1. Try reading some of this tale aloud. Does the dialect add to the story's humor? How?

2. Discuss the significance of Uncle Remus's animal characters. What kind of person is portrayed by the fox? The rabbit? What are the social and

psychological implications of these tales in which the rabbit invariably outwits the fox? Why do these stories have such great appeal for children?

3. Compare Brer Rabbit to other tricksters in our comic literature. What does he have in common with other members of minority groups, such as Malamud's Jewbird (see p. 45)?

Sut Lovingood's Lizards

George W. Harris

Sut Lovingood is by far the most hilarious prankster in southwestern humor. Ironically called "Lovingood," Sut is an unprincipled rascal, the foe of all civilized restraints. He seems a type of the devil incarnate, acknowledging, "I haint got nara a soul, nuffin but a whiskey proof gizzard." This "damned fool," as he calls himself, often battles with Christianity, represented by Parson Bullen, who sees Sut "a livin proof ove the hell-desarvin nater ove man." This excerpt from "Parson John Bullen's Lizards" describes the chaos unleashed when Sut puts lizards in the parson's pants. Americans have continued to enjoy the robust humor of these tales; since they were first published in 1867, the yarns of Sut Lovingood have seldom been out of print.

[Parson Bullen] cummenced ontu the sinners; he threaten'd em orful, tried tu skeer 'em wif all the wust varmints he cud think ove, an' arter a while he got ontu the idear ove Hell-sarpints, an' he dwelt on it sum. He tole 'em how the ole Hell-sarpints wud sarve 'em if they didn't repent; how cold they'd crawl over thar nakid bodys, an' how like untu pitch they'd stick tu 'em es they crawled; how they'd rap thar tails roun' thar naiks chokin clost, poke thar tungs up thar noses, an' hiss intu thar years. This wer the way they wer tu sarve men folks. Then he turned ontu the wimen: tole 'em how they'd quile intu thar buzzims, an' how they *wud* crawl down onder thar frock-strings, no odds how tite they tied 'em, an' how sum ove the oldes' an' wus ones wud crawl up thar laigs, an' travil *onder* thar garters, no odds how tight they tied *them,* an' when the two armys ove Hell-sarpints met, then—— That las' remark *fotch 'em.* Ove all the screamin, an' hollerin, an' loud cryin, I ever hearn, begun all at onst, all over the hole groun' jis' es he hollered out that word 'then.' He kep on a bellerin, but I got so buisy jis' then, that I didn't listen tu him much, fur I saw that my time fur ackshun hed cum. Now yu see, George, I'd cotch seven ur eight big pot-bellied lizzards, an' hed 'em in a littil narrer bag, what I had made a-purpus. Thar tails at the bottim, an' so crowdid fur room that they cudent turn roun'. So when he wer a-ravin ontu his tip-toes, an' a-poundin the pulpit wif his fis'—onbenowenst tu enybody, I ontied my bag ove reptiles, put the mouf ove hit onder the bottim ove his britches-laig, an' sot intu pinchin thar tails. Quick es gunpowder they all tuck up his bar laig, makin a nise like squirrils a-climbin a shell-bark hickory. He stop't preachin rite in the middil ove the word 'damnation,' an' looked fur a moment like he wer a listenin fur sumthin—sorter like a ole sow dus, when she hears yu a-whistlin fur the dorgs. The tarifick shape ove his feeters stop't the shoutin an' screamin; instuntly yu cud hearn a cricket chirp, I gin a long groan, an' hilt my head a-twixt my knees. He gin hisself sum orful open-handed slaps wif fust one han' an' then tuther, about the place whar yu cut the bes' steak outen a beef. Then he'd fetch a vigrus ruff rub whar a hosses tail sprouts; then he'd stomp one foot, then tuther, then bof at onst. Then he run his han' atween his waisbun an' his shut an' reach'd way down, an' roun' wif hit; then he spread his big laigs, an' gin his back a good rattlin rub agin the pulpit, like a hog scratches hissef agin a stump, leanin tu hit pow'ful, an' twitchin, an' squirmin all over, es ef he'd slept in a dorg bed, ur ontu a pisant hill. About this time, one ove my lizzards scared an' hurt by all this poundin' an' feelin, an' scratchin, popp'd out his head frum the passun's shut collar, an' his ole brown naik, an' wer a-surveyin the crowd, when old Bullin struck at 'im, jis' too late, fur he'd dodged back agin. The hell desarvin ole raskil's speech now cum tu 'im, an' sez he, 'Pray fur me brethren an' sisteren, fur I is a-rastilin wif the great inimy rite now!' an' his voice wer the mos' pitiful, trimblin thing I ever hearn. Sum ove the wimen fotch a painter yell, an' a young docter, wif ramrod laigs, lean'd toward me monstrus knowin like, an' sez he, 'Clar case ove Delishus Tremenjus.' I nodded my head an' sez I, 'Yas, spechuly the tremenjus part, an' Ise feard hit haint at hits worst.' Ole Bullin's eyes wer a-stickin out like ontu two buckeyes flung agin a mud wall, an' he wer a-cuttin up more shines nor a cockroach in a hot skillet. Off went the clamhammer coat, an' he flung hit ahine 'im like he wer a-gwine intu a fight; he hed no jackid tu take off, so he unbuttoned his galluses, an' vigrusly flung the ainds back over his head. He fotch his shut over-handed a durnd site faster nor I got outen my pasted one, an' then flung hit strait up in the air, like he jis' wanted hit tu keep on up furever; but hit lodged ontu a black-jack, an' I sed one ove my lizzards wif his tail up, a-racin about all over the ole dirty shut, skared too bad tu jump. Then he gin a sorter shake, an' a stompin kine ove twis', an' he cum outer his britches. He tuck 'em by the bottim ove the laigs, an' swung 'em roun' his head a time ur two, an' then fotch 'em down cherall-up over the frunt ove the pulpit. You cud a hearn the smash a quarter ove a mile! Ni ontu fifteen shorten'd biskits, a boiled chicken, wif hits laigs crossed, a big dubbil-bladed knife, a hunk ove terbacker, a cob-pipe, sum copper ore, lots ove broken glass, a cork, a sprinkil ove whisky, a squirt, an' three lizzards flew permiskusly all over that meetin-groun', outen the upper aind ove them big flax britches. One ove the smartes' ove my lizzards lit head-fust intu the buzzim ove a fat 'oman, es big es a skin'd hoss, an' ni ontu es ugly, who sot thuty yards a fannin hersef wif a tucky-tail. Smart tu the las', by golly, he imejuntly commenced runnin down the centre ove her breas'-bone, an' kep on, I speck. She wer jis' boun' tu faint; an' she did hit fust rate—flung the tucky-tail up in the air, grabbed the lap ove her gown, gin hit a big histin an' fallin shake, rolled down the hill, tangled her laigs an' garters in the top ove a huckilberry bush, wif her head in the branch an' jis' lay still. She wer interestin, she wer, ontil a serious-lookin, pale-faced 'oman hung a nankeen ridin skirt over the huckilberry bush. That wer all that wer dun to'ards bringin her too, that I seed. Now ole Bullin hed nuffin left ontu 'im but a par ove heavy, low quarter'd shoes, short woolen socks, an' eel-skin garters tu keep off the cramp. His skeer hed druv him plum crazy, fur he felt roun' in the air, abuv his head, like he wer huntin sumthin in the dark, an' he beller'd out, 'Brethren, brethren, take keer ove yerselves, the Hell-sarpints *hes got me!*' When this cum out, yu cud a-hearn the screams tu Halifax. He jis' spit in his han's, an' loped over the frunt ove the pulpit *kerdiff!* He lit on top ove, an' rite amung the mos' pius part ove the congregashun. Ole Misses Chaneyberry sot wif her back tu the pulpit, sorter stoopin forrid. He lit astradil ove her long naik, a shuttin her up wif a snap, her head atwix her knees, like shuttin up a jack-knife, an' he sot intu gittin away his levil durndest; he went in a heavy lumberin gallop, like a ole fat waggon hoss, skared at a locomotive. When he jumpt a bainch he shook the yeath. The bonnets, an' fans clar'd the way an' jerked most ove the children wif em, an' the rest he scrunched. He open'd a purfeckly clar track tu the woods, ove every livin thing. He weighed ni ontu three hundred, hed a black stripe down his back, like ontu a ole bridil rein, an' his belly wer 'bout the size an' color ove a beef paunch, an' hit a-swingin out frum side tu side; he leand back frum hit, like a littil feller a-totin a big drum, at a muster, an' I hearn hit plum tu whar I wer. Thar wer cramp-knots on his laigs es big es walnuts, an' mottled splotches on his shins; an' takin him all over, he minded ove a durnd crazy ole elephant, pussessed ove the devil, rared up on hits hind aind, an' jis' *gittin* frum sum imijut danger ur tribulashun. He did the loudest, an' skariest, an' fussiest runnin I ever seed, tu be no faster nur hit wer, since dad tried tu outrun the ho'nets.

"Well, he disapear'd in the thicket jis' bustin—an' ove all the noises yu ever hearn, wer made thar on that camp groun': sum wimen screamin— they wer the skeery ones; sum larfin—they wer the wicked ones; sum cryin—they wer the fool ones, (sorter my stripe yu know;) sum tryin tu git away wif thar faces red—they wer the modest ones; sum lookin arter ole Bullin—they wer the curious ones; sum hangin clost tu thar sweethearts—they wer the sweet ones; sum on thar knees wif thar eyes shot, but facin the way the old mud turtil wer a-runnin—they wer the 'saitful ones; sum duin nuthin—they wer the waitin ones; an' the mos' dangerus ove all ove em by a durnd long site.

"I tuck a big skeer mysef arter a few rocks, an' sich like fruit, spattered ontu the pulpit ni ontu my head; an' es the Lovingoods, durn em! knows nuffin but tu run, when they gits skeerd, I jis' put out fur the swamp on the krick. As I started, a black bottil ove bald-face smashed agin a tree furninst me, arter missin the top ove my head 'bout a inch. Sum durn'd fool professor dun this, who hed more zeal or sence; fur I say that eny man who wud waste a quart ove even mean sperrits, fur the chance ove knockin a poor ornary devil like me down wif the bottil, is a bigger fool nur ole Squire Mackmullen, an' he tried tu shoot hissef wif a onloaded hoe-handle."

"Did they catch you, Sut?"

"Ketch thunder! *No sir!* jis' look at these yere laigs! Skeer me, hoss, jis' skeer me, an' then watch me while I stay in site, an' yu'll never ax that fool question agin. Why, durn it, man, that's what the ait dullers am fur.

"Ole Barbelly Bullin, es they calls 'im now, never preached ontil yesterday, an' he hadn't the fust durn'd 'oman tu hear 'im, *they hev seed too much ove 'im.* Passuns ginerly hev a pow'ful strong holt on wimen; but, hoss, I tell yu thar ain't meny ove em kin run stark nakid over an' thru a crowd ove three hundred wimen an' not injure thar karacters *sum.* Enyhow, hits a kind ove show they'd ruther see one at a time, an' pick the passun at that. His tex' wer, 'Nakid I cum intu the world, an' nakid I'm gwine outen hit, ef I'm spard ontil then.' He sed nakidness warnt much ove a sin, purtickerly ove dark nights. That he wer a weak, frail wum ove the dus', an' a heap more sich truck. Then he totch ontu me; sed I wer a livin proof ove the hell-desarvin nater ove man, an' that thar warnt grace enuf in the whole 'sociation tu saften my outside rind; that I wer 'a lost ball' forty years afore I wer born'd, an' the bes' thing they cud du fur the church, wer tu turn out, an' still hunt fur me ontil I wer shot. An' he never said Hell-sarpints onst in the hole preach. I b'leve, George, the durnd fools am at hit.

"Now, I wants yu tu tell ole Barbelly this fur me, ef he'll let me an' Sall alone, I'll let him alone—a-while; an' ef he don't, eff I don't lizzard him agin, I jis' wish I may be dod durnd! *Skeer him if yu ken.*

"Let's go tu the spring an' take a ho'n.

"Say George, didn't that ar Hell-sarpint sermon ove his'n, hev sumthin like a Hell-sarpint aplicashun? Hit looks sorter so to me."

QUESTIONS

1. Describe what happens when Sut puts the lizards in the minister's pants. What does Parson Bullen do? How does he explain the lizards to his congregation? What is their reaction?

2. What was the text of the parson's sermon yesterday? What is his new name?

3. Why is Squire Mackmullen a fool? Why does Sut think the professor is a bigger fool?

4. What do we learn about Sut? Why does he set the lizards loose? What deal does he make with Parson Bullen? Compare Sut with Jim Doggett in "The Big Bear of Arkansas" (see p. 119).

5. What qualities of frontier humor does this sketch illustrate? Pay special attention to Sut's language. Give examples of his concrete descriptions. Though his dominant mode is exaggeration, where does Sut make use of understatement?

Diddling Considered as One of the Exact Sciences

Edgar Allan Poe

In this spoof of American materialism, the crude pranks of Sut Lovingood are replaced by the sophisticated strategies of the swindler, a popular figure in American humor. One critic associates the last diddler described here with the comic characterizations of W. C. Fields. Poe's elaborate definition of diddling parodies a scientific treatise. Although Poe wrote famous tales of terror—"The Tell-Tale Heart," "The Pit and the Pendulum," "The Narrative of Arthur Gordon Pym"—he was also a master of satire; his "King Pest" has been called one of the most brilliant burlesques in English.

> Hey, diddle diddle,
> The cat and the fiddle.
> *Mother Goose*

Since the world began there have been two Jeremys. The one wrote a Jeremiad about usury, and was called Jeremy Bentham. He has been much admired by Mr. John Neal, and was a great man in a small way. The other gave name to the most important of the Exact Sciences, and was a great man in a great way; I may say, indeed, in the very greatest of ways.

Diddling, or the abstract idea conveyed by the verb to diddle, is sufficiently well understood. Yet the fact, the deed, the thing, *diddling*, is somewhat difficult to define. We may get, however, at a tolerably distinct conception of the matter in hand, by defining—not the thing, diddling, in itself—but man, as an animal that diddles. Had Plato but hit upon this, he would have been spared the affront of the picked chicken.

Very pertinently it was demanded of Plato why a picked chicken, which was clearly a "biped without feathers," was not, according to his own definition, a man? But I am not to be bothered by any similar query. Man is an animal that diddles, and there is no animal that diddles *but* man. It will take an entire hen-coop of picked chickens to get over that.

What constitutes the essence, the nare, the principle of diddling is, in fact, peculiar to the class of creatures that wear coats and pantaloons. A crow thieves; a fox cheats; a weasel outwits; a man diddles. To diddle is his destiny. "Man was made to mourn," says the poet. But not so:—he was made to diddle. This is his aim—his object—his *end.* And for this reason when a man's diddled we say he's *done.*

Diddling, rightly considered, is a compound, of which the ingredients are minuteness, interest, perseverance, ingenuity, audacity, nonchalance, originality, impertinence, and *grin.*

Minuteness:—Your diddler is minute. His operations are upon a small scale. His business is retail, for cash or approved paper at sight. Should he ever be tempted into magnificent speculation, he then at once loses his distinctive features, and becomes what we term "financier." This latter word conveys the diddling idea in every respect except that of magnitude. A diddler may thus be regarded as a banker *in petto;* a "financial operation," as a diddle at Brobdingnag. The one is to the other as Homer to "Flaccus," as a mastodon to a mouse, as the tail of a comet to that of a pig.

Interest:—Your diddler is guided by self-interest. He scorns to diddle for the mere *sake* of the diddle. He has an object in view—his pocket—and yours. He regards always the main chance. He looks to Number One. You are Number Two, and must look to yourself.

Perseverance:—Your diddler perseveres. He is not readily discouraged. Should even the banks break he cares nothing about it. He steadily pursues his end, and

"Ut canis a corio nunquam absterrebitur uncto,"

so he never lets go of his game.

Ingenuity:—Your diddler is ingenious. He has constructiveness large. He understands plot. He invents and circumvents. Were he not Alexander, he would be Diogenes. Were he not a diddler, he would be a maker of patent rat-traps or an angler for trout.

Audacity:—Your diddler is audacious. He is a bold man. He carries the war into Africa. He conquers all by assault. He would not fear the daggers of the Frey Herren. With a little more prudence Dick Turpin would have made a good diddler; with a little less blarney, Daniel O'Connell; with a pound or two more brains, Charles the Twelfth.

Nonchalance:—Your diddler is nonchalant. He is not at all nervous. He never *had* any nerves. He is never seduced into a flurry. He is never put out—unless put out of doors. He is cool—cool as a cucumber. He is calm—"calm as a smile from Lady Bury." He is easy—easy as an old glove, or the damsels of ancient Baiæ.

Originality:—Your diddler is original—conscientiously so. His thoughts are his own. He would scorn to employ those of another. A stale trick is his aversion. He would return a purse, I am sure, upon discovering that he had obtained it by an unoriginal diddle.

Impertinence:—Your diddler is impertinent. He swaggers. He sets his arms akimbo. He thrusts his hands in his trousers' pockets. He sneers in your face. He treads on your corns. He eats your dinner, he drinks your wine, he borrows your money, he pulls your nose, he kicks your poodle, and he kisses your wife.

Grin:—Your *true* diddler winds up all with a grin. But this nobody sees but himself. He grins when his daily work is done—when his allotted labors are accomplished—at night in his own closet, and altogether for his own private entertainment. He goes home. He locks his door. He divests himself of his clothes. He puts out his candle. He gets into bed. He places his head upon the pillow. All this done, and your diddler *grins*. This is no hypothesis. It is a matter of course. I reason *a priori*, and a diddle would be *no* diddle without a grin.

The origin of the diddle is referable to the infancy of the Human Race. Perhaps the first diddler was Adam. At all events, we can trace the science back to a very remote period of antiquity. The moderns, however, have brought it to a perfection never dreamed of by our thick-headed progenitors. Without pausing to speak of the "old saws," therefore, I shall content myself with a compendious account of some of the more "modern instances."

A very good diddle is this. A housekeeper in want of a sofa, for instance, is seen to go in and out of several cabinet warehouses. At length she arrives at one offering an excellent variety. She is accosted, and invited to enter, by a polite and voluble individual at the door. She finds a sofa well adapted to her views, and, upon inquiring the price, is surprised and delighted to hear a sum named at least twenty per cent. lower than her expectations. She hastens to make the purchase, gets a bill and receipt, leaves her address, with a request that the article be sent home as speedily as possible, and retires amid a profusion of bows from the shop-keeper. The night arrives, and no sofa. The next day passes, and still none. A servant is sent to make inquiry about the delay. The whole transaction is denied. No sofa has been sold—no money received—except by the diddler, who played shop-keeper for the nonce.

Our cabinet warehouses are left entirely unattended, and thus afford every facility for a trick of this kind. Visitors enter, look at furniture, and depart unheeded and unseen. Should any one wish to purchase, or to inquire the price of an article, a bell is at hand, and this is considered amply sufficient.

Again, quite a respectable diddle is this. A well-dressed individual enters a shop; makes a purchase to the value of a dollar; finds, much to his vexation, that he has left his pocket-book in another coat pocket; and so says to the shop-keeper—

"My dear sir, never mind!—just oblige me, will you, by sending the bundle home? But stay! I really believe that I have nothing less than a five-dollar bill, even there. However, you can send four dollars in change with the bundle, you know."

"Very good, sir," replies the shop-keeper, who entertains at once a lofty opinion of the high-mindedness of his customer. "I know fellows," he says to himself, "who would just have put the goods under their arm, and walked off with a promise to call and pay the dollar as they came by in the afternoon."

A boy is sent with the parcel and change. On the route, quite accidentally, he is met by the purchaser, who exclaims:—

"Ah! this is my bundle, I see—I thought you had been home with it, long ago. Well, go on! My wife, Mrs. Trotter, will give you the five dollars—I left instructions with her to that effect. The change you might as well give to *me*—I shall want some silver for the Post Office. Very good! One, two, is this a good quarter?—three, four—quite right! Say to Mrs. Trotter that you met me, and be sure now and do not loiter on the way."

The boy doesn't loiter at all; but he is a very long time in getting back from his errand, for no lady of the precise name of Mrs. Trotter is to be discovered. He consoles himself, however, that he has not been such a fool as to leave the goods without the money, and, reëntering his shop with a self-satisfied air, feels sensibly hurt and indignant when his master asks him what has become of the change.

A very simple diddle, indeed, is this. The captain of a ship, which is about to sail, is presented by an official looking person with an unusually moderate bill of city charges. Glad to get off so easily, and confused by a hundred duties pressing upon him all at once, he discharges the claim forthwith. In about fifteen minutes, another and less reasonable bill is handed him by one who soon makes it evident that the first collector was a diddler, and the original collection a diddle.

And here, too, is a somewhat similar thing. A steamboat is casting loose from a wharf. A traveller, portmanteau in hand, is discovered, running towards the wharf at full speed. Suddenly, he makes a dead halt, stoops, and picks up something from the ground in a very agitated manner. It is a pocket-book, and—"Has any gentleman lost a pocket-book?" he cries. No one can say that he has exactly lost a pocket-book; but a great excitement ensues, when the treasure trove is found to be of value. The boat, however, must not be detained.

"Time and tide wait for no man," says the captain.

"For God's sake, stay only a few minutes," says the finder of the book—"the true claimant will presently appear."

"Can't wait!" replies the man in authority; "cast off there, d'ye hear?"

"What *am* I to do?" asks the finder, in great tribulation. "I am about to leave the country for some years, and I cannot conscientiously retain this large amount in my possession. I beg your pardon, sir" (here he addresses a gentleman on shore), "but you have the air of an honest man. *Will* you confer upon me the favor of taking charge of this pocket-book —I *know* I can trust you—and of advertising it? The notes, you see, amount to a very considerable sum. The owner will, no doubt, insist upon rewarding you for your trouble——"

"*Me!*—no, *you!*—it was *you* who found the book."

"Well, if you *must* have it so—*I* will take a small reward—just to satisfy your scruples. Let me see—why, these notes are all hundreds— bless my soul! a hundred is too much to take—fifty would be quite enough, I am sure——"

"Cast off there!" says the captain.

"But then I have no change for a hundred, and upon the whole *you* had better——"

"Cast off there!" says the captain.

"Never mind!" cries the gentleman on shore, who has been examining his own pocket-book for the last minute or so—"never mind! *I* can fix it—here is a fifty on the Bank of North America—throw me the book."

And the over-conscientious finder takes the fifty with marked reluctance, and throws the gentleman the book, as desired, while the steamboat fumes and fizzes on her way. In about half an hour after her departure the "large amount" is seen to be a "counterfeit presentment," and the whole thing a capital diddle.

A bold diddle is this. A camp-meeting, or something similar, is to be held at a certain spot which is accessible only by means of a free bridge. A diddler stations himself upon this bridge, respectfully informs all passers-by of the new county law, which establishes a toll of one cent for foot passengers, two for horses and donkeys, and so forth, and so forth. Some grumble, but all submit, and the diddler goes home a wealthier man by some fifty or sixty dollars well earned. This taking a toll from a great crowd of people is an excessively troublesome thing.

A neat diddle is this. A friend holds one of the diddler's promises to pay, filled up and signed in due form upon the ordinary blanks printed in red ink. The diddler purchases one or two dozen of these blanks, and every day dips one of them in his soup, makes his dog jump for it, and finally gives it to him as a *bonne bouche.* The note arriving at maturity, the diddler, with the diddler's dog, calls upon the friend, and the promise to pay is made the topic of discussion. The friend produces it from his *éscritoire,* and is in the act of reaching it to the diddler, when up jumps the diddler's dog and devours it forthwith. The diddler is not only surprised but vexed and incensed at the absurd behavior of his dog, and expresses his entire readiness to cancel the obligation at any moment when the evidence of the obligation shall be forthcoming.

A very minute diddle is this. A lady is insulted in the street by a diddler's accomplice. The diddler himself flies to her assistance, and, giving his friend a comfortable thrashing, insists upon attending the lady to her own door. He bows, with his hand upon his heart, and most respectfully bids her adieu. She entreats him, as her deliverer, to walk in and be introduced to her big brother and her papa. With a sigh, he declines to do so. "Is there no way, then, sir," she murmurs, "in which I may be permitted to testify my gratitude?"

"Why, yes, madam, there is. Will you be kind enough to lend me a couple of shillings?"

In the first excitement of the moment the lady decides upon fainting outright. Upon second thought, however, she opens her purse-strings and delivers the species. Now this, I say, is a diddle minute—for one entire moiety of the sum borrowed has to be paid to the gentleman who had the trouble of performing the insult, and who had then to stand still and be thrashed for performing it.

Rather a small, but still a scientific diddle is this. The diddler approaches the bar of a tavern, and demands a couple of twists of tobacco. There are handed to him, when, having slightly examined them, he says:—

"I don't much like this tobacco. Here, take it back, and give me a glass of brandy and water in its place."

The brandy and water is furnished and imbibed, and the diddler makes his way to the door. But the voice of the tavern-keeper arrests him.

"I believe, sir, you have forgotten to pay for your brandy and water."

"Pay for my brandy and water!—didn't I give you the tobacco for the brandy and water? What more would you have?"

"But, sir, if you please, I don't remember that you paid for the tobacco."

"What do you mean by that, you scoundrel?—Didn't I give you back your tobacco? Isn't *that* your tobacco lying *there?* Do you expect me to pay for what I did not take?"

"But, sir," says the publican, now rather at a loss what to say, "but, sir——"

"But me no buts, sir," interrupts the diddler, apparently in very high dudgeon, and slamming the door after him, as he makes his escape.— "But me no buts, sir, and none of your tricks upon travellers."

Here again is a very clever diddle, of which the simplicity is not its least recommendation. A purse, or pocket-book, being really lost, the loser inserts in *one* of the daily papers of a large city a fully descriptive advertisement.

Whereupon our diddler copies the *facts* of this advertisement, with a change of heading, of general phraseology, and *address*. The original, for instance, is long and verbose, is headed "A Pocket-Book Lost!" and requires the treasure when found, to be left at No. 1 Tom Street. The copy is brief and, being headed with "Lost" only, indicates No. 2 Dick, or No. 3 Harry Street, as the locality at which the owner may be seen. Moreover, it is inserted in at least five or six of the daily papers of the day, while in point of time it makes its appearance only a few hours after the original. Should it be read by the loser of the purse, he would hardly suspect it to have any reference to his own misfortune. But, of course, the chances are five or six to one that the finder will repair to the address given by the diddler, rather than to that pointed out by the rightful proprietor. The former pays the reward, pockets the treasure, and decamps.

Quite an analogous diddle is this. A lady of *ton* has dropped, somewhere in the street, a diamond ring of very unusual value. For its recovery, she offers some forty or fifty dollars' reward—giving in her advertisement a very minute description of the gem, and of its settings, and declaring that, upon its restoration to No. So and So, in such and such Avenue, the reward will be paid *instanter*, without a single question being asked. During the lady's absence from home, a day or two afterwards, a ring is heard at the door of No. So and So, in such and such Avenue; a servant appears; the lady of the house is asked for and is declared to be out, at which astounding information the visitor expresses the most poignant regret. His business is of importance and concerns the lady herself. In fact, he had the good fortune to find her diamond ring. But perhaps it would be as well that he should call again. "By no means!" says the servant; and "By no means!" say the lady's sister and the lady's sister-in-law, who are summoned forthwith. The ring is clamorously identified, the reward is paid, and the finder nearly thrust out of doors. The lady returns, and expresses some little dissatisfaction with her sister and sister-in-law, because they happen to have paid forty or fifty dollars for a fac-simile of her diamond ring—a fac-simile made out of real pinchbeck and unquestionable paste.

But, as there is really no end to diddling, so there would be none to this essay, were I even to hint at half the variations, or inflections, of which this science is susceptible. I must bring this paper, perforce, to a conclusion, and this I cannot do better than by a summary notice of a very decent but rather elaborate diddle, of which our own city was made the theatre, not very long ago, and which was subsequently repeated with success in other still more verdant localities of the Union. A middle-aged gentleman arrives in town from parts unknown. He is remarkably precise, cautious, staid, and deliberate in his demeanor. His dress is scrupulously neat, but plain, unostentatious. He wears a white cravat, an ample waistcoat, made with an eye to comfort alone; thick-soled cosey-looking shoes, and pantaloons without straps. He has the whole air, in fact, of your well-to-do, sober-sided, exact, and respectable "man of business," *par excellence*—one of the stern and outwardly hard, internally soft, sort of people that we see in the crack high comedies; fellows whose words are so many bonds, and who are noted for giving away guineas, in charity, with the one hand, while in the way of mere bargain, they exact the uttermost fraction of a farthing with the other.

He makes much ado before he can get suited with a boarding-house. He dislikes children. He has been accustomed to quiet. His habits are methodical—and then he would prefer getting into a private and respectable small family, piously inclined. Terms, however, are no object; only he must insist upon settling his bill on the first of every month (it is now the second), and begs his landlady, when he finally obtains one to his mind, *not* on any account to forget his instructions upon this point—but to send in a bill, *and* receipt, precisely at ten o'clock on the *first* day of every month, and under no circumstances to put it off to the second.

These arrangements made, our man of business rents an office in a reputable rather than in a fashionable quarter of the town. There is nothing he more despises than pretence. "Where there is much show," he says, "there is seldom anything very solid behind;" an observation which so profoundly impresses his landlady's fancy that she makes a pencil memorandum of it forthwith, in her great family Bible, on the broad margin of the Proverbs of Solomon.

The next step is to advertise, after some such fashion as this, in the principal business sixpennies of this city—the pennies are eschewed as not "respectable" and as demanding payment for all advertisements in advance. Our man of business holds it as a point of his faith that work should never be paid for until done.

"WANTED.—The advertisers, being about to commence extensive business operations in this city, will require the services of three or four intelligent and competent clerks, to whom a liberal salary will be paid. The very best recommendations, not so much for capacity, as for integrity, will be expected. Indeed, as the duties to be performed involve high responsibilities, and large amounts of money must necessarily pass through the hands of those engaged, it is deemed advisable to demand a deposit of fifty dollars from each clerk employed. No person need apply, therefore, who is not prepared to leave this sum in the possession of the advertisers, and who cannot furnish the most satisfactory testimonials of morality. Young gentlemen piously inclined will be preferred. Application should be made between the hours of ten and eleven, A.M., and four and five, P.M., of Messrs.

"Bogs, Hogs, Logs, Frogs, & Co.
"No. 110 Dog Street"

By the thirty-first day of the month, this advertisement has brought to the office of Messrs. Bogs, Hogs, Logs, Frogs, and Company, some fifteen or twenty young gentlemen piously inclined. But our man of business is in no hurry to conclude a contract with any—no man of business is *ever* precipitate—and it is not until the most rigid catechism, in respect to the piety of each young gentleman's inclination, that his services are engaged and his fifty dollars receipted for, *just* by way of proper precaution, on the part of the respectable firm of Bogs, Hogs, Logs, Frogs, and Company. On the morning of the first day of the next month, the landlady does *not* present her bill, according to promise; a piece of neglect for which the comfortable head of the house ending in *ogs* would no doubt have chided her severely, could he have been prevailed upon to remain in town a day or two for that purpose.

As it is, the constables have had a sad time of it, running hither and thither, and all they can do is to declare the man of business most emphatically a "hen knee high"—by which some persons imagine them to imply that, in fact he is n. e. i.—by which again the very classical phrase *non est inventus* is supposed to be understood. In the mean time the young gentlemen, one and all, are somewhat less piously inclined than before, while the landlady purchases a shilling's worth of the best Indian rubber, and very carefully obliterates the pencil memorandum that some fool has made in her great family Bible, on the broad margin of the Proverbs of Solomon.

QUESTIONS

1. What is diddling? Describe some of the more successful diddles Poe recounts.

2. What are the characteristics of a diddler? How does the true diddler wind up?

3. Study the style of Poe's opening paragraphs. How does he burlesque science?

4. Discuss the tone of this piece. What is Poe's attitude toward the diddlers? How do you feel about them? About their victims?

The Operation

Herman Melville

There is a striking similarity between Poe's "Diddling" and Melville's novel about a riverboat swindler, The Confidence Man. Like Poe, Melville was appalled by American morality and, though Moby Dick and Billy Budd explore metaphysical evil, they are also streaked with satire of social evils. White Jacket, from which the following selection comes, exposes the dreadful life of sailors aboard an American man-of-war. Not the least of the horrors they had to face were doctors of the sort Melville caricatures in Cadwallader Cuticle, Surgeon of the Fleet. The story dramatizes an old joke and the characters are exaggerated; even their names are ridiculous. Yet Melville's comedy, like that of Poe, has a serious purpose: exposing the absurdity of a materialistic society concerned with outward appearance, not inner worth.

Next morning, at the appointed hour, the surgeons arrived in a body. They were accompanied by their juniors, young men ranging in age from nineteen years to thirty. Like the senior surgeons, these young gentlemen were arrayed in their blue navy uniforms, displaying a profusion of bright buttons, and several broad bars of gold lace about the wristbands. As in honour of the occasion, they had put on their best coats; they looked exceedingly brilliant.

The whole party immediately descended to the half-deck, where preparations had been made for the operation. A large garrison-ensign was stretched across the ship by the mainmast, so as completely to screen the space behind. This space included the whole extent aft to the bulkhead of the commodore's cabin, at the door of which the marine orderly paced, in plain sight, cutlass in hand.

Upon two gun-carriages, dragged amidships, the death-board (used for burials at sea) was horizontally placed, covered with an old royal-stun'-sail. Upon this occasion, to do duty as an amputation-table, it was widened by an additional plank. Two match-tubs, near by, placed one upon another, at either end supported another plank, distinct from the table, whereon was exhibited an array of saws and knives of various and peculiar shapes and sizes; also, a sort of steel, something like the dinner-table implement, together with long needles, crooked at the end for taking up the arteries, and large darning-needles, thread and bee's-wax, for sewing up a wound.

At the end nearest the larger table was a tin basin of water, surrounded by small sponges, placed at mathematical intervals. From the long horizontal pole of a great-gun rammer—fixed in its usual place overhead —hung a number of towels, with "U. S." marked in the corners.

All these arrangements had been made by the "Surgeon's steward," a person whose important functions in a man-of-war will, in a future chapter, be entered upon at large. Upon the present occasion, he was bustling about, adjusting and readjusting the knives, needles, and carver, like an over-conscientious butler fidgeting over a dinner-table just before the convivialists enter.

But by far the most striking object to be seen behind the ensign was a human skeleton, whose every joint articulated with wires. By a rivet at the apex of the skull, it hung dangling from a hammock-hook fixed in a beam above. Why this object was here, will presently be seen; but why it was placed immediately at the foot of the amputation-table, only Surgeon Cuticle can tell.

While the final preparations were being made, Cuticle stood conversing with the assembled Surgeons and Assistant Surgeons, his invited guests.

"Gentlemen," said he, taking up one of the glittering knives and artistically drawing the steel across it; "Gentlemen, though these scenes are very unpleasant, and in some moods, I may say, repulsive to me—yet how much better for our patient to have the contusions and lacerations of his present wound—with all its dangerous symptoms—converted into a clean incision, free from these objections, and occasioning so much less subsequent anxiety to himself and the Surgeon. Yes," he added, tenderly feeling the edge of his knife, "amputation is our only resource. Is it not so, Surgeon Patella?" turning toward that gentleman, as if relying upon some sort of an assent, however clogged with conditions.

"Certainly," said Patella, "amputation is your only resource, Mr. Surgeon of the Fleet; that is, I mean, if you are fully persuaded of its necessity."

The other surgeons said nothing, maintaining a somewhat reserved air, as if conscious that they had no positive authority in the case, whatever might be their own private opinions; but they seemed willing to behold, and, if called upon, to assist at the operation, since it could not now be averted.

The young men, their Assistants, looked very eager, and cast frequent glances of awe upon so distinguished a practitioner as the venerable Cuticle.

"They say he can drop a leg in one minute and ten seconds from the moment the knife touches it," whispered one of them to another.

"We shall see," was the reply, and the speaker clapped his hand to his fob, to see if his watch would be forthcoming when wanted.

"Are you all ready here?" demanded Cuticle, now advancing to his steward; "have not those fellows got through yet?" pointing to three men of the carpenter's gang, who were placing bits of wood under the gun-carriages supporting the central table.

"They are just through, sir," respectfully answered the Steward, touching his hand to his forehead, as if there were a cap-front there.

"Bring up the patient, then," said Cuticle.

"Young gentlemen," he added, turning to the row of Assistant Surgeons, "seeing you here reminds me of the classes of students once under my instruction at the Philadelphia College of Physicians and Surgeons. Ah, those were happy days!" he sighed, applying the extreme corner of his handkerchief to his glass eye. "Excuse an old man's emotions, young gentlemen; but when I think of the numerous rare cases that then came under my treatment, I can not but give way to my feelings. The town, the city, the metropolis, young gentlemen, is the place for you students; at least in these dull times of peace, when the army and navy furnish no inducements for a youth ambitious of rising in our honorable profession. Take an old man's advice, and if the war now threatening between the States and Mexico should break out, exchange your Navy commissions for commissions in the army. From having no military marine herself, Mexico has always been backward in furnishing subjects for the amputation-tables of foreign navies. The cause of science has languished in her hands. The army, young gentlemen, is your best school; depend upon it. You will hardly believe it, Surgeon Bandage," turning to that gentleman, "but this is my first important case of surgery in a nearly three years' cruise. I have been almost wholly confined in this ship to doctor's practice—prescribing for fevers and fluxes. True, the other day a man fell from the mizzen-top-sail yard; but that was merely an aggravated case of dislocations and bones splintered and broken. No one, sir, could have made an amputation of it, without severely contusing his conscience. And mine—I may say it, gentlemen, without ostentation—is peculiarly susceptible."

And so saying, the knife and carver touchingly dropped to his sides, and he stood for a moment fixed in a tender reverie. But a commotion being heard beyond the curtain, he started, and, briskly crossing and recrossing the knife and carver, exclaimed, "Ah, here comes our patient; surgeons, this side of the table, if you please; young gentlemen, a little further off, I beg. Steward, take off my coat—so; my neckerchief now; I must be perfectly unencumbered, Surgeon Patella, or I can do nothing whatever."

These articles being removed, he snatched off his wig, placing it on the gun-deck capstan; then took out his set of false teeth, and placed it by the side of the wig; and, lastly, putting his forefinger to the inner angle of his blind eye, spirted out the glass optic with professional dexterity, and deposited that, also, next to the wig and false teeth.

Thus divested of nearly all inorganic appurtenances, what was left of the Surgeon slightly shook itself, to see whether any thing more could be spared to advantage.

"Carpenter's mates," he now cried, "will you never get through with that job?"

"Almost through, sir—just through," they replied, staring round in search of the strange, unearthly voice that addressed them; for the absence of his teeth had not at all improved the conversational tones of the Surgeon of the Fleet.

With natural curiosity, these men had purposely been lingering, to see all they could; but now, having no further excuse, they snatched up their hammers and chisels, and—like the stage-builders decamping from a public meeting at the eleventh hour, after just completing the rostrum in time for the first speaker—the Carpenter's gang withdrew.

The broad ensign now lifted, revealing a glimpse of the crowd of man-of-war's-men outside, and the patient, borne in the arms of two of his mess-mates, entered the place. He was much emaciated, weak as an infant, and every limb visibly trembled, or rather jarred, like the head of a man with the palsy. As if an organic and involuntary apprehension of death had seized the wounded leg, its nervous motions were so violent that one of the mess-mates was obliged to keep his hand upon it.

The top-man was immediately stretched upon the table, the attendants steadying his limbs, when, slowly opening his eyes, he glanced about at the glittering knives and saws, the towels and sponges, the armed sentry at the Commodore's cabin-door, the row of eager-eyed students, the meagre death's-head of a Cuticle, now with his shirt sleeves rolled up upon his withered arms and knife in hand, and, finally, his eye settled in horror upon the skeleton, slowly vibrating and jingling before him, with the slow, slight roll of the frigate in the water.

"I would advise perfect repose of your every limb, my man," said Cuticle, addressing him; "the precision of an operation is often impaired by the inconsiderate restlessness of the patient. But if you consider, my good fellow," he added, in a patronizing and almost sympathetic tone, and slightly pressing his hand on the limb, "if you consider how much better it is to live with three limbs than to die with four, and especially if you but knew to what torments both sailors and soldiers were subjected before the time of Celsus, owing to the lamentable ignorance of surgery then prevailing, you would certainly thank God from the bottom of your heart that *your* operation has been postponed to the period of this enlightened age, blessed with a Bell, a Brodie, and a Larrey. My man, before Celsus's time, such was the general ignorance of our noble science, that, in order to prevent the excessive effusion of blood, it was deemed indispensable to operate with a red-hot knife"—making a professional movement toward the thigh—"and pour scalding oil upon the parts"—elevating his elbow, as if with a tea-pot in his hand—"still further to sear them, after amputation had been performed."

"He is fainting!" said one of his mess-mates; "quick! some water!" The steward immediately hurried to the top-man with the basin.

Cuticle took the top-man by the wrist, and feeling it a while, observed, "Don't be alarmed, men," addressing the two mess-mates; "he'll recover presently; this fainting very generally takes place." And he stood for a moment, tranquilly eying the patient.

Now the Surgeon of the Fleet and the top-man presented a spectacle which, to a reflecting mind, was better than a church-yard sermon on the mortality of man.

Here was a sailor, who, four days previous, had stood erect—a pillar of life—with an arm like a royal-mast and a thigh like a windlass. But the slightest conceivable finger-touch of a bit of crooked trigger had eventuated in stretching him out, more helpless than an hour-old babe, with a blasted thigh, utterly drained of its brawn. And who was it that now stood over him like a superior being, and, as if clothed himself with the attributes of immortality, indifferently discoursed of carving up his broken flesh, and thus piecing out his abbreviated days? Who was it, that in capacity of Surgeon, seemed enacting the part of a Regenerator of life? The withered, shrunken, one-eyed, toothless, hairless Cuticle; with a trunk half dead—a *memento mori* to behold!

And while, in those soul-sinking and panic-striking premonitions of speedy death which almost invariably accompany a severe gun-shot wound, even with the most intrepid spirits; while thus drooping and dying, this once robust top-man's eye was now waning in his head like a Lapland moon being eclipsed in clouds—Cuticle, who for years had still lived in his withered tabernacle of a body—Cuticle, no doubt sharing in the common self-delusion of old age—Cuticle must have felt his hold of life as secure as the grim hug of a grizzly bear. Verily, Life is more awful than Death; and let no man, though his live heart beat in him like a cannon—let him not hug his life to himself; for, in the predestinated necessities of things, that bounding life of his is not a whit more secure than the life of a man on his death-bed. To-day we inhale the air with expanding lungs, and life runs through us like a thousand Niles; but to-morrow we may collapse in death, and all our veins be dry as the Brook Kedron in a drought.

"And now, young gentlemen," said Cuticle, turning to the Assistant Surgeons, "while the patient is coming to, permit me to describe to you the highly-interesting operation I am about to perform."

"Mr. Surgeon of the Fleet," said Surgeon Bandage, "if you are about to lecture, permit me to present you with your teeth; they will make your discourse more readily understood." And so saying, Bandage, with a bow, placed the two semicircles of ivory into Cuticle's hands.

"Thank you, Surgeon Bandage," said Cuticle, and slipped the ivory into its place.

"In the first place, now, young gentlemen, let me direct your attention to the excellent preparation before you. I have had it unpacked from its case, and set up here from my state-room, where it occupies the spare berth; and all this for your express benefit, young gentlemen. This skeleton I procured in person from the Hunterian department of the Royal College of Surgeons in London. It is a master-piece of art. But we have no time to examine it now. Delicacy forbids that I should amplify at a juncture like this"—casting an almost benignant glance toward the patient, now beginning to open his eyes; "but let me point out to you upon this thigh-bone"—disengaging it from the skeleton, with a gentle twist—"the precise place where I propose to perform the operation. *Here*, young gentlemen, *here* is the place. You perceive it is very near the point of articulation with the trunk."

"Yes," interposed Surgeon Wedge, rising on his toes, "yes, young gentlemen, the point of articulation with the *acetabulum* of the *os innominatum*."

"Where's your 'Bell on Bones,' Dick?" whispered one of the assistants to the student next him. "Wedge has been spending the whole morning over it, getting out the hard names."

"Surgeon Wedge," said Cuticle, looking round severely, "we will dispense with your commentaries, if you please, at present. Now, young gentlemen, you can not but perceive, that the point of operation being so near the trunk and the vitals, it becomes an unusually beautiful one, demanding a steady hand and a true eye; and, after all, the patient may die under my hands."

"Quick, Steward! water, water; he's fainting again!" cried the two mess-mates.

"Don't be alarmed for your comrade, men," said Cuticle, turning round. "I tell you it is not an uncommon thing for the patient to betray some emotion upon these occasions—most usually manifested by swooning; it is quite natural it should be so. But we must not delay the operation. Steward, that knife—no, the next one—there, that's it. He is coming to, I think"—feeling the top-man's wrist. "Are you all ready, sir?"

This last observation was addressed to one of the Neversink's assistant surgeons, a tall, lank, cadaverous young man, arrayed in a sort of shroud of white canvass, pinned about his throat, and completely enveloping his person. He was seated on a match-tub—the skeleton swinging near his head—at the foot of the table, in readiness to grasp the limb, as when a plank is being severed by a carpenter and his apprentice.

"The sponges, Steward," said Cuticle, for the last time taking out his teeth, and drawing up his shirt sleeve still further. Then, taking the patient by the wrist, "Stand by, now, you mess-mates; keep hold of his arms; pin him down. Steward, put your hand on the artery; I shall commence as soon as his pulse begins to—*now, now!*" Letting fall the wrist, feeling the thigh carefully, and bowing over it an instant, he drew the fatal knife unerringly across the flesh. As it first touched the part, the row of surgeons simultaneously dropped their eyes to the watches in their hands, while the patient lay, with eyes horribly distended, in a kind of waking trance. Not a breath was heard; but as the quivering flesh parted in a long, lingering gash, a spring of blood welled up between the living walls of the wound, and two thick streams, in opposite directions, coursed down the thigh. The sponges were instantly dipped in the purple pool; every face present was pinched to a point with suspense; the limb writhed; the man shrieked; his mess-mates pinioned him; while round and round the leg went the unpitying cut.

"The saw!" said Cuticle.

Instantly it was in his hand.

Full of the operation, he was about to apply it, when, looking up, and turning to the assistant surgeons, he said, "Would any of you young gentlemen like to apply the saw? A splendid subject!"

Several volunteered; when, selecting one, Cuticle surrendered the instrument to him, saying, "Don't be hurried, now; be steady."

While the rest of the assistants looked upon their comrade with glances of envy, he went rather timidly to work; and Cuticle, who was earnestly regarding him, suddenly snatched the saw from his hand. "Away, butcher! you disgrace the profession. Look at *me!*"

For a few moments the thrilling, rasping sound was heard; and then the top-man seemed parted in twain at the hip, as the leg slowly slid into the arms of the pale, gaunt man in the shroud, who at once made away with it, and tucked it out of sight under one of the guns.

"Surgeon Sawyer," now said Cuticle, courteously turning to the surgeon of the Buccaneer, "would you like to take up the arteries? They are quite at your service, sir."

"Do, Sawyer; be prevailed upon," said Surgeon Bandage.

Sawyer complied; and while, with some modesty, he was conducting the operation, Cuticle, turning to the row of assistants, said, "Young gentlemen, we will now proceed with our illustration. Hand me that bone, Steward." And taking the thigh-bone in his still bloody hands, and holding it conspicuously before his auditors, the Surgeon of the Fleet began:

"Young gentlemen, you will perceive that precisely at this spot—*here* —to which I previously directed your attention—at the corresponding spot precisely—the operation has been performed. About here, young gentlemen, *here*"—lifting his hand some inches from the bone—"about *here* the great artery was. But you noticed that I did not use the tourniquet; I never do. The forefinger of my steward is far better than a tourniquet, being so much more manageable, and leaving the smaller veins uncompressed. But I have been told, young gentlemen, that a certain Seignior Seignioroni, a surgeon of Seville, has recently invented an admirable substitute for the clumsy, old-fashioned tourniquet. As I understand it, it is something like a pair of *calipers*, working with a small Archimedes screw—a very clever invention, according to all accounts. For the padded points at the end of the arches"—arching his forefinger and thumb—"can be so worked as to approximate in such a way, as to—but you don't attend to me, young gentlemen," he added, all at once starting.

Being more interested in the active proceedings of Surgeon Sawyer, who was now threading a needle to sew up the overlapping of the stump, the young gentlemen had not scrupled to turn away their attention altogether from the lecturer.

A few moments more, and the top-man, in a swoon, was removed below into the sick-bay. As the curtain settled again after the patient had disappeared, Cuticle, still holding the thigh-bone of the skeleton in his ensanguined hands, proceeded with his remarks upon it; and having concluded them, added, "Now, young gentlemen, not the least interesting consequence of this operation will be the finding of the ball, which, in case of non-amputation, might have long eluded the most careful search. That ball, young gentlemen, must have taken a most circuitous route. Nor, in cases where the direction is oblique, is this at all unusual. Indeed, the learned Hennen gives us a most remarkable—I had almost said an incredible—case of a soldier's neck, where the bullet, entering at the part called Adam's Apple—"

"Yes," said Surgeon Wedge, elevating himself, "the *pomum Adami*."

"Entering the point called *Adam's Apple*," continued Cuticle, severely emphasizing the last two words, "ran completely round the neck, and, emerging at the same hole it had entered, shot the next man in the ranks. It was afterward extracted, says Hennen, from the second man, and pieces of the other's skin were found adhering to it. But examples of foreign substances being received into the body with a ball, young gentlemen, are frequently observed. Being attached to a United States ship at the time, I happened to be near the spot of the battle of Ayacucho, in Peru. The day after the action, I saw in the barracks of the wounded a trooper, who, having been severely injured in the brain, went crazy, and, with his own holster-pistol, committed suicide in the hospital. The ball drove inward a portion of his woolen night-cap—"

"In the form of a *cul-de-sac*, doubtless," said the undaunted Wedge.

"For once, Surgeon Wedge, you use the only term that can be employed; and let me avail myself of this opportunity to say to you, young gentlemen, that a man of true science"—expanding his shallow chest a little—"uses but few hard words, and those only when none other will answer his purpose; whereas the smatterer in science"—slightly glancing toward Wedge—"thinks, that by mouthing hard words, he proves that he understands hard things. Let this sink deep in your minds, young gentlemen; and, Surgeon Wedge"—with a stiff bow—"permit me to submit the reflection to yourself. Well, young gentlemen, the bullet was afterward extracted by pulling upon the external parts of the *cul-de-sac*—a simple, but exceedingly beautiful operation. There is a fine example, somewhat similar, related in Guthrie; but, of course, you must have met with it, in so well-known a work as his Treatise upon Gun-shot Wounds. When, upward of twenty years ago, I was with Lord Cochrane, then Admiral of the fleets of this very country"—pointing shoreward, out of a port-hole—"a sailor of the vessel to which I was attached, during the blockade of Bahia, had his leg—" But by this time the fidgets had completely taken possession of his auditors, especially of the senior surgeons; and turning upon them abruptly, he added, "But I will not detain you longer, gentlemen"—turning round upon all the surgeons— "your dinners must be waiting you on board your respective ships. But, Surgeon Sawyer, perhaps you may desire to wash your hands before you go. There is the basin, sir; you will find a clean towel on the rammer. For myself, I seldom use them"—taking out his handkerchief. "I must leave you now, gentlemen"—bowing. "To-morrow, at ten, the limb will be upon the table, and I shall be happy to see you all upon the occasion. Who's there?" turning to the curtain, which then rustled.

"Please, sir," said the Steward, entering, "the patient is dead."

"The body also, gentlemen, at ten precisely," said Cuticle, once more turning round upon his guests. "I predicted that the operation might prove fatal; he was very much run down. Good-morning;" and Cuticle departed.

"He does not, surely, mean to touch the body?" exclaimed Surgeon Sawyer, with much excitement.

"Oh, no!" said Patella, "that's only his way; he means, doubtless, that it may be inspected previous to being taken ashore for burial."

The assemblage of gold-laced surgeons now ascended to the quarter-deck; the second cutter was called away by the bugler, and, one by one, they were dropped aboard of their respective ships.

The following evening the mess-mates of the top-man rowed his remains ashore, and buried them in the ever-vernal Protestant cemetery, hard by the Beach of the Flamingoes, in plain sight from the bay.

QUESTIONS

1. What gory details does Melville give us about the operation? How does the patient look when he is brought in? Why does he keep fainting?

2. Describe the guests. What do they talk about? How do their names contribute to the story's comedy? Why does Patella echo Cuticle's words?

3. What is the significance of Cuticle's removing his wig, false teeth, and glass eye? What does he look like after he takes them off? How does he respond when he's told the patient is dead?

4. What does Cuticle advise the assistant surgeons to do if war breaks out? Why? In what ways does he remind you of your own doctor?

5. Discuss the irony in the story. How are the guests dressed? What does the surgeon's steward look like? The carpenter's gang? Consider Cuticle's claim that his conscience is "peculiarly susceptible."

Jealous

Paul Laurence Dunbar

"Jealous" also focuses on an American character type, but no one so grisly as Melville's Dr. Cuticle. The speaker is another incarnation of the trickster, and the poem turns on the familiar motif of the trickster tricked. But Dunbar regards the petty flaws of his characters with the same warm good humor that stamps most of his poetry. The son of a slave, Dunbar was considered by William Dean Howells "the first instance of an American Negro who had evinced innate distinction in literature."

Hyeah come Cæsar Higgins,
Don't he think he's fine?
Look at dem new riggin's
Ain't he tryin' to shine?
Got a standin' collar
An' a stove-pipe hat,
I'll jes' bet a dollar
Some one gin him dat.

Don't one o' you mention,
Nothin' 'bout his cloes,
Don't pay no attention,
Er let on you knows
Dat he's got 'em on him,
Why, 't 'll mek him sick,
Jes go on an' sco'n him,
My, ain't dis a trick!

Look hyeah, whut's he doin'
Lookin' t' othah way?
Dat ere move's a new one,
Some one call him, "Say!"
Can't you see no pusson—
Puttin' on you' airs,

Sakes alive, you's wuss'n
Dese hyeah millionaires.

Need n't git so flighty,
Case you got dat suit.
Dem cloes ain't so mighty,—
Second hand to boot,
I's a-tryin' to spite you!
Full of jealousy!
Look hyeah, man, I'll fight you,
Don't you fool wid me!

QUESTIONS

1. Even in such a short poem, Dunbar gives life to his characters. Describe the narrator and Caesar Higgins.

2. How is this a tale of a trickster tricked? What had the narrator planned to do to Caesar? What happens instead?

3. Give examples of Dunbar's use of dialect. Compare the dialect in this poem with that used by Joel Chandler Harris (see p. 130). How does dialect help us to visualize the characters?

4. Discuss Dunbar's attitude toward his characters. How can you tell how he feels about them?

The Fable of the Preacher
Who Flew His Kite,
but Not Because
He Wished to Do So

George Ade

Since Aesop, the fable has been a customary form for preaching wisdom. With George Ade it underwent a metamorphosis that made it peculiarly American. Ade's colloquial parables began appearing in his newspaper columns in 1897, and by 1920 he had published ten volumes of Fables in Slang. *Parodying the McGuffey readers, which were then widely used in elementary schools, Ade borrowed their heavy use of capital letters, but his morals were realistic, not idealistic. The preacher in this fable, another trickster, finds success by pandering to the vulgarity and stupidity of his congregation.*

A certain Preacher became wise to the Fact that he was not making a Hit with his Congregation. The Parishioners did not seem inclined to seek him out after Services and tell him he was a Daisy. He suspected that they were Rapping him on the Quiet.

The Preacher knew there must be something wrong with his Talk. He had been trying to Expound in a clear and straightforward Manner, omitting Foreign Quotations, setting up for illustration of his Points such Historical Characters as were familiar to his Hearers, putting the stubby Old English words ahead of the Latin, and rather flying low along the Intellectual Plane of the Aggregation that chipped in to pay his Salary.

But the Pew-Holders were not tickled. They could Understand everything he said, and they began to think he was Common.

So he studied the Situation and decided that if he wanted to Win them and make everybody believe he was a Nobby and Boss Minister he would have to hand out a little Guff. He fixed it up Good and Plenty.

On the following Sunday Morning he got up in the Lookout and read a Text that didn't mean anything, read from either Direction, and then he sized up his Flock with a Dreamy Eye and said: "We cannot more adequately voice the Poetry and Mysticism of our Text than in those familiar Lines of the great Icelandic Poet, Ikon Navrojk:

> To hold is not to have—
> Under the seared Firmament,
> Where Chaos sweeps, and Vast Futurity
> Sneers at these puny Aspirations—
> There is the full Reprisal."

When the Preacher concluded this Extract from the Well-Known Icelandic Poet he paused and looked downward, breathing heavily through his Nose, like Camille in the Third Act.

A Stout Woman in the Front Row put on her Eye-Glasses and leaned forward so as not to miss anything. A Venerable Harness Dealer over at the Right nodded his Head solemnly. He seemed to recognize the Quotation. Members of the Congregation glanced at one another as if to say: "This is certainly Hot Stuff!"

The Preacher wiped his Brow and said he had no Doubt that every one within the Sound of his Voice remembered what Quarolius had said, following the same Line of Thought. It was Quarolius who disputed the Contention of the great Persian Theologian Ramtazuk, that the Soul in its reaching out after the Unknowable was guided by the Spiritual Genesis of Motive rather than by mere Impulse of Mentality. The Preacher didn't know what all This meant, and he didn't care, but you can rest easy that the Pew-Holders were On in a minute. He talked it off in just the Way that Cyrano talks when he gets Roxane so Dizzy that she nearly falls off the Piazza.

The Parishioners bit their Lower Lips and hungered for more First-Class Language. They had paid their Money for Tall Talk and were prepared to solve any and all Styles of Delivery. They held on to the Cushions and seemed to be having a Nice Time.

The Preacher quoted copiously from the Great Poet Amebius. He recited 18 lines of Greek and then said: "How true this is!" And not a Parishioner batted an Eye.

It was Amebius whose Immortal Lines he recited in order to prove the Extreme Error of the Position assumed in the Controversy by the Famous Italian, Polenta.

He had them Going, and there wasn't a Thing to it. When he would get tired of faking Philosophy he would quote from a Celebrated Poet of Ecuador or Tasmania or some other Seaport Town. Compared with this Verse, all of which was of the same School as the Icelandic Masterpiece, the most obscure and clouded Passage in Robert Browning was like a Plate-Glass Front in a State Street Candy Store just after the Colored Boy gets through using the Chamois.

After that he became Eloquent, and began to get rid of long Boston Words that hadn't been used before that Season. He grabbed a rhetorical Roman Candle in each Hand and you couldn't see him for the Sparks.

After which he sunk his Voice to a Whisper and talked about the Birds and the Flowers. Then, although there was no Cue for him to Weep, he shed a few real Tears. And there wasn't a dry Glove in the Church.

After he sat down he could tell by the Scared Look of the People in Front that he had made a Ten-Strike.

Did they give him the Joyous Palm that Day? Sure!

The Stout Lady could not control her Feelings when she told how much the Sermon had helped her. The venerable Harness Dealer said he wished to indorse the Able and Scholarly Criticism of Polenta.

In fact, every one said the Sermon was Superfine and Dandy. The only thing that worried the Congregation was the Fear that if it wished to retain such a Whale it might have to Boost his Salary.

In the Meantime the Preacher waited for some one to come and ask about Polenta, Amebius, Ramtazuk, Quarolius and the great Icelandic Poet, Navrojk. But no one had the Face to step up and confess his Ignorance of these Celebrities. The Pew-Holders didn't even admit among themselves that the Preacher had rung in some New Ones. They stood Pat, and merely said it was an Elegant Sermon.

Perceiving that they would stand for Anything, the Preacher knew what to do after that.

MORAL: *Give the People what they Think they want.*

QUESTIONS

1. How did the preacher know his services had not been successful? What kind of sermon had he been delivering?

2. How does he change his sermon? Why does he breathe heavily? What does he do for a finale?

3. How does the congregation respond to the new sermon? What does the Stout Lady say? The Harness Dealer? What worries them now?

4. Discuss the lines from Ikon Navrojk. What do they mean? How are they similar to the sayings of Quarolius and Amebius?

5. Do you agree with Ade's moral? How effective is this parable as a satire of human nature?

Devil's Definitions and Two Fables

Ambrose Bierce

The fables of George Ade leave us unprepared for the Fantastic Fables *of Ambrose Bierce. Indeed, little in American humor before the dark comedy of our own age seems related to Bierce's corrosive, morbid wit. In addition to strange fables and stinging definitions, Bierce wrote stories of the supernatural, many of which, like "My Favorite Murder" and "Oil of Dog," are cast in an atmosphere of ludicrous horror. Bierce's disappearance into the Mexican wilderness in 1913 brought to a close the stormy career that had earned him the nickname "Bitter Bierce" and made him a literary legend.*

DELIBERATION, *n.* The act of examining one's bread to determine which side it is buttered on.

DENTIST, *n.* A prestidigitator who, putting metal into your mouth, pulls coins out of your pocket.

DICTIONARY, *n.* A malevolent literary device for cramping the growth of a language and making it hard and inelastic. This dictionary, however, is a most useful work.

DIE, *n.* The singular of "dice." We seldom hear the word, because there is a prohibitory proverb, "Never say die." At long intervals, however, some one says: "The die is cast," which is not true, for it is cut. The word is found in an immortal couplet by that eminent poet and domestic economist, Senator Depew:

> A cube of cheese no larger than a die
> May bait the trap to catch a nibbling mie.

DIPLOMACY, *n.* The patriotic art of lying for one's country.

HAPPINESS, *n.* An agreeable sensation arising from contemplating the misery of another.

HISTORIAN, *n.* A broad-gauge gossip.

HISTORY, *n.* An account mostly false, of events mostly unimportant, which are brought about by rulers mostly knaves, and soldiers mostly fools.

Of Roman history, great Niebuhr's shown
'Tis nine-tenths lying. Faith, I wish 'twere known,
Ere we accept great Niebuhr as a guide,
Wherein he blundered and how much he lied.
Salder Bupp.

LOVE, *n.* A temporary insanity curable by marriage or by removal of the patient from the influences under which he incurred the disorder. This disease, like *caries* and many other ailments, is prevalent only among civilized races living under artificial conditions; barbarous nations breathing pure air and eating simple food enjoy immunity from its ravages. It is sometimes fatal, but more frequently to the physicians than to the patient.

MAGPIE, *n.* A bird whose thievish disposition suggested to some one that it might be taught to talk.

MALE, *n.* A member of the unconsidered, or negligible sex. The male of the human race is commonly known (to the female) as Mere Man. The genus has two varieties: good providers and bad providers.

MALEFACTOR, *n.* The chief factor in the progress of the human race.

MAMMON, *n.* The god of the world's leading religion. His chief temple is in the holy city of New York.

He swore that all other religions were gammon,
And wore out his knees in the worship of Mammon.
Jared Oopf.

MAYONNAISE, *n.* One of the sauces which serve the French in place of a state religion.

MONDAY, *n.* In Christian countries, the day after the baseball game.

WOMAN, *n.* An animal usually living in the vicinity of Man, and having a rudimentary susceptibility to domestication. It is credited by many of the elder zoölogists with a certain vestigial docility acquired in a former state of seclusion, but naturalists of the postsusananthony period, having no knowledge of the seclusion, deny the virtue and declare that such as creation's dawn beheld, it roareth now. The species is the most widely distributed of all beasts of prey, infesting all habitable parts of the globe, from Greenland's spicy mountains to India's moral strand. The popular name (wolf-man) is incorrect, for the creature is of the cat kind. The woman is lithe and graceful in its movements, especially the American variety *(Felis pugnans)*, is omnivorous and can be taught not to talk.—*Balthasar Pober.*

TWO POLITICIANS

Two Politicians were exchanging ideas regarding the rewards for public service.

"The reward that I most desire," said the First Politician, "is the gratitude of my fellow citizens."

"That would be very gratifying, no doubt," said the Second Politician, "but, alas! in order to obtain it one has to retire from politics."

For an instant they gazed upon each other with inexpressible tenderness; then the First Politician murmured, "God's will be done! Since we cannot hope for reward let us be content with what we have."

And lifting their right hands for a moment from the public treasury they swore to be content.

A TALISMAN

Having been summoned to serve as a juror, a Prominent Citizen sent a physician's certificate stating that he was afflicted with softening of the brain.

"The gentleman is excused," said the Judge, handing back the certificate to the person who had brought it—"he has a brain."

QUESTIONS

1. What do Bierce's definitions reveal about his views on government? Religion? Women? Human nature in general?

2. How appropriate are these definitions today? Would you describe Bierce as cynical or merely realistic?

3. What is the moral of the fable about the two politicians? Explain how the tone of this anecdote contrasts with what it says. Why are the characters called simply First Politician and Second Politician?

The Storyteller

Vaudeville Sketch

From about 1880 to 1930, vaudeville was a national pastime in America. Though often regarded as unsophisticated and crude, it still attracted most of the great comic talent of the age and provided a forum for comic discussion of American culture. As waves of immigrants arrived in America, vaudeville acts frequently ridiculed the various racial or national groups; the Irish routines of Harrigan and Hart were well known, and the Italians, Jews, and blacks were subjects for comedy as well. "The Storyteller" was a popular routine. The decline of vaudeville, explains one comedian, was caused by "creeping atrophy of the box office muscles induced by the twin viruses, talking movies and radios."

Enter to Music which Dies down as You start speaking. Costume should consist of Prince Albert coat, striped trousers, and puffed tie. If you can not obtain these clothes, a plain business suit can be worn.

(*Laughingly*) We have a colored girl working for us at our house and her name is Mandy Brown. Well, the other evening she came home all excited. "What's the idea of all the joyousness, Mandy?" I asked her. "Why, I'se goin to git married," said Mandy. "Why Mandy, I didn't even know you had a beau," said I. "I ain't exactly had one, Mister (*use your name here*), but you know the fun-ral I'se went to last week; well, I'se goin to marry the corpse's husband. He says I was the life of the fun'ral." (*This should be done with a Negro dialect when coming to the colored girl's part of the conversation, and in your own natural voice when doing the straight stuff*)

Which reminds me of the time my friend Si Slimkin from up in Maine came to New York. When he landed in the Big City, the first thing he noticed were some laborers digging up the streets. He walked over to the excavation and looked down the deep hole in the street, and could see some of the men working. (*In rube dialect*) "Hey, there," shouted Si, "what are you doing down there?" "Building the subway," came the answer from below. (*This should be done in Italian or Irish dialect*) "How soon will it be finished?" asked Si. "In five years," they shouted back. "Well, never mind, then. I'll take the elevated train," said Si as he walked away.

I must tell you about my good friends, Pat and Mike. Mike was sick in the hospital and Pat thought it was his duty to visit Mike in the hospital and make him forget his pains by telling him funny stories. Before going to the hospital Pat stopped off in a few thirst emporiums and by the time he reached Mike's bedside he had a nice brannigan on. When he finally reached the hospital and got to Mike's side he told him a story of what happened to him at church the past Sunday. "Ah," sighed Mike, "will you tell me that story again?" Pat repeated the story. "Would ye mind leaning over a bit, Pat, me hearing ain't what it used to be, and tell me that story again," said Mike. And Pat repeated the same story again. "Tell it again," begged Mike, and after Pat told the same story a dozen times, he said to Mike, "Mike, that story ain't so good as to be worth me tellin it to ye so many times, is it?" "Sure it ain't the story," sez Mike, "it's your breath that is like a whiff from Heaven." (*This story should be told with two different Irish voices. A thin voice for Pat and a deep voice for Mike, or vice versa*)

And speaking about Mike reminds me of the time he sent his young daughter Bridget to Sunday school for the first time. Mike instructed her in case the teacher should ask her some questions. Mike said, "Now, Bridget, if the teacher asks your name, say Bridget Doolan. If she asks you how old you are, say seven years old. And if she asks you who made you, say God made me." Well sir, when Bridget got to Sunday school and was questioned by the teacher, she made the correct responses to all the questions until the teacher asked her who made her and she answered (*in a kid's voice*), "Papa told me his name, but I've forgotten."

I believe I'll lay off the Irish and tell you a story about my old friend Ikey Cohen. Ikey was a pretty rich man and he was showing his daughter the family jewels that were kept in a large trunk in the house. The daughter was admiring a particularly valuable necklace when two burglars rushed in, brandished revolvers, and carried the trunk out of the door. "Oy, Oy," shouted Cohen. "All our jewelry is gone. Everything is lost." "Not everything, Papa," said his daughter Sadie. "Look, I still have the pearl necklace." "Sadie, mine child, you saved the pearls. How did you manage to do it?" "Easy, Papa," said Sadie. "When the burglars came in, I just put the necklace down and sat on it." "Oy, Sadie," sighed Cohen, "if your mama was here we could have saved the whole trunk." (*This story should be told in Hebrew dialect when the Hebrew characters are speaking*)

Ikey had a brother named Jake who went one evening to visit his oldest sister, who was married and had young triplets. Before Jake started for home a heavy storm blew up. "You can't go out in this awful rain, Jake," his sister said. "You'll get all wet. Better you stay here tonight. You can sleep in the next room with the triplets." So Jake did, and the next morning she asked him if he had a good night's rest with the triplets. "Oy, I slept alright," said Jake, "but I may as well have went home through the rain."

A few days ago my friend Bill Tomkins had a few drinks too many and was driving down Broadway and in attempting to turn around in the middle of the street was side-swiped and upset by a hook-and-ladder truck. Walking over to Bill's overturned flivver, a traffic officer poked his head through the window and said *(in Irish dialect)*, "What do you mean by blocking traffic like this? Come outta there, you're pinched." *(Speaking as if you're under the influence of liquor; muss your hair up a little)* "Shay, offisher," sez Bill, "how did I know them drunken painters were going to run into me?" *(Hic.)* *(Rearrange hair and bow as music plays "Auld Lang Syne" for Exit)*

QUESTIONS

1. Vaudeville stories frequently capitalize on ethnic humor. How does the storyteller poke fun at blacks? The Irish? The Jews?

2. Another favorite American motif found in vaudeville is the tale of the rube in the Big City. What does the story about Si Slimkin suggest about the country bumpkin? Judging from his name, what do you think he looks like?

3. Describe the costume recommended for the raconteur. Do you think this would be effective? Why?

A Medieval Romance

Mark Twain

The burlesque stories of vaudeville comedians often mocked ethnic groups, but this burlesque by Mark Twain, like his "Fenimore Cooper's Limitations," has a literary target—the romance. With a melodramatic situation, passionate characters, and ominous subtitles, Twain parodies the romance form, but his exaggeration creates a story of sustained absurdity. The greatest absurdity is saved for the conclusion, at which anticlimax is substituted for climax. Dramatic tension dissolves at precisely the point we expect it to be highest. Twain also uses these techniques, in stories like "The Double-barreled Detective Story" and "The Stolen White Elephant," to lampoon detective fiction.

1 THE SECRET REVEALED

It was night. Stillness reigned in the grand old feudal castle of Klugenstein. The year 1222 was drawing to a close. Far away up in the tallest of the castle's towers a single light glimmered. A secret council was being held there. The stern old lord of Klugenstein sat in a chair of state meditating. Presently he said, with a tender accent: "My daughter!"

A young man of noble presence, clad from head to heel in knightly mail, answered: "Speak, father!"

"My daughter, the time is come for the revealing of the mystery that hath puzzled all your young life. Know, then, that it had its birth in the matters which I shall now unfold. My brother Ulrich is the great Duke of Brandenburgh. Our father, on his deathbed, decreed that if no son were born to Ulrich the succession should pass to my house, provided a *son* were born to me. And further, in case no son were born to either, but only daughters, then the succession should pass to Ulrich's daughter if she proved stainless; if she did not, my daughter should succeed if she retained a blameless name. And so I and my old wife here prayed fervently for the good boon of a son, but the prayer was vain. You were born to us. I was in despair. I saw the mighty prize slipping from my grasp—the splendid dream vanishing away! And I had been so hopeful! Five years had Ulrich lived in wedlock, and yet his wife had borne no heir of either sex.

" 'But hold,' I said, 'all is not lost.' A saving scheme had shot athwart my brain. You were born at midnight. Only the leech, the nurse, and six waiting-women knew your sex. I hanged them every one before an hour sped. Next morning all the barony went mad with rejoicing over the proclamation that a *son* was born to Klugenstein—an heir to mighty Brandenburgh! And well the secret has been kept. Your mother's own sister nursed your infancy, and from that time forward we feared nothing.

"When you were ten years old a daughter was born to Ulrich. We grieved, but hoped for good results from measles, or physicians, or other natural enemies of infancy, but were always disappointed. She lived, she throve—Heaven's malison upon her! But it is nothing. We are safe. For, ha! ha! have we not a son? And is not our son the future duke? Our well-beloved Conrad, is it not so?—for woman of eight-and-twenty years as you are, my child, none other name than that hath ever fallen to *you!*

"Now it hath come to pass that age hath laid its hand upon my brother, and he waxes feeble. The cares of state do tax him sore, therefore he wills that you shall come to him and be already duke in act, though not yet in name. Your servitors are ready—you journey forth to-night.

"Now listen well. Remember every word I say. There is a law as old as Germany, that if any woman sit for a single instant in the great ducal chair before she hath been absolutely crowned in presence of the people—SHE SHALL DIE! So heed my words. Pretend humility. Pronounce your judgments from the Premier's chair, which stands at the *foot* of the throne. Do this until you are crowned and safe. It is not likely that your sex will ever be discovered, but still it is the part of wisdom to make all things as safe as may be in this treacherous earthly life."

"Oh, my father! is it for this my life hath been a lie? Was it that I might cheat my unoffending cousin of her rights? Spare me, father, spare your child!"

"What, hussy! Is this my reward for the august fortune my brain has wrought for thee? By the bones of my father, this puling sentiment of thine but ill accords with my humor. Betake thee to the duke instantly, and beware how thou meddlest with my purpose!"

Let this suffice of the conversation. It is enough for us to know that the prayers, the entreaties, and the tears of the gentle-natured girl availed nothing. Neither they nor anything could move the stout old lord of Klugenstein. And so, at last, with a heavy heart, the daughter saw the castle gates close behind her, and found herself riding away in the darkness surrounded by a knightly array of armed vassals and a brave following of servants.

The old baron sat silent for many minutes after his daughter's departure, and then he turned to his sad wife, and said:

"Dame, our matters seem speeding fairly. It is full three months since I sent the shrewd and handsome Count Detzin on his devilish mission to my brother's daughter Constance. If he fail we are not wholly safe, but if he do succeed no power can bar our girl from being duchess, e'en though ill fortune should decree she never should be duke!"

"My heart is full of bodings; yet all may still be well."

"Tush, woman! Leave the owls to croak. To bed with ye, and dream of Brandenburgh and grandeur!"

2   FESTIVITY AND TEARS

Six days after the occurrences related in the above chapter, the brilliant capital of the Duchy of Brandenburgh was resplendent with military pageantry and noisy with the rejoicings of loyal multitudes, for Conrad, the young heir to the crown, was come. The old duke's heart was full of happiness, for Conrad's handsome person and graceful bearing had won his love at once. The great halls of the palace were thronged with nobles, who welcomed Conrad bravely; and so bright and happy did all things seem that he felt his fears and sorrows passing away and giving place to a comforting contentment.

But in a remote apartment of the palace a scene of a different nature was transpiring. By a window stood the duke's only child, the Lady Constance. Her eyes were red and swollen and full of tears. She was alone. Presently she fell to weeping anew, and said aloud:

"The villain Detzin is gone—has fled the dukedom! I could not believe it at first, but, alas! it is too true. And I loved him so. I dared to love him though I knew the duke, my father, would never let me wed him. I loved him—but now I hate him! With all my soul I hate him! Oh, what is to become of me? I am lost, lost, lost! I shall go mad!"

3   THE PLOT THICKENS

A few months drifted by. All men published the praises of the young Conrad's government, and extolled the wisdom of his judgments, the mercifulness of his sentences, and the modesty with which he bore himself in his great office. The old duke soon gave everything into his hands, and sat apart and listened with proud satisfaction while his heir delivered the decrees of the crown from the seat of the Premier. It seemed plain that one so loved and praised and honored of all men as Conrad was could not be otherwise than happy. But, strangely enough, he was not. For he saw with dismay that the Princess Constance had begun to love him! The love of the rest of the world was happy fortune for him, but this was freighted with danger! And he saw, moreover, that the delighted duke had discovered his daughter's passion likewise, and was already dreaming of a marriage. Every day somewhat of the deep sadness that had been in the princess's face faded away; every day hope and animation beamed brighter from her eye; and by and by even vagrant smiles visited the face that had been so troubled.

Conrad was appalled. He bitterly cursed himself for having yielded to the instinct that had made him seek the companionship of one of his own sex when he was new and a stranger in the palace—when he was sorrowful and yearned for a sympathy such as only women can give or feel. He now began to avoid his cousin. But this only made matters worse, for, naturally enough, the more he avoided her the more she cast herself in his way. He marveled at this at first, and next it startled him. The girl haunted him; she hunted him; she happened upon him at all times and in all places, in the night as well as in the day. She seemed singularly anxious. There was surely a mystery somewhere.

This could not go on forever. All the world was talking about it. The duke was beginning to look perplexed. Poor Conrad was becoming a very ghost through dread and dire distress. One day as he was emerging from a private anteroom attached to the picture-gallery Constance confronted him, and seizing both his hands in hers, exclaimed:

"Oh, why do you avoid me? What have I done—what have I said, to lose your kind opinion of me—for surely I had it once? Conrad, do not despise me, but pity a tortured heart? I cannot, cannot hold the words unspoken longer, lest they kill me—I LOVE YOU, CONRAD! There, despise me if you must, but they *would* be uttered!"

Conrad was speechless. Constance hesitated a moment, and then, misinterpreting his silence, a wild gladness flamed in her eyes, and she flung her arms about his neck and said:

"You relent! you relent! You *can* love me—you *will* love me! Oh, say you will, my own, my worshiped Conrad!"

Conrad groaned aloud. A sickly pallor overspread his countenance, and he trembled like an aspen. Presently, in desperation, he thrust the poor girl from him, and cried:

"You know not what you ask! It is forever and ever impossible!" And then he fled like a criminal, and left the princess stupefied with amazement. A minute afterward she was crying and sobbing there, and Conrad was crying and sobbing in his chamber. Both were in despair. Both saw ruin staring them in the face.

By and by Constance rose slowly to her feet and moved away, saying:

"To think that he was despising my love at the very moment that I thought it was melting his cruel heart! I hate him! He spurned me—did this man—he spurned me from him like a dog!"

4   THE AWFUL REVELATION

Time passed on. A settled sadness rested once more upon the countenance of the good duke's daughter. She and Conrad were seen together no more now. The duke grieved at this. But as the weeks wore away Conrad's color came back to his cheeks, and his old-time vivacity to his eye, and he administered the government with a clear and steadily ripening wisdom.

Presently a strange whisper began to be heard about the palace. It grew louder; it spread farther. The gossips of the city got hold of it. It swept the dukedom. And this is what the whisper said:

"The Lady Constance hath given birth to a child!"

When the lord of Klugenstein heard it he swung his plumed helmet thrice around his head and shouted:

"Long live Duke Conrad!—for lo, his crown is sure from this day forward! Detzin has done his errand well, and the good scoundrel shall be rewarded!"

And he spread the tidings far and wide, and for eight-and-forty hours no soul in all the barony but did dance and sing, carouse and illuminate, to celebrate the great event, and all proud and happy at old Klugenstein's expense.

5   THE FRIGHTFUL CATASTROPHE

The trial was at hand. All the great lords and barons of Brandenburgh were assembled in the Hall of Justice in the ducal palace. No space was left unoccupied where there was room for a spectator to stand or sit. Conrad, clad in purple and ermine, sat in the Premier's chair, and on either side sat the great judges of the realm. The old duke had sternly commanded that the trial of his daughter should proceed without favor, and then had taken to his bed broken-hearted. His days were numbered. Poor Conrad had begged, as for his very life, that he might be spared the misery of sitting in judgment upon his cousin's crime, but it did not avail.

The saddest heart in all that great assemblage was in Conrad's breast.

The gladdest was in his father's, for, unknown to his daughter "Conrad," the old Baron Klugenstein was come, and was among the crowd of nobles triumphant in the swelling fortunes of his house.

After the heralds had made due proclamation and the other preliminaries had followed, the venerable Lord Chief Justice said: "Prisoner, stand forth!"

The unhappy princess rose, and stood unveiled before the vast multitude. The Lord Chief Justice continued:

"Most noble lady, before the great judges of this realm it hath been charged and proven that out of holy wedlock your Grace hath given birth unto a child, and by our ancient law the penalty is death excepting in one sole contingency, whereof his Grace the acting duke, our good Lord Conrad, will advertise you in his solemn sentence now; wherefore give heed."

Conrad stretched forth his reluctant scepter, and in the selfsame moment the womanly heart beneath his robe yearned pityingly toward the doomed prisoner, and the tears came into his eyes. He opened his lips to speak, but the Lord Chief Justice said quickly:

"Not there, your Grace, not there! It is not lawful to pronounce judgment upon any of the ducal line SAVE FROM THE DUCAL THRONE!"

A shudder went to the heart of poor Conrad, and a tremor shook the iron frame of his old father likewise. CONRAD HAD NOT BEEN CROWNED—dared he profane the throne? He hesitated and turned pale with fear. But it must be done. Wondering eyes were already upon him. They would be suspicious eyes if he hesitated longer. He ascended the throne. Presently he stretched forth the scepter again, and said:

"Prisoner, in the name of our sovereign Lord Ulrich, Duke of Brandenburgh, I proceed to the solemn duty that hath devolved upon me. Give heed to my words. By the ancient law of the land, except you produce the partner of your guilt and deliver him up to the executioner you must surely die. Embrace this opportunity—save yourself while yet you may. Name the father of your child!"

A solemn hush fell upon the great court—a silence so profound that men could hear their own hearts beat. Then the princess slowly turned, with eyes gleaming with hate, and, pointing her finger straight at Conrad, said:

"Thou art the man!"

An appalling conviction of his helpless, hopeless peril struck a chill to Conrad's heart like the chill of death itself. What power on earth could save him! To disprove the charge he must reveal that he was a woman, and for an uncrowned woman to sit in the ducal chair was death! At one and the same moment he and his grim old father swooned and fell to the ground.

The remainder of this thrilling and eventful story will NOT be found in this or any other publication, either now or at any future time.

The truth is, I have got my hero (or heroine) into such a particularly close place that I do not see how I am ever going to get him (or her) out of it again, and therefore I will wash my hands of the whole business, and leave that person to get out the best way that offers—or else stay there. I thought it was going to be easy enough to straighten out that little difficulty, but it looks different now.

QUESTIONS

1. How does Twain burlesque the romance genre? In what ways are the characters and plot exaggerated? Consider his use of ominous subtitles.

2. Discuss the ending of the story. Why does Twain speak directly to the reader? How does this contribute to the story's joke? Compare the trick Twain plays on the reader with the one Washington Irving uses at the conclusion of "Adventure of the German Student" (see p. 111).

3. A thin line separates melodrama from farce. Have you read any romances that were not intended as spoofs but that were so unbelievable as to be funny? What is your reaction to radio and TV soap operas?

The Day the Dam Broke

James Thurber

When he visited England in 1958, James Thurber had the honor of being the first American since Mark Twain to be "called to the table" for the Wednesday luncheon of Punch, the famous humor magazine. The recognition thus given him was perspicacious, for Thurber may well be to twentieth-century American humor what Mark Twain was to nineteenth—the comic genius who draws together the strains of his age. Parodying Wordsworth's famous definition of poetry as "emotion recollected in tranquillity," Thurber defined humor as "emotional chaos told about calmly and quietly in retrospect." This aptly characterizes My Life and Hard Times, *the best of Thurber's early books. Besides "The Day the Dam Broke," it contains such Thurber classics as "The Night the Bed Fell" and "The Night the Ghost Got In." The theme of the story that follows, like that of so many American stories, is comic disorder. The story's effect depends on the calm, understated manner in which Thurber reports the anarchy that overwhelms the eccentric characters in his peculiar comic world.*

My memories of what my family and I went through during the 1913 flood in Ohio I would gladly forget. And yet neither the hardships we endured nor the turmoil and confusion we experienced can alter my feeling toward my native state and city. I am having a fine time now and wish Columbus were here, but if anyone ever wished a city was in hell it was during that frightful and perilous afternoon in 1913 when the dam broke, or, to be more exact, when everybody in town thought that the dam broke. We were both ennobled and demoralized by the experience. Grandfather especially rose to magnificent heights which can never lose their splendor for me, even though his reactions to the flood were based upon a profound misconception; namely, that Nathan Bedford Forrest's cavalry was the menace we were called upon to face. The only possible means of escape for us was to flee the house, a step which grandfather sternly forbade, brandishing his old army sabre in his hand. "Let the sons — —— come!" he roared. Meanwhile hundreds of people were streaming by our house in wild panic, screaming "Go east! Go east!" We had to stun grandfather with the ironing board. Impeded as we were by the inert form of the old gentleman—he was taller than six feet and weighed almost a hundred and seventy pounds—we were passed, in the first half-mile, by practically everybody else in the city. Had grandfather not come to, at the corner of Parsons Avenue and Town Street, we would unquestionably have been overtaken and engulfed by the roaring waters—that is, if there had *been* any roaring waters. Later, when the panic had died down and people had gone rather sheepishly back to their homes and their offices, minimizing the distances they had run and offering various reasons for running, city engineers pointed out that even if the dam had broken, the water level would not have risen more than two additional inches in the West Side. The West Side was, at the time of the dam scare, under thirty feet of water—as, indeed, were all Ohio river towns during the great spring floods of twenty years ago. The East Side (where we lived and where all the running occurred) had never been in any danger at all. Only a rise of some ninety-five feet could have caused the flood waters to flow over High Street—the thoroughfare that divided the east side of town from the west—and engulf the East Side.

The fact that we were all as safe as kittens under a cookstove did not, however, assuage in the least the fine despair and the grotesque desperation which seized upon the residents of the East Side when the cry spread like a grass fire that the dam had given way. Some of the most dignified, staid, cynical, and clear-thinking men in town abandoned their wives, stenographers, homes, and offices and ran east. There are few alarms in the world more terrifying than "The dam has broken!" There are few persons capable of stopping to reason when that clarion cry strikes upon their ears, even persons who live in towns no nearer than five hundred miles to a dam.

The Columbus, Ohio, broken-dam rumor began, as I recall it, about noon of March 12, 1913. High Street, the main canyon of trade, was loud with the placid hum of business and the buzzing of placid businessmen arguing, computing, wheedling, offering, refusing, compromising. Darius Conningway, one of the foremost corporation lawyers in the Middle-West, was telling the Public Utilities Commission in the language of Julius Caesar that they might as well try to move the Northern star as to move him. Other men were making their little boasts and their little gestures. Suddenly somebody began to run. It may be that he had simply remembered, all of a moment, an engagement to meet his wife, for which he was now frightfully late. Whatever it was, he ran east on Broad Street (probably toward the Maramor Restaurant, a favorite place for a man to meet his wife). Somebody else began to run, perhaps a newsboy in high spirits. Another man, a portly gentleman of affairs, broke into a trot. Inside of ten minutes, everybody on High Street, from the Union Depot to the Courthouse was running. A loud mumble gradually crystallized into the dread word "dam." "The dam has broke!" The fear was put into words by a little old lady in an electric, or by a traffic cop, or by a small boy: nobody knows who, nor does it now really matter. Two thousand people were abruptly in full flight. "Go east!," was the cry that arose—east away from the river, east to safety. "Go east! Go east! Go east!"

Black streams of people flowed eastward down all the streets leading in that direction; these streams, whose headwaters were in the drygoods stores, office buildings, harness shops, movie theatres, were fed by trickles of housewives, children, cripples, servants, dogs, and cats, slipping out of the houses past which the main streams flowed, shouting and screaming. People ran out leaving fires burning and food cooking and doors wide open. I remember, however, that my mother turned out all the fires and that she took with her a dozen eggs and two loaves of bread. It was her plan to make Memorial Hall, just two blocks away, and take refuge somewhere in the top of it, in one of the dusty rooms where war veterans met and where old battle flags and stage scenery were stored. But the seething throngs, shouting "Go east!" drew her along and the rest of us with her. When grandfather regained full consciousness, at Parsons Avenue, he turned upon the retreating mob like a vengeful prophet and exhorted the men to form ranks and stand off the Rebel dogs, but at length he, too, got the idea that the dam had broken and, roaring "Go east!" in his powerful voice, he caught up in one arm a small child and in the other a slight clerkish man of perhaps forty-two and we slowly began to gain on those ahead of us.

A scattering of firemen, policemen, and army officers in dress uniforms—there had been a review at Fort Hayes, in the northern part of town—added color to the surging billows of people. "Go east!" cried a little child in a piping voice, as she ran past a porch on which drowsed a lieutenant-colonel of infantry. Used to quick decisions, trained to immediate obedience, the officer bounded off the porch and, running at full tilt, soon passed the child, bawling "Go east!" The two of them emptied rapidly the houses of the little street they were on. "What is it? What is it?" demanded a fat, waddling man who intercepted the colonel. The officer dropped behind and asked the little child what it was. "The dam has broke!" gasped the girl. "The dam has broke!" roared the colonel. "Go east! Go east! Go east!" He was soon leading, with the exhausted child in his arms, a fleeing company of three hundred persons who had gathered around him from living-rooms, shops, garages, backyards, and basements.

Nobody has ever been able to compute with any exactness how many people took part in the great rout of 1913, for the panic, which extended from the Winslow Bottling Works in the south end to Clintonville, six miles north, ended as abruptly as it began and the bobtail and ragtag and velvet-gowned groups of refugees melted away and slunk home, leaving the streets peaceful and deserted. The shouting, weeping, tangled evacuation of the city lasted not more than two hours in all. Some few people got as far east as Reynoldsburg, twelve miles away; fifty or more reached the Country Club, eight miles away; most of the others gave up,

exhausted, or climbed trees in Franklin Park, four miles out. Order was restored and fear dispelled finally by means of militiamen riding about in motor lorries bawling through megaphones: "The dam has *not* broken!" At first this tended only to add to the confusion and increase the panic, for many stampeders thought the soldiers were bellowing "The dam has now broken!," thus setting an official seal of authentication on the calamity.

All the time, the sun shone quietly and there was nowhere any sign of oncoming waters. A visitor in an airplane, looking down on the straggling, agitated masses of people below, would have been hard put to it to divine a reason for the phenomenon. It must have inspired, in such an observer, a peculiar kind of terror, like the sight of the *Marie Celeste*, abandoned at sea, its galley fires peacefully burning, its tranquil decks bright in the sunlight.

An aunt of mine, Aunt Edith Taylor, was in a movie theatre on High Street when, over and above the sound of the piano in the pit (a W. S. Hart picture was being shown), there rose the steadily increasing tromp of running feet. Persistent shouts rose above the tromping. An elderly man, sitting near my aunt, mumbled something, got out of his seat, and went up the aisle at a dogtrot. This started everybody. In an instant the audience was jamming the aisles. "Fire!" shouted a woman who always expected to be burned up in a theatre; but now the shouts outside were louder and coherent. "The dam has broke!" cried somebody. "Go east!" screamed a small woman in front of my aunt. And east they went, pushing and shoving and clawing, knocking women and children down, emerging finally into the street, torn and sprawling. Inside the theatre, Bill Hart was calmly calling some desperado's bluff and the brave girl at the piano played "Row! Row! Row!" loudly and then "In My Harem." Outside, men were streaming across the Statehouse yard, others were climbing trees, a woman managed to get up onto the "These Are My Jewels" statue, whose bronze figures of Sherman, Stanton, Grant, and Sheridan watched with cold unconcern the going to pieces of the capital city.

"I ran south to State Street, east on State to Third, south on Third to Town, and out east on Town," my Aunt Edith has written me. "A tall spare woman with grim eyes and a determined chin ran past me down the middle of the street. I was still uncertain as to what was the matter, in spite of all the shouting. I drew up alongside the woman with some effort, for although she was in her late fifties, she had a beautiful easy running form and seemed to be in excellent condition. 'What is it?' I puffed. She gave me a quick glance and then looked ahead again, stepping up her pace a trifle. 'Don't ask me, ask God!' she said.

"When I reached Grant Avenue, I was so spent that Dr. H. R. Mallory—you remember Dr. Mallory, the man with the white beard who looks like Robert Browning?—well, Dr. Mallory, whom I had drawn away from at the corner of Fifth and Town, passed me. 'It's got us!' he shouted, and I felt sure that whatever it was *did* have us, for you know what conviction Dr. Mallory's statements always carried. I didn't know at the time what he meant, but I found out later. There was a boy behind him on roller-skates, and Dr. Mallory mistook the swishing of the skates for the sound of rushing water. He eventually reached the Columbus School for Girls, at the corner of Parsons Avenue and Town Street, where he collapsed, expecting the cold frothing waters of the Scioto to sweep him into oblivion. The boy on the skates swirled past him and Dr. Mallory realized for the first time what he had been running from. Looking back up the street, he could see no signs of water, but nevertheless, after resting a few minutes, he jogged on east again. He caught up with me at Ohio Avenue, where we rested together. I should say that about seven hundred people passed us. A funny thing was that all of them were on foot. Nobody seemed to have had the courage to stop and start his car; but as I remember it, all cars had to be cranked in those days, which is probably the reason."

The next day, the city went about its business as if nothing had happened, but there was no joking. It was two years or more before you dared treat the breaking of the dam lightly. And even now, twenty years after, there are a few persons, like Dr. Mallory, who will shut up like a clam if you mention the Afternoon of the Great Run.

QUESTIONS

1. What happens on the afternoon of the Great Run? How does the panic begin? How does it finally end?

2. Thurber is well known for his comic portraits of friends and relatives in Columbus. Describe Dr. Mallory. What had he mistaken for the sound of rushing waters? Why did Grandfather need to be stunned with the ironing board? What was Mrs. Thurber's plan?

3. Much of Thurber's humor depends on incongruous description. For instance, while the mob is frantically fleeing the expected disaster, "all the time, the sun shone quietly and there was nowhere any sign of oncoming waters." What other examples of incongruity do you find?"

The Auction of the Spotted Horses

William Faulkner

For all the chaos in "The Day the Dam Broke," no one is hurt; though Grandfather is stunned by the ironing board, the incident seems painless. In this excerpt from "Spotted Horses," however, slapstick comedy incongruously mingles with deep suffering. Faulkner's tale, set in the mythical Mississippi county of Yoknapatawpha, has the flavor of American backwoods humor. The pattern is a traditional one: the farmer meets the flimflam man. The auctioneer, descended from a long line of cheats that includes Poe's diddlers, preys on the greed and gullibility of his victims. "Spotted Horses," acclaimed by one critic as the greatest comic story since Mark Twain, recalls the cruel and exaggerated humor of the frontier. Faulkner, winner of the Nobel Prize, has won wide praise for his novels The Sound and the Fury, The Hamlet, As I Lay Dying, *and* Sanctuary.

"All right," the Texan said. He was still breathing harshly, but now there was nothing of fatigue or breathlessness in it. He shook another cake into his palm and inserted it beneath his moustache. "All right, I want to get this auction started. I ain't come here to live, no matter how good a country you folks claim you got. I'm going to give you that horse." For a moment there was no sound, not even that of breathing except the Texan's.

"You going to give it to me?" Eck said.

"Yes. Provided you will start the bidding on the next one." Again there was no sound save the Texan's breathing, and then the clash of Mrs. Littlejohn's pail against the rim of the pot.

"I just start the bidding," Eck said. "I don't have to buy it lessen I ain't over-topped." Another wagon had come up the lane. It was battered and paintless. One wheel had been repaired by crossed planks bound to the spokes with baling wire and the two underfed mules wore a battered harness patched with bits of cotton rope; the reins were ordinary cotton plowlines, not new. It contained a woman in a shapeless gray garment and a faded sunbonnet, and a man in faded and patched though clean overalls. There was not room for the wagon to draw out of the lane so the man left it standing where it was and got down and came forward—a thin man, not large, with something about his eyes, something strained and washed-out, at once vague and intense, who shoved into the crowd at the rear, saying,

"What? What's that? Did he give him that horse?"

"All right," the Texan said. "That wall-eyed horse with the scarred neck belongs to you. Now. That one that looks like he's had his head in a flour barrel. What do you say? Ten dollars?"

"Did he give him that horse?" the newcomer said.

"A dollar," Eck said. The Texan's mouth was still open for speech; for an instant his face died so behind the hard eyes.

"A dollar?" he said. "One dollar? Did I actually hear that?"

"Durn it," Eck said. "Two dollars then. But I ain't——"

"Wait," the newcomer said. "You, up there on the post." The Texan looked at him. When the others turned, they saw that the woman had left the wagon too, though they had not known she was there since they had not seen the wagon drive up. She came among them behind the man, gaunt in the gray shapeless garment and the sunbonnet, wearing stained canvas gymnasium shoes. She overtook the man but she did not touch him, standing just behind him, her hands rolled before her into the gray dress.

"Henry," she said in a flat voice. The man looked over his shoulder.

"Get back to that wagon," he said.

"Here, missus," the Texan said. "Henry's going to get the bargain of his life in about a minute. Here, boys, let the missus come up close where she can see. Henry's going to pick out that saddle-horse the missus has been wanting. Who says ten——"

"Henry," the woman said. She did not raise her voice. She had not once looked at the Texan. She touched the man's arm. He turned and struck her hand down.

"Get back to that wagon like I told you." The woman stood behind him, her hands rolled again into her dress. She was not looking at anything, speaking to anyone.

"He ain't no more despair than to buy one of them things," she said. "And us not but five dollars away from the poorhouse, he ain't no more despair." The man turned upon her with that curious air of leashed, of dreamlike fury. The others lounged along the fence in attitudes gravely inattentive, almost oblivious. Mrs. Littlejohn had been washing for some time now, pumping rhythmically up and down above the washboard in the sud-foamed tub. She now stood erect again, her soap-raw hands on her hips, looking into the lot.

"Shut your mouth and get back in that wagon," the man said. "Do you want me to take a wagon stake to you?" He turned and looked up at the Texan. "Did you give him that horse?" he said. The Texan was looking at the woman. Then he looked at the man; still watching him, he tilted the paper carton over his open palm. A single cake came out of it.

"Yes," he said.

"Is the fellow that bids in this next horse going to get that first one too?"

"No," the Texan said.

"All right," the other said. "Are you going to give a horse to the man that makes the first bid on the next one?"

"No," the Texan said.

"Then if you were just starting the auction off by giving away a horse, why didn't you wait till we were all here?" The Texan stopped looking at the other. He raised the empty carton and squinted carefully into it, as if it might contain a precious jewel or perhaps a deadly insect. Then he crumpled it and dropped it carefully beside the post on which he sat.

"Eck bids two dollars," he said. "I believe he still thinks he's bidding on them scraps of bob-wire they come here in instead of on one of the horses. But I got to accept it. But are you boys——"

"So Eck's going to get two horses at a dollar a head," the newcomer said. "Three dollars." The woman touched him again. He flung her hand off without turning and she stood again, her hands rolled into her dress across her flat stomach, not looking at anything.

"Misters," she said, "we got chaps in the house that never had shoes last winter. We ain't got corn to feed the stock. We got five dollars I earned weaving by firelight after dark. And he ain't no more despair."

"Henry bids three dollars," the Texan said. "Raise him a dollar, Eck, and the horse is yours." Beyond the fence the horses rushed suddenly and for no reason and as suddenly stopped, staring at the faces along the fence.

"Henry," the woman said. The man was watching Eck. His stained and broken teeth showed a little beneath his lip. His wrists dangled into fists below the faded sleeves of his shirt too short from many washings.

"Four dollars," Eck said.

"Five dollars!" the husband said, raising one clenched hand. He shouldered himself forward toward the gatepost. The woman did not follow him. She now looked at the Texan for the first time. Her eyes were a washed gray also, as though they had faded too like the dress and the sunbonnet.

"Mister," she said, "if you take that five dollars I earned my chaps a-weaving for one of them things, it'll be a curse on you and yours during all the time of man."

"Five dollars!" the husband shouted. He thrust himself up to the post, his clenched hand on a level with the Texan's knees. He opened it upon a wad of frayed banknotes and silver. "Five dollars! And the man that raises it will have to beat my head off or I'll beat hisn."

"All right," the Texan said. "Five dollars is bid. But don't you shake your hand at me."

At five o'clock that afternoon the Texan crumpled the third paper carton and dropped it to the earth beneath him. In the copper slant of the levelling sun which fell also upon the line of limp garments in Mrs. Littlejohn's backyard and which cast his shadow and that of the post on which he sat long across the lot where now and then the ponies still rushed in purposeless and tireless surges, the Texan straightened his leg and thrust his hand into his pocket and took out a coin and leaned down to the little boy. His voice was now hoarse, spent. "Here, bud," he said. "Run to the store and get me a box of gingersnaps." The men still stood along the fence, tireless, in their overalls and faded shirts. Flem Snopes was there now, appeared suddenly from nowhere, standing beside the fence with a space the width of three or four men on either side of him, standing there in his small yet definite isolation, chewing tobacco, in the same gray trousers and minute bow tie in which he had departed last summer but in a new cap, gray too like the other, but new, and overlaid with a bright golfer's plaid, looking also at the horses in the lot. All of them save two had been sold for sums ranging from three dollars and a half to eleven and twelve dollars. The purchasers, as they had bid them in, had gathered as though by instinct into a separate group on the other side of the gate, where they stood with their hands lying upon the top strand of the fence, watching with a still more sober intensity the animals which some of them had owned for seven and eight hours now but had not yet laid hands upon. The husband, Henry, stood beside the post on which the Texan sat. The wife had gone back to the wagon, where she sat gray in the gray garment, motionless, looking at nothing, still, she might have been something inanimate which he had loaded into the wagon to move it somewhere, waiting now in the wagon until he should be ready to go on again, patient, insensate, timeless.

"I bought a horse and I paid cash for it," he said. His voice was harsh and spent too, the mad look in his eyes had a quality glazed now and even sightless. "And yet you expect me to stand around here till they are all sold before I can get my horse. Well, you can do all the expecting you want. I'm going to take my horse out of there and go home." The Texan looked down at him. The Texan's shirt was blotched with sweat. His big face was cold and still, his voice level.

"Take your horse then." After a moment Henry looked away. He stood with his head bent a little, swallowing from time to time.

"Ain't you going to catch him for me?"

"It ain't my horse," the Texan said in that flat still voice. After a while Henry raised his head. He did not look at the Texan.

"Who'll help me catch my horse?" he said. . . .

"Well, what are we waiting for?" Freeman said. "For them to go to roost?" . . .

"I reckon the best way will be for us all to take and catch them one at a time," Freeman said.

"One at a time," the husband, Henry, said. Apparently he had not moved since the Texan had led his mules through the gate, save to lift his hands to the top of the gate, one of them still clutching the coiled rope. "One at a time," he said. He began to curse in a harsh, spent monotone. "After I've stood around here all day, waiting for that—" He cursed. He began to jerk at the gate, shaking it with spent violence until one of the others slid the latch back and it swung open and Henry entered it, the others following, the little boy pressing close behind his father until Eck became aware of him and turned.

"Here," he said. "Give me that rope. You stay out of here."

"Aw, paw," the boy said.

"No sir. Them things will kill you. They almost done it this morning. You stay out of here."

"But we got two to catch." For a moment Eck stood looking down at the boy.

"That's right," he said. "We got two. But you stay close to me now. And when I holler run, you run. You hear me?"

"Spread out, boys," Freeman said. "Keep them in front of us." They began to advance across the lot in a ragged crescent-shaped line, each one with his rope. The ponies were now at the far side of the lot. One of them snorted; the mass shifted within itself but without breaking. Freeman, glancing back, saw the little boy. "Get that boy out of here," he said.

"I reckon you better," Eck said to the boy. "You go and get in the wagon yonder. You can see us catch them from there." The little boy turned and trotted toward the shed beneath which the wagon stood. The line of men advanced, Henry a little in front.

"Watch them close now," Freeman said. "Maybe we better try to get them into the barn first—" At that moment the huddle broke. It parted and flowed in both directions along the fence. The men at the ends of the line began to run, waving their arms and shouting. "Head them," Freeman said tensely. "Turn them back." They turned them, driving them back upon themselves again; the animals merged and spun in short, huddling rushes, phantom and inextricable. "Hold them now," Freeman said. "Don't let them get by us." The line advanced again. Eck turned; he did not know why—whether a sound, what. The little boy was just behind him again.

"Didn't I tell you to get in that wagon and stay there?" Eck said.

"Watch out, paw!" the boy said. "There he is! There's ourn!" It was the one the Texan had given Eck. "Catch him, paw!"

"Get out of my way," Eck said. "Get back to that wagon." The line was still advancing. The ponies milled, clotting, forced gradually backward toward the open door of the barn. Henry was still slightly in front, crouched slightly, his thin figure, even in the mazy moonlight, emanating something of that spent fury. The splotchy huddle of animals seemed to be moving before the advancing line of men like a snowball which they might have been pushing before them by some invisible means, gradually nearer and nearer to the black yawn of the barn door. Later it was obvious that the ponies were so intent upon the men that they did not realize the barn was even behind them until they backed into the shadow of it. Then an indescribable sound, a movement desperate and despairing, arose among them; for an instant of static horror men and animals faced one another, then the men whirled and ran before a gaudy vomit of long wild faces and splotched chests which overtook and scattered them and flung them sprawling aside and completely obliterated from sight Henry and the little boy, neither of whom had moved though Henry had flung up both arms, still holding his coiled rope, the herd sweeping on across the lot, to crash through the gate which the last man through it had neglected to close, leaving it slightly ajar, carrying all of the gate save the upright to which the hinges were nailed with them, and so among the teams and wagons which choked the lane, the teams springing and lunging too, snapping hitch-reins and tongues. Then the whole inextricable mass crashed among the wagons and eddied and divided about the one in which the woman sat, and rushed on down the lane and into the road, dividing, one half going one way and one half the other.

The men in the lot, except Henry, got to their feet and ran toward the gate. The little boy once more had not been touched, not even thrown off his feet; for a while his father held him clear of the ground in one hand, shaking him like a rag doll. "Didn't I tell you to stay in that wagon?" Eck cried. "Didn't I tell you?"

"Look out, paw!" the boy chattered out of the violent shaking, "there's ourn! There he goes!" It was the horse the Texan had given them again. It was as if they owned no other, the other one did not exist; as if by some absolute and instantaneous rapport of blood they had relegated to oblivion the one for which they had paid money. They ran to the gate and down the lane where the other men had disappeared. They saw the horse the Texan had given them whirl and dash back and rush through the gate into Mrs. Littlejohn's yard and run up the front steps and crash once on the wooden veranda and vanish through the front door. Eck and the boy ran up onto the veranda. A lamp sat on a table just inside the door. In its mellow light they saw the horse fill the long hallway like a pinwheel, gaudy, furious and thunderous. A little further down the hall there was a varnished yellow melodeon. The horse crashed into it; it produced a single note, almost a chord, in bass, resonant and grave, of deep and sober astonishment; the horse with its monstrous and antic shadow whirled again and vanished through another door. It was a bedroom; Ratliff, in his underclothes and one sock and with the other sock in his hand and his back to the door, was leaning out the open window facing the lane, the lot. He looked back over his shoulder. For an instant he and the horse glared at one another. Then he sprang through the window as the horse backed out of the room and into the hall again and whirled and saw Eck and the little boy just entering the front door, Eck still carrying his rope. It whirled again and rushed on down the hall and onto the back porch just as Mrs. Littlejohn, carrying an armful of clothes from the line and the washboard, mounted the steps.

"Get out of here, you son of a bitch," she said. She struck with the washboard; it divided neatly on the long mad face and the horse whirled and rushed back up the hall, where Eck and the boy now stood.

"Get to hell out of here, Wall!" Eck roared. He dropped to the floor, covering his head with his arms. The boy did not move, and for the third time the horse soared above the unwinking eyes and the unbowed and untouched head and onto the front veranda again just as Ratliff, still carrying the sock, ran around the corner of the house and up the steps. The horse whirled without breaking or pausing. It galloped to the end of the veranda and took the railing and soared outward, hobgoblin and floating, in the moon. It landed in the lot still running and crossed the lot and galloped through the wrecked gate and among the overturned wagons and the still intact one in which Henry's wife still sat, and on down the lane and into the road.

A quarter of a mile further on, the road gashed pallid and moony between the moony shadows of the bordering trees, the horse still galloping, galloping its shadow into the dust, the road descending now toward the creek and the bridge. It was of wood, just wide enough for a single vehicle. When the horse reached it, it was occupied by a wagon coming from the opposite direction and drawn by two mules already asleep in the harness and the soporific motion. On the seat was Tull and his wife, in splint chairs in the wagon behind them sat their four daughters, all returning belated from an all-day visit with some of Mrs. Tull's kin. The horse neither checked nor swerved. It crashed once on the wooden bridge and rushed between the two mules which waked lunging in opposite directions in the traces, the horse now apparently scrambling along the wagon-tongue itself like a mad squirrel and scrabbling at the end-gate of the wagon with its forefeet as if it intended to climb into the wagon while Tull shouted at it and struck at its face with his whip. The mules were now trying to turn the wagon around in the middle of the bridge. It slewed and tilted, the bridge-rail cracked with a sharp report above the shrieks of the women; the horse scrambled at last across the back of one of the mules and Tull stood up in the wagon and kicked at its face. Then the front end of the wagon rose, flinging Tull, the reins now wrapped several times about his wrist, backward into the wagon bed among the overturned chairs and the exposed stockings and undergarments of his women. The pony scrambled free and crashed again on the wooden planking, galloping again.

The wagon lurched again; the mules had finally turned it on the bridge where there was not room for it to turn and were now kicking themselves free of the traces. When they came free, they snatched Tull bodily out of the wagon. He struck the bridge on his face and was dragged for several feet before the wrist-wrapped reins broke. Far up the road now, distancing the frantic mules, the pony faded on. While the five women still shrieked above Tull's unconscious body, Eck and the little boy came up, trotting, Eck still carrying his rope. He was panting. "Which way'd he go?" he said.

In the now empty and moon-drenched lot, his wife and Mrs. Littlejohn and Ratliff and Lump Snopes, the clerk, and three other men raised Henry out of the trampled dust and carried him into Mrs. Littlejohn's backyard. His face was blanched and stony, his eyes were closed, the weight of his head tautened his throat across the protruding larynx; his teeth glinted dully beneath his lifted lip. They carried him on toward the house, through the dappled shade of the chinaberry trees. Across the dreaming and silver night a faint sound like remote thunder came and ceased. "There's one of them on the creek bridge," one of the men said.

"It's that one of Eck Snopes'," another said. "The one that was in the house." Mrs. Littlejohn had preceded them into the hall. When they entered with Henry, she had already taken the lamp from the table and she stood beside an open door, holding the lamp high.

"Bring him in here," she said. She entered the room first and set the lamp on the dresser. They followed with clumsy scufflings and pantings and laid Henry on the bed and Mrs. Littlejohn came to the bed and stood looking down at Henry's peaceful and bloodless face. "I'll declare," she said. "You men." They had drawn back a little, clumped, shifting from one foot to another, not looking at her nor at his wife either, who stood at the foot of the bed, motionless, her hands folded into her dress. "You all get out of here, V. K.," she said to Ratliff. "Go outside. See if you can't find something else to play with that will kill some more of you."

"All right," Ratliff said. "Come on, boys. Ain't no more horses to catch in here." They followed him toward the door, on tiptoe, their shoes scuffling, their shadows monstrous on the wall.

"Go get Will Varner," Mrs. Littlejohn said. "I reckon you can tell him it's still a mule." They went out; they didn't look back. They tiptoed up the hall and crossed the veranda and descended into the moonlight. Now that they could pay attention to it, the silver air seemed to be filled with faint and sourceless sounds—shouts, thin and distant, again a brief thunder of hooves on a wooden bridge, more shouts faint and thin and earnest and clear as bells; once they even distinguished the words: "Whooey. Head him."

QUESTIONS

1. Explain how the Texan gets the men to buy the wild horses.

2. Discuss Henry and his wife. Why doesn't she want him to buy a horse? How does he treat her? What happens to him? In what way, if any, is Henry's story humorous?

3. How does the auction bring out certain traits in each of the characters? In Eck? Henry? The Texan? To what extent can these traits be labeled American?

4. Describe the events that occur when the men round up their horses. What happens in Mrs. Littlejohn's house? On the bridge?

5. How does Faulkner's story reflect a tradition of native American humor? Consider his diction, his use of violence, his mixture of pathos and slapstick. Refer to the essay by Louis D. Rubin, Jr., especially its last pages, in the "Theories and Criticism" section.

Our Mrs. Parker

Alexander Woollcott

The brilliant, famous, and wealthy Dorothy Parker was an engaging heroine for any story. As a poet and short-story writer, she belonged to a coterie of the most influential intellectuals in America during the twenties and thirties. Alexander Woollcott, in this popular sketch from While Rome Burns, *relishes the biting witticisms that made Parker one of the most colorful writers and characters of her time. Woollcott, her friend and colleague, was himself the celebrated subject of the play* The Man Who Came to Dinner.

When William Allen White, Jr., son of Emporia's pride, was a verdant freshman ten years ago, he spent the Christmas vacation in New York and was naturally assumed as a public charge by all his father's friends in the newspaper business. He had been at Harvard only a few months, but the pure Kansas of his speech was already seriously affected. He fastidiously avoided anything so simple as a simple declarative.

For example, he would never indulge in the crude directness of saying an actress was an actress. No, she was *by way of being* an actress. You see, they were going in for that expression at Harvard just then. Nor could he bring himself to ask outright if such and such a building was the Hippodrome. No, indeed. Subjunctive to the last, he preferred to ask, "And that, sir, would be the Hippodrome?"

I myself took him to the smartest restaurant of the moment, filled him to the brim with costly groceries, and escorted him to a first night. As we loped up the aisle during the intermission rush for a dash of nicotine, I pointed out celebrities in the manner of a barker on a Chinatown bus. Young Bill seemed especially interested in the seamy lineaments of a fellow Harvard man named Robert Benchley, then, as now, functioning on what might be called the lunatic fringe of dramatic criticism. Seated beside him was a little and extraordinarily pretty woman with dark hair, a gentle, apologetic smile, and great reproachful eyes. "And that, I suppose," said the lad from Emporia, "would be Mrs. Benchley." "So I have always understood," I replied crossly, "but it *is* Mrs. Parker."

In the first part of this reply, I was in error. At the time I had not been one of their neighbors long enough to realize that, in addition to such formidable obstacles as Mrs. Benchley, Mr. Parker, and the laws of the commonwealth, there was also a lack of romantic content in what was then, and ever since has been, a literary partnership seemingly indissoluble. At least it has had a good run. Mrs. Parker's latest and finest volume of poems carries on the flyleaf the simple dedication: "To Mr. Benchley," and even a dozen years ago, these two shared a microscopic office in the crumby old building which still houses the Metropolitan Opera.

There was just about room in it for their two typewriters, their two chairs, and a guest chair. When both were supposed to be at work, merely having the other one there to talk to provided a splendid excuse for not working at all. But when Benchley would be off on some mischief of his own, the guest chair became a problem. If it stood empty, Mrs. Parker would be alone with her thoughts and—good God!—might actually have to put some of them down on paper. And, as her desperate editors and publishers will tell you, there has been, since O. Henry's last carouse, no American writer so deeply averse to doing some actual writing. That empty guest chair afflicted her because the Parker-Benchley office was then so new a hideaway that not many of their friends had yet found a path to it, and even Mrs. Parker, having conscientiously chosen an obscure cubby-hole so that she might not be disturbed in her wrestling with *belles-lettres*, was becomingly reluctant to telephone around and suggest that everyone please hurry over and disturb her at once.

However, this irksome solitude did not last long. It was when the sign painter arrived to letter the names of these new tenants on the glass door that she hit upon a device which immediately assured her a steady stream of visitors, and gave her the agreeable illusion of presiding over as thronged a salon as even Madame Récamier knew. She merely bribed the sign painter to leave their names off the door entirely and print there instead the single word "Gentlemen."

Thus pleasantly distracted through the years, Mrs. Parker's published work does not bulk large. But most of it has been pure gold and the five winnowed volumes on her shelf—three of poetry, two of prose—are so potent a distillation of nectar and wormwood, of ambrosia and deadly nightshade, as might suggest to the rest of us that we all write far too much. Even though I am one who does not profess to be privy to the intentions of posterity, I do suspect that another generation will not share the confusion into which Mrs. Parker's poetry throws so many of her contemporaries, who, seeing that much of it is witty, dismiss it patronizingly as "light" verse, and do not see that some of it is thrilling poetry of a piercing and rueful beauty.

I think it not unlikely that the best of it will be conned a hundred years from now. If so, I can foresee the plight of some undergraduate in those days being maddened by an assignment to write a theme on what manner of woman this dead and gone Dorothy Parker really was. Was she a real woman at all? he will naturally want to know. And even if summoned from our tombs, we will not be sure how we should answer that question.

Indeed, I do not envy him his assignment, and in a sudden spasm of sympathy for him, herewith submit a few miscellaneous notes, though, mark you, he will rake these yellowing files in vain for any report on her most salient aspects. Being averse to painting the lily, I would scarcely attempt a complete likeness of Mrs. Parker when there is in existence, and open to the public, an incomparable portrait of her done by herself. From the nine matchless stanzas of "The Dark Girl's Rhyme"—one of them runs:

> There I was, that came of
> Folk of mud and flame—
> I that had my name of
> Them without a name—

to the mulish lyric which ends thus:

> But I, despite expert advice,
> Keep doing things I think are nice,
> And though to good I never come—
> Inseparable my nose and thumb!

her every lyric line is autobiographical.

From the verses in *Enough Rope, Sunset Gun,* and *Death and Taxes,* the toiling student of the year 2033 will be able to gather, unaided by me, that she was, for instance, one who thought often and enthusiastically of death, and one whose most frequently and most intensely felt emotion was the pang of unrequited love. From the verses alone he might even construct, as the paleontologist constructs a dinosaur, a picture of our Mrs. Parker wringing her hands at sundown beside an open grave and looking pensively into the middle-distance at the receding figure of some golden lad—perhaps some personable longshoreman—disappearing over the hill with a doxy on his arm.

Our Twenty-First Century student may possibly be moved to say of her, deplorably enough, that, like Patience, our Mrs. Parker yearned her living, and he may even be astute enough to guess that the moment the aforesaid golden lad wrecked her favorite pose by showing some sign of interest, it would be the turn of the sorrowing lady herself to disappear in the other direction just as fast as she could travel. To this shrewd guess, I can only add for his information that it would be characteristic of the sorrowing lady to stoop first by that waiting grave, and with her finger trace her own epitaph: "Excuse my dust."

But if I may not here intrude upon the semiprivacy of Mrs. Parker's lyric lamentation, I can at least supply some of the data of her outward life and tell the hypothetical student how she appeared to a neighbor who has often passed the time of day with her across the garden wall and occasionally run into her at parties. Well, then, Dorothy Parker (née Rothschild) was born of a Scotch mother and a Jewish father. Her people were New Yorkers, but when she came into the world in August 1893, it was, to their considerable surprise and annoyance, a trifle ahead of schedule. It happened while they were staying at West End, which lies on the Jersey shore a pebble's throw from Long Branch, and it was the last time in her life when she wasn't late.

Her mother died when she was still a baby. On the general theory that it was a good school for manners, she was sent in time to a convent in New York, from which she was eventually packed off home by an indignant Mother Superior who took umbrage when her seemingly meek charge, in writing an essay on the miracle of the Immaculate Conception, referred to that sacred mystery as spontaneous combustion. When, at her father's death a few years later, she found herself penniless, she tried her hand at occasional verse, and both hands at playing the piano for a dancing school.

Then she got a job writing captions on a fashion magazine. She would write "Brevity is the Soul of Lingerie" and things like that for ten dollars a week. As her room and breakfast cost eight dollars, that left an inconsiderable margin for the other meals, to say nothing of manicures, dentistry, gloves, furs, and traveling expenses. But just before hers could turn into an indignant O. Henry story, with General Kitchener's grieving picture turned to the wall and a porcine seducer waiting in the hall below, that old marplot, her employer, doubled her salary. In 1918, she was married to the late Edwin Parker, a Connecticut boy she had known all her life. She became Mrs. Parker a week before his division sailed for France. There were no children born of this marriage.

Shortly after the armistice, the waiting bride was made dramatic critic of *Vanity Fair*, from which post she was forcibly removed upon the bitter complaints of sundry wounded people of the theater, of whose shrieks, if memory serves, Billie Burke's were the most penetrating. In protest against her suppression, and perhaps in dismay at the prospect of losing her company, her coworkers, Robert E. Sherwood and Robert Benchley, quit *Vanity Fair* at the same time in what is technically known as a body, the former to become editor of *Life*, and the latter its dramatic critic.

Since then Mrs. Parker has gone back to the aisle seats only when Mr. Benchley was out of town and someone was needed to substitute for him. It would be her idea of her duty to catch up the torch as it fell from his hand—and burn someone with it. I shall never forget the expression on the face of the manager who, having recklessly produced a play of Channing Pollock's called *The House Beautiful*, turned hopefully to

Benchley's next *feuilleton*, rather counting on a kindly and even quotable tribute from that amiable creature. But it seems Benchley was away that week, and it was little Mrs. Parker who had covered the opening. I would not care to say what she had covered it with. The trick was done in a single sentence. *"The House Beautiful,"* she had said with simple dignity, "is the play lousy."

And more recently she achieved an equal compression in reporting on *The Lake*. Miss Hepburn, it seems, had run the whole gamut from A to B.

But for the most part, Mrs. Parker writes only when she feels like it or, rather, when she cannot think up a reason not to. Thus once I found her in hospital typing away lugubriously. She had given her address as Bed-pan Alley, and represented herself as writing her way out. There was the hospital bill to pay before she dared get well, and downtown an unpaid hotel bill was malignantly lying in wait for her. Indeed, at the preceding Yuletide, while the rest of us were all hanging up our stockings, she had contented herself with hanging up the hotel.

Tiptoeing now down the hospital corridor, I found her hard at work. Because of posterity and her creditors, I was loath to intrude, but she, being entranced at any interruption, greeted me from her cot of pain, waved me to a chair, offered me a cigarette, and rang a bell. I wondered if this could possibly be for drinks. "No," she said sadly, "it is supposed to fetch the night nurse, so I ring it whenever I want an hour of uninterrupted privacy."

Thus, by the pinch of want, are extracted from her the poems, the stories, and criticisms which have delighted everyone except those about whom they were written. There was, at one time, much talk of a novel to be called, I think, *The Events Leading Up to the Tragedy*, and indeed her publisher, having made a visit of investigation to the villa where she was staying at Antibes, reported happily that she had a great stack of manuscript already finished. He did say she was shy about letting him see it. This was because that stack of alleged manuscript consisted largely of undestroyed carbons of old articles of hers, padded out with letters from her many friends.

Then she once wrote a play with Elmer Rice. It was called *Close Harmony*, and thanks to a number of circumstances over most of which she had no control, it ran only four weeks. On the fourth Wednesday she wired Benchley: "CLOSE HARMONY DID A COOL NINETY DOLLARS AT THE MATINEE STOP ASK THE BOYS IN THE BACK ROOM WHAT THEY WILL HAVE."

The outward social manner of Dorothy Parker is one calculated to confuse the unwary and unnerve even those most addicted to the incomparable boon of her company. You see, she is so odd a blend of Little Nell and Lady Macbeth. It is not so much the familiar phenomenon of a hand of steel in a velvet glove as a lacy sleeve with a bottle of vitriol concealed in its folds. She has the gentlest, most disarming demeanor of anyone I know. Don't you remember sweet Alice, Ben Bolt? Sweet Alice wept with delight, as I recall, when you gave her a smile, and if memory serves, trembled with fear at your frown. Well, compared with Dorothy Parker, Sweet Alice was a roughshod bully, trampling down all opposition. But Mrs. Parker carries—as everyone is uneasily aware—a dirk which knows no brother and mighty few sisters. "I was so terribly glad to see you," she murmurs to a departing guest. "Do let me call you up sometime, won't you, please?" And adds, when this dear chum is out of hearing, "That woman speaks eighteen languages, and can't say No in any of them." Then I remember her comment on one friend who had lamed herself while in London. It was Mrs. Parker who voiced the suspicion that this poor lady had injured herself while sliding down a barrister. And there was that wholesale libel on a Yale prom. If all the girls attending it were laid end to end, Mrs. Parker said, she wouldn't be at all surprised.

Mostly, as I now recall these cases of simple assault, they have been muttered out of the corner of her mouth while, to the onlooker out of hearing, she seemed all smiles and loving-kindness. For as she herself has said (when not quite up to par), a girl's best friend is her mutter. Thus I remember one dreadful week-end we spent at Nellie's country home. Mrs. Parker radiated throughout the visit an impression of humble gratitude at the privilege of having been asked. The other guests were all of the kind who wear soiled batik and bathe infrequently, if ever. I could not help wondering how Nellie managed to round them up, and where they might be found at other times. Mrs. Parker looked at them pensively. "I think," she whispered, "that they crawl back into the woodwork."

Next morning we inspected nervously the somewhat inadequate facilities for washing. These consisted of a single chipped basin internally decorated with long-accumulated evidences of previous use. It stood on a bench on the back porch with something that had apparently been designed as a toothbrush hanging on a nail above it. "In God's name," I cried, "what do you suppose Nellie does with that?" Mrs. Parker studied it with mingled curiosity and distaste, and said: "I think she rides on it on Halloween."

It will be noted, I am afraid, that Mrs. Parker specializes in what is known as the dirty crack. If it seems so, it may well be because disparagement is easiest to remember, and the fault therefore, if fault there be, lies in those of us who—and who does not?—repeat her sayings. But it is quite true that in her writing—at least in her prose pieces—her most effective vein is the vein of dispraise. Her best word portraits are dervish dances of sheer hate, equivalent in the satisfaction they give her to the waxen images which people in olden days fashioned of their enemies in order, with exquisite pleasure, to stick pins into them. Indeed, disparagement to Mrs. Parker is so habitual that she has no technique for praise, and when she feels admiration, can find no words for it.

Thus when she fain would burn incense to her gods—Ernest Hemingway and D. H. Lawrence—she cannot make herself heard at all, and becomes as gauche as an adoring shopgirl in the presence of Clark Gable. But just let her get a shot at a good, easy target like A. A. Milne, and the whole town listens. Including, of course, the time when, as Constant Reader in the *New Yorker*, she was so overcome by Mr. Milne's elfin whimsicality that Tonstant Weader fwowed up.

It should be added that that inveterate dislike of her fellow creatures which characterizes so many of Mrs. Parker's utterances is confined to the human race. All other animals have her enthusiastic support. It is only fair to her eventual biographer to tip him off that there is also a strong tinge of autobiography in that sketch of hers about a lady growing tearful in a speak-easy because her elevator man would be stuffy if she should pick up a stray horse and try to bring him to her apartment.

While she has never quite managed this, any home of hers always has the aspects and aroma of a menagerie. Invariably there is a dog. There was Amy, an enchanting, woolly, four-legged coquette whose potential charm only Dorothy Parker would have recognized at first meeting. For at that first meeting Amy was covered with dirt and a hulking truckman was kicking her out of his way. This swinish biped was somewhat taken aback to have a small and infuriated poetess rush at him from the sidewalk and kick him smartly in the shins—so taken aback that he could only stare open-mouthed while she caught the frightened dog up in her arms, hailed a taxi, and took her up to Neysa McMein's studio to wash her in the bathtub. There Amy regained her trust in the human race, achieved a fearful air of harlotry by eating all the rose-madder paint, of which a good deal lingered to incarnadine her face, and eventually won her way to a loving home on Long Island.

Then there was a Scottie named Alexander Woollcott Parker who reversed the customary behavior of a namesake by christening *me*—three times, as I recall—in a single automobile ride. More recently there has been Robinson, a softhearted and languishing dachshund who was chewed up by a larger dog. The brute's owner said that Robinson had started it. Mrs. Parker turned on him with great bitterness. "I have no doubt," she said, "that he was also carrying a revolver." Robinson's successor is a Blue Bedlington named John. Woodrow Wilson was, I think, the name of the dog at the end of her leash when I first knew her. This poor creature had a distressing malady. Mrs. Parker issued bulletins about his health—confidential bulletins, tinged with skepticism. He *said* he got it from a lamp post.

Of her birds, I remember only an untidy canary whom she named Onan for reasons which will not escape those who know their Scriptures. And then there were the two alligators which she found in her taxi, where someone had been shrewd enough to abandon them. Mrs. Parker brought them home and thoughtfully lodged them in the bathtub. When she returned to her flat that night, she found that her dusky handmaiden had quit, leaving a note on the table which read as follows: "I will not be back. I cannot work in a house where there are alligators. I would have told you this before, but I didn't suppose the question would ever come up."

Well, I had thought here to attempt, if not a portrait, then at least a dirty thumb-nail sketch, but I find I have done little more than run around in circles quoting Mrs. Parker. I know a good many circles where, by doing just that, one can gain quite a reputation as a wit. *One* can? Several can. Indeed, several I know do.

But I have not yet told here my favorite of all the Dorothy Parker stories. It was about the belated baby girl who, as the daughter of a successful playwright, is now an uppity miss at a fancy school. It seemed to those of us on Broadway that she was forever being born. For months the whole town had been kept uneasily aware of her approach. For months the little mother had filled the public eye with a kind of aggressive fragility. Until the last, she would pointedly rise at first nights and conspicuously leave the theater whenever the play became too intense for one in her sedulously delicate condition.

Long after Marc Connelly, in behalf of an exhausted neighborhood, had taken the expectant mother aside and gravely advised her to drop the whole project, we were still waiting for the news from that spotlighted confinement. At last it came, and the telegrams of relief and congratulations poured in from every direction. "Good work, Mary," our Mrs. Parker wired collect. "We all knew you had it in you."

QUESTIONS

1. Why does Woollcott describe Dorothy Parker as "so odd a blend of Little Nell and Lady Macbeth"? What are some of the less kind remarks for which she is famous? How did she guarantee that her office had many visitors?

2. Do you think Woollcott's hypothetical student would gain a clear picture of Mrs. Parker from this article? Why?

3. Much of Parker's wit, as Woollcott reports it, depends on punning ("a girl's best friend is her mutter") or literalism ("to catch up the torch as it fell from his hand—and burn someone with it"). Find additional examples of these techniques. What other humorous strategies does she use?

4. Woollcott's own style makes use of phrases like "well, then" and "you see." What effect does this have on the tone of the story? On our feelings toward him? Toward Mrs. Parker?

The Adventures of Mark Time, Star Detective of the Circum-Solar Federation

The Firesign Theatre

From the beginning of our comic tradition, American storytellers have delighted in poking fun at their own art. In "Adventure of the German Student" (see p. 111), Washington Irving lampooned the melodramatic fiction popular in his day, as Mark Twain did later in "A Medieval Romance" (p. 168). This contemporary radio play about Mark Time, detective of the "circum-solar federation," parodies two genres that enjoy a wide audience today—detective fiction and science fiction. Author David Ossman, along with Philip Austin, Peter Bergman, and Philip Proctor, belongs to the zany comedy team known as the Firesign Theatre. Their burlesques are included in The Firesign Theatre's Big Book of Plays *and* The Firesign Theatre's Big Mystery Joke Book.

MUSIC: "MARK TIME" THEME IN AND UNDER.

SOUND: SPACE NOISE.

ANNOUNCER: As you will remember from our last episode, Mark Time, Star Detective of the Circum-Solar Federation, and his Rocket-Jockey sidekick Bob Bunny, have been taken as prisoners to the subterranean ice caverns on Jupiter, where the Warlord, Prince Arcturus, keeps his court and council. Let's join them! Ready? Here we go through Time Warp Two-o-o-o-o-o!!

SOUND: TIME WARP ON ECHO.

BOB: Holy Moon rocks, Mr. Time! It looks like I've stoked my last Atom Furnace! There's nothin' in the System that I can get to help us down here!

MARK: If only I hadn't let Doc Technical go off with that stray asteroid by himself—he's so old and stupid!

BOB: Well, that's fuel under the reactor now, Mr. Time! Prince Arcturus has us by the thrusters! With you as bait, half the Federation Navy's gonna come blastin' in, and the Prince'll have 'em trapped like Mars flies in a Klein Bottle!

MARK: Ah! That's where you're wrong, Bob! You see, the Lunar Council knows we've been captured. It's up to those Navy boys now to confuse Arcturus and his Moth Men into letting us get control of the Communications Reactor!

BOB: Well, scramble my feedback! But what about Doc?

MARK: Dr. Technical is on his own, Bob! Right in the middle of the biggest battlefield this old Universe has ever seen!

BOB: Oh, golly gamma rays! I wish I could scan him on my Video, Mr. Time! He must be mighty hot around the collar . . .

SOUND: ROCKET PASS AND SPACE NOISE.

ANNOUNCER: In the black reaches of Space, a glistening little rocket-sub turns slowly, end over end. A power failure has left her helpless!

SOUND: INTERIOR OF ROCKET-SUB.

ANNOUNCER: Inside, Dr. Technical races against the Sidereal Clock to find out the source of the trouble . . .

DOC: Ouch! Ding-blast it to blazes! The trouble ain't in my Piles, and it ain't in the Converter. I wish ta' Sunrise I'd never learned how to pilot one of these Space-rafts! Never worth a Martian nickel anyway! (Working hard) If I can just jerry-rig a new water pump . . .

SOUND: COMMUNICATOR VIDEO ON.

DOC: Oh, my glory! There goes the Video! How do ya' turn the darn thing on here . . .

ARCTURUS: (On Video) Attention! This is Prince Arcturus! Men of the Federation, wherever you are! I am now in command! It was useless to send Mark Time and his redheaded friend to spy on me! They have been captured and languish in caves of methane ice, a thousand miles below my fortified palace! You must surrender, Men of the Federation! I, Prince Arcturus, command it!

SOUND: VIDEO WARP OUT.

DOC: Well, if that don't take the rings off a Boomer! Mark's in a heap o' hot gas now, and I can't do a thing but go 'round and 'round in this tin box!

SOUND: COMMUNICATOR VIDEO ON.

DOC: Agh! Here comes another one!

DEMOS: (On Video) Prince Arcturus! Commander Demos of the Federation Navy speaking! A thousand men, mutants and just plain Joes from little Moons all over the Universe are ready to chase you back to whatever evil world you came from! Batten down the hatches, Arcturus! Here we come!

SOUND: VIDEO WARP OUT AND ROCKET PASS.

DOC: Well, my stars! Looks like I'm gonna miss out on all the exposition, and the biggest thing since the Eagle landed. If I could just get this dad-blamed water pump to turn over . . . (Fading)

SOUND: ROCKET PASS AND SPACE NOISE.

MARK: (Fading in) Alright, Bob! You know the plan. The attack's set for daybreak, Lunar Time—that's about two minutes from now.

BOB: Oh, boy!

MARK: Alright, you get the guard's attention by urinating through the window in the cell door and I'll knock him out when he comes in. Ready?

BOB: I guess if I'm not in orbit now, I'll never be, Mr. Time!

MARK: Good! Hold on the pad! . . . Ignition! . . . Blast off!

SOUND: BLAST OFF AND TIME WARP ON ECHO.

ANNOUNCER: Can Mark Time and Bob make their childish trick work? Can Doctor Technical get out of the Asteroid Belt before two mighty rocket fleets launch their attacks around him? Who knows! Who cares! Listen next week, same fire time, same fire station, to Ma-a-a-a-rk Ti-i-i-i-me!!

SOUND: ROCKET PASS.

MUSIC: IN, UP AND OUT.

QUESTIONS

1. How is each character satirized by his name? By his language? Consider such expressions as Bob's "Holy Moon rocks" and "golly gamma rays," and Doc's "dad-blamed" and "ding-blast it to blazes."

2. Discuss Mark Time as a comic figure. Compare his plan of escape with Jim Doggett's unsuccessful bear hunt (see p. 119). Why is reference to excretory functions a stock device in humor?

3. An audience can be made to laugh only if it does not identify too closely with the events and characters on stage. What techniques are used in this play to create comic distance? Refer particularly to Mark's comments about Doc Technical, Demos's description of his men, and the announcer's final speech.

4. Try reading this skit aloud, with sound effects if possible. How does the play exaggerate the typical plots of science fiction and detective stories?

"*All right, have it your way—you heard a seal bark.*"

part 4

The Little Soul

In his essay "Laughter," the philosopher Henri Bergson suggests that comedy is generated when what is human becomes mechanical. Man is vital, flexible, dynamic; pit him against what is rigid or fixed, and the end result is a comic dilemma. If Bergson's notion is valid, surely no time has been so fertile for comedy as our own, for never before has the clash between man and machine been so dramatic, so full of ominous forebodings. And in America, where we are known by our social security numbers and our driver's license numbers and our student numbers, helplessness in the face of technocracy is perhaps felt more keenly than anywhere else in the world. It is precisely this frustration that is personified in the figure of the little soul.

Whereas comedy in the past has enabled Americans to reduce obstacles to manageable proportions, the new comedy functions in reverse. The little soul is tormented by trifles that are, at best, discomfitting. Robert Benchley is convinced that post-office regulations are made for the sole purpose of achieving "general confusion," and suburbanite Judith Viorst worries over plumbers, diaper service, "and other drab necessities that got ignored in / Great literature and philosophy." At worst, the little soul is driven to desperate straits: the main character in Ring Lardner's "Large Coffee," for instance, becomes suicidal over the impossibility of dealing successfully with hotel room service.

What is reduced in this brand of humor is the comic persona. As Russell Baker concludes of New York's Consolidated Edison Company: "I do not believe they are in the electrical business at all. I believe they are in the business of training corporate workers to be assigned to berserk corporations all over America to speed up the breaking of the human spirit." The little soul as husband and father is perennially dominated by overbearing women and monstrous little children; as wage earner is generally subservient to a tyrannical boss. He seems indeed—this Dagwood Bumstead or Caspar Milquetoast—to be brainless, spineless, often sexless. Dressed in chiffon after bridge, or wearing nothing but red sandals and a Martex bath towel for goat hunting in Hawaii, the narrator of E. B. White's whimsical reverie on the world of fashionable society seems both masculine and feminine. Sheepish, forever tottering on the verge of mental breakdown, the little soul bumbles and fumbles through a variety of elementary tasks, only to have efforts—and ego—topple. Though he dreams of exotic penthouses, White finds himself down on his knees trying to repair the radiator. Similarly, S. J. Perelman, defeated in his endeavor to assemble a simple child's toy, winds up on all fours whinnying. And poor Peter De Vries's carefully rehearsed jokes are all doomed. As wife and mother, the little soul also feels let down. "I saw us walking hand-in-hand through life," muses Viorst. "But now it's clear we really need two cars."

More important, the reduction of the individual signifies a widespread cultural collapse. In the nineteenth century, Huckleberry Finn, sick of civilization, lit out for the Territory. But today the mountains have all been crossed. What used to be frontier country is now a place where split-level houses stand in tidy rows and telephone wires crisscross farms relying on government price supports, where factories make soft drinks in throwaway cans. In Dick Allen's *Anon*, the story of a modern American Everyman, the legendary figures of the past are now called "Powermaniacs" and are being cared for by a psychiatrist, who explains:

> . . . "They thought
> too big. They lived

in fantasy. They hoped
to rule the world
by quantity. But now
they're out of fashion. . . ."

Not out of fashion, however, is the habit of living in fantasy. In the cynical, world-weary voice she assumes in her poetry, Dorothy Parker, having decided finally "You might as well live," rehearses the part she will play. After meeting their neighbors, the Viorsts face the overwhelming problem that "we can't decide / Who we want them to think / We are." Don Marquis's cat, mehitabel, has been reduced by reincarnation, but she recalls her former station as Cleopatra, and the cockroach, archy, though he cannot work the capital letters on the typewriter, writes free-verse poetry. To survive, the little soul must invent triumphant alter egos. The archetypal twentieth-century comic hero is portrayed in James Thurber's fables—the husband who conjures up mythical beasts to defeat his virago of a wife. In a profound sense, the little soul is the American Superman switching identities, as it were, in an imaginary telephone booth.

Anon Visits the Home of Heroes

Dick Allen

In the second canto of Dick Allen's popular epic, Anon, the modern American, symbolically nameless, discovers what has become of the legendary figures of the past: they have been retired. Allen's real achievement in these lines is to show the change in American values. The Home of Heroes, an old-age home for outworn ideals, inverts our myths to become the setting for comic contrasts—Paul Bunyan takes thyroid treatments, Slue-Foot Sue sucks a lollipop, and Casey Jones drives a child's choo-choo. The winner of several distinguished awards for poetry, Dick Allen has recently published the much-praised Regions with No Proper Names.

"Paul Bunyan! Glad
to meet you," Anon said.
"How goes the world?"

"They're cutting down my trees!"
the great boy cried. "The wilderness
is almost gone, and what

will I do then?" His big blue ox
was snorting by his side. "The darn
Commies did it, bless my soul.

They're bad!" Then Paul
chopped one more tree. He used
it for a toothpick. When

he finished eating Bunyan dumped
his garbage in the river. Babe
went after it

but couldn't turn
the river blue again
although she tried.

"Oh Anon, gosh," Paul said,
"Gee whiz, whatever happened to
the guys like me

and Pecos Bill
and Slue-Foot Sue
and Stormalong?

You know," he rambled on,
"they fenced me in. They say
I'm unfair competition. Yesterday

they organized my men!
The whole darn bunch of them
got *union* cards!

And now
I've even got to pay
them wages, not to mention give

them food.
And everytime I want
to go out walking, some

guy follows me.
'Don't *step* on anything,' that's all
he says all day.

Now just
a week ago
I figured I'd get rid of that

grand timberland
along Big Sur. This guy
he says there's something wrong. It seems

some people want to *look* at it.
Beats me.
I don't know *what* we're coming to."

He scratched his dimpled chin. Old Babe
came bouncing over. Paul
looked down at her

and slapped her hide. "I read
Ayn Rand and all
and even voted for

The Arizona Kid. But it
seems nothing helps. By Jiminy,
I'm goin' to Australia. *There's*

a place a man's a man.
What's more,
they don't let any niggers in.

This country's getting so
you can't do anything
you want.

My friends, the Minutemen,
can't even keep their guns. Anon,
something's *wrong.*"

The bird of Paradise
flew up his nose.
Paul sneezed.

The bird of Paradise
flew out again
but dropped

because its wings
were weighted down
with snot.

"Darn birds," said Paul.
"I thought we got
rid of all the doves.

The only birds I liked
were eagles but
they too are growing bald."

Anon tried to call
an answer up to Paul.
However, Anon found

he was too small
and anyway, the time
had come

for Bunyan's thyroid treatments. After that
the doctor let him play
some basketball

with boulders and silos. They kept
him busy building dams.
His foe,

a giant Black
John Henry Uncle Tom
was also occupied

with drilling H-bomb shelters in
the Colorado mountainside, while Stormalong

was used for charting underwater paths
the submarines
could follow as they ran

from Sonar, missiles, other submarines.
The whole
thing was a game,

the Ultimate in treating all
the sickened human race,
the doctors said.

Anon shook his head. The last
heroes that he saw
were Casey Jones

who drove the choo-choo train
around the reservation,
Slue-Foot Sue

who sucked a lollipop;
Pecos Bill
who mowed the lawns

and Moby Dick
who blubbered as the doctors pulled
out his harpoons.

"In God's name, what
happened to them all?"
he asked the chief

psychiatrist. "It's simple, really," was
the man's reply. "They thought
too big. They lived

in fantasy. They hoped
to rule the world
by quantity. But now

they're out of fashion. Power's not
the going thing. You've got
to think of everybody else

to live. Not one of them
could ever be at home
in an apartment house.

They have to learn
to give and take
and mostly how to give."

He hemhawed on: "The U.S.A.,
yes, yes, needs mighty men
but also we

must keep our eyes on how
these men behave."
He closed his eyes. "If you

would stay the night
you'd hear them raving on
and on

on Liberty and Freedom, all
that *rot*.
Big Sue

kicks up a storm. She wants
to not wear clothes,
and Casey Jones, he thinks

it's perfectly all right
to ride his train
the whole long night

and John—why if
we didn't take the hammer from his hand
he'd drive himself to death. These patients here

have suffered from
the Puritan
Work Ethic. All

they want to do is work
and sort of play
whenever *they*

decide.
Of course
you see what's wrong with that.

The law decrees
it's best
we keep them out of sight."

The doctor smiled. "I've got
a name for them," he said.
"They're Powermaniacs

living in a world
before
the Civil War.

It's sad but true
we've got too many ordinary men
to tolerate

the legendary heroes.
The people in our world
are sinking. We cannot afford

to let them swim.
Perhaps . . . if we could breathe on Mars. . . ."
His voice trailed off.

Anon thanked him, drove
down from the institution.
The sunset was a brilliant red.

QUESTIONS

1. What has happened to the giant figures from our comic folklore?
Casey Jones? Slue-Foot Sue? Pecos Bill? Moby Dick? What other Powermaniacs
from American history might Anon meet in the Home of Heroes?

2. What does Paul Bunyan complain about? What's happening to the
wilderness? His men? Why does he take thyroid treatments? Where does he
want to go? Why?

3. How does the chief psychiatrist analyze our old-fashioned heroes?
What do they have to learn? According to him, what is it the U.S.A. needs now?

4. Who is Ayn Rand? How does her philosophy relate to Allen's poem?
What is the Puritan work ethic?

5. Describe the sunset at the end of the poem. Is it appropriate?
Explain why you agree or disagree with the following lines: "The people in our
world / are sinking. We cannot afford / to let them swim."

6. What happens to the bird of paradise? How does Allen's humor
reflect an irreverence typical of our comic tradition?

archy and mehitabel

Don Marquis

As the "cosmic cockroach," archy suggests the limited vision of the little soul. The intellectual roach, a poet in a former life, now scrambles along the typewriter keys hammering out philosophic verses that belie his puny existence. Initially the literary bug jabbed at fashionable beliefs in reincarnation and free verse, but archy's commentary soon touched on the plight of the twentieth-century American and on the policies of Franklin Roosevelt. "Toujours gai," the motto of the promiscuous mehitabel, the cat, was a thrust at contemporary morality. Although he also created the characters of Hermione, with her Little Group of Serious Thinkers, and the Old Soak, Marquis's most memorable character continues to be archy.

i   the coming of archy

Dobbs Ferry possesses a rat which slips out of his lair at night and runs a typewriting machine in a garage. Unfortunately, he has always been interrupted by the watchman before he could produce a complete story.

It was at first thought that the power which made the typewriter run was a ghost, instead of a rat. It seems likely to us that it was both a ghost and a rat. Mme. Blavatsky's ego went into a white horse after she passed over, and someone's personality has undoubtedly gone into this rat. It is an era of belief in communications from the spirit land.

And since this matter had been reported in the public prints and seriously received we are no longer afraid of being ridiculed, and we do not mind making a statement of something that happened to our own typewriter only a couple of weeks ago.

We came into our room earlier than usual in the morning, and discovered a gigantic cockroach jumping about upon the keys.

He did not see us, and we watched him. He would climb painfully upon the framework of the machine and cast himself with all his force upon a key, head downward, and his weight and the impact of the blow were just sufficient to operate the machine, one slow letter after another. He could not work the capital letters, and he had a great deal of difficulty operating the mechanism that shifts the paper so that a fresh line may be started. We never saw a cockroach work so hard or perspire so freely in all our lives before. After about an hour of this frightfully difficult literary labor he fell to the floor exhausted, and we saw him creep feebly into a nest of the poems which are always there in profusion.

Congratulating ourself that we had left a sheet of paper in the machine the night before so that all this work had not been in vain, we made an examination, and this is what we found:

expression is the need of my soul
i was once a vers libre bard
but i died and my soul went into the body of a cockroach
it has given me a new outlook upon life
i see things from the under side now
thank you for the apple peelings in the wastepaper basket
but your paste is getting so stale i cant eat it
there is a cat here called mehitabel i wish you would have
removed she nearly ate me the other night why dont she
catch rats that is what she is supposed to be for
there is a rat here she should get without delay

most of these rats here are just rats
but this rat is like me he has a human soul in him
he used to be a poet himself
night after night i have written poetry for you
on your typewriter
and this big brute of a rat who used to be a poet
comes out of his hole when it is done
and reads it and sniffs at it
he is jealous of my poetry
he used to make fun of it when we were both human
he was a punk poet himself
and after he has read it he sneers
and then he eats it

i wish you would have mehitabel kill that rat
or get a cat that is onto her job
and i will write you a series of poems showing how things look
to a cockroach
that rats name is freddy
the next time freddy dies i hope he wont be a rat
but something smaller i hope i will be a rat
in the next transmigration and freddy a cockroach
i will teach him to sneer at my poetry then
dont you ever eat any sandwiches in your office
i havent had a crumb of bread for i dont know how long
or a piece of ham or anything but apple parings

and paste leave a piece of paper in your machine
every night you can call me archy

ii   mehitabel was once cleopatra

boss i am disappointed in
some of your readers they
are always asking how does
archy work the shift so as to get a
new line or how does archy do
this or do that they
are always interested in technical
details when the main question is
whether the stuff is
literature or not
i wish you would leave
that book of george moores on
the floor

mehitabel the cat and i want to
read it i have discovered that
mehitabel s soul formerly inhabited a
human also at least that
is what mehitabel is claiming these
days it may be she got jealous of
my prestige anyhow she and
i have been talking it over in a
friendly way who were you
mehitabel i asked her i was
cleopatra once she said well i said i
suppose you lived in a palace you bet
she said and what lovely fish dinners
we used to have and licked her chops

mehitabel would sell her soul for
a plate of fish any day i told her i thought
you were going to say you were
the favorite wife of the emperor
valerian he was some cat nip eh
mehitabel but she did not get me
                                    archy

QUESTIONS

1. Explain transmigration. Do you believe in it? What would you like to be? What do you think you may have been? How does Marquis use the doctrine of transmigration as a vehicle for satire?

2. What human characteristics do archy and mehitabel have? What complaints? What aspirations? Why does archy think he is superior to mehitabel?

3. Who is freddy? What does he do with archy's poetry? What is Marquis ridiculing through the figure of freddy?

4. "archy and mehitabel" is a kind of frame story, in which archy's poems are reported to us by a narrator. Describe this narrator. In what way is he like archy? How does he influence our reaction to the poetry?

5. How does the language of the poems contribute to their humor? Pay particular attention to archy's choice of words.

Back in Line

Robert Benchley

Although he may be no more than a thinking cockroach like archy, the little soul often pretends to be a sophisticate. Robert Benchley, largely responsible for popularizing this kind of comic figure, has been praised as "perhaps the most finished master of the technique of literary fun in America." Benchley's fun often depends on total nonsense, as in the titles of his books, for example 20,000 Leagues Under the Sea, or, David Copperfield. *But his ridiculous translations of foreign words, his habit of asserting something with brash self-confidence and then qualifying or even denying it, his non sequiturs and repetitions—all these tricks of style satirize the superficial mentality of Benchley's persona, a little man trying to stay rational in a complex and hostile world.*

For a nation which has an almost evil reputation for bustle, bustle, bustle, and rush, rush, rush, we spend an enormous amount of time standing around in line in front of windows, just waiting. It would be all right if we were Spanish peasants and could strum guitars and hum, or even stab each other, while we were standing in line, or East Indians who could just sit cross-legged and simply stare into space for hours. Nobody expects anything more of Spanish peasants or East Indians, because they have been smart enough to build themselves a reputation for picturesque lethargy.

But we in America have built ourselves reputations for speed and dash, and are known far and wide as the rushingest nation in the world. So when fifty of us get in a line and stand for an hour shifting from one foot to the other, rereading the shipping news and cooking recipes in an old newspaper until our turn comes, we just make ourselves look silly.

Most of this line-standing is the fault of the Government, just as everything else which is bad in our national life is the fault of the Government, including stone bruises and tight shoes. We would have plenty of time to rush around as we are supposed to do, if the Government did not require 500 of us to stand in one line at once waiting for two civil service employees to weigh our letters, thumb our income-tax blanks, tear off our customs slips or roll back our eyelids. Of course, there are times when we stand in line to see a ball game or buy a railroad ticket, but that is *our* affair, and in time we get enough sense to stop going to ball games or traveling on railroads.

The U.S. Post Office is one of the most popular line-standing fields in the country. It has been estimated that six-tenths of the population of the United States spend their entire lives standing in line in a post office. When you realize that no provision is made for their eating or sleeping or intellectual advancement while they are thus standing in line, you will understand why six-tenths of the population look so cross and peaked. The wonder is that they have the courage to go on living at all.

This congestion in the post offices is due to what are technically known as "regulations" but what are really a series of acrostics and anagrams devised by some officials who got around a table one night and tried to be funny. "Here's a good gag!" one of them probably cried. "Let's make it so that as soon as a customer reaches the window with his package after his forty-five minutes in line, he has to go home again, touch some object made of wood, turn around three times, and then come back and stand in line again!" "No, no, that's too easy!" another objected. "Let's make it compulsory for the package to be wrapped in paper which is watermarked with Napoleon's coat of arms. We won't say anything about it until they get right up to the window, so there will be no danger of their bringing that kind of paper with them. Then they will have to go away again with their bundles, find some paper watermarked with Napoleon's coat of arms (of which there is none that I ever heard of), rewrap their bundles, and come back and stand in line again. What do you say to that!" This scheme probably threw the little group of officials into such a gale of merriment that they had to call the meeting off and send down for some more White Rock.

You can't tell me that the post-office regulations (to say nothing of those of the Custom House and Income Tax Bureau) were made with anything else in mind except general confusion. It must be a source of great chagrin to those in charge to think of so many people being able to stick a stamp on a letter and drop it into a mail box without any trouble or suffering at all. They are probably working on that problem at this very minute, trying to devise some way in which the public can be made to fill out a blank, stand in line, consult some underling who will refer them to a superior, and then be made to black up with burned cork before they can mail a letter. And they'll figure it out, too. They always have.

But at present their chief source of amusement is in torturing those unfortunates who find themselves with a package to send by mail. And with Christmas in the offing, they must be licking their chops with glee in very anticipation. Although bundles of old unpaid bills is about all anyone will be sending this Christmas, it doesn't make any difference to the P.O. Department. A package is a package, and you must suffer for it.

It wouldn't be a bad idea for those of us who have been through the fire to get together and cheat the officials out of their fun this year by sending out lists of instructions (based on our own experience) to all our friends, telling them just what they have got to look out for before they start to stand in line. Can you imagine the expression on the face of a post-office clerk if a whole line of people came up to his window, one by one, each with his package so correctly done up that there was no fault to find with it? He would probably shoot himself in the end, rather than face his superiors with the confession that he had sent no one home to do the whole thing over. And if his superiors shot themselves too it would not detract one whit from the joyousness of the Christmas tide.

So here are the things I have learned in my various visits to the Post Office. If you will send me yours and get ten friends to make a round robin of their experiences, we may thwart the old Government yet.

Packages to be mailed abroad must be:

1. Wrapped in small separate packages, each weighing no more than one pound and seven-eighths (Eastern Standard Time), and each package to be tied with blue ribbon in a sheepshank knot. (Any sailor of fifteen years' experience will teach you to tie a sheepshank.)

2. The address must be picked out in blue, and re-enforced with an insertion of blue ribbon, no narrower than three-eighths of an inch and no wider than five-eighths of an inch, (and certainly not exactly four-eighths or one-half), or else you may have to stay and write it out a hundred times after the post office has closed.

3. The package, no matter what size, will have to be made smaller.

4. The package, no matter what size, will have to be made larger.

(In order to thwart the clerk on these last two points, it will be necessary to have packages of *all* sizes concealed in a bag slung over your back.)

5. The person who is mailing the package must approach the window with the package held in his right hand extended toward the clerk one foot from the body, while with the left hand he must carry a small bunch of lilies of the valley, with a tag on them reading: "Love from—[name of sender]—to the U.S. Post Office."

6. The following ritual will then be adhered to, a deviation by a single word subjecting the sender to a year in Leavenworth or both:

CLERK'S QUESTION: Do you want to mail a package?
SENDER'S ANSWER: No, sir.
Q. What *do* you want to do?
A. I don't much care, so long as I can be with you.
Q. Do.you like tick-tack-toe?
A. I'm crazy mad for it.
Q. Very well. We won't play that.
A. Aren't you being just a little bit petty?
Q. Are you criticizing *me*?

A. Sorry.
Q. And high time. Now what do you want?
A. *You,* dear.
Q. You get along with yourself. What's in your hand?
A. Flowers for you—*dear.*
Q. I know that. What's in the other hand?
A. I won't tell.
Q. Give it here this minute.
A. You won't like it.
Q. Give-it-here-this-minute, I say.
The sender reluctantly gives over the parcel.
Q. What do you want to do with this?
A. I want to take it home with me and wrap it up again.
Q. You leave it here, and *like it.*
A. Please give it back. Please, pretty please?
Q. I will do no such thing. You leave it here and I will mail it for you. And shut up!
The sender leaves the window, sobbing. The clerk, just to be mean, mails the package.

QUESTIONS

1. Why do Americans look silly standing in line? Why would it be all right if we were Spanish peasants or East Indians?

2. Describe the hypothetical meeting of post-office officials. Why was it called off? What disturbs officials about the way letters are mailed? How will this problem be solved?

3. What has the narrator learned from his visits to the post office? How should packages be addressed? Why is it necessary to have packages of all sizes concealed in a bag? How should the sender leave the window? Why will the clerk mail the package?

4. Benchley suggests that if we "get ten friends to make a round robin of their experiences, we may thwart the old Government yet." In what situations do you share his attitude of wanting to "thwart" the government? What kinds of things does Benchley blame on the government?

5. How does Benchley's comedy depend on exaggeration? Confusion? Nonsense? Consider such statements as that each package should weigh "no more than one pound and seven-eighths (Eastern Standard Time)."

Insert Flap "A" and Throw Away

S. J. Perelman

According to no less an authority than Robert Benchley, S. J. Perelman has taken over the "dementia praecox" field. When a scriptwriter for the Marx Brothers, Perelman achieved fame as a talented creator of wild humor. Yet beneath the mask of his typical narrator—aptly characterized by the proposed title of his memoirs, "Forty Years a Boob"—we glimpse the efforts of a sensitive, intelligent soul struggling to maintain his sanity. The odds are against him, and often, as in this piece in which he cannot follow directions, he comes perilously close to slipping over the edge. Perelman's finest burlesques are collected in The Most of Perelman.

One stifling summer afternoon last August, in the attic of a tiny stone house in Pennsylvania, I made a most interesting discovery: the shortest, cheapest method of inducing a nervous breakdown ever perfected. In this technique (eventually adopted by the psychology department of Duke University, which will adopt anything), the subject is placed in a sharply sloping attic heated to 340°F. and given a mothproof closet known as the Jiffy-Cloz to assemble. The Jiffy-Cloz, procurable at any department store or neighborhood insane asylum, consists of half a dozen gigantic sheets of red cardboard, two plywood doors, a clothes rack, and a packet of staples. With these is included a set of instructions mimeographed in pale-violet ink, fruity with phrases like "Pass Section F through Slot AA, taking care not to fold tabs behind washers (see Fig. 9)." The cardboard is so processed that as the subject struggles convulsively to force the staple through, it suddenly buckles, plunging the staple deep into his thumb. He thereupon springs up with a dolorous cry and smites his knob (Section K) on the rafters (RR). As a final demonic touch, the Jiffy-Cloz people cunningly omit four of the staples necessary to finish the job, so that after indescribable purgatory, the best the subject can possibly achieve is a sleazy, capricious structure which would reduce any self-respecting moth to helpless laughter. The cumulative frustration, the tropical heat, and the soft, ghostly chuckling of the moths are calculated to unseat the strongest mentality.

In a period of rapid technological change, however, it was inevitable that a method as cumbersome as the Jiffy-Cloz would be superseded. It was superseded at exactly nine-thirty Christmas morning by a device called the Self-Running 10-Inch Scale-Model Delivery-Truck Kit Powered by Magic Motor, costing twenty-nine cents. About nine on that particular morning, I was spread-eagled on my bed, indulging in my favorite sport of mouth-breathing, when a cork fired from a child's air gun mysteriously lodged in my throat. The pellet proved awkward for a while, but I finally ejected it by flailing the little marksman (and his sister, for good measure) until their welkins rang, and sauntered in to breakfast. Before I could choke down a healing fruit juice, my consort, a tall, regal creature indistinguishable from Cornelia, the Mother of the Gracchi, except that her foot was entangled in a roller skate, swept in. She extended a large, unmistakable box covered with diagrams.

"Now don't start making excuses," she whined. "It's just a simple cardboard toy. The directions are on the back—"

"Look, dear," I interrupted, rising hurriedly and pulling on my overcoat, "it clean slipped my mind. I'm supposed to take a lesson in crosshatching at Zim's School of Cartooning today."

"On Christmas?" she asked suspiciously.

"Yes, it's the only time they could fit me in," I countered glibly. "This is the big week for crosshatching, you know, between Christmas and New Year's."

"Do you think you ought to go in your pajamas?" she asked.

"Oh, that's O.K.," I smiled. "We often work in our pajamas up at Zim's. Well, goodbye now. If I'm not home by Thursday, you'll find a cold snack in the safe-deposit box." My subterfuge, unluckily, went for naught, and in a trice I was sprawled on the nursery floor, surrounded by two lambkins and ninety-eight segments of the Self-Running 10-Inch Scale-Model Delivery-Truck Construction Kit.

The theory of the kit was simplicity itself, easily intelligible to Kettering of General Motors, Professor Millikan, or any first-rate physicist. Taking as my starting point the only sentence I could comprehend, "Fold down on all lines marked 'fold down'; fold up on all lines marked 'fold up,'" I set the children to work and myself folded up with an album of views of Chili Williams. In a few moments, my skin was suffused with a delightful tingling sensation and I was ready for the second phase, lightly referred to in the directions as "Preparing the Spring Motor Unit." As nearly as I could determine after twenty minutes of mumbling, the Magic Motor ("No Electricity—No Batteries—Nothing to Wind—Motor Never Wears Out") was an accordion-pleated affair operating by torsion, attached to the axles. "It is necessary," said the text, "to cut a slight notch in each of the axles with a knife (see Fig. C). To find the exact place to cut this notch, lay one of the axles over diagram at bottom of page."

"Well, *now* we're getting someplace!" I boomed, with a false gusto that deceived nobody. "Here, Buster, run in and get Daddy a knife."

"I dowanna," quavered the boy, backing away. "You always cut yourself at this stage." I gave the wee fellow an indulgent pat on the head that flattened it slightly, to teach him civility, and commandeered a long, serrated bread knife from the kitchen. "Now watch me closely, children," I ordered. "We place the axle on the diagram as in Fig. C, applying a strong downward pressure on the knife handle at all times." The axle must have been a factory second, because an instant later I was in the bathroom grinding my teeth in agony and attempting to stanch the flow of blood. Ultimately, I succeeded in contriving a rough bandage and slipped back into the nursery without awaking the children's suspicions. An agreeable surprise awaited me. Displaying a mechanical aptitude clearly inherited from their sire, the rascals had put together the chassis of the delivery truck.

"Very good indeed," I complimented (naturally, one has to exaggerate praise to develop a child's self-confidence). "Let's see—what's the next step? Ah, yes. 'Lock into box shape by inserting tabs C, D, E, F, G, H, J, K, and L into slots C, D, E, F, G, H, J, K, and L. Ends of front axle should be pushed through holes A and B.' " While marshaling the indicated parts in their proper order, I emphasized to my rapt listeners the necessity of patience and perseverance. "Haste makes waste, you know," I reminded them. "Rome wasn't built in a day. Remember, your daddy isn't always going to be here to show you."

"Where *are* you going to be?" they demanded.

"In the movies, if I can arrange it," I snarled. Poising tabs C, D, E, F, G, H, J, K, and L in one hand and the corresponding slots in the other, I essayed a union of the two, but in vain. The moment I made one set fast and tackled another, tab and slot would part company, thumbing their noses at me. Although the children were too immature to understand, I saw in a flash where the trouble lay. Some idiotic employee at the factory had punched out the wrong design, probably out of sheer spite. So that was his game, eh? I set my lips in a grim line and, throwing one hundred and fifty-seven pounds of fighting fat into the effort, pounded the component parts into a homogeneous mass.

"There," I said with a gasp, "that's close enough. Now then, who wants candy? One, two, three—everybody off to the candy store!"

"We wanna finish the delivery truck!" they wailed. "Mummy, he won't let us finish the delivery truck!" Threats, cajolery, bribes were of no avail. In their jungle code, a twenty-cent gewgaw bulked larger than a parent's love. Realizing that I was dealing with a pair of monomaniacs, I determined to show them who was master and wildly began locking the cardboard units helter-skelter, without any regard for the directions. When sections refused to fit, I gouged them with my nails and forced them together, cackling shrilly. The side panels collapsed; with a bestial oath, I drove a safety pin through them and lashed them to the roof. I used paper clips, bobby pins, anything I could lay my hands on. My fingers fairly flew and my breath whistled in my throat. "You want a delivery truck, do you?" I panted. "All right, I'll show you!" As merciful blackness closed in, I was on my hands and knees, bunting the infernal thing along with my nose and whinnying, "Roll, confound you, roll!"

"Absolute quiet," a carefully modulated voice was saying, "and fifteen of the white tablets every four hours." I opened my eyes carefully in the darkened room. Dimly I picked out a knifelike character actor in pince-nez lenses and a morning coat folding a stethoscope into his bag. "Yes," he added thoughtfully, "if we play our cards right, this ought to be a long, expensive recovery." From far away, I could hear my wife's voice bravely trying to control her anxiety.

"What if he becomes restless, Doctor?"

"Get him a detective story," returned the leech. "Or better still, a nice, soothing picture puzzle—something he can do with his hands."

QUESTIONS

1. What is the Jiffy-Cloz? Where can it be purchased? What is distinctive about the cardboard from which it is made? What is the final "demonic touch" provided by the manufacturer?

2. Describe what happens when Perelman attempts to assemble the truck. What is the only sentence he can comprehend? When sections refuse to fit, what does he do? Why does he end up in the bathroom?

3. How is the narrator dominated by his wife? Children? Doctor? What attempts to escape does he make? How effective are they?

4. Discuss the comic incongruities in this essay: between the name of the truck, for example, and its price; between the narrator's tone and the events he recounts; between his diction and his son's. What other comic strategies does Perelman make use of?

Large Coffee

Ring Lardner

Ring Lardner first became popular with his slang-filled, misspelled letters of a bush-league baseball player, published as You Know Me Al, *but in "Large Coffee" he pokes fun at a writer, a clever type who is first cousin to Perelman's narrator. As Lardner tries to explain himself clearly, the veneer of sophisticated competence wears thin, revealing another fallible and frightened American. The impact of the story derives from a peculiar blend of the fantastic and the real, typical of much of Lardner's fiction. As Dorothy Parker observes, his art "teeters on the edge of the fantasy which lies at the heart of all realism." His collection* Round Up *contains such well-known stories as "Alibi Ike" and "The Golden Honeymoon."*

Note: Readers of the daily papers will recall a paragraph printed earlier this week to the effect that the body of a Mr. Lardner was found in a New York hotel room by a house officer who had broken in after the chambermaids had reported that they had rapped on the door every day for over a fortnight and had received no response, and were disposed to believe that the occupant of the room would need a clean towel if living, and perhaps two of them if dead. The occupant was in the last-named condition or worse. Dressed as usual in pajamas, he was sprawled out on the floor, his head crushed in by a blow from some blunt instrument, probably another hotel. At the time the item appeared, there was mention of the discovery of a diary. It now develops that one really was unearthed and turned over to the police, who used parts of it as curl papers for Grover Whalen. We have acquired the mechanical rights to the balance and herewith publish extracts from it as a human document of particular interest to men and women who, like the writer thereof, have been battered and broken by an insensate world.

Friday, May 31

Today I registered and was assigned this room, 657, which is to be my home through most of the summer. At a conference of my wife and children, it was decided that I ought to contribute something to their support and they recommended that I do a little writing for the magazines or newspapers. I told them this would be impossible in our hut on Long Island unless they and the neighbors agreed to become hermits so that my mind would not be constantly distracted by the knowledge that other people were having fun. It is my plan to visit the family one day in the middle of each week, not at the week-end when there seems to be a tendency to drink cocktails and expect you to sit by, look on and like it. The hotel is giving me a rate of $4.00 a day, really a bargain because the room has a window. You can look right into other people's rooms on the courtyard if they don't keep their shades down. O diary, I hope it's a hot summer. (Editors' Note: Did he get his hope?)

Sunday, June 2

I spent so much thought yesterday and this morning on what I would have sent up for breakfast that when I sat down at the typewriter, my mind was too tired to work. I spoke of this over the telephone (my only means of communication with the outside world) to a friend and he advised me to make a selection of a few nourishing and inoffensive victuals, commit them to memory and order them every morning. I then asked him what to do about the coffee problem, which is something of a problem to me. You see, when you drink lots of coffee you can kind of kid yourself into believing it's something else, so for breakfast I always want four cups. What I mean is enough coffee to fill one cup four times. Yesterday morning I said to the order clerk, "Two orders of coffee," and the result was two small pots of coffee, each containing enough for two cups. But the set-up, as I believe they call it, was for two people; there were two cereal dishes, two plates for my bacon and eggs and two cups for my coffee. This lay-out congested the table, leaving no space for my shoe tree. So this morning I said, "Two orders of coffee, but served for one person." The result was a small pot of coffee, containing enough for two cups. Well, my friend said I would have to work this out for myself; the only advice he could give me was ridiculous—that I give up coffee. This evening I will try to think of a solution and also select a permanent breakfast so there will be no more brain fag or waste of time.

Friday, June 7

The breakfast I have picked out for the summer consists of orange juice, corn flakes, medium hard boiled eggs, and buttered toast. Boiled eggs are preferable to other kinds because they don't bring you two plates for them even if your coffee order makes them believe you are two people. I selected toast instead of plain rolls or sweet rolls because the sweet ones are too filling and messy, and the plain ones are made in Bethlehem, Pa. The toast is also immune, but you have to say something when the order clerk insists. The coffee situation is just as baffling as a week ago. One morning I said, "I am living alone, but I drink four cups of coffee." I got a large pot of coffee and four cups. Another morning I said, "Double coffee, served for one." I got a large pot of coffee, two cups, and two orders of tooth-proof toast. Yesterday I asked the waiter how much a large pot of coffee cost. He said it was sixty cents. So this morning I said to the order clerk, "One orange juice, one corn flakes, one medium hard boiled eggs, one buttered toast, and sixty cents worth of coffee." "Coffee," she replied, "is only thirty cents a pot." "But I want twice as much as that." "Oh, all right. You want two orders." "Yes, but I'm not two people." I got one small pot of coffee.

Monday, July 8

It is the hottest summer in history. Everybody on our court is free and easy. Formality and modesty have been thrown to the winds, if there are any. A business woman who looks like Tom Heeney and has a red splotch under her left shoulder blade is occupying the room just opposite. She is out all day and goes to bed at eight and reads the Brooklyn telephone directory. The electric light in my bathroom wouldn't work today and I wanted to shave on account of the waiters. I told the floor clerk to send me the electrician. Pretty soon a plumber came and turned on everything but the light. "I don't see anything wrong," he said. "The light won't turn on," I said. "Oh," said he. "You want the electrician." The electrician came. I said, "The light won't turn on in the bathroom and I know the bulb isn't burned out because I tried another bulb and it wouldn't work." So the electrician tried another bulb and found it wouldn't work. "It must be something else," he said. He found the trouble and fixed it. This may have no bearing on the case, but I want to tell all.

I have been getting my large pot of coffee every morning, but never with less than two cups and nearly always with two egg cups, two dishes for cereal, and two orders of toast.

Double coffee, large coffee, enough coffee for four cups, sixty cents worth of coffee, enough coffee for two people served for one person. I have thought I might ask Percy Hammond to come and room with me, but that would only mean six or eight cups on the same-sized table. An assistant manager called me up at twenty minutes to three this morning and said somebody had just complained that I was using a typewriter. What the hell does Mrs. Heeney think I moved in here for, to be near Gimbel Brothers?

Thursday, August 22

Yesterday morning I got what I wanted and I called right back and asked for the order clerk. "Are you the only order clerk?" "Oh, no." "Well, are you the one that just took the order for 657?" "Yes. Was it wrong?" "No. It was right. Now listen, I'm not trying to start a flirtation, but what is your name?" "If there's any complaint, I'll connect you with the superintendent." "There's no complaint, but I want your name so I can give you my order every morning." "Well, my name is Foley." "Thanks, Miss Foley. And when I call you tomorrow and other mornings, please do as you just did—send me a large pot of coffee and only one cup."

Every day the paper says cooler tomorrow. They ought to put that with the rest of the comics. A mystifying combination of tenants has taken the room across the court. There are two young women and a man. They can't be going to stay in town very long because the women apparently haven't brought anything but nightgowns and when the man isn't in B.V.D.'s he's out of them. I feel as if some time I would almost have to shout at them, "Don't you want a fourth for bridge?"

Monday, September 2

The worst has happened. Miss Foley "isn't here any more." My house was built on sand. I've got to start all over again and work up from the bottom.

And I'm pretty sure that late tonight I will lean out the window and holler, "Hey! Don't you want a fourth for strip bridge?"

QUESTIONS

1. How does the note at the beginning of the essay set the stage for what follows? What is its tone? What serious issues does it raise? How is it nonsensical?

2. Describe the character of the narrator. How does his confident manner contrast with the events he relates? How is his life controlled by his family? The hotel manager? Room service? What advice does his friend give him about drinking coffee?

3. "Large Coffee" is rich in irony. For instance, why doesn't Lardner do his writing at home? What is ironic about his stay at the hotel? What other examples are there of defeated expectations?

4. Discuss Lardner's neighbors at the hotel. How do they contribute to the humor of the story?

5. How does the author generate comedy through exaggeration? Look at the passage beginning "The worst has happened."

On Conning Ed

Russell Baker

In a nation that has been mechanized and ultimately dehumanized, the voice of the individual is ignored. This article about New York's Consolidated Edison Company has significance far beyond the matter of whether or not Russell Baker is to leave a deposit for his electric service. It depicts the epic struggle between the small soul and the unapproachable forces that control society. As with Lardner, Baker's self-assurance is incongruous alongside his inability to explain his needs to a giant corporation. A syndicated columnist, Baker has also written Poor Russell's Almanac, *a parody of* Poor Richard.

In New York they have the Consolidated Edison electrical company. When I lived elsewhere, New Yorkers would come and bore me with tales of this berserk corporate monster, and I would dismiss it as New York hysteria and laugh a bored and torpid laugh.

Corporations are berserk all over America, I would tell them. You cannot scare me with what is after all only a small, localized nightmare. Me, I have gone up against the Columbia Record Club and the Sears, Roebuck computer. I have seen American Express run wild, have struggled with the friendly skies of United Airlines.

As one who had been buffeted by corporate incompetence on the continental scale, how could I be anything but bored by tales of a local nuisance known as the Consolidated Edison electrical company? It was to laugh. A cosmic corporate monster might break my spirit some day, and probably would, but a piffling Consolidated Edison electrical company? Never.

Insouciantly, I moved to New York for a stay. I arrived on a fourth of December. On the fifth, I received a letter from the Consolidated Edison electrical company. It announced that my electricity was going to be turned off for nonpayment of $325.

"Look here," I said on the telephone, in the voice which had crushed many a computer at the Chesapeake & Potomac Telephone Company, "since I have been in the house less than 24 hours, it is impossible that I can already have used $325 worth of Consolidated Edison electricity."

The uncrushed voice of the Consolidated Edison electrical company replied that the $325 was not for electricity used during the night previous, but was a deposit the company required of new customers.

But $325! That would have paid the bill for 18 months in my previous residence, which was three times as big, I explained. "That is our standard deposit charge for small-business establishments," the voice said.

"This is not a small business. Only a very small house."

"We will call you back," said the voice.

Sure enough, another voice called back. "We have made a mistake and will accept a smaller deposit."

"How much?"

"How much do you want to pay?" it replied.

I said I would think about it, proceeding on my theory that when dealing with idiot corporations nothing works like the stall.

A few hours later, I was rewarded. The Consolidated Edison electrical company telephoned again. "It is all a mistake," said the voice. "You needn't pay anything in advance. The deposit has been waived."

I called a number of New Yorkers and crowed about the ease with which a skilled guerrilla could defeat the local monster. It was the top of the world. New York was beautiful.

Eight days later came another letter from the Consolidated Edison electrical company. It was my final warning. The juice would stop flowing almost instantly unless I came across with the deposit. It was accompanied by a statement of my legal rights. If I could afford Louis Nizer's fee, I apparently had a fighting chance to avoid a percentage of the company gouge.

I went back to the stall. If I didn't call attention to myself, they might forget me in their own confusion. December gave way to January, and the electricity flowed. I had forgotten the matter entirely by the time the first snowstorm of the winter occurred when out of the gale in dead of night crept an ancient gnarled gentleman to ring the doorbell.

He was from the Consolidated Edison electrical company, he said. He had come to see about terminating the juice on my small-business establishment. I showed him that it was only a small house. He was delighted.

"Do not worry," he said, "for all is well. There is no need for a deposit payment." He vanished in the snow. I celebrated.

The following week, the Consolidated Edison electrical company wrote threatening to black me out in 10 days unless I forked over $110. I have just written the check and blotted it with tears, for I am certain that the Consolidated Edison electrical company will phone back soon and tell me the check is not required and, the week after that, will come to cut off the power on the ground that they haven't received my check.

I do not believe they are in the electrical business at all. I believe they are in the business of training corporate workers to be assigned to berserk corporations all over America to speed up the breaking of the human spirit.

Tell me, Consolidated Edison electrical company, how did a smart man like Edison ever get mixed up with you?

QUESTIONS

1. Why was Baker confident he could successfully battle with New York's electrical company? Discuss the significance of the essay's title.

2. Explain what happens. What conclusion does Baker come to concerning Consolidated Edison? Why?

3. How does Baker blot his check? Contrast the tone of his essay with the events he recounts. What does this difference imply about the little soul?

Laughter in the Basement

Peter De Vries

As an epigraph to his novel The Tents of Wickedness, *Peter De Vries writes, "You must not think me necessarily foolish because I am facetious, nor will I consider you necessarily wise because you are grave." This might be the epigraph for all his fiction, which, more often than not, is laden with deep social or religious significance. In the following definition of "prepartee," we hear again the voice of a pseudo sophisticate trying to deceive himself about his chances for success. Regarded by some critics as the best living American satirist, De Vries has also written* The Tunnel of Love, The Mackerel Plaza, Let Me Count the Ways, The Blood of the Lamb, *and* Reuben, Reuben.

"She has no mind, merely a mind of her own" is something I recently said in open conversation, with less profit than I had anticipated. When I say anticipated, I mean over a fairly long stretch, for the remark is one of a repertory of retorts I carry about in my head, waiting for the chance to spring them. This is a form of wit I call prepartee—prepared repartee for use in contingencies that may or not arise. For instance, I have been waiting for years for some woman to dismiss a dress she has on as "just something I slipped into," so that I can say, behind my hand, "Looks more like something she slipped and *fell* into."

There are two types of prepartee: the kind you can wangle an opening for, and the kind you can't. The sally about the woman who had no mind, merely a mind of her own, required no specific straight line but only a general one, in a context I was able to steer the conversation to after bringing the woman into it myself. But my plan to retort dryly when next I hear somebody say that money doesn't matter, "No, provided one has it," is something else again. I can, of course, bring up the *subject* of money any time I choose, but though you can lead a stooge to water, you can't make him drink, and unless somebody says, "Money doesn't matter," in so many words, or virtually that, I will never get to use the riposte.

The chances of my getting a feeder for it are slimmer than you might think. Clichés are like cops, in that you can never find one when you want one. This applies to trite questions as well as trite statements. I have been waiting since 1948 for some poor devil to ask, "What does a woman want most in a man?," so that I can come back, quick as a flash, with "Fiscal attraction." And I have been lying in wait even longer to hear so much as the vaguest reference to current realistic fiction as a reflection of our time, so that I can murmur, "I had thought it rather a reflection *on* it."

I almost murmured that one in Cos Cob. I was at a buffet supper in the home of friends there, and found myself in the library with the hostess and a couple of other guests. It was a week after my quip about the woman with no mind, and I had been trying to analyze just why it had failed. I had finally diagnosed my waggeries as, texturally, the suave and underplayed sort, requiring small groups and an intimate, offhand delivery, so I was happy to find myself in the snug library with just a handful of people, well away from the general commotion in the living room, so reminiscent of the previous week's mob. Coffee had been poured and brandy was passed. I began setting up the conversation for my little mot about realistic novels. Having lit my pipe, I squeezed from the packed shelves a volume of fiction suited to my design and casually asked the hostess, "Have you read this?"

She nodded briskly. "Yes, I thought it pretty good of its kind," she said.

"Ah, of its kind. But what good is its kind?" I asked.

By dint of such questions, by tirelessly jockeying the discussion this way and that, by nudging, cuing, and tinkering with her responses, I succeeded in maneuvering her to within striking distance of my aphorism. Prepartee is very much like those games in which, over a course beset with delays, digressions, "penalties," and other pitfalls, one tries to move a disc to a goal marked "Home." After a quarter of an hour, I heard the hostess say, "Well, I mean realistic novels of this sort, whatever you may think of them artistically, do have some value for our time."

I sat on the edge of my chair. One more jump and I would be Home. Very carefully, very deliberately, I said, "How do you mean?"

At that moment, a hearty character in tweeds boomed into the room. "Just a minute," I snapped. "Ethel here is talking. Go on, Ethel. What was it you were saying? What are these novels in connection with our time?"

"They hold a mirror up to it," she said.

I sat back in my chair. "I see," I said, and reached for my cold cup of coffee.

With Home so hard to gain in manipulable contexts, the chances of scoring with rejoinders depending on straight lines you can't even *begin* to finagle are discouraging indeed. Thus the odds against my ever being told, by a newcomer to my community, "We'd like to meet some people who count," in order that I may answer, "Well, I can introduce you to a couple of bank tellers," are really astronomical. And I long ago decided not to hold my breath till I hear someone refer to a third party as "my cousin twice removed," so I can say, "I didn't know he was your cousin, but I knew he was twice removed—once as treasurer of his firm and later to the state prison at Ossining."

Recognizing all this, I eventually scaled my ambitions down to where I bluntly *asked* people to stooge for me, as you do in putting a riddle. This is a tawdry substitute for the real thing, but better than nothing when you're bent on making an impression, as I was recently at a party where I found myself *à deux* with a toothsome girl, a house guest of the host and hostess. We were sitting together on the floor, through which the sound of laughter from the basement game room occasionally seeped. We sat leaning against chairs, with our elbows hitched up on the seats, having a pleasant chat. I had spotted her from the first as a merry, responsive sort, a kid who could go along with a joke. In no connection, I turned to her and said, "Did I ever tell you about my cousin twice removed?"

She shook her head, tossing a wealth of black hair. "No. What about him?" she asked.

"Well, as I say, he was twice removed—once as treasurer of the bank he was connected with and later to the state prison at Ossining."

She laughed gaily, throwing her head back. "So you've got a banker in jail in your family?" she said. "Well, we've got a congressman at large in ours."

Having failed with large groups, then with small, and finally with a single companion (the less said about that brash chit the better), there seemed nothing left for me to do but talk to myself, a state to which frustration has brought stronger men than I. However, I rallied after making what you might call one more strategic retreat. I thought I would apply the technique I had evolved to the lowest common denominator— the practical joke.

We know a couple, living in one of the suburban towns near Westport, named Moses. They are of impressive Yankee extraction, and moved down from Vermont six years ago. One of the nuisances of living in the country is, of course, power failures, and I got the notion of ringing them up sometime when the electricity was off, and asking, "Where was Moses when the lights went out?" This is admittedly a far cry from my early high ideals for prepartee—so far, indeed, as to be not true prepartee at all. Nevertheless, as some philosopher or other has said, a difference in quantity, if great enough, becomes a difference in quality, and this gag depended on such a number of factors going just right—that is to say, just wrong—that I felt it to be qualitatively unique. It required, to begin with, a meteorological mishap of such extent and duration as to plunge into darkness an area wide enough to embrace Westport, where I live, and the town where the Moseses' place is, a good ten miles inland.

It called for the most perfect timing, in that it would have to be pulled when falling limbs had broken the power lines, which are strung along the tops of the poles, but not yet the telephone connections underneath. It would depend on the Moseses and ourselves being brought simultaneously to the same pass. Having met these conditions, it would still require the phone's being answered by Mrs. Moses and not Moses himself. (I couldn't say, "Where were you when the lights went out?") So the sporting odds against my getting Home were actually greater than they had been across more cerebral courses.

It wasn't until the ice storm early last January, or three and a half years after the gag's conception, that the necessary factors coincided. I thought I saw my chance during the big blow of '51, when the winds attained hurricane force, but our power and phone lines were both reduced to spaghetti before I could get my wits about me. However, in this winter's glacéed adventure, our juice went at dusk, taking with it light, heat, and cooking power. The phone still worked, but, of course, it was being monopolized for the time being by housewives on the party line making unnecessary calls.

During dinner, which consisted of shredded wheat crouched over by candlelight, I mentally reviewed the situation. Everything was in order; it remained to be seen only whether the Moseses could be got through to by phone. (That they had no power was a fair certainty, for it had been knocked out or shut off for miles around.) I vibrated like a scientist for whom every long-awaited element is fortuitously aligning itself in his favor, hurrying him toward the exquisite moment of experiment. Dinner over, I slipped into our dark vestibule and sat down at the phone. I found it alive and free, and, what was more, the operator got me the number I wanted after only a few moments' delay. Hearing the ring at the other end, I sat erect, realizing I had forgotten there was still a final requisite beyond that of the other phone's working—a woman's voice would have to answer.

I heard the phone picked up. "Hello?" a voice said. It was a woman's.

"Where was Moses when the lights went out?" I asked.

"In bed," she said. "He hasn't been at all well."

"Aw, gosh, that's too bad. I'm sorry to hear that," I said. "What seems to be the trouble?"

"Oh, the usual—flu, grippe, or whatever you want to call it," Mrs. Moses said. "Who is this?"

I told her. Then I added, "I've had a cold myself, which is probably why you didn't recognize my voice. Well, we were just wondering how you two were making out over there. Is there anything we can . . ."

Thus prepartee, in either its pure or debased form, is no indolent hobby, no pastime for the weak-nerved. The life of a parlor desperado, with its long hours in ambush, is a hard and often wearing one. It has its

midnight post-mortems just like its more familiar counterpart, departee
—which is, I think, the proper term for remarks thought up on the way
home. I don't know which is the more frustrating, moments to which one
has proved unequal or stunners for which no occasion arose, but I have
found both abrasive. My little tittup about Moses and the lights came to
an end when I hung up to find my wife behind me with a flashlight, a
child clinging to either leg. "Who was that?" she asked, playing the beam
on me. I told her. I also told her why I had phoned, and said that I
wondered why Mrs. Moses hadn't been more on the ball. I asked my wife
whether *she* didn't think the line was funny. *"Funny!"* she said. "Don't
make me laugh."

QUESTIONS

1. What is prepartee? Explain its purpose. Give examples of both
types. How do they differ? What is a feeder? What examples of departee have
you ever thought of?

2. What kind of game is prepartee like? How does the narrator
maneuver Ethel? The girl at the party? What are the results?

3. Why does De Vries phone Mrs. Moses? What factors are just right?
What does she say to him?

4. Describe how De Vries's ambitions are reduced. To what state does
frustration bring him?

5. How does the humor of the essay depend on puns? Anticlimax?
Clichés?

Dusk in Fierce Pajamas

E. B. White

E. B. White, described by James Thurber as the "number one wheel horse" of The New Yorker, joined the magazine's staff in 1926 and became one of its most influential writers and editors. In many of his essays, especially those collected in The Second Tree from the Corner, White urges a return to a simple agrarian economy in which the calm beauty of the natural world will help the bedraggled urbanite regain his sanity. In the following parody from Quo Vadimus? or, The Case for the Bicycle, White's exaggerated descriptions often give way to complete nonsense, but the humor depends largely on the incongruity between the narrator's real life and his dreams. In addition to his celebrated book of essays, One Man's Meat, White is widely known for Charlotte's Web and Stuart Little, children's stories that have gained popularity with adults as well.

Ravaged by pink eye, I lay for a week scarce caring whether I lived or died. Only Wamba, my toothless old black nurse, bothered to bring me food and quinine. Then one day my strength began to return, and with it came Wamba to my bedside with a copy of *Harper's Bazaar* and a copy of *Vogue*. "Ah brought you couple magazines," she said proudly, her red gums clashing.

In the days that followed (happy days of renewed vigor and reawakened interest), I studied the magazines and lived, in their pages, the gracious lives of the characters in the ever-moving drama of society and fashion. In them I found surcease from the world's ugliness, from disarray, from all unattractive things. Through them I escaped into a world in which there was no awkwardness of gesture, no unsuitability of line, no people of no importance. It was an enriching experience. I realize now that my own life is by contrast an unlovely thing, with its disease, its banalities, its uncertainties, its toil, its single-breasted suits, and its wine from lesser years. I am aware of a life all around me of graciousness and beauty, in which every moment is a tiny pearl of good taste, and in which every acquaintance has the common decency to possess a good background.

Lying here in these fierce pajamas, I dream of the *Harper's Bazaar* world, the *Vogue* life; dream of being a part of it. In fancy I am in Mrs. Cecil Baker's pine-panelled drawing-room. It is dusk. (It is almost always dusk in the fashion magazines.) I have on a Gantner & Mattern knit jersey bathing suit with a flat-striped bow and an all-white buck shoe with a floppy tongue. No, that's wrong. I am in chiffon, for it is the magic hour after bridge. Suddenly a Chippendale mahogany hors-d'oeuvre table is brought in. In its original old blue-and-white Spode compartments there sparkle olives, celery, hard-boiled eggs, radishes—evidently put there by somebody in the employ of Mrs. Baker. Or perhaps my fancy wanders away from the drawing-room: I am in Mrs. Baker's dining-room, mingling unostentatiously with the other guests, my elbows resting lightly on the dark polished oak of the Jacobean table, my fingers twiddling with the early Georgian silver. Or perhaps I am not at Mrs. Baker's oak table in chiffon at all—perhaps instead I am at Mrs. Jay Gould's teakwood table in a hand-knitted Anny Blatt ensemble in diluted tri-colors and an off-the-face hat.

It is dusk. I am dining with Rose Hobart at the Waldorf. We have lifted our champagne glasses. "To sentiment!" I say. And the haunting dusk is shattered by the clean glint of jewels by Cartier.

It is dusk. I am seated on a Bruce Buttfield pouf, for it is dusk.

Ah, magazine dreams! How dear to me now are the four evenings in the life of Mrs. Allan Ryan, Junior. I have studied them one by one, and I feel that I know them. They are perfect little crystals of being—static, precious. There is the evening when she stands, motionless, in a magnificent sable cape, her left arm hanging gracefully at her side. She is ready to go out to dinner. What will this, her first of four evenings, bring of romance, or even of food? Then there is the evening when she just sits on the edge of the settee from the Modernage Galleries, the hard bright gleam of gold lamé topping a slim, straight, almost Empire skirt. I see her there (the smoke from a cigarette rising), sitting, sitting, waiting. Or the third evening—the evening with books. Mrs. Ryan is in chiffon; the books are in morocco. Or the fourth evening, standing with her dachshund, herself in profile, the dog in full face.

So I live the lives of other people in my fancy: the life of the daughter of Lord Curzon of Kedleston, who has been visiting the Harold Talbotts on Long Island. All I know of her is that she appeared one night at dinner, her beauty set off by the lustre of artificial satin and the watery fire of aquamarine. It is all I know, yet it is enough; for it is her one perfect moment in time and space, and I know about it, and it is mine.

It is dusk. I am with Owen Johnson over his chafing dish. It is dusk. I am with Prince Matchabelli over his vodka. Or I am with the Countess de Forceville over her bridge tables. She and I have just pushed the tables against the wall and taken a big bite of gazpacho. Or I am with the Marquis de Polignac over his Pommery.

How barren my actual life seems, when fancy fails me, here with Wamba over my quinine. Why am I not to be found at dusk, slicing black bread very thin, as William Powell does, to toast it and sprinkle it with salt? Why does not twilight find me (as it finds Mrs. Chester Burden) covering a table with salmon-pink linens on which I place only white objects, even to a white salt shaker? Why don't I learn to simplify my entertaining, like the young pinch-penny in *Vogue*, who has all his friends in before the theatre and simply gives them champagne cocktails, caviar, and one hot dish, then takes them to the show? Why do I never give parties after the opera, as Mr. Paul Cravath does, at which I have the prettiest women in New York? Come to think of it, why don't the prettiest women in New York ever come down to my place, other than that pretty little Mrs. Fazaenzi, whom Wamba won't let in? Why haven't I a butler named Fish, who makes a cocktail of three parts gin to one part lime juice, honey, vermouth, and apricot brandy in equal portions—a cocktail so delicious that people like Mrs. Harrison Williams and Mrs. Goodhue Livingston seek him out to get the formula? And if I *did* have a butler named Fish, wouldn't I kid the pants off him?

All over the world it is dusk! It is dusk at Armando's on East Fifty-fifth Street. Armando has taken up his accordion; he is dreaming over the keys. A girl comes in, attracted by the accordion, which she mistakes for Cecil Beaton's camera. She is in stiff green satin, and over it she wears a silver fox cape which she can pull around her shoulders later in the evening if she gets feeling like pulling a cape around her shoulders. It is dusk on the Harold Castles' ranch in Hawaii. I have risen early to shoot a goat, which is the smart thing to do in Hawaii. And now I am walking silently through hedges of gardenias, past the flaming ginger flowers, for I have just shot a goat. I have on nothing but red sandals and a Martex bath towel. It is dusk in the Laurentians. I am in ski togs. I feel warm and safe, knowing that the most dangerous pitfall for skiers is *color*, knowing that although a touch of brilliance against the snow is effective, too much of it is the sure sign of the amateur. It is the magic hour before cocktails. I am in the modern penthouse of Monsieur Charles de Beistegui. The staircase is entirely of cement, spreading at the hemline and trimmed with padded satin tubing caught at the neck with a bar of milk chocolate. It is dusk in Chicago. I am standing beside Mrs. Howard Linn, formerly Consuelo Vanderbilt, formerly Sophie M. Gay, formerly Ellen Glendinning, formerly Saks-Fifth Avenue. It is dusk! A pheasant has Julian Street down and is pouring a magnificent old red Burgundy down his neck. Dreams, I'm afraid. It is really dusk in my own apartment. I am down on my knees in front of an airbound radiator, trying to fix it by sticking pins in the vent. Dusk in these fierce pajamas. Kneeling here, I can't help wondering where Nancy Yuille is, in her blue wool pants and reefer and her bright red mittens. For it is dusk. I said *dusk*, Wamba! Bring the quinine!

QUESTIONS

1. Explain the significance of the title "Dusk in Fierce Pajamas." Why is it usually dusk in the fashion magazines? In what sense are White's pajamas "fierce"?

2. The essay begins "Ravaged by pink eye . . ." How is this phrase anticlimactic? What light does it shed on the narrator?

3. What kind of butler does White wish for? What does he suspect he'd do if he had such a butler? Why?

4. To what extent does White's prose trail off into nonsense? Consider, for example, his description of the modern penthouse of Monsieur Charles de Beistegui.

5. This essay burlesques dreams inspired by fashion magazines. In a deeper sense, does it poke fun at the process of dreaming itself? At people who need to dream? Why does White's persona seem at times feminine, at times masculine?

The Little Man

James Thurber

One of E. B. White's most valuable contributions to The New Yorker *was to bring to its staff in 1927 the young cartoonist and writer James Thurber. Probably with greater success than any of his contemporaries, Thurber fleshed out an image of the American little soul. These well-known parables from* Fables for Our Time *express the two interrelated conflicts that motivate almost all of Thurber's work: the struggle between men and women, and that between fantasy and reality. In both, the shy, imaginative, typically Thurberesque hero is threatened by an aggressive, shallow woman. The moral of "The Shrike and the Chipmunks" burlesques the practicality of Ben Franklin's* Poor Richard's Almanack, *but both fables spoof the values of Puritanism and capitalism.*

THE UNICORN IN THE GARDEN

Once upon a sunny morning a man who sat in a breakfast nook looked up from his scrambled eggs to see a white unicorn with a gold horn quietly cropping the roses in the garden. The man went up to the bedroom where his wife was still asleep and woke her. "There's a unicorn in the garden," he said. "Eating roses." She opened one unfriendly eye and looked at him. "The unicorn is a mythical beast," she said, and turned her back on him. The man walked slowly downstairs and out into the garden. The unicorn was still there; he was now browsing among the tulips. "Here, unicorn," said the man, and he pulled up a lily and gave it to him. The unicorn ate it gravely. With a high heart, because there was a unicorn in his garden, the man went upstairs and roused his wife again. "The unicorn," he said, "ate a lily." His wife sat up in bed and looked at him, coldly. "You are a booby," she said, "and I am going to have you put in the booby-hatch." The man, who had never liked the words "booby" and "booby-hatch," and who liked them even less on a shining morning when there was a unicorn in the garden, thought for a moment. "We'll see about that," he said. He walked over to the door. "He has a golden horn in the middle of his forehead," he told her. Then he went back to the garden to watch the unicorn; but the unicorn had gone away. The man sat down among the roses and went to sleep.

As soon as the husband had gone out of the house, the wife got up and dressed as fast as she could. She was very excited and there was a gloat in her eye. She telephoned the police and she telephoned a psychiatrist; she told them to hurry to her house and bring a strait-jacket. When the police and the psychiatrist arrived they sat down in chairs and looked at her, with great interest. "My husband," she said, "saw a unicorn this morning." The police looked at the psychiatrist and the psychiatrist looked at the police. "He told me it ate a lily," she said. The psychiatrist looked at the police and the police looked at the psychiatrist. "He told me it had a golden horn in the middle of its forehead," she said. At a solemn signal from the psychiatrist, the police leaped from their chairs and seized the wife. They had a hard time subduing her, for she put up a terrific struggle, but they finally subdued her. Just as they got her into the strait-jacket, the husband came back into the house.

"Did you tell your wife you saw a unicorn?" asked the police. "Of course not," said the husband. "The unicorn is a mythical beast." "That's all I wanted to know," said the psychiatrist. "Take her away. I'm sorry, sir, but your wife is as crazy as a jay bird." So they took her away, cursing and screaming, and shut her up in an institution. The husband lived happily ever after.

MORAL: *Don't count your boobies until they are hatched.*

THE SHRIKE AND THE CHIPMUNKS

Once upon a time there were two chipmunks, a male and a female. The male chipmunk thought that arranging nuts in artistic patterns was more fun than just piling them up to see how many you could pile up. The female was all for piling up as many as you could. She told her husband that if he gave up making designs with the nuts there would be room in their large cave for a great many more and he would soon become the wealthiest chipmunk in the woods. But he would not let her interfere with his designs, so she flew into a rage and left him. "The shrike will get you," she said, "because you are helpless and cannot look after yourself." To be sure, the female chipmunk had not been gone three nights before the male had to dress for a banquet and could not find his studs or shirt or suspenders. So he couldn't go to the banquet, but that was just as well, because all the chipmunks who did go were attacked and killed by a weasel.

The next day the shrike began hanging around outside the chipmunk's cave, waiting to catch him. The shrike couldn't get in because the doorway was clogged up with soiled laundry and dirty dishes. "He will come out for a walk after breakfast and I will get him then," thought the shrike. But the chipmunk slept all day and did not get up and have breakfast until after dark. Then he came out for a breath of air before beginning work on a new design. The shrike swooped down to snatch up the chipmunk, but could not see very well on account of the dark, so he batted his head against an alder branch and was killed.

A few days later the female chipmunk returned and saw the awful mess the house was in. She went to the bed and shook her husband. "What would you do without me?" she demanded. "Just go on living, I guess," he said. "You wouldn't last five days," she told him. She swept the house and did the dishes and sent out the laundry, and then she made the chipmunk get up and wash and dress. "You can't be healthy if you lie in bed all day and never get any exercise," she told him. So she took him for a walk in the bright sunlight and they were both caught and killed by the shrike's brother, a shrike named Stoop.

MORAL: *Early to rise and early to bed makes a male healthy and wealthy and dead.*

QUESTIONS

1. How are the wives in both fables alike? The husbands? Does Thurber portray males or females more sympathetically? Do you think his portrayals are accurate? Explain.

2. Thurber's animals represent different traits. What is symbolized by the unicorn? The chipmunks? The shrike? Compare this shrike with the editor named Shrike in "Miss Lonelyhearts, Help me, Help Me" (see p. 38).

3. Both parables are highly ironic; characterizations and events are often contrary to our expectations. For instance, why is the chipmunk saved while his wife is away? How is he eventually killed? How are the morals examples of reversal? What other ironies can you find?

4. Though the fables begin like fairy tales and are told tongue in cheek, what do they say about American values? How does Thurber use parody as a vehicle for satire? Compare Thurber's satiric use of the parable with George Ade's (see p. 159). With Ambrose Bierce's (see p. 162).

The Little Woman

Dorothy Parker

As if in response to Thurber, New Yorker writer Dorothy Parker gives us the distaff side of the battle of the sexes. These poems sparkle not with the imaginative zaniness of Thurber's parables, but with the sardonic wit that brands all of Parker's writing. Somerset Maugham thought it was her "common sense that gives her poems their singular and characteristic savor," adding, "What is it but common sense that makes this uncertain, absurd, hard and transitory life not only tolerable, but amusing?" Hers is the common sense of a woman who is worldly wise, and her argument against men is tinged with more than a little cynicism. In addition to the poems collected in Enough Rope, Sunset Gun, *and* Death and Taxes, *she is well known for her mordant short stories about pathetic victimized women.*

EXPERIENCE

Some men break your heart in two,
    Some men fawn and flatter,
Some men never look at you;
    And that cleans up the matter.

COMMENT

Oh, life is a glorious cycle of song,
A medley of extemporanea;
And love is a thing that can never go wrong;
And I am Marie of Roumania.

UNFORTUNATE COINCIDENCE

By the time you swear you're his,
　Shivering and sighing,
And he vows his passion is
　Infinite, undying—
Lady, make a note of this:
　One of you is lying.

SOCIAL NOTE

Lady, lady, should you meet
One whose ways are all discreet,
One who murmurs that his wife
Is the lodestar of his life,
One who keeps assuring you
That he never was untrue,
Never loved another one . . .
Lady, lady, better run!

RÉSUMÉ

Razors pain you;
Rivers are damp;
Acids stain you;
And drugs cause cramp.
Guns aren't lawful;
Nooses give;
Gas smells awful;
You might as well live.

QUESTIONS

1. Describe the male characteristics that annoy Parker. What do men always brag about to her? What is her attitude toward "true love"? What recommendations does she have for women?

2. Contrast the view of men presented in these poems with the one given by James Thurber (see p. 240). Which do you think is closer to the truth? Are both inaccurate? Explain.

3. As Alexander Woollcott explains (see p. 188), Dorothy Parker is well known for her urbane, witty style. What examples of the famous Parker style do you find in these poems?

The Wife

Judith Viorst

Judith Viorst, a contributing editor of Redbook, *also projects an image of the little woman—now married and hemmed in by diaper pails and supermarket shelves. Like her male counterpart, this antiheroine is disturbed by the gap between the real and the ideal. The title of Viorst's best-selling book explains her dilemma:* It's Hard to Be Hip over Thirty. *But though her verse is rich in social satire, her jabs are at best delivered gingerly. "Married Is Better," announces one poem, and, while she may be repressed, hassled, sometimes neurotic, she still opts for husband, children, and mother-in-law—for someone to "step on a cockroach whenever I need him."*

MONEY

Once I aspired to
Humble black turtleneck sweaters
And spare unheated rooms
With the Kama Sutra, a few madrigals, and
Great literature and philosophy.

Once I considered money
Something to be against
On the grounds that
Credit cards,
Installment-plan buying,
And a joint checking account
Could never coexist with
Great literature and philosophy.

Once I believed
That the only kind of marriage I could respect
Was a spiritual relationship
Between two wonderfully spiritual human beings
Who would never argue about money
Because they would be too busy arguing about
Great literature and philosophy.

I changed my mind,
Having discovered that

Spiritual is hard without the cash
To pay the plumber to unstop the sink
And pay a lady to come clean and iron
So every other Friday I can think about
Great literature and philosophy.

No one ever offers us a choice
Between the Kama Sutra and a yacht.
We're always selling out for diaper service
And other drab necessities that got ignored in
Great literature and philosophy.

A jug of wine, a loaf of bread, and thou
No longer will suffice, I must confess
My consciousness is frequently expanded
By Diners' Club, American Express, and things undreamed of in
Great literature and philosophy.

I saw us walking hand-in-hand through life,
But now it's clear we really need two cars.
I looked with such contempt at power mowers,
And now, alas, that power mower's ours.
It seems I'm always reaching for my charge plates,
When all I'd planned to reach for were the stars,
Great literature and philosophy.

CHOICES

We've met the fun couples
Who own works of art
That are strawberry malteds in plaster,
And watch television
Only to see the commercials
And use words like life style and panache.

And we've met the boycott-the-supermarket people
Who oppose certain conservative instant puddings
And support certain progressive canned vegetables
In addition to voter registration, busing, and immediate withdrawal.

And we've met the above-reproach crowd
Who are signed up for
Cancer,
Heart disease,
Stroke,
A booth at the annual book fair,
And he goes to sewer meetings in tweed jackets
With leather elbow patches
While she exchanges recipes
At brunches.

And we've met the social leaders
Who know how to act at horse shows,
And their ancestors always come from the British Isles.

And we've met the self-improvers
Who buy quality paperbacks,
Season tickets to theaters in the round,
And Brentano reproductions.

And we can't decide
Who we want them to think
We are.

QUESTIONS

1. Describe the people Viorst meets in suburbia. What is her dilemma?

2. Explain how Viorst's attitude toward money has changed. Discuss the humorous incongruities in "Money." How do your own ideas on the subject agree or disagree with those expressed in the poem?

3. Compare her comic strategies with those used by such writers as Thurber and Benchley. What use does she make of comic lists, understatement, exaggeration, and distortion?

The comic figures that have captured the popular imagination tell us much about our national character. One of the most beloved is Snoopy, the spirited dog who stars in Charles Schulz's comic strip, "Peanuts." Since the strip first appeared in 1950, millions of American adults have been fascinated with its children: dirty Pig Pen; Lucy, domineering and shrewish; the trusting and invariably defeated Charlie Brown; Schroeder with his toy piano; Linus, who carries his blanket with him for security. As for Snoopy, his vivacious personality has become legend. Schulz, like the nineteenth-century cartoonist Thomas Nast (see p. 62), uses the animal as a vehicle for satire, but his humor is far more gentle than Nast's. What Schulz's art reveals about us is the subject of Arthur Asa Berger's essay included in this section, "Peanuts: The Americanization of Augustine." (© 1960 by United Features Syndicate, Inc.)

part 5

Theories and Criticism

. . . more time and effort have been invested in attempting to study and to understand American tragedy than American comedy, and humorous writing is customarily relegated to a subordinate role. In so doing, we have been guilty of neglecting a valuable insight into the understanding of American society. For not only have many American writers been comic writers, but the very nature of comedy would seem to make it particularly useful in studying life in the United States.

In his essay "The Great American Joke," Louis D. Rubin, Jr., strikes the keynote of Part 5: the relationship between American comedy and American culture. The link is strong, he contends, for incongruity, the essence of comedy, is also the essence of American life. The essential problem faced by a democracy is how to include all citizens in the decision-making process without "cheapening and vulgarizing its highest social, cultural and ethical ideals." The inevitable clashes between different social and intellectual levels, between reality and ideality, are represented by the clash of language modes, literary and vernacular, that is a hallmark of American literature.

Louis Kronenberger also relates our comic perceptions to our national life, but he insists that "America, in the deep sense, has neither irony nor humor." Our lack of profound humor, he suggests, reflects our lack of seriousness; the American spirit is youthful, expansive, busy, devoted to the "twin gospels of Belonging and of Getting Ahead." Kronenberger locates the heart of humor in suffering. We have suffered little, thought little, he points out, and so, unlike many of the have-not peoples of the world, we have become jokesters, rather than humorists.

But American comedy reflects more than American reality: the patterns in our humor trace the shapes of our fantasies. So Constance Rourke explains the evolution of the American tall-tale heroes, noting of Mike Fink: "He was in fact a Mississippi river-god, one of those minor deities whom men create in their own image and magnify to magnify themselves." In "Comedy's Greatest Era," James Agee explores the techniques used by the great stars of silent-film comedies to expose "secret hopes." Similarly, Arthur Asa Berger, in his discussion of Charles Schulz's popular comic strip, "Peanuts," reminds us that we live vicariously through Snoopy: "What Snoopy demonstrates, to all his readers, is that ultimately we are all free to create ourselves as we wish, no matter what our status on the Great Chain of Being might be." Finally, Horace Newcomb finds in TV situation comedy a "one-sided world" in which unrealistic characters show us the possibilities of "magical paths out of our troubles."

As we approach the last decades of the twentieth century, the troubles faced by Americans proliferate. Even our comic sense has been colored by what is often termed "the imagination of disaster." Some critics have already announced the death of American humor. Others, more cautious, have been content to pronounce it sick—very sick, perhaps fatally so. Kenneth Rexroth writes in *The Nation* on "The Decline of American Humor," and a full-length study of our comic tradition by Jesse Bier is more elaborately titled *The Decline and Fall of American Humor.* Melvin Maddocks speculates in a *Time* essay that we may be victims of "cataplexity," a "disease" that renders us unable to laugh. And James Thurber, in "The Future, if any, of comedy or, where do we non-go from here?," remarks that comedy has identified itself with the "tension and terror" it once worked to alleviate. "Comedy didn't die," he concludes, "it just went crazy." But critic Ihab Hassan is not so pessimistic. In "Echoes of Dark Laughter: The Comic Sense in Contemporary American Fiction," he sees the new comedy as "the birth of a new sense of reality, a new knowledge of error and of incongruity, an affirmation of life under the aspect of comedy."

Thalia, the muse of comedy, has always been something of a wallflower in critical circles, and the attention has gone principally to Melpomene and her more glamorous celebrants of tragedy. In large part, of course, this is because in the hierarchy of letters comedy has always occupied a position below and inferior to tragedy. We have tended to equate gravity with importance. The highest accolade we give to a humorist is when we say that even so he is a "serious" writer—which is to say that although he makes us laugh, his ultimate objective is to say something more about the human condition than merely that it is amusing. This implies that comedy is "un-serious"—we thus play a verbal trick, for we use "serious" to mean both "important" and "without humor," when the truth is that there is no reason at all why something cannot be at once very important and very comic.

In any event, more time and effort have been invested in attempting to study and to understand American tragedy than American comedy, and humorous writing is customarily relegated to a subordinate role. In so doing, we have been guilty of neglecting a valuable insight into the understanding of American society. For not only have many American writers been comic writers, but the very nature of comedy would seem to make it particularly useful in studying life in the United States. When Mark Twain speaks of "the calm confidence of a Christian holding four aces," he makes a joke and notes a human incongruity of interest to historians of American Protestantism. The essence of comedy is incongruity, the perception of the ridiculous. The seventeenth-century English critic Dennis's remark, that "the design of Comedy is to amend the follies of Mankind, by exposing them," points to the value of humor in searching out the shortcomings and the liabilities of society. In a democracy, the capacity for self-criticism would seem to be an essential function of the body politic, and surely this has been one of the chief tasks of the American writer. Thus H. L. Mencken, himself a newspaperman, rebukes the American press. The brain of the average journalist, he reports, "is a mass of trivialities and puerilities; to recite it would be to make even a barber beg for mercy." From colonial times onward, we have spent a great deal of time and effort criticizing ourselves, pointing out our shortcomings, exploring the incongruities and the contradictions within American society. As the novelist and poet Robert Penn Warren put it, "America was based on a big promise—a great big one: the Declaration of Independence. When you have to live with that in the house, that's quite a problem—particularly when you've got to make money and get ahead, open world markets, do all the things you have to, raise your children, and so forth. America is stuck with its self-definition put on paper in 1776, and that was just like putting a burr under the metaphysical saddle of America—you see, that saddle's going to jump now and then and it pricks." Literature has been one of the important ways whereby the American people have registered their discomfort at

Whether humor in America is in fact dying, declining, or simply finding new dimensions, each reader will need to decide. The question is a compelling one; indeed, our answer will eventually determine how we define our entire culture.

The Great American Joke

Louis D. Rubin, Jr.

Most critics of American literature tend either to ignore our comic tradition or to treat it patronizingly. On the contrary, scholar Louis Rubin explores the essence of humor to show its unique value in a democracy. His definition of the Great American Joke points out the dichotomy between the ideal and the real in our culture. Rubin is the editor of The Comic Imagination in America, *a collection of critical essays.*

> He took a pen and some paper. "Now—name of the elephant?"
> "Hassan Ben Ali Selim Abdallah Mohammed Moise Alhammal Jamsetjejeebhoy Dhuleep Sultan Ebu Bhudpoor."
> "Very well. Given name?"
> "Jumbo."
>
> —Mark Twain, "The Stolen White Elephant"

The American literary imagination has from its earliest days been at least as much comic in nature as tragic. Perhaps this is only as might be expected; for while the national experience has involved sadness, disappointment, failure and even despair, it has also involved much joy, hopefulness, accomplishment. The tragic mode, therefore, could not of itself comprehend the full experience of the American people. From the moment that the colonists at Jamestown were assailed by the arrows of hostile Indians, and one Mr. Wynckfield "had one shott cleane through his bearde, yet scaped hurte," there has been too much to smile at. The type of society that has evolved in the northern portion of the western hemisphere bears no notable resemblance either to Eden or to Utopia, of course. From the start it has been inhabited by human beings who have remained most human and therefore most fallible. Even so, if one views American history as a whole it would be very difficult to pronounce it a tragedy, or to declare that the society of man would have been better off if it had never taken place (though Mark Twain once suggested as much).

Yet for all that, it is remarkable how comparatively little attention has been paid to American humor, and to the comic imagination in general, by those who have chronicled and interpreted American literature.

those pricks, and repeatedly the discomfort has been expressed in the form of humor—often enough through just such a homely metaphor as Warren used. For if we look at Warren's remark, what we will notice is that it makes use of a central motif of American humor—the contrast, the incongruity between the ideal and the real, in which a common, vernacular metaphor is used to put a somewhat abstract statement involving values—self-definition, metaphysical—into a homely context. The statement, in other words, makes its point through working an incongruity between two modes of language—the formal, literary language of traditional culture and learning, and the informal, vernacular language of everyday life.

This verbal incongruity lies at the heart of American experience. It is emblematic of the nature and the problem of democracy. On the one hand there are the ideals of freedom, equality, self-government, the conviction that ordinary people can evince the wisdom to vote wisely, and demonstrate the capacity for understanding and cherishing the highest human values through embodying them in their political and social institutions. On the other hand there is the *Congressional Record*—the daily exemplary reality of the fact that the individual citizens of a democracy are indeed ordinary people, who speak, think and act in ordinary terms, with a suspicion of abstract ideas and values. Thus Senator Simon Cameron of Pennsylvania, after his Committee on Foreign Relations had rejected the nomination of Richard Henry Dana as U.S. Ambassador to England, could exult because his country would not be represented at the Court of St. James's by "another of those damned literary fellows." The problem of democracy and culture is one of how, in short, a democracy can reach down to include all its citizens in its decision-making, without at the same time cheapening and vulgarizing its highest social, cultural and ethical ideals. Who, that is, will, in a democracy, commission the Esterhazy quartets? Confronting this problem, Thomas Jefferson called for an *aristoi*, an aristocracy of intellect; he believed that through public education the civilized values of truth, knowledge and culture that he cherished would be embodied and safeguarded in the democratic process so that leadership could be produced which would not be demagogic and debasing. His good friend John Adams was skeptical of this ever coming to pass, and Adams's great-grandson, Henry Adams, lived to chronicle and deplore a time when the workings of political and economic democracy made heroes of the vulgar and the greedy, and had no place in the spectrum of power, he thought, for an Adams who by virtue of inbred inheritance still believed in the disinterested morality, as he saw it, of the Founding Fathers. What Henry Adams could not fathom was why the public could nominate for the presidency of the United States a Ulysses Grant, a James A. Garfield, a James G. Blaine, and then vote for him. He could only conclude that "the moral law had expired—like the Constitution."

"The progress of evolution from President Washington to President Grant," he concluded, "was alone evidence enough to upset Darwin." The problem has been part of American experience from the start, and it is at least as crucial today as in the past. Though it is by no means purely or uniquely American, it is nevertheless distinctively so, and if we look at American literary history we will quickly recognize that the writers have been dealing with it all along the way. Herman Melville's famous invocation to the muses in *Moby-Dick* faces it squarely:

> If, then, to meanest mariners, and renegades and castaways, I shall hereafter ascribe high qualities, though dark; weave round them tragic graces; if even the most mournful, perchance the most abased, among them all, shall at times lift himself to the exalted mounts; if I shall spread a rainbow over his disastrous set of sun; then against all mortal spirits bear me out in it, thou just Spirit of Equality, which hast spread one royal mantle of humanity over all my kind! Bear me out in it, thou great democratic God! . . .

Melville wanted to create a tragedy along metaphysical lines, and yet he wanted to write about the Nantucket whaling fleet; his problem was how to render the everyday experience of life aboard a whaling vessel while creating a tragic protagonist, one who, in Aristotle's classic formula, could arouse pity and terror through his fall from eminence. Obviously such a protagonist, Aristotle declared, "must be one who is highly renowned and prosperous,—a personage like Oedipus, Thyestes, or other illustrious men of such families." How to give a whaling captain such heroic stature? Melville's solution was partly one of language. He separated the two elements. He used a literary, highly poetic, Shakespearean diction to chronicle Ahab, and a much more vernacular, colloquial diction to report on the activities of the crew. He made the language distance between tragic captain and motley crew serve his ultimate meaning.

In so doing, however, Melville was forced to distort and impoverish the experience of a whaling captain. He could not make (nor did he wish to make) Captain Ahab into a "typical" Nantucket whaling skipper. He had to leave out a great deal of what an ordinary whaling captain does and says and thinks. The Captain of the *Pequod* must not cuss out the cabin boy in approved Nantucket style. To achieve the magnificent tragedy of Ahab against the universe, Melville was forced to sacrifice much of what a whaling captain was *as a whaling captain*. The "realism" of *Moby-Dick* does not extend to the Captain of the *Pequod*. No one would lament the loss; *Moby-Dick* is worth whatever it cost to make it possible. But all the same, the problem remains. How does the writer evoke the civilized values—of language, religion, philosophy, culture in general—that have traditionally been used to give order and delineate meaning in society, while at the same time remaining faithful to the everyday texture of "low life" experience? How may a whaling captain grapple with the eternal verities and yet be shown doing it in the terms in which such things would confront a whaling captain, and in a mode of language that can reproduce his experience *as* a whaling captain? How many Nantucket whaling skippers, upon confronting their prey, would be heard declaring "Aye, breach your last to the sun, Moby Dick . . . thy hour and thy harpoon are at hand"? How to make a whaling captain into a tragic hero, in other words, without using as model the literary image of a Shakespearean tragedy? This has been the dilemma of the American writer from colonial times onward.

Henry James, in a famous passage about Nathaniel Hawthorne, expressed the cultural problem quite (I will not say succinctly, since that is no word for the style of even the early Henry James) appropriately. Taking his cue from something that Hawthorne himself wrote, James declared that

> one might enumerate the forms of high civilization, as it exists in other countries, which are absent from the texture of American life, until it should be a wonder to know what was left. No State, in the European sense of the word, and indeed barely a specific national name. No sovereign, no court, no personal loyalty, no aristocracy, no church, no clergy, no army, no diplomatic service, no country gentlemen, no palaces, no castles, nor manors, nor old country-houses, nor parsonages, not thatched cottages nor ivied ruins; no cathedrals, nor abbeys, nor little Norman churches; no great Universities nor public schools—no Oxford, nor Eton, nor Harrow; no literature, no novels, no museums, no pictures, no political society, no sporting class—no Epsom nor Ascot! Some such list as that might be drawn up of the absent things in American life—especially in the American life of forty years ago, the effect of which, upon an English or a French imagination, would probably as a general thing be appalling.

But James does not stop there. "The American knows that a good deal remains," he continues; "what it is that remains—that is his secret, his joke, as one may say. It would be cruel, in this terrible denudation, to deny him the consolation of his national gift, that 'American humor' of which of late years we have heard so much." James's words are appropriately chosen, for so much of American literature has focused upon just that national "joke"—by which I take him to mean the fact that in a popular democracy the customary and characteristic institutions that have traditionally embodied cultural, social and ethical values are missing from the scene, and yet the values themselves, and the attitudes that derive from and serve to maintain them, remain very much part of the national experience. This is what Robert Penn Warren meant by the "burr under the metaphysical saddle of America," which pricks whenever the saddle jumps. Out of the incongruity between mundane circumstance and heroic ideal, material fact and spiritual hunger, democratic, middle-class society and desire for cultural definition, theory of equality and fact of social and economic inequality, the Declaration of Independence and the Mann Act, the Gettysburg Address and the Gross National Product, the Battle Hymn of the Republic and the Union Trust Company, the Horatio Alger ideal and the New York Social Register—between what men would be and must be, as acted out in American experience, has come much pathos, no small amount of tragedy, and also a great deal of humor. Both the pathos and the humor have been present from the start, and the writers have been busy pointing them out. This, then, has been what has been called "the great American joke," which comedy has explored and imaged.

One of the more amusing sketches in Joseph Glover Baldwin's *The Flush Times of Alabama and Mississippi* (1853) is that entitled "Simon Suggs, Jr., Esq: A Legal Biography." Baldwin took his character's name from that given to the old scoundrel in Johnson Jones Hooper's Simon Suggs stories. Like his father, Suggs, Jr., is semiliterate and a complete rogue. The sketch opens with some correspondence between Suggs, Jr., and the promoters of a New York biographical magazine, who write to inform him that he has been honored by having been chosen to have his biographical sketch appear in public print, and asking him to furnish biographical details and a suitable daguerreotype. The letter to Suggs, Jr., is couched in the most formal and flowery of terms, but its message is in effect a suggestion that by having his biography appear in the magazine suitably worded, Suggs, Jr., will perhaps be chosen to be a judge some day. To this elaborately worded invitation—"We know from experience, that the characteristic diffidence of the profession, in many instances, shrinks from the seeming, though falsely seeming, indelicacy of an egotistical parade of one's own talents and accomplishments . . ."— Suggs, Jr., responds with misspelled alacrity: "I'm obleeged to you for your perlite say so, and so forth. I got a friend to rite it—my own ritin being mostly perfeshunal. He done it—but he rites such a cussed bad hand I cant rede it: I reckon its all kerrect tho'." He doesn't have a daguerreotype available, but the engraving of his famous father appearing in Hooper's *Some Adventures of Simon Suggs* will do for him if retouched to make him look a bit younger. He then receives another letter from the publisher, thanking him for his sketch, "the description of a lawyer distinguished in the out-door labors of his profession, and directing great energies to the preparation of proof." In a postscript, however, the editor informs Suggs, Jr., that "our delicacy caused us to omit . . . to mention what we suppose was generally understood, viz., the fact that the cost to us of preparing engravings &c. &c., for the sketches or memoirs, is one hundred and fifty dollars, which sum it is expected, of course, the gentleman who is perpetuated in our work, will forward to us before the insertion of his biography. . . ."

Suggs, Jr., now realizes what is going on, and he writes, "*Dear Mr. Editor*—In your p.s. which seems to be the creem of your correspondents you say I can't get in your book without paying one hundred and fifty dollars—pretty tall entrants fee!" He tells them "I believe I will pass. I'll enter a nolly prossy q. O-n-e-h-u-n-d-r-e-d-dollars and fifty better! Je-whellikens." He has begun "to see the pint of many things which was very vague and ondefinit before." And so on.

Following this exchange of correspondence, we then get the text of the biographical sketch which was prepared by Simon Suggs, Jr.'s friend for inclusion in the magazine. It is cast in the elegiac, flowery tone of such self-adulatory biographical sketches, and it makes the most of a very checkered career, putting the kindest construction possible on the events of that career. What is described is the story of various slick dealings by a consummate rogue and trickster, involving much swindling, knavery, and dishonesty, and couched throughout in the most formal and literary of tones. The humor consists of the self-important pomposity of the literary method of narration as it contrasts with the very undignified vernacular antics being described. To wit:

> Col. Suggs also extricated a client and his sureties from a forfeited recognizance, by having the defaulting defandant's obituary notice somewhat prematurely inserted in the newspapers; the solicitor, seeing which, discontinued proceedings; for which service, the deceased, immediately after the adjournment of court, returned to the officer his particular acknowledgements. . . .

The sketch concludes with Simon Suggs, Jr., in Washington attempting to settle claims on behalf of the Choctaw Indians, and with the suggestion that "may the Indians live to get their dividends of the arrears paid to their agent."

Now the humor of this sketch, like that of most of the writings of the humorists of the old nineteenth-century Southern frontier, comes out of the clash of language modes. Baldwin is perhaps the most extreme of all of them in this respect. A well-educated and highly literate man, he adopts the persona of a cultivated gentleman in order to describe the wild, untutored, catch-as-catch-can doings of the old frontier regions. The tone is that of condescension, and the humor arises out of the inappropriateness of the way in which vernacular and usually crass activities are described in quite ornate and pompous language. But although the author's spokesman is a man of culture and refinement who is amused by and somewhat contemptuous of the uninhibited, semicivilized crudeness of the frontier folk, there is also an element of respect for the way that the low-life characters can get right to the point and deal directly with experience. Suggs, Jr.'s shrewdness in spotting what the invitation to submit a sketch for the magazine really involves, his failure to be taken in by the flowery language and erudite circumlocutions of the thing, are, in the context, quite admirable. Suggs, Jr., is a rogue, to be sure, as his biographical sketch admirably demonstrates, but he does not pretend to be anything other than that. The New York entrepreneur, by contrast, is every bit as dishonest. Though his magazine is supposedly designed to supply "a desideratum in American literature, namely, the commemoration and perpetuation of the names, characters, and personal and professional traits and histories of American lawyers and jurists," and though he says that Simon, Jr., has been selected for inclusion by "many of the most prominent gentlemen in public and private life, who have the honor of your acquaintance," what he is really doing is selling self-advertisements in the guise of biographical sketches. Unlike Simon, Jr., however, he pretends to be doing so "from motives purely patriotic and disinterested," in order that "through our labors, the reputation of distinguished men of the country, constituting its moral treasure, may be preserved for the admiration and direction of mankind, not for a day, but for all time." Suggs, Jr., in brief, is a crude but honest rogue, and the editor of the magazine is a civilized but hypocritical confidence man.

Here, indeed, is the elementary, basic American humorous situation— the "great American joke," and in one very obvious form. The humor arises out of the gap between the cultural ideal and the everyday fact, with the ideal shown to be somewhat hollow and hypocritical, and the fact crude and disgusting.

The so-called frontier humor was admirably constituted to image the problems of meaning and existence in a society that was very much caught up in the process of formation. In the Old Southwest—Georgia, West Florida, Alabama, Mississippi—of the 1820's, 1830's, and 1840's, virgin wilderness was almost overnight being converted into farmland, and towns and cities coming into being where the forest trails crossed. New wealth was being created, and old fortunes either vastly augmented or lost overnight. Rich and poor flocked into the new lands, and the social distinctions brought from the older society of the Eastern seaboard were very much disordered and distorted by the new circumstance. The ability to parse a Latin verb or ride to the hounds would be less than completely useful in the fashionable parlors of Tuscaloosa, Alabama, and Columbus, Mississippi, for some time to come. Society, in other words, was being reordered, and former distinctions of class and caste rearranged in accordance with the realities of wealth and power in a changed community. Since language, education, culture are always ultimately grounded in social position, the social confusion of an open frontier society is reflected in a confusion of language and cultural modes and attitudes. It will take several generations for the descendants of a

Simon Suggs, Jr., to acquire the social polish and cultural sophistication that educational advantages made possible by new wealth can ultimately afford them; and the effort to chronicle the checkered career of an opportunistic rascal in the sophisticated language appropriate to a biographical sketch in an Eastern magazine provides the rich incongruity that Baldwin could draw on for purposes of humor.

The clash between the ideal and the real, between value and fact, is of course not an exclusively American motif. Cervantes rang the changes on it in *Don Quixote*, and Aristophanes before him. But a society based theoretically upon the equality of all men, yet made up of human beings very unequal in individual endowment, and containing within it many striking social, economic and racial differences, is more than ordinarily blessed with such problems in human and social definition, and the incongruities are likely to be especially observable. The very conditions of a frontier society, with its absence of settled patterns and with its opportunities for freedom and individuality, are ideally suited for this kind of humor. One finds it already in flower long before the Declaration of Independence. Consider a work such as William Byrd II's *History of the Dividing Line*. An English-educated planter, trained for the law in the Middle Temple, member of the Royal Society, one accustomed to command and to receiving the deference due a wealthy planter, goes off with a surveying party to determine the boundary line between the Virginia and the North Carolina colonies. There in the Dismal Swamp he encounters rustics who are without culture, refinement, ambition, or wealth, and who moreover do not seem to feel the lack of such commodities very much. His response is to poke fun at them, to use ridicule to rebuke the failure of the vulgar fact to approximate the cultural and social ideal. So he adopts a mode of language that through its inappropriateness to the triviality of the occasion, makes the settlers appear ludicrous: they "stand leaning with both their arms upon the cornfield fence, and *gravely consider* whether they had best go and take a small heat at the hoe . . ." [italics mine]. Here again is the same clash of modes that Baldwin and the Southwestern Humorists would use to chronicle the New Men in the New Territory. In both instances the fact—the ordinary man, as he is, unregenerate and uncaring—is satirized by being described in a language mode customarily reserved for more elevated subject matter. But where in Byrd the satire is all directed at the low-life objects, in Baldwin it is not so one-sided. For though Baldwin is a Virginian and a Whig and a man of education and culture, he is enough of a democratic American to admire the independence and the practicality of his low-life characters just a little, and so he does not confine his ridicule to them. He turns the language mode, the elevated diction, back on itself. He is consciously over-elegant, overly genteel in his choice of phraseology, so that the formal diction, the language of Culture, is also being mocked. The Great American Joke thus works both ways, and the incongruity illuminates the shortcomings of both modes.

Neither Byrd's *History of the Dividing Line* nor Baldwin's *Flush Times in Alabama and Mississippi* is, strictly speaking, literature, so much as subliterature. The one is narrative history, the other humorous journalism. Neither was designed purely or primarily as full-fledged artistic statement. But the same kind of incongruity they offer, the clash of genteel and vulgar modes, has been incorporated into the comic art of many of America's best and most respected writers. A single example will suffice to illustrate. The twentieth-century novelist William Faulkner has not only written certain novels that are possibly the only genuine literary tragedy produced by an American author in this century, but he is also one of the finest comic writers in American literature. In his comic masterpiece, *The Hamlet*, Flem Snopes and a Texan bring a herd of wild Texas horses to Mississippi and offer them for sale at very low prices. They are snapped up by the inhabitants, who are then invited to claim the horses they have purchased. Before very long wild horses are being pursued all over the landscape; they jump fences, leap over people, run into houses, overturn wagons, until as nighttime comes they are scattered over miles of countryside. One hapless purchaser, felled by the stampeding Texas herd, is carried unconscious into a house by some of his friends. Afterwards they go outside:

> They went out; they didn't look back. They tiptoed up the hall and crossed the veranda and descended into the moonlight. Now that they could pay attention to it, the silver air seemed to be filled with faint and sourceless sounds—shouts, thin and distant, again a brief thunder of hooves on a wooden bridge, more shouts faint and thin and earnest and clear as bells; once they even distinguished the words: "Whooey. Head him."

Once again, both language modes are at work: the heightened literary diction, drawing on the full resources of cadenced prose and metaphor, and the vivid colloquial counterthrust. The haunting, beautiful description of the pursuit over the pastoral landscape is undercut by the broad vulgar comedy of the actual fact itself—the hoodwinked farmers vainly attempting to corral their untamable purchases. But Faulkner is not satirizing his characters; the human dignity he has given them as they go about the activities that are the plot of *The Hamlet* is such that, though they are "low-life," they are not thereby debased. Thus when, with the escape of the wild horses and their pursuit, he moves into the mode of formal literary diction and metaphor to describe what happens, the effect of incongruity does not produce satire and ridicule, so much as a delightful counterpoint of modes that plays them back and forth, against and around and along with each other. The shouting *is* "faint and thin and earnest and clear as bells," even as they *do* call out "Whooey. Head him." The contrast of literary language and poetic description with vernacular fact and colloquial speech is developed into as marvelously comic a scene as any in American literature. Both elements are at work, and in their juxtaposition each delineates the other. It is a masterful intensification of the same brand of humor as that of Byrd's *Dividing Line*, Baldwin's *Flush Times*, Irving's *Knickerbocker History*, Long-street's *Georgia Scenes*, Clemens's *Connecticut Yankee*, Hemingway's *Torrents of Spring*, Barth's *Sot-Weed Factor*, and many another work of American comedy. It is the interplay of the ornamental and the elemental, the language of culture and the language of sweat, the democratic ideal and the mulishness of fallen human nature—the Great American Joke. To quote the business partner of Thomas Wolfe's Bascom Pentland in *Of Time and the River*, "the Reverend knows words the average man aint never heard. He knows words that aint even in the dictionary. Yes, sir!—an' uses them too—all the time!"

QUESTIONS

1. According to Rubin, what is the highest praise we give a humorist? What does this imply about comedy?

2. How does Rubin define the essence of comedy? Why is comedy especially important in a democracy?

3. Explain the quotation from Robert Penn Warren. How does it express a central motif in American humor? Discuss the relationship between the style of Warren's remark and its substance.

4. What is "the problem of democracy and culture"? How did Jefferson hope to solve it? How successful has Jefferson's plan been? What do you think Henry Adams would say if he could comment on contemporary politics?

5. What was Melville's problem in *Moby-Dick*? How was it resolved? Name other American writers who have faced a similar dilemma.

6. What is the Great American Joke? Explain how it works two ways. How is it illustrated in the anecdote about Simon Suggs, Jr.?

7. How is the Great American Joke central in Faulkner's "The Auction of the Spotted Horses"? How important is it in other selections in this book?

The American Sense of Humor

Louis Kronenberger

The broad societal implications of our comic tradition are taken up again in this article by Louis Kronenberger, who is critical of what our sense of humor—or lack of it—reveals about us. Paradoxically, he suggests that we lack great wit precisely because we have suffered so little, and he foresees a dim future for American humor. By contrasting the American brand of comedy with that of other nations, he helps us gain a broader perspective on both our humor and our culture. This essay is included in Kronenberger's well-known collection Company Manners.

There is perhaps nothing we Americans feel more certain of than our sense of humor. In partial proof we can point to a vital humorous tradition and to a long, still-flourishing line of humorists. For the rest, it is indisputable that we have a famous method of joking. That method—very logical in a young, expansive, bumptious people—has been one of overstatement and exaggeration, of the tall tale and the woolly yarn, of bringing to our jests something of that giantism that has molded our dreams: we even joke, as it were, in six figures. Ours has been, almost entirely, a humor of release rather than reflectiveness, a fizz rather than a *fine*. There is little that is wise, there is little that is melancholy, about American humor—little, even, that can be called rueful. Possibly the best thing about it is the disbelief that gets hitched on behind the bragging, the "Sez you" that is tossed after the "And I said to him." But the snorting has much the same crudity as the boastfulness. We meet the braggart too much on his own terms: for though a world of humor can be insinuated into a mock bow, not much is possible to a Bronx cheer. Nor is the breezy manner at all a mask of seriousness. It's precisely because we are not, in the best sense, a serious people that we have ceased, in the best sense, to be a humorous one. At our worst, we have made our humor the handle of our acquisitiveness, a trick way of getting our foot in the door. Not only do we precede the moment of sale with the one about the two Irishmen, but signing on the dotted line is itself a quip.

It is because there is no longer a deeply self-critical quality in our humor that it is so much less cathartic. Our humor has become a confederate of our faults rather than their prosecutor. This has partly to do with our being such cocks of the walk, such top dogs in the struggle of life. The underprivileged, the downtrodden, the disreputable crack jokes that tell consciously against themselves or that make a sad fun of their betters. "If this is how Her Majesty treats her prisoners," said Oscar Wilde, standing handcuffed in the pouring rain, "she doesn't deserve to have any." With such humor there will often go a certain self-pity as well, or a certain twisted contempt—the sharper's contempt for the sucker, the rogue's for the gull. But the humor of such people, even where it is cruel, is the badge of their humanity, of what makes them despise, equally, their victim and themselves. Such people have usually suffered enough, sinned enough, faced the truth about themselves enough, to *feel* the joke. In most good jokes about crooks, about failures, about trades or races or groups that are looked down on or discriminated against, there is an element to be shared, as it were, between *professionals:* they share and react to the joke as two artisans share and react to a piece of technical skill. Americans, in this sense, seldom "experience" a joke; they merely get the point of it.[1] Their jokes have become a kind of surface communication—the latest gag is a way out of having to find something to talk about, or a mere preamble to getting down to business. The breezy approach enables one, without changing the tone of one's voice, to change the basis of one's talk. Our national joke is the one about the traveling salesman and the farmer's obligingly innocent daughter—and fittingly so, since that is our dream *business* relationship as well as sexual one.

Yet even here we have covered up our tracks, transposed our symbol; for the difference between us and more serious or self-accepting races is that where their jokes are a way of acknowledging their true motives, ours are frequently a way of trying to conceal them. We try to suggest that there is a strong playful element in all our business dealings, but increasingly, I think, there is a certain self-seeking in all our playfulness. We "entertain" clients; we hand over tricky contracts with a "better have a damn smart lawyer give *this* the once-over"; we crack wise to take advantage of an employee—"Gotta chain you to the galleys tonight"; we make gags as a way of minimizing resentment. Originally much of this sprang from something genuinely friendly and democratic in American life, but more and more—and all the more for having the appearance of real humor—it is becoming a device.

We possess a certain natural good humor, but no great sense of humor about ourselves, no very rueful appreciation of our plights. We are not at all an ironic people, so that once our humor loses its disinterestedness it tends to become cynical and hard-boiled, a sort of cold chuckle. Our

---

[1] Which is not unrelated to our already obsessive and yet increasing enjoyment of the gag—a form of humor that for the most part has point *without* substance.

breezy averageness robs us, moreover, of stance and style. No American, faced with the proofs of his grand-scale buccaneering, would confess himself like Clive, "amazed at my own moderation." Our modern sports-jacket approach to the world—so youthful, playful, *un*business-like—is a touch misleading. To begin with, though it seems to break with a stuffy, over-solemn tradition, it is much more the product of an *arriviste* business class that never knew any such tradition and that, finding shirt sleeves comfortable, have gone on to make them respectable.

As for our brand of humor, the tall tale of the nineteenth century, being the expression of a young, healthy, hell-raising frontier people, gave something new and exhilarating to the humor of the world. Our contributions in the twentieth century—the gag, the wisecrack, the comeback, the nifty, the clincher—are nowhere so good. As long as it was expertly used—indeed, scrupulously stylized—in old vaudeville routines; as long, too, as it represented a second stage of American humor, a kind of retort on the tall tale's boastfulness, the American gag had its real virtues. But we have turned the gag into a mechanical, ubiquitous, incessant national tool so brassy as to be vulgar, so unchanging as to be dull. As for the comeback, though fond of it, we have never been very good at it; in terms of cussing and repartee alike, our truck drivers are mere duffers by comparison with even the average cockney. After all, the essence of a good comeback is a certain delayed sting, a certain perfection of surface politeness. Two Frenchmen who had been brilliant and bitterly hostile rivals at school went on to become a famous general and a distinguished cardinal. The cardinal, seeing the general, after many years, on a railway platform, approached him haughtily and said, "Mr. Stationmaster, when does the next train leave for Bordeaux?" The general paused, smiled, said, "At half past two, madame." By comparison, how very American at bottom is the most famous of modern comebacks; how lacking in all subtlety and in any final wit is Whistler's [remark, in response to Wilde's "I wish I'd said that"] "You will, Oscar, you will."

There is a reason, I think, why our comebacks are so crudely, so overtly abusive. The comeback flowers best in a class-ridden society where people must preserve at least the *form* of knowing their place and are thus driven in their retorts into understatement, or double meanings, or irony. Or it flowers in a cultivated formal society, where the urbanity of the language is wholly at variance with the brutality of the sentiment. In a democracy, where one is free to speak one's mind, one is prevented, as it were, from being insolent. We heckle rather than insinuate, and we *borrow* forms of abuse rather than invent them. We have even a sort of defensive guile about our lack of polish and subtlety in these matters. "An epigram," Oscar Levant once said, "is a wisecrack that has played

Carnegie Hall." But it is not, and in his heart Mr. Levant must be quite aware that it is not.

That our humor isn't deep or cleansing would seem belied by a great many things—though it is perhaps just those things that bear out my contention. We are humor-conscious much as we are culture-conscious; we are extremely worried that we won't seem to show sense of humor enough (particularly as a "sense of humor" has become a synonym for being a good sport). We joke incessantly—but partly from having reduced an attitude to a mere habit, and partly because, conversationally, we have so little to say. We shop for humor, we constantly listen to humor—on radio and TV, at movies and shows; but that is from lacking more serious cultural interests and from being so bored with ourselves when left alone. We have, generally, a brisk manner; we many of us lead bustling lives; we are still a "youthful" and often boisterous, slangy, sassy nation; and all this would seem to make us notably humorous. But a moment's reflection (a rare American trait) would suggest that humor is not a matter of being brisk, but of being reflective.

And though we once were open and hearty, were we ever—at any significant level—deeply humorous? In fact, could we have been? I say this rather to characterize than disparage us: humor, for one thing, isn't all pure gain; and for another, though purgative and health-giving, it often bulks largest in people who themselves are not healthy. Humor must largely constitute an appreciation, even an airing, of one's own and one's community's and one's country's faults, rather than a tribute to their virtues; or if that comes too close to defining satire, then humor is a gay confession and a wry acceptance of what makes us fools and sinners, goatish as well as godlike. Humor simultaneously wounds and heals, indicts and pardons, diminishes and enlarges; it constitutes inner growth at the expense of outer gain, and those who possess and honestly practice it make themselves more through a willingness to make themselves less.

Perhaps no young race can, in the very best sense, *be* humorous for the crueler, cruder, more boyish, prankish, exuberant forms of humor neither greatly express nor truly educate. And it has been our misfortune as we have grown older not to have had, in our personal lives, misfortune enough, not to have been compelled to reflect or made to suffer. Creatures of noise and hurry, of hope and assurance, we have not had the time, we have never felt the need, to think hard on our problems or to confess our weaknesses. We have kept certain dead donkeys in our stables so as not to have to flay the living ones—and certain standard "goats" as well. Our national jokes are the umpire, the Milquetoast, the henpecked husband, the interfering mother-in-law, longhairs and sissies (whom we don't accurately define), suckers for gold bricks (the fool, not the knave!), and not the city slicker but the hick. All the symbols of push, of philistinism, of sharp practice—the joiner, the yes-man, the salesman, the Chamber of Commerce—are satiric figures created by an enlightened minority and objects of laughter to but a relative few. We laugh at polish (that is to say, Harvard) rather than push, at high-brows sooner than louts. Our humor is largely at the expense of what it is safe and indeed quite proper to despise: of what we don't want to be, can afford not to be, can with impunity make fun of. Even corruption thrives as a joke at the expense of those who *can't* horn in on it. We don't make fun of ourselves—only of our minorities and failures, of those who don't conform or assert themselves or measure up. Our humor, where it is directed inward and not at mere "goats," is almost completely flattering. We kid ourselves for being such reckless spenders and sports, such suckers for a good-looking girl, such soft touches for a hard-luck story; or, worse, we jest about what is wrong in terms that would make it seem right—just overgrown "boys" at reunions and conventions; just "cards" for perpetrators of various cruelties. We are really apologists for ourselves, as opposed to races that, like Negroes and Italians, have humility, or, like the Spaniards and Scots, have pride. In any important context, we tend to fear and fight off humor: Adlai Stevenson's Presidential campaign was a real anomaly and one that the nation felt sure could backfire.

No doubt humor, in the personal sense, is a distillate of suffering and, in the poetic sense, of melancholy; and it is no coincidence that we so often find it among the have-not races. More fortunate races, given to contemplate their blessings and to wonder how much they truly bless, are more likely to become ironic than humorous. America, in the deep sense, has neither irony nor humor. It is, on the one hand, still too naive; on the other, too shallow; in its ambitions and aggressions it is too much consumed with self-importance. Americans don't habitually see the wry humor of their plight, the sad irony of their triumphs; they go right on affirming the values that, even at the beginning, they hardly so much chose as had foisted upon them. They are only saved morally in the degree that they are so genuinely and wistfully lost. They haven't the melancholy of humor, but are the more lost, and more melancholy, for lacking it.

If we lack profound humor for lacking this poetic sense of melancholy, we lack it too from having so largely ceased to be spectators of life. We are much more a part of the game itself, or of the crowd who themselves insist on being looked at. And we seem destined to become a less humorous people because our twin gospels of Belonging and of Getting Ahead foster a sense of self-importance. Says a character in Sholem Aleichem: "I was, with God's help, a poor man." Americans, far from savoring such remarks, would quite fail to grasp their meaning. Humor, to most Americans, is not an inward way of looking at life, but an outward, good-guy way of living it. Humor, to most Americans, means grinning rather than getting sore when somebody hits you with a snowball, or laughing at yourself when you lose out through carelessness or anger. Humor, in other words, is for most Americans a matter of conduct rather than character, of the proper reaction rather than the owned-up-to-motive, and is but another facet of conformity. It is also a tactic at the other fellow's expense—a way of side-stepping sensibility and shame rather than feeling them. We hope—indeed often expect—that the wronged person will laugh the thing off so that we can join in, that *his* "seeing the humor in it" will take us off the spot. Increasingly, our humor shows a vital lack of criticism and insight, fails to educate either the heart or the mind; it is chiefly a salve or poultice for easing tensions, preventing scenes and snarls. Humor, it seems to me, has become a kind of national front, as politeness is with the French.

QUESTIONS

1. Why does Kronenberger feel that Americans seldom "experience" a joke, but merely get the point of it? What is our national joke? How does it fit us?

2. Why do we shop for humor? What is the relationship between comedy and reflection? Between comedy and suffering?

3. Describe our brand of humor in the nineteenth century. In the twentieth. How are the two related?

4. What is the essence of a good comeback? How is it revealed in the conversation between the two Frenchmen? In what kinds of societies do comebacks flourish? Why does Kronenberger disagree with Oscar Levant's definition of an epigram?

5. "We have kept certain dead donkeys in our stables so as not to have to flay the living ones—and certain standard 'goats' as well." What are these "goats"? Which real ones does Kronenberger think we ignore? Do you agree that our humor is almost completely flattering? Explain.

6. In what way is our humor a kind of "national front"? What evidence supports the claim that we are destined to become an even less humorous people?

The Tall Tale

Constance Rourke

Since it first appeared in 1931, Constance Rourke's American Humor: A Study of the National Character *has become a classic, praised as highly for its lively style as for its original interpretation of our cultural history. In the following selection she defines the tall tale, explaining how it both reflected American society and influenced its development. Other books by Rourke include* Davy Crockett *and* The Roots of American Culture.

The backwoodsman's fancy roamed over two figures of his own kind: Davy Crockett, the hunter and backwoods oracle, and Mike Fink, known in legend as the first flatboatman who dared to take a broadhorn over the Falls of the Ohio. Fink's frolics and pranks, his feats of strength, his marksmanship, became themes for endless story-telling. He had ridden a moose like a horse through wild country. In a canoe on the Mississippi he had grasped a she-wolf swimming to attack him, and had held her under water until she drowned. As an Indian stood on a hill proudly silhouetted against the sky with his scalp lock and hawk's feather etched clear, Fink—below him and many yards distant—raised his rifle: the Indian leapt high into the air and fell to the ground. The act was as cruel as deliberate murder, for Fink—as he intended—had severed the Indian's scalp lock. Many of the tales exhibited the broad, blind cruelty of the backwoods; yet many of them insisted that Fink was good. The abstract quality was habitually attached to shaggy backwoods heroes in later tales.

Mike Fink passed into legend not only because of his early exploits on the rivers but because he was the last of the boatmen—or so he was called—clinging contentiously to his broadhorn long after the steamboats came, when men could not be induced to travel in a low wooden ark. The tales about him became an elegy to wild days that were past or passing. "What's the use of improvements? Where's the fun, the frolicking, the fighting?" he cried in one of them. "Gone! All gone!" The sad noisy sentiment mounted through twenty years or more. The exploits of Fink were still being celebrated during the '50's by the western almanacs. He even passed into literary discussion: one writer said that if he had lived in early Greece his feats would have rivaled those of Jason,

and that among the Scandinavians he would have become a river-god.
He was in fact a Mississippi river-god, one of those minor deities
whom men create in their own image and magnify to magnify
themselves. Gradually he grew super-sized; he had eaten a buffalo robe,
but New England rum had ruined his stomach. He became Mike Finch,
Mike Finx, Mike Wing, in a hundred minor tales. Driven at last from the
Mississippi, he moved into the unknown regions of the farther West,
achieving the final glory of heroes, a death wrapped in mystery, indeed
many deaths, for the true story was lost, and others sprang up.

Mike Fink embodied the traditional history of the hero, but he never
attained the nation-wide fame of Crockett, nor did he embody so many
aspects of life on the frontier, or slip—as Crockett did—into poetic
legend. Crockett first emerged as a coonskin follower of Jackson; he later
became Jackson's opponent, and was transformed into an oracle
throughout the land, with a position similar to that of Jack Downing.
Squibs and stories were contrived, purporting to reveal discussions
between them—the legendary and the living figure. Crockett's philosophy was simple: he wanted to save the land from the speculator. In this
early phase he was rather more the settler than the huntsman. In his
autobiography, which seems to have been taken down as he did it,
fragments of old dance and labor songs appeared—"Now weed corn,
kiver taters, double shuffle!" He repeated other songs reminiscent of
work in the fields and of old country games—

> We are on our way to Baltimore
> With two behind and two before,
> Around, around, around we go,
> Where oats, peas, beans, and barley grow,
>   In waiting for somebody. (A *kiss*)

> 'Tis thus the farmer sows his seed,
> Folds his arms and takes his ease,
> Stamps his feet and claps his hands,
> Wheels around and thus he stands,
>   In waiting for somebody. (A *kiss*)

The whir of the spinning wheel could be heard in this narrative, and the
phrases of homely proverbs. "A short horse is soon curried." "If a fellow
is born to be hung he will never be drowned."

But hog and hominy were soon mixed with air and thunder. Even in
the autobiography Crockett's magnified exploits of marksmanship and
strength were pictured—by himself. Soon still greater feats were attached
to him. He had climbed a tree upwards of a hundred times that rose
thirty feet without branches, sliding down and climbing up again to
break the chill after a plunge into icy water. He was "shaggy as a bear,

wolfish about the head, and could grin like a hyena until the bark would curl off a gum log." He had fiercely grinned at what he took to be a raccoon in the topmost crotch of a tree, but the beast failed to fall before his spell, and the striped circle proved to be a knothole from which his grin had stripped the bark. He was full of "quirky humors," and fought and neighed and crowed and proclaimed himself the "yallerest blossom of the forest." He could whip his weight in wild cats. "Gentlemen," the legendary Crockett boasted, "I'm the darling branch of old Kentuck that can eat up a painter, hold a buffalo out to drink, and put a rifle-ball through the moon."

Crockett became a myth even in his own lifetime. Other spurious autobiographies were offered as his own; he was made the hero of a hundred popular tales repeated by word of mouth and circulated in newspapers and almanacs. After his death in 1836 he was boldly appropriated by the popular fancy. His heroic stand at the Alamo was richly described; and laments arose in the western wilderness. "That's a great rejoicin' among the bears of Kaintuck, and the alligators of the Mississippi rolls up thar shinin' ribs to the sun, and has grown so fat and lazy that they will hardly move out of the way for a steamboat. The rattlesnakes come up out of thar holes and frolic within ten foot of the clearings, and the foxes goes to sleep in the goose-pens. It is bekos the rifle of Crockett is silent forever, and the print of his moccasins is found no more in our woods."

Then Crockett reappeared in popular stories as though he had never died, assuming an even bolder legendary stature than before. The story of his life in one of the almanacs began by picturing him as a baby giant planted in a rock bed as soon as he was born and watered with wild buffalo's milk. Another declared that as a boy he tied together the tails of two buffaloes and carried home five tiger cubs in his cap. In another he wrung the tail off a comet, and announced that he could "travel so all lightnin' fast that I've been known to strike fire agin the wind." Lightning glanced through all the stories. By leaping astride the lightning Crockett escaped from a tornado on the Mississippi when houses came apart and trees walked out by their roots. He could make lightning by striking his own eye. He could make fire by rubbing a flint with his knuckles. On one of his adventures he was barred by an "Injun rock so 'tarnal high, so all flinty hard that it will turn off a common streak of lightnin' and make it point downward and look as flat as a cow's tail." Once he escaped up Niagara Falls on an alligator. "The alligator walked up the great hill of water as slick as a wild cat up a white oak."

For the most part Crockett was a wanderer, moving westward, to Texas, across the plains, to California, to Japan—for pearls—and to the South Seas. Diving there, he came to a cave, crawled until he reached dry land in the deepest depths beneath the ocean, made a lampwick out of his hair, soaked it in elbow-grease, and struck a light with his knuckles on a rock.

"Now I tell you what," people would say of some strange happening, "it's nothing to Crockett."

In the end he became a demigod, or at least a Prometheus. "One January morning it was so all screwen cold that the forest trees were stiff and they couldn't shake, and the very daybreak froze fast as it was trying to dawn. The tinder box in my cabin would no more ketch fire than a sunk raft at the bottom of the sea. Well, seein' daylight war so far behind time I thought creation war in a fair way for freezen fast: so, thinks I, I must strike a little fire from my fingers, light my pipe, an' travel out a few leagues, and see about it. Then I brought my knuckles together like two thunderclouds, but the sparks froze up afore I could begin to collect 'em, so out I walked, whistlin' 'Fire in the mountains!' as I went along in three double quick time. Well, arter I had walked about twenty miles up the Pcak o' Day and Daybreak Hill I soon discovered what war the matter. The airth had actually friz fast on her axes, and couldn't turn round; the sun had got jammed between two cakes o' ice under the wheels, an' thar he had been shinin' an' workin' to get loose till he friz fast in his cold sweat. C-r-e-a-t-i-o-n! thought I, this ar the toughest sort of suspension, an' it mustn't be endured. Somethin' must be done, or human creation is done for. It war then so anteluvian an' premature cold that my upper and lower teeth an' tongue war all collapsed together as tight as a friz oyster; but I took a fresh twenty-pound bear off my back that I'd picked up on my road, and beat the animal agin the ice till the hot ile began to walk out on him at all sides. I then took an' held him over the airth's axes an' squeezed him till I'd thawed 'em loose, poured about a ton on't over the sun's face, give the airth's cog-wheel one kick backward till I got the sun loose—whistled 'Push along, keep movin'!' an' in about fifteen seconds the airth gave a grunt, an' began movin'. The sun walked up beautiful, salutin' me with sich a wind o' gratitude that it made me sneeze. I lit my pipe by the blaze o' his top-knot, shouldered my bear, an' walked home, introducin' people to the fresh daylight with a piece of sunrise in my pocket."

As the tall tale came into its great prime in the early '30's a sudden contagion was created. A series of newspaper hoaxes sprang into life in the East. The scale was western, the tone that of calm, scientific exposition of wonders such as often belonged to western comic legend. Explorations of the moon by telescope, voyages to the moon or across the Atlantic by balloon, were explained in the imperturbable manner of the tall tale, verging aggressively toward the appearance of truth and sheering away again. They were circumstantial, closely colored; yet they broke all possible bounds and reached toward poetry, making snares out of natural elements or even from the cosmos. No single character dominated them, and they went off at a long tangent from popular lingo; yet the alliance seems clear. Similar monstrous practical jokes were being played with the sun, moon, stars, winds, waves, and water in the tall talk of the West.

The new inflation crept into New England: and Uncle Zeke sat on the bottom of the river pouring powder from one horn into another. Improbable reverberations were heard in Philadelphia, which quickly became a fountainhead of American jokes. An old gentleman was so absent-minded that he tucked his pantaloons into bed one night and hung himself on the back of his chair, where he froze to death. Another had whiskey so good that when he drank it he spoke broad Scotch. A man was so tall that he had to get up on a ladder to shave himself. There was the immemorial oyster, so large that two men were required to swallow it. Many of these tall tales in miniature have never died, and there was a reason for their sturdy continuance. Consciousness of native humor had dawned; and these little tall tales were pristine; they wore the lustrous air of new birth. They were therefore appropriated with loyalty and preserved as carefully as the old men hung up in bags in one of Hawley's Rocky Mountain stories. Again and again they were taken out, like the old men, and revived. Dry and wispy as they became, they continued for years to betray the sense of jubilant discovery.

With them came a long sequence of stories—chiefly hunting stories— in which the hunter killed or captured a bagful of game at a single stroke. In danger from the onslaught of a bear and a moose, he aimed at a sharp-edged rock; the split bullet killed both, and fragments of rock flew into a tree and killed a squirrel. The recoil knocked him backward into a river; swimming to the shore, he found his coat full of trout, and other fish flopped from his trousers. Such tales were told throughout the century and perhaps have never died. Their lineage is long: they appear in shy forms on the New England frontier of the eighteenth century. No doubt they have a far older ancestry, going back to fairy tales of Europe in which a hunter or a poor man wanders all day without finding game, and then encounters magical events in the forest. Touches of natural magic remain in the later inventions, but the excess belongs to the American frontier. It was in the West that these tales took on their final inflation; and from the West they spread over the country.

Not only the expansive effect but strange new words came rolling out of the West. The backwoodsman may have gained his freedom with language from that large era of the sixteenth or early seventeenth century out of which many of his progenitors had stepped, passing so soon into the wilderness as to preserve their habits of speech, and to be uninfluenced, presumably, by the later stability of the English language. At least he was full of free inventions. "Absquatulate," "slantendiclur," "cahoot," "catawampus," "spyficated," "flabbergasted," "tarnacious," "rampagious," "concussence," "supernatiousness," "rumsquattle," and dozens of other ear-splitting syllables were among his novelties—sudden comic shouts or mock pompous words. Some of these passed into common use and moved eastward to join with the drawling speech of New England, mixing with the less marked vernacular.

Tall talk echoed from Florida to Oregon with whoops and boasting, and a larger verbal thunder rose to match it in the fantasy of western oratory. "What orator," said a Kentuckian, "can deign to restrain his imagination within a vulgar and sterile state of facts?" Said another, "The eloquence of the East is sober, passionless, condensed, metaphysical; that of the West is free, lofty, agitating, grand, impassioned. . . . The West defies and transcends criticism."

"The literature of a young and free people will of course be declamatory," said an oratorical writer in 1834, who was drenched in western ideas. "Deeper learning will no doubt abate its verbosity and intumescence; but our natural scenery and our liberal political and social institutions must long continue to maintain its character of floridness. And what is there in this that should excite regret in ourselves, or raise derision in others?" he queried—with remembrance of the parent critics across the sea. "Ought not the literature of a free people to be declamatory?" he reasoned. "Whenever the literature of a new country loses its metaphorical and declamatory character, the institutions which depend on public sentiment will languish and decline. . . . A people who have fresh and lively feelings will always relish oratory."

The American people relished oratory. With the beginnings of the Jacksonian democracy public speech burst forth in a never-ending flood. "And how, sir, shall I speak of him," said a member from Mississippi of Calhoun in 1840—"he who is so justly esteemed the wonder of the world, the astonisher of mankind? Like the great Niagara, he goes dashing and sweeping on, bidding all created things give way, and bearing down, in his resistless course, all who have the temerity to oppose his onward career. He, sir, is indeed the cataract, the political Niagara of America; and, like that noblest work of nature and of nature's God, he will stand through all after-time no less the wonder than the admiration of the world. His was the bright star of genius that in early life shot madly forth, and left the lesser satellites that may have dazzled in its blaze to that impenetrable darkness to which nature's stern decree had destined them; his the broad expansive wing of genius, under which his country sought political protection. . . . He stands beneath the consecrated arch, defended by a lightning shut up in the hearts of his countrymen—by a lightning that will not slumber but will leap forth to avenge even a word, a thought, a look, that threatens him with insult. The story of his virtuous fame is written in the highest vault of our political canopy, far above the reach of groveling speculation, where it can alone be sought upon the eagle's pinions and be gazed at by an eagle's eye. . . ."

This encomium was offered as "buncombe"—as burlesque. It sprang from a region where tall tales flourished. In similar set pieces every feather of the eagle was accounted for and magnified. Orators kept the bird so continuously in flight from the peak of the Alleghanies to the top of Mount Hood that its shadow was said to have worn a trail across the basin of the Mississippi. Niagara continued to roar; the inevitable lightning flashed. The thunderous echoes were heard in New England, and the Yankee as well as the backwoodsman learned the art of comic oratory. Barnum enjoyed it in his early years. Dickens regarded it with indignation. Serious oratory rose and fell in similar cascades, but so far-reaching was the burlesque that it was often impossible to tell one from the other without a wide context of knowledge as to the subject and the speakers. Popular declamation of the '30's and '40's has often been considered as bombast when it should be taken as comic mythology.

An exhilarated and possessive consciousness of a new earth and even of the wide universe ran through this tall talk and the tall tales; they were striated by a naturalistic poetry. Inflation appeared with an air of wonder, which became mock wonder at times but maintained the poetic mode. The Crockett stories even distantly approached the realm of the epic, not merely because of the persistent effect of scale or because of their theme of wandering adventure, but because they embodied something of those interwoven destinies of gods and men which have made the great epical substance. The tales were brief and scattered; the bias was comic; a perverse and wayward spirit was abroad. The animistic might take the place of the godlike presence, appearing in the spirit which sent the squash vines chasing pigs or hoisted Brother Joe to the skies through the medium of shrinking leather. But half-gods had taken shape and walked the earth with a familiar look in the later Davy Crockett and Mike Fink; and around them faint shapes emerged of a similar large mold.

"I saw a little woman streaking it along through the woods like all wrath," said Crockett in one of the almanac stories. Sally Ann Thunder Ann Whirlwind Crockett wore a hornet's nest trimmed with wolves' tails for a bonnet and a dress of a whole bear's hide with the tail for a train; she could shoot a wild goose flying, wade the Mississippi without wetting her shift, and stamp on a litter of wild cats. Mike Fink had a huge daughter who could whistle with one corner of her mouth, eat with the other, and scream with the middle, and who had tamed a full-grown bear. Another figure appeared as an occasional companion of Crockett's, Ben Hardin, a well-known character in Kentucky who claimed that he had been a sailor on far seas and had consorted with mermaids. It was with Hardin in tow that Crockett performed some of his boldest exploits. The outlines of a supernatural hierarchy were sketched in these figures; and beyond them lay dim others belonging to local legend who might grow into a dynamic stature.

The whole history of these tales can never be traced, so transient were they, so quickly passed on and embellished, so rarely recorded. They belonged to that wide portion of the West known as the old Southwest, which spread from Kentucky and Tennessee in a broad encirclement through Georgia and the Gulf States to Texas and Arkansas, reaching beyond the Mississippi as the scout and huntsman and pioneer moved from his first base of the dark and bloody ground. The tales spread indeed over the entire country. The Crockett almanacs, widely circulated in the West, were reprinted in New England; and the stories which they contained were often caught up by other local almanacs and newspapers. Some of the almanac stories were clearly the work of sophisticated minds, but even when the hand of the skilled writer shows, a homely origin is usually plain. Many of them appear as direct transcriptions of tales current in the West. They were linked at times to make a consistent legend, but fragments were given place which sound like casual talk picked up first hand; and gross inconsistency in tone or handling was uncommon. The talk was that southern talk with a mellowed roughness which became the popular speech of the West.

Even on their own ground these tales took on finish, for they flourished not only among boatmen and backwoodsmen, but at the annual meetings of the bar in the West and Southwest, where the members, who often lived in remote isolation, joined in bouts of story-telling as after long drouth. The strangest, most comic experiences, quiddities, oddities, tales, and bits of novel expression were treasured and matched one against another.

These fabulous stories underwent the many changes to which popular legends have always been subject, but they never coalesced into large forms. The more extravagant of the Crockett legends were unattached to the older body of the Crockett story; they slipped into oblivion as the almanacs were scattered and lost. They exist now only in fragments.

QUESTIONS

1. Recount some of Mike Fink's "frolics and pranks." Why did Fink become a legend? What effect do these minor deities have on the men who create them?

2. What was Crockett's philosophy? Which great adventures became part of the Crockett myth? How did he save "human creation"?

3. Describe the characters who surrounded the demigods: Sally Ann Thunder Ann Whirlwind Crockett, Mike Fink's daughter, and Ben Hardin.

4. Discuss the western tall tales. How are they related to European fairy tales? Why is it difficult to distinguish between serious oratory and burlesque? What were some of the new words used by the backwoodsmen?

5. What effect did the western tall tales have in the East? What kinds of hoaxes sprang up? Jokes?

Comedy's Greatest Era

James Agee

In this bit of nostalgia from the 1940s, James Agee surveys the silent comedies, poking into the studios to see how these films were made, comparing the artists who achieved spectacular success in the medium, and contrasting the silent films with the talkies that brought their era to an end. Most important, Agee brings alive for us the brilliance and magic of one of America's great comic art forms. In addition to the collection of essays, Agee on Film, *he wrote the best-selling novel* A Death in the Family.

In the language of screen comedians four of the main grades of laugh are the titter, the yowl, the bellylaugh and the boffo. The titter is just a titter. The yowl is a runaway titter. Anyone who has ever had the pleasure knows all about a bellylaugh. The boffo is the laugh that kills. An ideally good gag, perfectly constructed and played, would bring the victim up this ladder of laughs by cruelly controlled degrees to the top rung, and would then proceed to wobble, shake, wave and brandish the ladder until he groaned for mercy. Then, after the shortest possible time out for recuperation, he would feel the first wicked tickling of the comedian's whip once more and start up a new ladder.

The reader can get a fair enough idea of the current state of screen comedy by asking himself how long it has been since he has had that treatment. The best of comedies these days hand out plenty of titters and once in a while it is possible to achieve a yowl without overstraining. Even those who have never seen anything better must occasionally have the feeling, as they watch the current run or, rather, trickle of screen comedy, that they are having to make a little cause for laughter go an awfully long way. And anyone who has watched screen comedy over the past ten or fifteen years is bound to realize that it has quietly but steadily deteriorated. As for those happy atavists who remember silent comedy in its heyday and the bellylaughs and boffos that went with it, they have something close to an absolute standard by which to measure the deterioration.

When a modern comedian gets hit on the head, for example, the most he is apt to do is look sleepy. When a silent comedian got hit on the head he seldom let it go so flatly. He realized a broad license, and a ruthless discipline within that license. It was his business to be as funny as possible physically, without the help or hindrance of words. So he gave us a figure of speech, or rather of vision, for loss of consciousness. In other words he gave us a poem, a kind of poem, moreover, that everybody understands. The least he might do was to straighten up stiff as a plank and fall over backward with such skill that his whole length seemed to slap the floor at the same instant. Or he might make a cadenza of it—look vague, smile like an angel, roll up his eyes, lace his fingers, thrust his hands palms downward as far as they would go, hunch his shoulders, rise on tiptoe, prance ecstatically in narrowing circles until, with tallow knees, he sank down the vortex of his dizziness to the floor, and there signified nirvana by kicking his heels twice, like a swimming frog.

Startled by a cop, this same comedian might grab his hatbrim with both hands and yank it down over his ears, jump high in the air, come to earth in a split violent enough to telescope his spine, spring thence into a coattail-flattening sprint and dwindle at rocket speed to the size of a gnat along the grand, forlorn perspective of some lazy back boulevard.

Those are fine clichés from the language of silent comedy in its infancy. The man who could handle them properly combined several of the more difficult accomplishments of the acrobat, the dancer, the clown and the mime. Some very gifted comedians, unforgettably Ben Turpin, had an immense vocabulary of these clichés and were in part so lovable because they were deep conservative classicists and never tried to break away from them. The still more gifted men, of course, simplified and invented, finding out new and much deeper uses for the idiom. They learned to show emotion through it, and comic psychology, more eloquently than most language has ever managed to, and they discovered beauties of comic motion which are hopelessly beyond reach of words.

It is hard to find a theater these days where a comedy is playing; in the days of the silents it was equally hard to find a theater which was not showing one. The laughs today are pitifully few, far between, shallow, quiet and short. They almost never build, as they used to, into something combining the jabbering frequency of a machine gun with the delirious momentum of a roller coaster. Saddest of all, there are few comedians now below middle age and there are none who seem to learn much from picture to picture, or to try anything new.

To put it unkindly, the only thing wrong with screen comedy today is that it takes place on a screen which talks. Because it talks, the only comedians who ever mastered the screen cannot work, for they cannot combine their comic style with talk. Because there is a screen, talking comedians are trapped into a continual exhibition of their inadequacy as screen comedians on a surface as big as the side of a barn.

At the moment, as for many years past, the chances to see silent comedy are rare. There is a smattering of it on television—too often treated as something quaintly archaic, to be laughed at, not with. Some two hundred comedies—long and short—can be rented for home projection. And a lucky minority had access to the comedies in the collection of New York's Museum of Modern Art, which is still incomplete but which is probably the best in the world. In the near future, however, something of this lost art will return to regular theaters. A thick straw in the wind is the big business now being done by a series of revivals of W. C. Fields's memorable movies, a kind of comedy more akin to the old silent variety than anything which is being made today. Mack Sennett now is preparing a sort of pot-pourri variety show called *Down Memory Lane* made up out of his old movies, featuring people like Fields and Bing Crosby when they were movie beginners, but including also interludes from silents. Harold Lloyd has re-released *Movie Crazy*, a talkie, and plans to revive four of his best silent comedies (*Grandma's Boy, Safety Last, Speedy* and *The Freshman*). Buster Keaton hopes to remake at feature length, with a minimum of dialogue, two of the funniest short comedies ever made, one about a porous homemade boat and one about a prefabricated house.

Awaiting these happy events we will discuss here what has gone wrong with screen comedy and what, if anything, can be done about it. But mainly we will try to suggest what it was like in its glory in the years from 1912 to 1930, as practiced by the employees of Mack Sennett, the father of American screen comedy, and by the four most eminent masters: Charlie Chaplin, Harold Lloyd, the late Harry Langdon and Buster Keaton.

Mack Sennett made two kinds of comedy: parody laced with slapstick, and plain slapstick. The parodies were the unceremonious burial of a century of hamming, including the new hamming in serious movies, and nobody who has missed Ben Turpin in *A Small Town Idol*, or kidding Erich von Stroheim in *Three Foolish Weeks* or as *The Shriek of Araby*, can imagine how rough parody can get and still remain subtle and roaringly funny. The plain slapstick, at its best, was even better: a profusion of hearty young women in disconcerting bathing suits, frisking around with a gaggle of insanely incompetent policemen and of equally certifiable male civilians sporting museum-piece mustaches. All these people zipped and caromed about the pristine world of the screen as jazzily as a convention of water bugs. Words can hardly suggest how energetically they collided and bounced apart, meeting in full gallop around the corner of a house; how hard and how often they fell on their backsides; or with what fantastically adroit clumsiness they got themselves fouled up in folding ladders, garden hoses, tethered animals and each other's headlong cross-purposes. The gestures were ferociously emphatic; not a line or motion of the body was wasted or inarticulate. The reader may remember how splendidly upright wandlike old Ben Turpin could stand for a Renunciation Scene, with his lampshade mustache twittering and his sparrowy chest stuck out and his head flung back like Paderewski assaulting a climax and the long babyish back hair trying to look lionlike, while his Adam's apple, an orange in a Christmas stocking, pumped with noble emotion. Or huge Mack Swain, who looked like a hairy mushroom, rolling his eyes in a manner patented by French Romantics and gasping in some dubious ecstasy. Or Louise Fazenda, the perennial farmer's daughter and the perfect low-comedy housemaid, primping her spit curl; and how her hair tightened a good-looking face into the incarnation of rampant gullibility. Or snouty James Finlayson, gleefully foreclosing a mortgage, with his look of eternally tasting a spoiled pickle. Or Chester Conklin, a myopic and inebriated little walrus stumbling around in outsize pants. Or Fatty Arbuckle, with his cold eye and his loose, serene smile, his silky manipulation of his bulk and his satanic marksmanship with pies (he was ambidextrous and could simultaneously blind two people in opposite directions).

The intimate tastes and secret hopes of these poor ineligible dunces were ruthlessly exposed whenever a hot stove, an electric fan or a bulldog took a dislike to their outer garments: agonizingly elaborate drawers, worked up on some lonely evening out of some Godforsaken lace curtain; or men's underpants with big round black spots on them. The Sennett sets—delirious wallpaper, megalomaniacally scrolled iron beds, Grand Rapids in extremis—outdid even the underwear. It was their business, after all, to kid the squalid braggadocio which infested the domestic interiors of the period, and that was almost beyond parody. These comedies told their stories to the unaided eye, and by every means possible they screamed to it. That is one reason for the India-ink silhouettes of the cops, and for convicts and prison bars and their shadows in hard sunlight, and for barefooted husbands, in tigerish pajamas, reacting like dervishes to stepped-on tacks.

The early silent comedians never strove for or consciously thought of anything which could be called artistic "form," but they achieved it. For Sennett's rival, Hal Roach, Leo McCarey once devoted almost the whole of a Laurel and Hardy two-reeler to pie-throwing. The first pies were thrown thoughtfully, almost philosophically. Then innocent bystanders began to get caught into the vortex. At full pitch it was Armageddon. But everything was calculated so nicely that until late in the picture, when havoc took over, every pie made its special kind of point and piled on its special kind of laugh.

Sennett's comedies were just a shade faster and fizzier than life. According to legend (and according to Sennett) he discovered the sped tempo proper to screen comedy when a green cameraman, trying to save money, cranked too slow. . . . Realizing the tremendous drumlike power of mere motion to exhilarate, he gave inanimate objects a mischievous life of their own, broke every law of nature the tricked camera would serve him for and made the screen dance like a witches' Sabbath. The thing one is surest of all to remember is how toward the end of nearly every Sennett comedy, a chase (usually called the "rally") built up such a majestic trajectory of pure anarchic motion that bathing girls, cops, comics, dogs, cats, babies, automobiles, locomotives, innocent by- standers, sometimes what seemed like a whole city, an entire civilization, were hauled along head over heels in the wake of that energy like dry leaves following an express train.

"Nice" people, who shunned all movies in the early days, condemned the Sennett comedies as vulgar and naive. But millions of less preten- tious people loved their sincerity and sweetness, their wild-animal innocence and glorious vitality. They could not put these feelings into words, but they flocked to the silents. The reader who gets back deep enough into that world will probably even remember the theater: the barefaced honky-tonk and the waltzes by Waldteufel, slammed out on a mechanical piano; the searing redolence of peanuts and demircp perfumery, tobacco and feet and sweat; the laughter of unrespectable people having a hell of a fine time, laughter as violent and steady and deafening as standing under a waterfall.

Sennett wheedled his first financing out of a couple of ex-bookies to whom he was already in debt. He took his comics out of music halls, burlesque, vaudeville, circuses and limbo, and through them he tapped in on that great pipeline of horsing and miming which runs back unbroken through the fairs of the Middle Ages at least to ancient Greece. He added all that he himself had learned about the large and spurious gesture, the late decadence of the Grand Manner, as a stage-struck boy in East Berlin, Connecticut and as a frustrated opera singer and actor. The only thing he claims to have invented is the pie in the face, and he insists, "Anyone who tells you he has discovered something new is a fool or a liar or both."

The silent-comedy studio was about the best training school the movies have ever known, and the Sennett studio was about as free and easy and as fecund of talent as they came. All the major comedians we will mention worked there, at least briefly. So did some of the major stars of the twenties and since—notably Gloria Swanson, Phyllis Haver, Wallace Beery, Marie Dressler and Carole Lombard. Directors Frank Capra, Leo McCarey and George Stevens also got their start in silent comedy; much that remains most flexible, spontaneous and visually alive in sound movies can be traced, through them and others, to this silent apprenticeship. Everybody did pretty much as he pleased on the Sennett lot, and everybody's ideas were welcome. Sennett posted no rules, and the only thing he strictly forbade was liquor. A Sennett story conference was a most informal affair. During the early years, at least, only the most important scenario might be jotted on the back of an envelope. Mainly Sennett's men thrashed out a few primary ideas and carried them in their heads, sure the better stuff would turn up while they were shooting, in the heat of physical action. This put quite a load on the prop man; he had to have the most improbable apparatus on hand—bombs, trick telephones, what not—to implement whatever idea might suddenly turn up. All kinds of things did—and were recklessly used. Once a low-comedy auto got out of control and killed the cameraman, but he was not visible in the shot, which was thrilling and undamaged; the audience never knew the difference.

Sennett used to hire a "wild man" to sit in on his gag conferences, whose whole job was to think up "wildies." Usually he was an all but brainless, speechless man, scarcely able to communicate his idea; but he had a totally uninhibited imagination. He might say nothing for an hour; then he'd mutter "You take . . ." and all the relatively rational others would shut up and wait. "You take this cloud . . ." he would get out, sketching vague shapes in the air. Often he could get no further; but thanks to some kind of thought-transference, saner men would take this cloud and make something of it. The wild man seems in fact to have functioned as the group's subconscious mind, the source of all creative energy. His ideas were so weird and amorphous that Sennett can no longer remember a one of them, or even how it turned out after rational processing. But a fair equivalent might be one of the best comic sequences in a Laurel and Hardy picture. It is simple enough—simple and real, in fact, as a nightmare. Laurel and Hardy are trying to move a piano across a narrow suspension bridge. The bridge is slung over a sickening chasm, between a couple of Alps. Midway they meet a gorilla.

Had he done nothing else, Sennett would be remembered for giving a start to three of the four comedians who now began to apply their sharp individual talents to this newborn language. The one whom he did not train (he was on the lot briefly but Sennett barely remembers seeing him around) wore glasses, smiled a great deal and looked like the sort of eager young man who might have quit divinity school to hustle brushes. That was Harold Lloyd. The others were grotesque and poetic in their screen characters in degrees which appear to be impossible when the magic of silence is broken. One, who never smiled, carried a face as still and sad as a daguerreotype through some of the most preposterously ingenious and visually satisfying physical comedy ever invented. That was Buster Keaton. One looked like an elderly baby and, at times, a baby dope fiend; he could do more with less than any other comedian. That was Harry Langdon. One looked like Charlie Chaplin, and he was the first man to give the silent language a soul.

When Charlie Chaplin started to work for Sennett he had chiefly to reckon with Ford Sterling, the reigning comedian. Their first picture together amounted to a duel before the assembled professionals. Sterling, by no means untalented, was a big man with a florid Teutonic style which, under this special pressure, he turned on full blast. Chaplin defeated him within a few minutes with a wink of the mustache, a hitch of the trousers, a quirk of the little finger.

With *Tillie's Punctured Romance*, in 1914, he became a major star. Soon after, he left Sennett when Sennett refused to start a landslide among the other comedians by meeting the raise Chaplin demanded. Sennett is understandably wry about it in retrospect, but he still says, "I was right at the time." Of Chaplin he says simply, "Oh well, he's just the greatest artist that ever lived." None of Chaplin's former rivals rate him much lower than that; they speak of him no more jealously than they might of God. We will try here only to suggest the essence of his supremacy. Of all comedians he worked most deeply and most shrewdly within a realization of what a human being is, and is up against. The Tramp is as centrally representative of humanity, as many-sided and as mysterious, as Hamlet, and it seems unlikely that any dancer or actor can ever have excelled him in eloquence, variety or poignancy of motion. As for pure motion, even if he had never gone on to make his magnificent feature-length comedies, Chaplin would have made his period in movies a great one singlehanded even if he had made nothing except *The Cure*, or *One A.M.* In the latter, barring one immobile taxi driver, Chaplin plays alone, as a drunk trying to get upstairs and into bed. It is a sort of inspired elaboration on a soft-shoe dance, involving an angry stuffed wildcat, small rugs on slippery floors, a Lazy Susan table, exquisite footwork on a flight of stairs, a contretemps with a huge, ferocious pendulum and the funniest and most perverse Murphy bed in movie history—and, always made physically lucid, the delicately weird mental processes of a man ethereally sozzled.

Before Chaplin came to pictures people were content with a couple of gags per comedy; he got some kind of laugh every second. The minute he began to work he set standards—and continually forced them higher. Anyone who saw Chaplin eating a boiled shoe like brook trout in *The Gold Rush*, or embarrassed by a swallowed whistle in *City Lights*, has seen perfection. Most of the time, however, Chaplin got his laughter less from the gags, or from milking them in any ordinary sense, than through his genius for what may be called *inflection*—the perfect, changeful shading of his physical and emotional attitudes toward the gag. Funny as his bout with the Murphy bed is, the glances of awe, expostulation and helpless, almost whimpering desire for vengeance which he darts at this infernal machine are even better.

A painful and frequent error among tyros is breaking the comic line with a too-big laugh, then a letdown; or with a laugh which is out of key or irrelevant. The masters could ornament the main line beautifully; they never addled it. In *A Night Out* Chaplin, passed out, is hauled along the sidewalk by the scruff of his coat by staggering Ben Turpin. His toes trail; he is as supine as a sled. Turpin himself is so drunk he can hardly drag him. Chaplin comes quietly to, realizes how well he is being served by his struggling pal, and with a royally delicate gesture plucks and savors a flower.

The finest pantomime, the deepest emotion, the richest and most poignant poetry were in Chaplin's work. He could probably pantomime Bryce's *The American Commonwealth* without ever blurring a syllable and make it paralyzingly funny into the bargain. At the end of *City Lights* the blind girl who has regained her sight, thanks to the Tramp, sees him for the first time. She has imagined and anticipated him as princely, to say the least; and it has never seriously occurred to him that he is inadequate. She recognizes who he must be by his shy, confident, shining joy as he comes silently toward her. And he recognizes himself, for the first time, through the terrible changes in her face. The camera just exchanges a few quiet close-ups of the emotions which shift and intensify in each face. It is enough to shrivel the heart to see, and it is the greatest piece of acting and the highest moment in movies.

Harold Lloyd worked only a little while with Sennett. During most of his career he acted for another major comedy producer, Hal Roach. He tried at first to offset Chaplin's influence and establish his own individuality by playing Chaplin's exact opposite, a character named Lonesome Luke who wore clothes much too small for him and whose gestures were likewise as unChaplinesque as possible. But he soon realized that an opposite in itself was a kind of slavishness. He discovered his own comic identity when he saw a movie about a fighting parson: a hero who wore glasses. He began to think about those glasses day and night. He decided on horn rims because they were youthful, ultravisible on the screen and on the verge of becoming fashionable (he was to make them so). Around these large lensless horn rims he began to develop a new character, nothing grotesque or eccentric, but a fresh, believable young man who could fit into a wide variety of stories.

Lloyd depended more on story and situation than any of the other major comedians (he kept the best stable of gagmen in Hollywood, at one time hiring six); but unlike most "story" comedians he was also a very funny man from inside. He had, as he has written, "an unusually large comic vocabulary." More particularly he had an expertly expressive body and even more expressive teeth, and out of his thesaurus of smiles he could at a moment's notice blend prissiness, breeziness and asininity, and still remain tremendously likable. His movies were more extroverted and closer to ordinary life than any others of the best comedies: the vicissitudes of a New York taxi driver; the unaccepted college boy who, by desperate courage and inspired ineptitude, wins the Big Game. He was especially good at putting a very timid, spoiled or brassy young fellow through devastating embarrassments. He went through one of his most uproarious Gethsemanes as a shy country youth courting the nicest girl in town in *Grandma's Boy*. He arrived dressed "strictly up to date for the Spring of 1862," as a subtitle observed, and found that the ancient colored butler wore a similar flowered waistcoat and moldering cutaway. He got one wandering, nervous forefinger dreadfully stuck in a fancy little vase. The girl began cheerfully to try to identify that queer smell which dilated from him; Grandpa's best suit was rife with mothballs. A tenacious litter of kittens feasted off the goose grease on his home-shined shoes.

Lloyd was even better at the comedy of thrills. In *Safety Last*, as a rank amateur, he is forced to substitute for a human fly and to climb a medium-sized skyscraper. Dozens of awful things happen to him. He gets fouled up in a tennis net. Popcorn falls on him from a window above, and the local pigeons treat him like a cross between a lunch wagon and St. Francis of Assisi. A mouse runs up his britches-leg, and the crowd below salutes his desperate dance on the window ledge with wild applause of the daredevil. A good deal of this full-length picture hangs thus by its eyelashes along the face of a building. Each new floor is like a new stanza in a poem; and the higher and more horrifying it gets, the funnier it gets.

In this movie Lloyd demonstrates beautifully his ability to do more than merely milk a gag, but to top it. (In an old, simple example of topping, an incredible number of tall men got, one by one, out of a small closed auto. After as many have clambered out as the joke will bear, one more steps out: a midget. That tops the gag. Then the auto collapses. That tops the topper.) In *Safety Last* Lloyd is driven out to the dirty end of a flagpole by a furious dog; the pole breaks and he falls, just managing to grab the minute hand of a huge clock. His weight promptly pulls the hand down from IX to VI. That would be more than enough for any ordinary comedian, but there is further logic in the situation. Now, hideously, the whole clockface pulls loose and slants from its trembling springs above the street. Getting out of difficulty with the clock, he makes still further use of the instrument by getting one foot caught in one of these obstinate springs.

A proper delaying of the ultrapredictable can of course be just as funny as a properly timed explosion of the unexpected. As Lloyd approaches the end of his horrible hegira up the side of the building in *Safety Last*, it becomes clear to the audience, but not to him, that if he raises his head another couple of inches he is going to get murderously conked by one of the four arms of a revolving wind gauge. He delays the evil moment almost interminably, with one distraction and another, and every delay is a suspense-tightening laugh; he also gets his foot nicely entangled in a rope, so that when he does get hit, the payoff of one gag sends him careening head downward through the abyss into another. Lloyd was outstanding even among the master craftsmen at setting up a gag clearly, culminating and getting out of it deftly, and linking it smoothly to the next. Harsh experience also taught him a deep and fundamental rule: never try to get "above" the audience.

Lloyd tried it in *The Freshman*. He was to wear an unfinished, basted-together tuxedo to a college party, and it would gradually fall apart as he danced. Lloyd decided to skip the pants, a low-comedy cliché, and lose just the coat. His gagmen warned him. A preview proved how right they were. Lloyd had to reshoot the whole expensive sequence, build it around defective pants and climax it with the inevitable. It was one of the funniest things he ever did.

When Lloyd was still a very young man he lost about half his right hand (and nearly lost his sight) when a comedy bomb exploded prematurely. But in spite of his artificially built-out hand he continued to do his own dirty work, like all of the best comedians. The side of the building he climbed in *Safety Last* did not overhang the street, as it appears to. But the nearest landing place was a roof three floors below him, as he approached the top, and he did everything, of course, the hard way, that is, the comic way, keeping his bottom stuck well out, his shoulders hunched, his hands and feet skidding over perdition.

If great comedy must involve something beyond laughter, Lloyd was not a great comedian. If plain laughter is any criterion—and it is a healthy counterbalance to the other—few people have equaled him, and nobody has ever beaten him.

Chaplin and Keaton and Lloyd were all more like each other, in one important way, than Harry Langdon was like any of them. Whatever else the others might be doing, they all used more or less elaborate physical comedy; Langdon showed how little of that one might use and still be a great silent-screen comedian. In his screen character he symbolized something as deeply and centrally human, though by no means as rangily so, as the Tramp. There was, of course, an immense difference in inventiveness and range of virtuosity. It seemed as if Chaplin could do literally anything, on any instrument in the orchestra. Langdon had one queerly toned, unique little reed. But out of it he could get incredible melodies.

Like Chaplin, Langdon wore a coat which buttoned on his wishbone and swung out wide below, but the effect was very different: he seemed like an outsized baby who had begun to outgrow his clothes. The crown of his hat was rounded and the brim was turned up all around, like a little boy's hat, and he looked as if he wore diapers under his pants. His walk was that of a child which has just gotten sure on its feet, and his body and hands fitted that age. His face was kept pale to show off, with the simplicity of a nursery-school drawing, the bright, ignorant, gentle eyes and the little twirling mouth. He had big moon cheeks, with dimples, and a Napoleonic forelock of mousy hair; the round, docile head seemed large in ratio to the cream-puff body. Twitchings of his face were signals of tiny discomforts too slowly registered by a tinier brain; quick, squirty little smiles showed his almost prehuman pleasures, his incurably premature trustfulness. He was a virtuoso of hesitations and of delicately indecisive motions, and he was particularly fine in a high wind, rounding a corner with a kind of skittering toddle, both hands nursing his hatbrim.

He was as remarkable a master as Chaplin of subtle emotional and mental process and operated much more at leisure. He once got a good three hundred feet of continuously bigger laughs out of rubbing his chest, in a crowded vehicle, with Limburger cheese, under the misapprehension that it was a cold salve. In another long scene, watching a brazen showgirl change her clothes, he sat motionless, back to the camera, and registered the whole lexicon of lost innocence, shock, disapproval and disgust, with the back of his neck. His scenes with women were nearly always something special. Once a lady spy did everything in her power (under the Hays Office) to seduce him. Harry was polite, willing, even flirtatious in his little way. The only trouble was that he couldn't imagine what in the world she was leering and pawing at him for, and that he was terribly ticklish. The Mata Hari wound up foaming at the mouth.

There was also a sinister flicker of depravity about the Langdon character, all the more disturbing because babies are premoral. He had an instinct for bringing his actual adulthood and figurative babyishness into frictions as crawley as a fingernail on a slate blackboard, and he wandered into areas of strangeness which were beyond the other comedians. In a nightmare in one movie he was forced to fight a large, muscular young man; the girl Harry loved was the prize. The young man was a good boxer; Harry could scarcely lift his gloves. The contest took place in a fiercely lighted prize ring, in a prodigious pitch-dark arena. The only spectator was the girl, and she was rooting against Harry. As the fight went on, her eyes glittered ever more brightly with blood lust and, with glittering teeth, she tore her big straw hat to shreds.

Langdon came to Sennett from a vaudeville act in which he had fought a losing battle with a recalcitrant automobile. The minute Frank Capra saw him he begged Sennett to let him work with him. Langdon was almost as childlike as the character he played. He had only a vague idea of his story or even of each scene as he played it; each time he went before the camera Capra would brief him on the general situation and then, as this finest of intuitive improvisers once tried to explain his work, "I'd go into my routine." The whole tragedy of the coming of dialogue, as far as these comedians were concerned—and one reason for the increasing rigidity of comedy ever since—can be epitomized in the mere thought of Harry Langdon confronted with a script.

Langdon's magic was in his innocence, and Capra took beautiful care not to meddle with it. The key to the proper use of Langdon, Capra always knew, was "the principle of the brick." "If there was a rule for writing Langdon material," he explains, "it was this: his only ally was God. Langdon might be saved by the brick falling on the cop, but it was *verboten* that he in any way motivate the brick's fall." Langdon became quickly and fantastically popular with three pictures, *Tramp, Tramp, Tramp, The Strong Man* and *Long Pants*; from then on he went downhill even faster. "The trouble was," Capra says, "that high-brow critics came around to explain his art to him. Also he developed an interest in dames. It was a pretty high life for such a little fellow." Langdon made two more pictures with high-brow writers, one of which *(Three's a Crowd)* had some wonderful passages in it, including the prize-ring nightmare; then First National canceled his contract. He was reduced to mediocre roles and two-reelers which were more rehashes of his old gags; this time around they no longer seemed funny. "He never did really understand what hit him," says Capra. "He died broke [in 1944]. And he died of a broken heart. He was the most tragic figure I ever came across in show business."

Buster Keaton started work at the age of three and one-half with his parents in one of the roughest acts in vaudeville ("The Three Keatons"); Harry Houdini gave the child the name Buster in admiration for a fall he took down a flight of stairs. In his first movies Keaton teamed with Fatty Arbuckle under Sennett. He went on to become one of Metro's biggest stars and earners; a Keaton feature cost about $200,000 to make and reliably grossed $2,000,000. Very early in his movie career friends asked him why he never smiled on the screen. He didn't realize he didn't. He had got the dead-pan habit in variety; on the screen he had merely been so hard at work it had never occurred to him there was anything to smile about. Now he tried it just once and never again. He was by his whole style and nature so much the most deeply "silent" of the silent comedians that even a smile was as deafeningly out of key as a yell. In a way his pictures are like a transcendent juggling act in which it seems that the whole universe is in exquisite flying motion and the one point of repose is the juggler's effortless, uninterested face.

Keaton's face ranked almost with Lincoln's as an early American archetype; it was haunting, handsome, almost beautiful, yet it was irreducibly funny; he improved matters by topping it off with a deadly horizontal hat, as flat and thin as a phonograph record. One can never forget Keaton wearing it, standing erect at the prow as his little boat is being launched. The boat goes grandly down the skids and, just as grandly, straight on to the bottom. Keaton never budges. The last you see of him, the water lifts the hat off the stoic head and it floats away.

No other comedian could do as much with the dead pan. He used this great, sad, motionless face to suggest various related things: a one-track mind near the track's end of pure insanity; mulish imperturbability under the wildest of circumstances; how dead a human being can get and still be alive; an awe-inspiring sort of patience and power to endure, proper to granite but uncanny in flesh and blood. Everything that he was and did bore out his rigid face and played laughs against it. When he moved his eyes, it was like seeing them move in a statue. His short-legged body was all sudden, machinelike angles, governed by a daft aplomb. When he swept a semaphorelike arm to point, you could almost hear the electrical impulse in the signal block. When he ran from a cop his transitions from accelerating walk to easy jogtrot to brisk canter to headlong gallop to flogged-piston sprint—always floating, above this frenzy, the untroubled, untouchable face—were as distinct and as soberly in order as an automatic gearshift.

Keaton was a wonderfully resourceful inventor of mechanistic gags (he still spends much of his time fooling with Erector sets); as he ran afoul of locomotives, steamships, prefabricated and over-electrified houses, he put himself through some of the hardest and cleverest punishment ever designed for laughs. In *Sherlock Jr.*, boiling along on the handlebars of a motorcycle quite unaware that he has lost his driver, Keaton whips through city traffic, breaks up a tug-of-war, gets a shovelful of dirt in the face from each of a long line of Rockette-timed ditch-diggers, approaches a log at high speed which is hinged open by dynamite precisely soon enough to let him through and, hitting an obstruction, leaves the handlebars like an arrow leaving a bow, whams through the window of a shack in which the heroine is about to be violated, and hits the heavy feet-first, knocking him through the opposite wall. The whole sequence is as clean in motion as the trajectory of a bullet.

Much of the charm and edge of Keaton's comedy, however, lay in the subtle leverages of expression he could work against his nominal dead pan. Trapped in the side-wheel of a ferryboat, saving himself from drowning only by walking, then desperately running, inside the accelerating wheel like a squirrel in a cage, his only real concern was, obviously, to keep his hat on. Confronted by Love, he was not as dead-pan as he was cracked up to be, either; there was an odd, abrupt motion of his head which suggested a horse nipping after a sugar lump.

Keaton worked strictly for laughs, but his work came from so far inside a curious and original spirit that he achieved a great deal besides, especially in his feature-length comedies. (For plain hard laughter his nineteen short comedies—the negatives of which have been lost—were even better.) He was the only major comedian who kept sentiment almost entirely out of his work, and he brought pure physical comedy to its greatest heights. Beneath his lack of emotion he was also uninsistently sardonic; deep below that, giving a disturbing tension and grandeur to the foolishness, for those who sensed it, there was in his comedy a freezing whisper not of pathos but of melancholia. With the humor, the craftsmanship and the action there was often, besides, a fine, still and sometimes dreamlike beauty. Much of his Civil War picture *The General* is within hailing distance of Mathew Brady. And there is a ghostly, unforgettable moment in *The Navigator* when, on a deserted, softly rolling ship, all the pale doors along a deck swing open as one behind Keaton and, as one, slam shut, in a hair-raising illusion of noise.

Perhaps because "dry" comedy is so much more rare and odd than "dry" wit, there are people who never much cared for Keaton. Those who do cannot care mildly.

As soon as the screen began to talk, silent comedy was pretty well finished. The hardy and prolific Mack Sennett made the transfer; he was the first man to put Bing Crosby and W. C. Fields on the screen. But he was essentially a silent-picture man, and by the time the Academy awarded him a special Oscar for his "lasting contribution to the comedy technique of the screen" (in 1938), he was no longer active. As for the comedians we have spoken of in particular, they were as badly off as fine dancers suddenly required to appear in plays.

Harold Lloyd, whose work was most nearly realistic, naturally coped least unhappily with the added realism of speech; he made several talking comedies. But good as the best were, they were not so good as his silent work, and by the late thirties he quit acting. A few years ago he returned to play the lead (and play it beautifully) in Preston Sturges's *The Sin of Harold Diddlebock*, but this exceptional picture—which opened, brilliantly, with the closing reel of Lloyd's *The Freshman*—has not yet been generally released.

Like Chaplin, Lloyd was careful of his money; he is still rich and active. Last June, in the presence of President Truman, he became Imperial Potentate of the A.A.O.N.M.S. (Shriners). Harry Langdon, as we have said, was a broken man when sound came in.

Up to the middle thirties Buster Keaton made several feature-length pictures (with such players as Jimmy Durante, Wallace Beery and Robert Montgomery); he also made a couple of dozen talking shorts. Now and again he managed to get loose into motion, without having to talk, and for a moment or so the screen would start singing again. But his dark, dead voice, though it was in keeping with the visual character, tore his intensely silent style to bits and destroyed the illusion within which he worked. He gallantly and correctly refuses to regard himself as "retired." Besides occasional bits, spots and minor roles in Hollywood pictures, he has worked on summer stages, made talking comedies in France and Mexico and clowned in a French circus. This summer he has played the straw hats in *Three Men on a Horse*. He is planning a television program. He also has a working agreement with Metro. One of his jobs there is to construct comedy sequences for Red Skelton.

The only man who really survived the flood was Chaplin, the only one who was rich, proud and popular enough to afford to stay silent. He brought out two of his greatest nontalking comedies, *City Lights* and *Modern Times*, in the middle of an avalanche of talk, spoke gibberish and, in the closing moments, plain English in *The Great Dictator*, and at last made an all-talking picture, Monsieur Verdoux, creating for that purpose an entirely new character who might properly talk a blue streak. Verdoux is the greatest of talking comedies though so cold and savage that it had to find its public in grimly experienced Europe.

Good comedy, and some that was better than good, outlived silence, but there has been less and less of it. The talkies brought one great comedian, the late, majestically lethargic W. C. Fields, who could not possibly have worked as well in silence; he was the toughest and the most warmly human of all screen comedians, and It's a Gift and The Bank Dick, fiendishly funny and incisive white-collar comedies, rank high among the best comedies (and best movies) ever made. Laurel and Hardy, the only comedians who managed to preserve much of the large, low style of silence and who began to explore the comedy of sound, have made nothing since 1945. Walt Disney, at his best an inspired comic inventor and teller of fairy stories, lost his stride during the war and has since regained it only at moments. Preston Sturges has made brilliant, satirical comedies, but his pictures are smart, nervous comedy-dramas merely italicized with slapstick. The Marx Brothers were sidesplitters but they made their best comedies years ago. Jimmy Durante is mainly a nightclub genius; Abbott and Costello are semiskilled laborers, at best; Bob Hope is a good radio comedian with a pleasing presence, but not much more, on the screen.

There is no hope that screen comedy will get much better than it is without new, gifted young comedians who really belong in movies, and without freedom for their experiments. For everyone who may appear we have one last, invidious comparison to offer as a guidepost.

One of the most popular recent comedies is Bob Hope's The Paleface. We take no pleasure in blackening The Paleface; we single it out, rather, because it is as good as we've got. Anything that is said of it here could be said, with interest, of other comedies of our time. Most of the laughs in The Paleface are verbal. Bob Hope is very adroit with his lines and now and then, when the words don't get in the way, he makes a good beginning as a visual comedian. But only the beginning, never the middle or the end. He is funny, for instance, reacting to a shot of violent whisky. But he does not know how to get still funnier (i.e., how to build and milk) or how to be funniest last (i.e., how to top or cap his gag). The camera has to fade out on the same old face he started with.

One sequence is promisingly set up for visual comedy. In it, Hope and a lethal local boy stalk each other all over a cow town through streets which have been emptied in fear of their duel. The gag here is that through accident and stupidity they keep just failing to find each other. Some of it is quite funny. But the fun slackens between laughs like a weak clothesline, and by all the logic of humor (which is ruthlessly logical) the biggest laugh should come at the moment, and through the way, they finally spot each other. The sequence is so weakly thought out that at that crucial moment the camera can't afford to watch them; it switches to Jane Russell.

Now we turn to a masterpiece. In *The Navigator* Buster Keaton works with practically the same gag as Hope's duel. Adrift on a ship which he believes is otherwise empty, he drops a lighted cigarette. A girl finds it. She calls out and he hears her; each then tries to find the other. First each walks purposefully down the long, vacant starboard deck, the girl, then Keaton, turning the corner just in time not to see each other. Next time around each of them is trotting briskly, very much in earnest; going at the same pace, they miss each other just the same. Next time around each of them is going like a bat out of hell. Again they miss. Then the camera withdraws to a point of vantage at the stern, leans its chin in its hand and just watches the whole intricate superstructure of the ship as the protagonists stroll, steal and scuttle from level to level, up, down and sidewise, always managing to miss each other by hair's-breadths, in an enchantingly neat and elaborate piece of timing. There are no subsidiary gags to get laughs in this sequence and there is little loud laughter; merely a quiet and steadily increasing kind of delight. When Keaton has got all he can out of this fine modification of the movie chase he invents a fine device to bring the two together: the girl, thoroughly winded, sits down for a breather, indoors, on a plank which workmen have left across sawhorses. Keaton pauses on an upper deck, equally winded and puzzled. What follows happens in a couple of seconds at most: air suction whips his silk topper backward down a ventilator; grabbing frantically for it, he backs against the lip of the ventilator, jackknifes and falls in backward. Instantly the camera cuts back to the girl. A topper falls through the ceiling and lands tidily, right side up, on the plank beside her. Before she can look more than startled, its owner follows, head between his knees, crushes the topper, breaks the plank with the point of his spine and proceeds to the floor. The breaking of the plank smacks Boy and Girl together.

It is only fair to remember that the silent comedians would have as hard a time playing a talking scene as Hope has playing his visual ones, and that writing and directing are as accountable for the failure as Hope himself. But not even the humblest journeymen of the silent years would have let themselves off so easily. Like the masters, they knew, and sweated to obey, the laws of their craft.

QUESTIONS

1. Define the four main grades of laugh evoked by screen comedians. How does an ideally good gag work?

2. How does a modern comedian generally look when he gets hit on the head? What happened when a silent comedian got hit on the head? When he was startled by a cop?

3. Describe the Sennett studio. How did Sennett discover the faster tempo used for silent comedies? What effect did this speed have on the audience? How did most Sennett comedies end? What was the function of the "wild man"?

4. Discuss the two kinds of comedies Sennett made. What kinds of characters appeared in the slapstick films? What kinds of underwear and stage sets were used in the parodies? Why were these so important?

5. How did Chaplin change comedy? Why is the Tramp similar to Hamlet? What does Agee think is the highest moment in movies?

6. Compare the comic characters created by Buster Keaton, Harold Lloyd, and Harry Langdon. How are they alike? Different? Give some examples of the "comedy of thrills."

7. What does Agee think of talking film comedy? How does he describe Walt Disney? The Marx Brothers? Abbott and Costello? How does he compare similar scenes by Bob Hope and Buster Keaton? Do you agree with his conclusions? Explain.

Peanuts: The Americanization of Augustine

Arthur Asa Berger

In his introduction to The Comic-Stripped American, *Arthur Asa Berger notes that comic books and strips, read by hundreds of millions of Americans, have attracted little scholarly interest. He proposes that this important dimension of our culture deserves serious study. The following essay argues the literary and philosophic significance of one of America's most popular comic strips, Charles Schulz's "Peanuts."*

> His heroes are not animals but preschool-age children, "led" by Charlie Brown, whose faith in human nature (and in that of his little comrades) is always cruelly deceived. His chief tormentor is a scowling, cynical little girl, a real child shrew, named Lucy van Pelt. Linus, Lucy's brother, is a precocious, delicate intellectual whose nerves give way with the loss of the blanket he always carries around with him to reassure himself. Schroeder, whose greatest pleasure is to play Beethoven on his toy piano, the dirty Pig-Pen, and several others complete this childish team, to which must be added Snoopy, the hedonistic young puppy who is very pleased with living.
>
> —Pierre Couperie and Maurice C. Horn, *A History of the Comic Strip*

Charles Schulz, the creator of *Peanuts*, is a rather shy person who personifies the American Dream. When he was graduating from high school, he saw an ad for an art school on a match-book cover. He sent away for information, took the course, and what do you know—he now makes more than three million dollars a year. Schulz used to be what we would now call "straight"—a crew-cut, clean-living midwesterner, dedicated to his family and his religion.

That was before the exploitation and the commercialization of the strip reached its present stage. *Peanuts* is now so ubiquitous that it is literally part of the fabric of modern American society, and Schulz is the spokesman for millions of mute Americans. This success has had its effect on "Sparky" (as he is known to his friends), and his image is now much cooler. His hair is longer, he wears tinted aviator glasses, and was recently separated from his wife. But the strip remains the same.

Because the comic strip does not have much status as an art form, and because the characters in *Peanuts* are little children and a dog, we tend to underestimate Schulz's achievement, even though almost everybody admires his work. *I believe that Schulz is one of the greatest humorists of the twentieth century.* Over the course of some two dozen years of drawing the strip (it started in 1950) and thinking up the gags, he has developed a distinctive style of art work, an incredible assortment of characters, and a positively amazing command of the techniques of humor.

His *ouvrage* is monumental. And though his earlier work was not particularly exceptional, he has developed his talent to an extraordinary level over the years. We find his work all about us—on school lunch boxes, on sheets and pillowcases, on dolls, calendars, in the theater, and on television. The strip is also popular abroad—some hundred million people read it daily—though I believe it is essentially American in its spirit.

We enjoy *Peanuts* because it is extremely funny. Schulz mixes graphic, verbal, and ideational humor in a genuinely inventive manner. He is a master of representing expressions in his characters. His characters tend to be monomaniacs who pursue their destinies with all the zany abandon of divinely inspired zealots. We seldom see them this way, however, because we have been taught to regard children (and dogs) as innocent and mildly amusing.

Schulz does not accept this notion; he portrays children in all their Augustinian corruptness. The characters in *Peanuts* exist after the fall of man from the Garden of Eden. They are corrupted by original sin and therefore can be selfish egoists without any strain on our credulity.

There are no adults in the strip; there are no authority figures, though Lucy, by virtue of her domineering personality and ready resort to fisticuffs, is probably the locus of power for all practical purposes. The strip is a fascinating study in anarchy. Without any central organizing power to set limits and establish boundaries, we find a collection of self-important petty sovereigns—or perhaps petty tyrants. A peanut is an "insignificant or tiny person," and Schulz's characters are in reality peanuts in both senses of the word. As far as their self-image is concerned, however, they are giants.

They are also lovable. Guilt does not make people nasty or hateful. Robert L. Short explains this in his analysis of "Original Sin" in *The Gospel According to Peanuts*:

> First of all, the doctrine of Original Sin (including the Garden of Eden story) is not so much concerned with *how* the human predicament got the way it is, as it is concerned to show *what* the human predicament is. And what is the "human predicament"? Is it that each one of us, every man born of a woman, is *born* under the *curse* of sin ("A curse comes to being/As a child is formed"), that we all have our personal origins in

sin, that we all *originate* this way in life—and hence the term *"Original Sin."* (This is also why some churches call Original Sin, "Birth-Sin.") But this sinfulness does not necessarily manifest itself in meanness or hatefulness. . . .

Just the opposite, in fact, may be the case. A man who accepts sin as a reality of the human condition has a much more philosophical attitude toward man's frailties than the man who sets a standard of sin-free perfection. Consequently, he is more understanding in human relations.

The love in *Peanuts* is based upon understanding, not illusion; Schulz is a supreme realist. One of the strip's charms is that it openly acknowledges pride and stupidity and gullibility and all the other evil qualities (or nasty ones) in man, and still is able to be accepting. Somehow we all feel that Schulz accepts man for what he is, not what he claims to be. Schulz relieves us of the awesome burden of innocence, and we are all grateful.

Schulz's characters are only innocent in the sense they are asexual and pregenital; they have all the vices of adults in every other aspect. They are subject to passions, susceptible to whims, motivated by greed or love, and they never learn. Lucy pursues Schroeder relentlessly, never understanding (or admitting to herself) that he does not particularly like her. Linus is insecure, and an emotional cripple without his blanket. Charlie Brown is continually suffering ignominious defeats on the baseball diamond and is victimized by people who take advantage of his trusting nature.

Since the characters are children (and animals), we are not offended by the light they throw on our vices. Naive commentators have long been used as a literary device by humorists to point out our shortcomings. Huck Finn is a case in point. But Twain's humor has a savage intensity, founded on a sense of moral outrage that we do not find in Schulz, whose satire is infinitely more gentle and genial. Schulz deals with a wider perspective and operates at a higher level of abstraction.

Peanuts is a commentary on the human condition, from the perspective of a person who understands human nature and man's invincible ignorance and propensity toward folly. The comic strip format does not easily lend itself to the more biting satire of Twain or Swift, but it does lend itself to satire and social commentary, and Schulz is probably the king of popular psychologists and lighthearted critics of man in America.

And though we are exposed to Schulz in bits and pieces, one strip per day, over the years the characters have taken on a certain identity—so that their adventures have more meaning to us after we have followed them for a number of years. All of the characters have changed too. They have not grown older (that is a convention of the comic strip); but as Schulz has perfected his style, they have changed their appearance and developed their personalities considerably. As I pointed out earlier, the first strips were rather bland. Schulz had not yet developed his characters nor mastered the techniques of humor.

An important element behind humor—an insight we get from Freud and psychoanalysis—is that it serves to mask aggression. The energy that we expend laughing at the ridiculous releases pent-up hostilities. Under the guise of wit, Schulz says things we would rather not hear. He does this by defining things in an amusing way. "Happiness," he tells us, "is a warm puppy," or "happiness is feeling the wind and rain in your hair." These definitions, which have a folksy quality to them, are really like proverbs—and Schulz is following a long line of humorists in America from Benjamin Franklin on, who cloaked their moralizing in witty phrases and comic maxims. Humor is implicitly social, and we must expect a certain amount of moralizing from our humorists. Proverbs, really, are moral directives. Schulz disguises this ethical element in his work so beautifully that we seldom see it.

Snoopy, from atop his doghouse, is very much a commentator from a mock-pulpit, calling man to see his errors and return to the straight and narrow path. In one episode, Snoopy has allowed four homeless birds to use his doghouse as a temporary refuge. They become so noisy playing bridge that Snoopy has to drive them away (the last one carrying a little bridge table on his head). Snoopy then comments: "A Friend is NOT someone who takes advantage of you!" There is something about being on doghouses, pulpits, or even soapboxes that brings out the moralist in man—and dogs like Snoopy.

Schulz is a mirthful moralist; he continues to point out our frailties and calls upon us to lead the good life. His particular instrument is his comic genius and the remarkable collection of many characters he has created in his strip. He does not sentimentalize childhood, and perhaps goes a step or two in the opposite direction at times, but then childhood is a period with many bitter and painful experiences.

Peanuts does a number of things for us. It points out, by implication, the danger of a society full of egoists who pursue their particular passions; it offers us little homilies and morality plays to help us maintain our righteousness; it offers us insights into the many frailties of man and human nature; and it enables us to release our aggressions by having a remarkable assortment of comic characters and fools for us to laugh at. It is no wonder that the strip is so popular with adults, for it is very reassuring. It says, "Don't feel so guilty about your children! Children are born with guilt, and people are fools anyway!" This relieves adults of a great deal of responsibility, and justifies the occasional feelings of anger and hostility people may feel toward their children.

Actually, *Peanuts* is full of inversions. We find children who act like adults, dogs who act like humans, and a comic strip which deals with many of the profundities of life and does not sentimentalize children. Inversion is also central to the pastoral, and I believe we must understand *Peanuts* as a kind of pastoral. When we think of the pastoral, we usually imagine shepherds and maidens frolicking on the grass. But in its modern manifestations we can interpret the pastoral as a device which uses inversion and puts the complex into the simple. Schulz's children act like adults in a society where adults often act like children.

There is a certain abstract quality to the strip. The characters do not seem to live in society *per se*—though society is intimated in the form of schools and psychiatrists and holidays. Much of the action takes place beyond society in a state of nature, with modern shepherds and shepherdesses playing out their roles.

I have, in the course of this discussion, described Schulz's characters as *fools*. There are many aspects of the various characters which are foolish, as the dictionary defines fool:

> A person lacking in judgment or prudence; a retainer formerly kept in great households to provide casual entertainment and commonly dressed in motley with cap, bells and bauble; one who is victimized or made to appear foolish (a dupe).

Certainly Snoopy and Charlie Brown and Linus and all the other characters have this element about them. But in addition they have a certain inflexibility in their character which verges on monomania and becomes the central element of their foolishness. Their obsessions are patently absurd, and it is this rather mechanical rigidity that does a great deal to create the humor in the strip.

In *The Anatomy of Criticism*, Northrop Frye explains how the humor of characterization works. He points out that there are four basic comedy types:

> 1. *alazones* or impostors
> 2. *eirons* or self-deprecators
> 3. *bomolochoi* or buffoons
> 4. *agroikos* or churls

The basis of comedy, which he says frequently deals with defeated characters, is

> a victory of arbitrary plot over consistency of character. Thus, in striking contrast to tragedy, there can hardly be such a thing as inevitable comedy, as far as the action of the individual play is concerned. That is, we may know that the convention of comedy will make some kind of a happy ending inevitable, but still for each play the dramatist must produce a distinctive "gimmick" or "weenie," to use disrespectful Hollywood terms. . . .

Schulz's genius, then, is in finding ways of manipulating his stock characters so that unexpected resolutions occur or that the resolutions that we anticipate do not occur.

He is aided by the fact that we all learn certain conventions as we are socialized, and by the fact that the characters—after a while—take on a comic dimension regardless of what they do. At a certain point the pattern takes over, and we decide (on the unconscious level) that whatever the characters do is funny. As Frye says ". . . laughter is partly a reflex, and like other reflexes, it can be conditioned by a simple repeated pattern." That explains in part the significance of the compulsive nature of Schulz's characters (and most other comic characters)— they are a means toward conditioning us to laugh.

By all odds the greatest of Schulz's characters, and the one he relies most upon, is Snoopy. Snoopy is the latest and one of the greatest manifestations of the talking animal convention. Not only does he talk, but he has a brilliant personality—he carries on human relationships, he is a *bon vivant*, he participates in history, he has an incredible imagination, he is witty, he expresses himself with virtuosity in any number of ways (eye movements, ear movements, tail movements, wisecracks, facial expressions), and he is superb as mimic and dancer. He has energy and spirit and a heart overflowing with kindness, though he has been known to boot a bird or two, or snatch a blanket.

There is, in fact, an existential dimension to Snoopy. He is an existential hero in every sense of the term. He strives, with dogged persistence and unyielding courage, to overcome what seems to be his fate—that he is a dog; that he is *just* a dog. And somehow he does it! I think we see Snoopy as a "person" who happens to be a dog, rather than a dog who happens to become a person—as is the case in Mikhail Bulgakov's brilliant satire *Heart of a Dog*.

"Existence precedes essence" says the distinguished French philosopher Jean-Paul Sartre—and if Snoopy's existence is that of a human is it not reasonable to think of him as one? Dogs don't fight the Red Baron or cruise around in dark glasses looking for chicks in the dorms. Nor do dogs write novels or develop phobias.

What Snoopy demonstrates, to all his readers, is that ultimately we are all free to create ourselves as we wish, no matter what our status on the Great Chain of Being might be. We can all be authentic if only we will have the courage *to* be what we can be. And this applies even to dogs.

Snoopy is an animal who has transcended his limitations, though he still has some. How curious that in a society characterized (so many social scientists tell us) by a growing sense of alienation and apathy, a dog in a comic strip is just bursting with *joie de vivre*, vitality, and hope. Perhaps we have reached the stage in which we live vicariously through Snoopy—and all the other characters in the strip. This is the ultimate inversion—a multitude of lifeless (in the sense of being de-energized and neurasthenic) and mute humans leading a kind of vicarious existence in the lives of comic strip characters . . . as well as through other entertainments offered by the mass media.

This is somewhat farfetched, but there is little question in my mind that one of the reasons for the popularity of *Peanuts* is that it helps assuage our hunger for *personality* in a world that is full of dehumanizing forces and in which identity is so much under attack. Snoopy shows that man's spirit has resiliency and that there is hope yet.

Schulz has said that his greatest ambition is to create a comic strip as good as *Krazy Kat,* probably the greatest comic strip produced to date. There is little question, I think, that he has come close to this goal. Schulz has transformed a comic strip into part of the very essence of American life. Charlie Brown and Linus and Snoopy and their cohorts are not just comic strip characters; they have long since transcended their roles and now are part of the galaxy of great comic creations, in any form of popular art. His characters have become legends in their own comic strip lifetimes.

QUESTIONS

1. Do you agree that "Peanuts" is essentially American in spirit? Explain. How is Schulz's humor similar to Ben Franklin's?

2. How are Schulz's characters "peanuts"? In what sense are they giants? What qualities are embodied by Lucy? Linus? Charlie Brown?

3. Why is the strip so popular with adults? What elements of satire and social comedy does it contain? What does it say about the concept of Original Sin?

4. What inversions are in "Peanuts"? What is the "ultimate" inversion? How does inversion make "Peanuts" a kind of pastoral?

5. Discuss Northrop Frye's definition of comedy. What are the four basic character types? How does this view apply to "Peanuts"?

6. Describe Snoopy's personality. In what way is he an existential hero? What does Snoopy demonstrate to his readers?

TV Situation Comedies

Horace Newcomb

In TV: The Most Popular Art, critic Horace Newcomb analyzes the formulas that bring success to various types of TV shows. Defining the situation comedy, he notes that it begins with a stereotyped situation, adds complication, and then offers an unrealistic, often magical unraveling of the difficulty. Newcomb relates TV "sitcoms" to the recurrent desire for easy solutions to our problems.

Lucy's daughter, Kim, arrives home to find her mother preparing for a date. She is thrilled that her mother is going out, and her pleasure is heightened by her mother's enthusiasm. Lucy has met a suave, handsome, polite man—everything a middle-aged television widow could wish for. In the next scene Kim meets the date at the door. Played by Robert Cummings, he is indeed everything her mother has indicated. The two of them make polite conversation until Lucy comes downstairs, reversing the classic pattern of parent waiting for daughter's dramatic appearance. Lucy is glowing in a new dress, her hair strikingly done. As the couple leaves, the daughter calls them back and explains to Bob that her mother is to be dealt with carefully and returned home at a reasonable hour, furthering the reversal of roles. Big laugh on the sound track. Kim waits up for her mother, who promises to tell all in the morning.

The following morning—scene shifted to the kitchen—Kim is having breakfast alone before Lucy's entrance. The milkman, a neighborhood gossip, arrives with the daily delivery. The daughter asks if he delivers Bob's milk. Of course, replies the milkman, and he begins to supply frightening details concerning the young women who are in and out of the apartment at all hours. Kim is increasingly alarmed; the milkman is increasingly comic. He envies the bachelor's freedom, his lack of responsibility, and his consequent harem. With each detail he sighs with desire as Kim cringes in fright. As Lucy comes in for breakfast, Kim hurries out of the house. She rushes to her mother's office and there solicits the aid of Uncle Harry in a plot to protect her mother from the menacing Bob. They plan a dinner party that will demonstrate Lucy's "true" nature and consequently frighten away the deceiving bachelor.

The wolf is met at the door by Uncle Harry, who casually reveals Lucy's wedding gown, hung prominently in the coat closet. It is kept there, he explains, in perpetual readiness. While Lucy is out of the room, Bob is told that she is actually older than he had been led to believe and is quite hard of hearing. He will have to speak loudly to her. Kim, meanwhile, has prepared a plate of special canapés for Bob, spiked with great quantities of hot sauce and pepper.

The following scene is the classic: yelling, mugging, strangling, confusion, and the gulping of huge glasses of water, all to the accompaniment of riotous laughter supplied by the sound track. Following a commercial break, we return to the scene. There, in summary form, we learn that the problem has been remedied. All characters are present and apologetic, for Lucy has explained that Bob is an agent for a modeling firm and does indeed use his apartment for interviews. She had known this all along. Kim and Uncle Harry are somewhat chagrined, but all in all it was a funny show and no one was ever really worried. The fade-out comes to a cast enjoying one another's company and laughing at its own misunderstandings, laughing at itself.

This is television's own form of comedy. Its roots go deep, of course, to farce, slapstick, to the confused comedies of the eighteenth-century stage, to the raucous silent films, even to Punch and Judy. But it is a standard format for television. No season is without a supply of new versions, but no season removes all of its old faithful, star-supported series, either. So stable—and so staple—is situation comedy that it has given rise to the parallel form, the domestic comedy. The only other comic forms on television are the monologue, a form not essentially visual, and the skit, usually a parody in situation comedy form.

The fact that Lucille Ball has starred in some type of situation comedy for over twenty years, however, does not mean simply that the form is a profitable time filler. More than any other television personality, she has found herself in situations like that described above. How many times has the audience watched in delight as she leaves the boss's theater tickets in a suit destined for the cleaners, calls the police to search for the kidnapped chimpanzee which turns up asleep in the neighbor's house? How many times have we marveled at the responses, the wide-eyed mugging, the bawling tears, the gleam of conspiracy? And there is something here that goes deeper than a superficial level of appeal.

This form allows Lucy to excel and in it we find many of the elements essential to any understanding of television as popular art. It is a paradigm for what occurs in more complex program types, and its perennial popularity is probably due to the relatively simple outline it follows. There is something here that allows us to do more than enjoy and laugh. Something makes us "love" Lucy.

In the delineation of the elements of the formula present here we can discern a meaning that goes beyond the element of "story." . . . the formula becomes the particular way of ordering and defining the world. Much of that ordering in situation comedy and in other television forms will have a strong sense of the "unreal." I suggest, however, that in situation comedy and in all of television there is the creation of a "special" sense of reality. The total effect of specific formulas is this reality. Each has its own meaning, its own structure, its own system of values. Indeed, . . . to break with this reality is to create a new formula, and in some cases a new form of television art. We begin with situation comedy precisely because its rigid structure is so apparent and because we find elements there that will carry through to other television formulas. A shift in emphasis, of focus, a different tone, a different sort of content, and we may find many of these same elements in mysteries, Westerns, doctor and lawyer shows, and many others.

Like all television forms, situation comedy creates its own special physical world. In part the worlds are defined by what is economical and what is feasible depending on varying advertisers and budgets. The southern California locale, for instance, predominates because that is the home of the film industry. But because content must be molded to this world, the physical circumstances take on a primary importance in defining the special nature of the formulas. As we will see, any change in setting—a movement, a change in decor, in design—reflects a change in attitude and in the meaning of the formula. These physical limitations, though they appear to limit the possibilities, delineate a great deal of the formulaic meaning that we are searching for.

The situation comedy depends on the one-room set. In the Lucy show recounted above, there are three of these sets: the living room, the kitchen, and the office in which Lucy and Uncle Harry work. For the eye of the viewer there is nothing of substance "between" these sets—that is, there is no concrete, physical world of things. Movement is always accomplished by means of a fade-out–fade-in sequence, and to move from house to office the viewer is never allowed to see the street, to "enter" a car or a subway. We see no houses, no yards, no trees. The formula is, in this sense, internal. We become accustomed to the shift in scenes that occurs during the commercial break.

Stylistically, the rooms that we see in situation comedy are stale with repetition. Always middle to upper-middle class in tone, they are carefully crowded with stuffed couches and comfortable chairs, coffee tables on which there are small "objects," and walls on which hang conventional paintings. Somewhere in the room is a passageway to another part of the house, a stairway or a door to bedroom or kitchen. Because the most important rooms are the living rooms and the kitchens, the sets frequently depend on the "modern" suburban arrangement of these rooms, and our eye is allowed to flow through a dining "area" connecting the two important rooms in one space. Bedrooms and baths are hidden in the recesses, though in the more "sophisticated" series such as the Dick Van Dyke show, we may be admitted to them. In "The New

Dick Van Dyke Show" we may even see the star and his wife occupying a double bed, in contrast to the "old" show in which the couple discreetly slept in twins.

Such homes reflect prosperity but not elegance. The standard of living is based on comfort; the rule of existence is neatness. During the meal scenes there is always plenty to eat, and a teen-ager frequently opens a refrigerator to pour another glass of milk. There is shabbiness or disarray only when called for by the script, and in such circumstances care is taken to indicate that it is an arranged form of clutter; the audience is immediately cued by the laugh track and the opening shots that this episode depends on a rearranged set of physical expectations.

The severity of this middle-class rule is indicated for us by the upturned world of "The Beverly Hillbillies." There in the midst of the millionaire's luxury they reflect the values of rural America—or perhaps is it more accurate to say that they reflect the values of rural America as conceived by middle-class Americans. At any rate the mixture is decidedly more middle class as they insist on wearing their worn, but very neat and clean, overalls. Their food is exotic, true, but the recipes are from the mountains and stewed possum is a staple dish. Much of the show's success depends on the continuing praise of middle-class virtues and the rejection of luxury as a way of life.

When one thinks of the living rooms in which the shows are viewed, a mighty contrast comes to mind. Where, on the television programs, are the scattered magazines and newspapers; where are the stacks of toys left by rumbling children? Does anyone ever run out of milk? Such scenes and events do not appear for good reason. We are not concerned with characters and their homes as representations of what "we" are like, of what our homes are like. We are concerned with what happens to a set of characters, and only incidentally will that character's physical surroundings and his attitudes toward them reflect our own. Indeed, the television version of the American living-dining-kitchen complex reflects a sort of idealized version which many of the viewers would choose over their own if given the opportunity, a factor that takes on greater importance as we now discover what it is that happens in these rooms.

What, in "real" life, is a situation? More aptly, what in "real" life is not? It is a strange word with which to define a formula, to define a type of comedy. Clearly, it is not meant to be universally applicable or we could find ourselves with situation tragedies or situation mysteries. In situation comedy the situation is simply the broad outline of events, the special funny "thing" that is happening this week to a special set of characters. The characters will appear at the same time the following week in another funny situation which will be entirely nondependent on what happens tonight. In the Lucy show episode the situation might be stated as follows: a reversal of the parent (mother) protects child (daughter) situation. In such terms this is a totally undeveloped situation, but clearly it has humorous possibilities.

In one sense the elaborate development of situation as it occurs in the Lucy show is rather roundabout; some minutes and three scenes are required to establish the situation fully. These scenes are required to define this episode's comic difficulty. In another manner, however, producers take a more direct route with the "built-in" situation. What happens when a man discovers that his beautiful young wife is a witch with incredible supernatural powers? Anything happens, and with great regularity. As the idea begins to wear a bit thin, there is always the possibility of introducing the mother-in-law, delightfully increasing the humor of the "my mother-in-law is a witch" idea. Similarly, it is possible for the young couple to have a child who is also a witch and who uses her "powers" in a typically childish fashion. If such a situation seems too extreme, one can always populate Beverly Hills with a family of mountain folk or marry a liberated Jew to a liberated Irish Catholic. Shipwreck a couple of millionaires, an actress, a professor, and a young girl with their pleasure boat crew, an inane captain and his zany crewman, and leave them on an island for a few years.

In such form, however, these descriptions are only bald outlines. In order for the situation to develop into something resembling a story, two other elements common to the formula must be added: complication and confusion. The complicating element in the Lucy episode is Kim's discovery of the suitor's "true" nature. The show cannot remain the same from this point on. Given the situation, the daughter must take it on herself to protect her mother, and to do this she must enlist the aid of the uncle. His concern, adult wisdom, maleness, and age are crucial. Basically, the complication of any situation is any element that begins the events of the particular show. It comes early, as soon as possible after the situation has been established. In an episode of "Bewitched," for example, where the situation is built in, Samantha and her daughter, Tabitha, shop for a doll. When the mother goes to pay for the item, the salesman chats with the small witch, remarking that he would like to be a child again. The laugh track begins to chuckle in anticipation and is rewarded when the little girl wiggles her nose manually and the salesman gapes at himself in the body of a nine-year-old boy. In the action that follows we are taken through all the contortions of convincing Tabitha that the man really wishes to be a grown-up again so that she can remove the spell.

Complications in situation comedies may take many forms, but most generally they are involved with some sort of human error or mistake. The source of the complication on the Lucy show has to do with the daughter's well-intended attempts at protection, but it rises basically out of the misinformation of the milkman. He is the low-comedy character, sighing and dreaming of a fuller life as he offers detail after detail which seem to indict Lucy's date. With each tidbit the daughter gasps and the milkman leers. It is an eloquent scene and the audience can thoroughly enjoy both performances, for the audience knows that this scene is the one that will precipitate the action that follows. Similarly, we may be treated to errors of a more physical nature. When Lucy leaves a winning lottery ticket in her boss's trousers, it is to the great delight of the audience that she must follow them through the entire cleaning process, emerging at last stiffened with starch.

It is such action that I refer to as confusion, the heart of what is comic about situation comedy. Situation comedy, like most television formulas, does not conform to the artistic standards of "high" art in the development of action, character, event, and conclusion. Events, the things that "happen" in sitcom, are composed solely of confusion, and the more thorough the confusion, the more the audience is let in on a joke that will backfire on the characters, the more comic the episode. Individual shows are frequently structured on various layers of confusion that can be generated out of a single complication. Like parentheses within parentheses, the characters slip into deeper and deeper confusion. Expression and reaction follow complication, gesture follows reaction, slapstick follows gesture. The broader the element, the louder the laughter.

After Bob has gulped several glasses of water in his attempt to drench the fiery canapés, he runs for the door and escapes. Lucy, who still does not understand what has been created by her guardians, eats one of the spiked appetizers. Before her daughter and Uncle Harry can stop her—their attempts are elaborately comic gestures—she swallows it whole and begins to steam, reaches for a pitcher of water and drinks it down as the fade-out begins. This is what we have waited to see, this moment of ultimate confusion in which the star proves her ability to outmug the other members of her family. There is no development, the "plot" is not getting anywhere. There are simply characters involved with one another in confusing sequences. The only movement is toward the alleviation of the complication and the reduction of confusion.

At the center of the situation, complication, and confusion stand the characters of the situation comedy. They are cause and effect, creator and butt of joke, the audience's key to what the formula means. As we have seen, that formula allows for little real development, no exploration of idea or of conflict; the stars merely do what they have always done and will continue to do so well. The characteristics of these favorites, the things that identify them, cut across program types and create not individual actors, but situation comedy stars, a television unit. We expect these characters to behave in certain ways, and if we have our favorites—Lucy, Gilligan, Granny—they will more than likely do the same things, react in the same ways, within their stylistically individual manners.

Physically the stars are easy to identify. With the rural exceptions they are young American suburbanites. Lucy's TV age is around forty or forty-five. In her earlier shows she could not have been cast as over thirty. Only the older Clampetts, of "The Beverly Hillbillies," exceed this top limit, and their actions belie their age as the "eternally youthful" Granny outdoes her grandchildren in physical prowess and mental exasperation. As becomes such youth, the characters are beautiful and healthy. They match the neatness of their living rooms, and if the opening shots of a show depict a character as ill or frazzled, we know that it is called for in the script, that the situation depends on it.

All the characters are prosperous enough to afford their suburban "ranch-style" homes. The husbands are employed as advertising account executives, young lawyers, or doctors. Dick Van Dyke in his earlier show portrayed a comedy writer for a television variety show, and Jeannie's husband is a career officer in the Air Force. As with sickness, extreme fatigue is almost always a function of the script. These people simply do not work themselves out of the sitcom "look."

Emotionally, the characters correspond to this same standard. They are never troubled in profound ways. Sorrow cannot touch their lives. Stress, as the result of confusion, is always funny.

Surrounding these central characters are two sets of supporting characters. They offer a more natural spread of types. In some cases they are older or younger than the central characters—Uncle Harry and Kim in "The Lucy Show," for example. In other cases they are not as carefully "beautiful"; Miss Jane, the secretary, in "The Beverly Hillbillies" is typical of this class. Children of various ages, occasional cousins, aunts, and uncles appear as needed.

One group of supporting characters is almost incidental. These people most nearly represent the audience. They appear in shops, banks, or offices. They are run over by fleeing characters, amazed and bewildered by unnatural events and unusual circumstances. Though they "populate" the comedy world, they almost never realize what the "situation" is, and they are often victims of the central characters' foibles.

More important is the set of regular characters who serve as foils for the antics of the stars. Ricky Ricardo and Fred and Ethel Mertz, of the "I Love Lucy" series, fall into this category. So do Ann Marie's father and her boyfriend Don in "That Girl." Banker Drysdale and Miss Jane, of "The Beverly Hillbillies," are classic patterns for the type.

Given such solid established worlds, it would seem strange that the characters should find themselves in difficulty. But difficulty is a mild word for the confusion that reigns in this formula. Again and again we run into horrible complications, plots involving policemen and postmen, mistaken identities and misplaced objects. Our middle-class characters come into possession of clues threatening gangsters, or formulas for secret weapons. Though the gangsters turn out to be funnier than guys and dolls and secret weapons fizzle in actual tests, it seems for the moment that we are beset on all sides by maddening complexities and problems. Ultimately, this is because of the most prominent aspect of the central character's makeup, a lack of any sense of probability. They are, in some way, out of touch with our day-to-day sense of how things happen, with the set of laws that allows us to predict the outcome of our actions. Again, Lucy is the prime example. She has no such sense of probability—not because she is stupid, for her schemes demonstrate exactly the opposite, but because she is innocent. Gilligan and Ann Marie are similar examples. They are without malice, and if their actions precipitate a chain of events that weighs heavily on other characters, it is not because they are cruel, for just as often they suffer the consequences themselves. Indeed, as often as not they do not "do" anything, but act "naturally" and are consequently done to. What they lack, or what they refuse to recognize, is a knowledge of the order of the world. If one did not suspect that the word had been invented precisely for the advertising of a new situation comedy, they would have to be called "wacky."

The supporting characters live somewhere between the improbable world of the central characters and the world as most of the audience experiences it. Uncle Harry knows that his suit is very wet after Lucy tips the water cooler over him, but it is unlikely that he will break her jaw in response. It is probable that the humor of the formula would be apparent simply in the audience's comparison of the events of the show with the events of its own world. There is no doubt, however, that the placement of a set of characters in the show, who will react similarly to the audience, is an advantage.

Such characters are all the more important in the show that depends on the built-in situation. If the fractured sense of probability is a workable component, if the audience accepts a Lucy innocent of the consequences of her own actions, then there is no need for central characters to conform to the laws of probability and reality in any way. It is only a short step, then, to a world in which the suburbs are inhabited by witches and genies, and a shorter step still to rich hillbillies in a Beverly Hills mansion, complete with mountain folk values and barnyard menagerie. An uncharted island in the South Pacific, a small rural community complete with pet pigs within commuting distance of New York? No problem at all. In fact, the problems are eased, the plot is simplified. All that is necessary now is a misdirected nose wiggle and the boss is turned into a monkey.

The supporting character is caught directly in the middle. Darren knows that his wife, his daughter, and his mother-in-law are witches. He is surrounded by "situation." There is no way for him to avoid involvement and the continued jarring of his sense of the real. Finally, even he accepts the new order of reality as we see him pleading that Samantha not give up her powers in order to preserve their marriage. He married her for what she is, he says, and that means witchness along with everything else.

These supporting characters serve a crucial function in that they stand, dramatically, closer to the value structure of the audience than to that of the central characters. Uncle Harry is a tightwad. He will not give Lucy a raise, though he should know by now that every refusal to do so will result in a scheme on her part and that he will most likely suffer in the outcome. His straightforward attitude precipitates an often incoherent sequence of events. Similarly, Banker Drysdale of "The Beverly Hillbillies" stands in awe of both the Clampetts' money and their value structure. Because he does not share their simplistic view of the world, however, he cannot share their wealth, despite his attempts to do so. But, then, very few people in the audience are hillbillies, much less millionaires, and cannot see the relationship between their world and the "situation" that entertains them.

For the supporting characters and for the audience to whom they directly relate, the world of such situations is an amusing and frustrating one. It is an embarrassing sort of frustration because the audience always knows more than the characters involved and watches time after time as an innocent or not-so-innocent character walks into the trap of his or her own actions. If the situation comedy consisted solely of the antics of the characters, if we were repeatedly forced to involve ourselves merely in laughing at the pie-in-the-face aspects of the formula, it would remain at the level of embarrassment. But there is a recurring structure that outlines every episode of situation comedy, and that outline is ultimately the defining factor of the formula.

Lucy takes a fall and lodges her hand in a coffeepot just prior to serving at an exclusive social function. Gilligan swallows a radio that suddenly receives signals from a spacecraft. Jeannie, the genie, sends her husband to the base without his pants. How should a character behave under such circumstances? In many cases the stars of situation comedy avoid the most natural conclusion to such a sequence of events. Lucy, for example, never tells her hostess that a coffeepot is stuck on her wrist; Jeannie's husband never admits to having married a genie. For if natural solutions were sought, the stories could never exist. Finding contorted paths out of such inane thickets is precisely the business of situation comedy.

The action involved will fall into four basic parts: the establishment of the "situation," the complication, the confusion that ensues, and the alleviation of the complication. The essential factor is the remedying of the confusion. It is rather like a mathematical process, the removing of parentheses within parentheses. In some cases it is accomplished merely by the explanation scene. In the Lucy episode that has served as our primary example, the entire show was given over to the creation of confusion in a single central scene which gave full play to the talents of the central characters. The clarification of that confusion was accomplished in a simple verbal explanation following the final commercial. In the episode of "Bewitched," however, in which the salesman was changed into a small boy, there was much more to do. In the attempt to clarify the physical elements of the confusion, more confusion followed. The removal of the spell was not an easy task, and time was spent demonstrating that the man's life would be seriously impaired by his nine-year-old body. In addition, the man learned the foolishness of wishing for a world of eternal childhood. But in both cases, the structure finally brings us full circle to a state of "normalcy."

Such "normalcy" is obviously "unreal." What does it mean to return to the normal state in which the witches are behaving like the good humans who surround them? Each of these shows is built on a complication that could never arise in "real" life. What, then, accounts for the success of such a formula? Why does it sell so well? What sense of need does this pattern tap so that it draws audience after audience, year after year? Clearly, though there is a sense of entertainment in the fantastic nature of some of the situations, and in the antics of the comic stars whom we enjoy watching, there is more than that, too. I would suggest that the more fundamental appeal of the situation comedy is found precisely in the fact that everything always "comes out all right."

What we see in the situation comedy is the establishment of a problem and an absolutely thorough solution to that problem. As suggested earlier, the audience always knows that the solution will be found. It is impossible that Lucy will be hurt by a scheming Bob, out to take advantage of her middle-aged dreams. It is impossible that the toy salesman will remain forever bewitched, an adult trapped unwillingly in a young boy's body. Rather, we know that all the parties involved will not only solve their problems but laugh at them, and laugh together, at each other. There is a warmth that emerges from the corrected mistakes, a sort of ultimate human companionship.

Such a feeling arises from the basic formula of human failure and human response. No one intends to cause pain in the shows, no one intends evil. The problems exist solely at the level of misunderstanding. Drysdale may desire the Clampetts' money, but he is not willing to steal and kill for it. Uncle Harry may not be free with salary raises, but he is quick to defend Lucy from emotional harm. So what if it is a one-sided world populated by characters totally innocent of our reality, or even if the characters are not of our order of reality at all? The possibility of the fantastic solution, of the magical paths out of our troubles, is a recurring human dream. And it is . . . one of the basic characteristics of popular art. The audience is reassured in its beliefs; it is not challenged by choice, by ambiguity, or by speculation about what might happen under other "realistic" circumstances. The character is not forced to examine his or her values, nor is the audience. In the situation comedy, there is no particular set of beliefs to be dealt with. There is only the barest, most basic outline, the paradigm. Human beings create problems for themselves; human beings resolve those problems, even in nonhuman situations. It is the upturned line of comedy in its barest form, and the result is a sigh of relief along with the laughter.

QUESTIONS

1. How does "sitcom" differ from "high art"? Review the pattern of action in situation comedy. What is the essential element?

2. Describe the sets in situation comedy. How are they idealized? What middle-class values do they express?

3. Discuss the different groups of characters. What is their relationship to one another? To us?

4. How does the author explain the popularity of situation comedies? What needs of the TV audience does this type of comedy fulfill? Do you agree with Newcomb's analysis? Why?

5. Consider situation comedies not discussed in this article. In what ways are they similar to the shows Newcomb describes? Different?

Echoes of Dark Laughter: The Comic Sense in Contemporary American Fiction

Ihab Hassan

It is fashionable today to sound a dirge for American humor. Ihab Hassan does not succumb to this temptation. Instead, he compares the comedic styles thriving in our novels and stories, and notes that, though it is difficult to predict the future development of comedy in American fiction, there is a genre of comedy "intelligent as well as celebrant, that keeps the possibility of spiritual heroism alive, without mendacity or bombast." A noted critic of contemporary American literature, Hassan has written Radical Innocence *and* The Dismemberment of Orpheus.

I

The popular imagination has always been easy with black humor. In America, for instance, the ghoulish cartoons of Chas. Addams and the nasty stings of the sick joke ("And aside from that, Mrs. Lincoln, how did you like the play?") testify to the currency of the genre. Yet sometime during the fifties the sound of dark laughter became more seriously fashionable. There was, of course, *Dr. Strangelove*, subtitled "How I Learned to Stop Worrying and Love the Bomb," a box-office hit across the nation. But there were also many off-Broadway plays and experimental novels displaying a taste for crazy comedy. It was as if the Muses had all suddenly taken to dancing under the gallows, their emblem a fool's cap or grinning skull.

Consider some of the best novels of that period (1949–1962): John Hawkes, *The Cannibal* (1949); Carson McCullers, *The Ballad of the Sad Café* (1951); J. D. Salinger, *The Catcher in the Rye* (1951); Ralph Ellison, *Invisible Man* (1952); Flannery O'Connor, *Wise Blood* (1952); John Cheever, *The Wapshot Chronicle* (1957); Vladimir Nabokov, *Lolita* (1955, 1958); J. P. Donleavy, *The Ginger Man* (1955, 1958); John Barth, *The End of the Road* (1958); Saul Bellow, *Henderson the Rain King* (1959); James Purdy, *Malcolm* (1959); William Burroughs, *Naked Lunch* (1959); John Updike, *Rabbit Run* (1960); Joseph Heller, *Catch-22* (1961); and Thomas Berger, *Reinhart in Love* (1962). Though mainly comic or ironic in tone, these works show a deep knowledge of sadness, madness, mortality. Their use of dark laughter soon became a trend. Critics began to ask: is this the death or the rebirth of comedy that we see in our midst?

It was, I believe, the birth of a new sense of reality, a new knowledge of error and of incongruity, an affirmation of life under the aspect of comedy. For comedy, broadly conceived, may be understood as *a way of making life possible in this world, despite evil or death.* Comedy recognizes human limitations, neither in broken pride nor yet in saintly humility but in the spirit of ironic acceptance. It is, therefore, the antic child of realism. Comedy recognizes danger, too, which makes of us tightrope walkers to the future, and may also make clowns of us all. Yet clowns can have skill and vision. They can unite horror and humor and make men laugh in order to live.

Intuitively, writers of the fifties knew this. They sensed that the postwar world offered few occasions of authentic heroism or even tragedy. The hero of Miller's *Death of a Salesman* is a sad and broken man, probably more pathetic than tragic. The heroes of fiction, likewise, are seldom larger than life. At best, they are rogues with a heart or winsome adolescents—like Holden Caulfield. At worst, they are victims with a purpose—like most of us. Bemused by incongruities, besieged in their private as in their social life, they do not stand tall with the dignity of Achilles or Odysseus. Their conflicts seldom allow for final resolutions.

It is no great wonder, then, that postwar novelists were anxious to respond to the incoherence of life, to its openness and even to its absurdity, in new ways. They cultivated the picaresque or fantastic modes; they avoided the neat formulations of style or structure that formalist critics once pressed too hard. Their sense of order admitted of potential disorder. In short, they acquired a tolerance for the mixed, causeless quality of experience: its loose ends, its broken links, its surprises and reversals. Knowing how outrageous facts could be, they did not pretend to subdue them with a flourish and a symbol.

II

There are, of course, literary precedents to the dark humor of postwar American novelists. Dostoevski's *Notes from Underground*, a book that I have always considered a kind of manifesto of the modern disorderly sensibility, resounds with grotesque or demonic laughter. The novels of Joyce, Kafka, and Gide are full of comedy both clownish and satanic. The works of both dada and surrealism abound in black humor. And the fiction of Sartre, Malraux, and Camus shows how comedy may vanish behind the mask of irony, revealing the latter as an intellectual grimace. Finally, the drama of Beckett, Ionesco, or Brecht often renders life as an incongruous or absurd disaster. (The heritage of black humor goes back to Swift and Sade, as André Breton shows in his *Anthologie de l'humour noir*.)

In America, the comic spirit has taken both parallel and divergent forms. The gothic or supernatural strain in classic American fiction, black with laughter, has been noted by Leslie Fiedler. Faulkner extended this strain well into the twentieth century. Stories like "A Rose for Emily"—the proud woman who kills her lover and lies in bed by his putrefying corpse for forty years—and novels like *Sanctuary* and *As I Lay Dying* make capital use of macabre humor. Even in his jaunty series of books about the acquisitive Snopes family, *The Hamlet*, *The Town*, and *The Mansion*, Faulkner shoved that burlesque, whether in horse- or wife-trading, could serve as a thin disguise for chilling malevolence. But Faulkner was not alone in exploiting this particular strain of comedy in our time. Sherwood Anderson, that woeful master of the grotesque, focused on the poetry of deviation and infirmity and on their humor. A satirist and surrealist both, Nathanael West revealed in his stories about Hollywood or Manhattan freaks a unique gift for torture-house parody. And Henry Miller, a more sanguine surrealist, seemed often at his best when translating acute pain into impish or ribald pleasure.

There are many echoes of dark laughter in the literature of the world; and I should not want to reduce them all to a single sound. My purpose, however, is to note a certain event in the modern imagination: the deflection of laughter toward anguish. Ageless as this impulse may be, it is largely in our century that it becomes a dominant motif. Since the Second World War, particularly, dark comedy has exhibited various shades in American fiction, to which I must now turn.

III

A rapid survey of American fiction in the fifties and early sixties discloses a variety of comic attitudes. The range of these attitudes extends from horror to slapstick; in between, the grotesque, the ironic, and the quixotic stances take their place.

We all recall the shudders and giggles experienced in any good horror film, by Hitchcock, say. The feeling is akin to the mournful frolic of nightmares. But horror is not merely sensational. In the hands of such writers as John Hawkes, in *The Cannibal*, or William Burroughs, in *Naked Lunch*, it underscores the fact that insanity or evil often puts on an antic disposition. We move into the midnight terrain where Macbeth met the witches, and there reckon with the forces of human desires. The witches' heath may also lie in the heart of a modern state. There violations in every form—murder, cannibalism, rape, drug addiction, political control—enact a comedy of errors, at times both ludicrous and horrible.

If there is much warping in nightmare, there is only a little less in the grotesque figures who populate the fiction of Flannery O'Connor, Carson McCullers, and James Purdy. The aim of these writers is to describe spiritual distortion in our time; in so doing they focus on physical distortion. They create freaks of love or loneliness, or monsters of holiness. Thus, for instance, the hero of O'Connor's *Wise Blood* is both a murderer and an ascetic, a preacher in the "Church Without Christ" who blinds himself with quicklime and wears barbed wire next to his skin. But freaks and monsters are also the subject of veiled mockery; more subtly, their abnormality shocks and shames us into ironic laughter. This is why the comedy of the grotesque often seems acerb.

The ironic attitude lies close to the satiric. In the latter, the object of attention is not the monstrous, which is irremediable, but, rather, the follies or vices of men, things merely reprehensible. There is a combination of both attitudes in the comedy of Nabokov's *Lolita*; its hero still thinks of himself as a grotesque monster. But when satire appears in less extravagant forms, as it does in Barth's *The End of the Road* or Updike's *Rabbit, Run*, we are already moving toward the sunnier reaches of comedy. The scalpel is still sharp, but the patients to whom it is applied are not altogether beyond hope. Their maladies are ours, and in our heart of hearts few of us consider ourselves beyond healing.

It is this possibility of regeneration that we sense in diverse characters, rogues and innocents abroad, who masquerade as the descendants of gaunt Don Quixote. There is, to be sure, something quixotic and whimsical about them, an idea or illusion raised to the condition of a large truth. This is clearest in Bellow's *Henderson the Rain King*. But there is also a good deal of bitter passion, as in Ellison's *Invisible Man*, which depicts a Negro whom everyone manages not to see; or moral disgust, as in Donleavy's *The Ginger Man*, which portrays a scoundrel who boozes on the milk money of his children until they develop rickets. Comedy in these books can still have a rasping noise. Even in such zany and genuinely humorous "picaresques" as Salinger's *The Catcher in the Rye*, laughter trails into a wistful tremor. The smile on our lips is sad.

Still, the unrelieved exuberance of life comes through in a number of novels that make large use of fantasy and burlesque. Cheever's *The Wapshot Chronicle*, about a daft and indestructible Yankee family, attests to the continuities of human existence under the aspect of whimsy. Berger's *Reinhart in Love* employs farce and madcap humor to convey the abundance of love. And the buffoonery of Heller's *Catch-22* settles for nothing less than sanity and freedom. The sense of release, of possibility, is very large in these novels. But we should be doing their spirit violence were we to ignore their undertone of individual and even anarchic protest. The last novel in particular holds society, its norms, pieties, and organizations, holds death itself, in deep suspicion: Yossarian will accept nothing but the Self as sacred. It is as if comedy, finally freed from the dark constraints of the modern world, had suddenly over-reached itself to the borders of chaos.

There are, of course, many other novelists—most notably, Norman Mailer—who do not fit into this scheme. But my aim is not to be inclusive; it is, rather, to convey some sense of the diversity of the comic spirit, the range of attitudes it has exhibited. This range may be more circular than linear: Hawkes's *The Cannibal* and Heller's *Catch-22*, representing horror and slapstick respectively, do not really stand very far apart. Our path through the dark woods of laughter ends close to where we began. And that may be precisely the point: nightmare and slapstick do meet in that surreal comic vision that, recognizing the discrepancies in human life, expresses and mediates them.

IV

In the late sixties, however, there was evidence of certain changes in the comic mood. Black humor had become conventional, a way of evading true passion or perception. Dark laughter often seemed to freeze on the face of the novelist, turning into a sophisticated leer, a knowing grimace. It became that elaborate and decadent form of wit sometimes called Camp.

Yet an exception must be made in the case of certain gifted authors and their works. These include: Kurt Vonnegut, Jr.'s *Cat's Cradle* (1963) and *Slaughterhouse-Five* (1969); John Barth's *Lost in the Funhouse* (1968) and *Chimera* (1972); Thomas Pynchon's *V* (1963) and *The Crying of Lot 49* (1966); Donald Barthelme's *Snow White* (1967) and *City Life* (1970); Ishmael Reed's *The Free-lance Pallbearers* (1967) and *Yellow Back Radio Broke-Down* (1969).

The sense of comedy in these works, though often desperate, is metaphysical. The joke is epistemological; the joke is the joke itself, which has no other terms in which to explain itself. Very often, the artist makes his art form itself the butt of his problematic humor. Very often, the novelist creates and destroys his sense of human destiny in the same comic and complex narrative structure. The humor of these different works, though by no means identical, somehow raises the question of consciousness questioning itself, of art at the end of its tether making new art, of entropy formulating an enigmatic theory of verbal games. Thus beneath the sentimentality of Vonnegut, the absurdism of Barth, the mysteries of Pynchon, the zaniness of Barthelme, and the black dadaism of Reed there is a profound intellectual irony calling culture, calling the cosmos itself, into doubt.

It is difficult, of course, to predict how the comic sense will further develop in American fiction. For a time, the sounds of dark laughter were refreshing in the late fifties, dominated as that decade was by the conformist spirit of the Cold War. Through antic surrealism, the writer wanted to expand awareness. Through improvisations in literary forms, he hoped to assert his liberty as well as that of his readers. And through bawdiness and obscenity he intended to remind us of the corporeal nature of man, his instinctual being. Later, as black humor became a stereotype of evasion, perhaps even a kind of cowardice, many authors in the rebellious sixties shunned it. Some found their own form of outrageous and heroic humor, as Norman Mailer, the most significant American writer alive, did in *Why Are We in Vietnam?* (1967). For, as Mailer well knows, there is a genre of comedy that succeeds only in narrowing human possibilities, in diminishing our demands and appeasing our challenges—a genre that becomes popular only because it is an accommodation to failure. And there is another genre, intelligent as well as celebrant, that keeps the possibility of spiritual heroism alive, without mendacity or bombast.

QUESTIONS

1. How does Hassan view comedy? Why does he call it the "antic child of realism"?

2. Describe the range of American comic fiction in the fifties and early sixties. What examples does Hassan cite? What others would you add? Why does the author feel the range may be "more circular than linear"?

3. Why do writers such as Eudora Welty and Flannery O'Connor focus on physical distortion? What kinds of freaks do they create? What grotesque figures have you read about in modern American fiction? Describe them.

4. Contrast the satiric attitude with the ironic. What kinds of things is satire concerned with?

5. Discuss the change that occurred in the comedy of the late sixties. Why did many writers shun black humor? What is Camp?

6. What does Hassan say about the future of American comedy? Do you agree? Explain.

Glossary of Critical Terms

ANIMALISM   A satiric technique in which human beings are depicted as animals.

ANTICLIMAX   A humorous strategy marked by a sudden transition from a significant idea or action to one that is trivial or ridiculous.

BLACK HUMOR   A brand of grim comedy characterized by the mingling, in varying degrees, of the ludicrous and the terrible. Unlike satire, black humor is not primarily concerned with follies that can be remedied; its basic joke is far more profound—life is absurd or, at best, is an enigma. The characters are pathetic, often grotesque, and the situations painful; the endings, in contrast to those of more traditional comedy, do not suggest rebirth and renewal. Black-humor fiction has become especially popular since World War II.

BURLESQUE   In comic writing, an imitation of a literary form that mocks the original by ludicrously distorting it, often by treating a trivial subject seriously. The term has also come to refer to theatrical entertainments, such as vaudeville shows, that include short comic skits.

CARICATURE   A technique of both literature and the visual arts in which the characteristic features of a subject are exaggerated in a manner that makes the subject appear ridiculously distorted.

COMEDY   A drama or other narrative form that treats its subject in a light or satiric manner and that generally ends happily. *High comedy* is aimed at the intellect; it usually is witty or subtle, it can even be serious, and often its purpose is moral or instructive. *Low comedy* has a broader, more elemental appeal and is closer to burlesque or farce; its jokes are coarse, its characters often clowns or buffoons, its actions boisterous. High comedy elicits thoughtful laughter, or it may have little to do with laughter; low comedy frequently provokes guffaws.

DIALECT   The form of a language, not recognized as standard, that is characteristic of a particular region, social class, or ethnic group; most often dialect is transmitted orally.

EPIGRAM   A short poem, usually satiric, ending with an unexpected turn of thought; also, a terse, witty saying.

FABLE   A short tale used to illustrate a moral. The characters often are animals embodying human follies.

FARCE A light dramatic piece marked by horseplay, coarse jesting, an improbable plot, and exaggerated characters. The term is also applied to the broad satire characteristic of such plays.

HUMOR The quality that appeals to our sense of the ludicrous. Humor depends on incongruity—attitudes, characters, or situations that are unsuitably matched—and on irony, or the unexpected. As with comedy, there is a wide range in the laughter evoked by humor, but generally humor takes a genial, sympathetic attitude toward human weakness, as opposed to the aggressive, somewhat intolerant approach of wit.

IRONY A manner of expression in which the intended meaning is the reverse of what is usual or expected. Words might be used in such a way as to convey the opposite of their literal meaning, or the actual outcome of events might be a surprise. The ironic writer usually assumes an attitude of detached awareness of incongruity.

LAMPOON Satire, often bitter, usually directed against an individual. The term can also refer to a light, mocking satire.

MALAPROPISM Use of a word that sounds like the one intended but is humorously wrong in the context. The term is derived from Mrs. Malaprop, a character noted for her misuse of words, in Richard Sheridan's eighteenth-century English comedy *The Rivals.*

MOCK HEROIC Descriptive term for a type of burlesque that ridicules a trivial subject by overstating its importance. Usually it employs the conventions and elevated style of the classical epics for satiric purposes.

PARODY A literary form in which the distinctive style of an author or a work is closely imitated for comic effect.

PUN Humorous play on a word, or on words that look or sound alike, in such a way that two or more meanings are suggested at once.

SATIRE Writing that exposes and criticizes human vices and follies through the devices of ridicule, sarcasm, or irony. Its subjects are often sexual mores, social manners, or political practices, and its traditional targets are such human weaknesses as greed, pride, and stupidity. Usually satire aims to correct the evils it attacks.

SHAGGY-DOG STORY A funny, often rambling story that has a sudden and irrelevant ending; often called a "catch story."

SLAPSTICK A form of low comedy stressing farce and physical conflict.

STAND-UP COMEDY The kind of act, popular with TV and nightclub comedians, in which the performer "stands up" before an audience to deliver a routine.

TALL TALE An anecdote that stretches the imagination with larger-than-life characters, settings, and incidents. Usually common people, miraculously endowed with supernatural qualities, perform great feats of strength and skill in their battles with the wilderness. Tall stories, born largely in the American West, were passed along at first by word of mouth and were marked by the braggadocio and colorful vernacular of the frontier. The exaggeration of the tall tale is generally regarded as America's most characteristic comic mode.

TRAVESTY A literary work that ridicules a noble or dignified subject by treating it frivolously.

UNDERSTATEMENT The deliberate use of restrained language to achieve a greater effect; the opposite of exaggeration.

WIT An intellectual quality that frequently uses quick wordplay to evoke laughter. Humor is marked by geniality and sympathy, wit by cold and clever mockery; humor depends on the perception of incongruities, wit often on the perception of similarities.

Brief History of Humor in American Literature

To trace the growth of America's comic literature is to trace the growth of our culture, so closely are the two related. It is not surprising, therefore, to find little humor in the writings of the first colonists. They were preoccupied with establishing a new society in the wilderness, and their literature consisted largely of diaries, chronicles of travel, and religious tracts and sermons. Yet even in seventeenth-century America the comic spirit was not totally absent, for there was a growing popular interest in ballads and jest books, as well as in picaresque and satiric narratives. Funny tales were told about such figures as Miles Standish, and, even so early in our history, women were objects of ridicule, mocked by New England preachers for being more concerned with fashion and manners than with Puritan ethics.

Satire, which began as an undercurrent in our national literature, soon became its chief form; during the eighteenth century, in America as in England, it flourished everywhere. Ebenezer Cook burlesqued Marylanders in his poem "The Sot-Weed Factor" (1708); North Carolinians were the target in William Byrd II's *History of the Dividing Line* (1728); Sarah Kemble Knight wrote a comic chronicle of her journey from Boston to New Haven (1704–05). Then, as the new political democracy took root, the country was flooded by political lampoons, many penned by the Connecticut group known as the "Hartford Wits." The most popular satire of the day, John Trumbull's mock-heroic *M'Fingal* (1776), described the fate of a Tory who was tarred and feathered by his Whig neighbors; Hugh Henry Brackenridge's lengthy, picaresque fiction, *Modern Chivalry* (1792–1815), exposed inconsistencies of democratic government. These writers were not full-time humorists or even full-time men of letters but, for the most part, active statesmen and civic leaders, and their burlesques had utilitarian ends. So did the clever political squibs of their celebrated contemporary, Benjamin Franklin.

Yet it is not Franklin's political satires but his portrayals of American character types that have led to his being dubbed the father of American humor. As "Silence Dogood," for instance, the young Franklin contributed essays to his brother James's *New England Courant*, which was modeled after the *Spectator* essays then popular in England. But the gossipy Widow Dogood was no Englishwoman; she was an American, commenting on Boston life and manners in accents that were unmistakably those of New England. Franklin later created another American woman, the promiscuous Polly Baker, and under her signature scandalized both Europe and America with his defense of "natural and useful actions." His most successful creation, though, was the genial homespun philosopher and almanac maker Richard Saunders (1732–57), the prototype of the American common man.

Franklin had pointed the way, and now other writers began to depict the idiosyncracies of American life and habits. The most important of them was Washington Irving, whose letters signed "Jonathan Oldstyle, Gent." (1802) gave new social status to the stock Yankee rustic figure of Jonathan. With Irving's creation of Diedrich Knickerbocker and his rambunctious comic epic, *The History of New York from the Beginning of the World to the End of the Dutch Dynasty* (1809), "a fresh new era in American humor began," as scholar Lewis Leary has observed. The *History*'s mingling of robust exaggeration and placid understatement, its presentation of the frontiersman as a humorous character, its unexpected moments of biting wit anticipated important elements of later American comedy. Similarly, the characters in Irving's "Legend of Sleepy Hollow," "Rip Van Winkle," and other fictions struck vital chords in the American imagination.

Though Irving, like Franklin, was still too greatly influenced by foreign models to be regarded as a native writer, he did indicate the possibilities for an authentically American humor. Concurrently, a comic folklore was gathering. Yankee Doodle already walked abroad in song. The country bumpkin Jonathan, first introduced to the theater in Royall Tyler's *Contrast* (1787), became a common stage figure. Tales were being told about the shrewd Yankee peddler and his backwoodsman brother. The *Farmer's Almanack* and others like it portrayed comic characters dispensing advice in the vernacular. Travelers recorded sectional differences in American life, and native characters appeared in the novels of James Fenimore Cooper. Finally, around 1830, in the East and in what was then the Southwest, the types, the techniques, and the themes seemed to fuse. As if full grown, an indigenously American humor emerged.

One pattern that would be repeated time and again was set by newspaper editor Seba Smith, in his letters signed "Major Jack Downing of Downingville, Away Down East in the State of Maine." Smith originated neither the character of the Yankee nor the idea of having a provincial comment on city life, but he did have his democratic hero become an intimate of President Andrew Jackson, he introduced an array of sharply defined comic figures, and he had a fine ear for salty New England speech. The idiomatic language and countrified types Smith helped to popularize were quickly picked up by others. Sam Slick, for instance, the itinerant Yankee peddler created by Thomas Chandler Haliburton, amused readers in the 1830s and '40s with his sly business dealings and witty aphorisms. As the tradition of Yankee humor developed, its methods gained refinement and its portraits gained variety and life. Women appeared—Frances Whitcher's Mrs. Bedott with her execrable poetry, Benjamin Shillaber's Mrs. Partington with her malapropisms. Even the Brahmins Oliver Wendell Holmes and James Russell Lowell invented comic characters for their satires: Holmes, the autocrat and the professor; Lowell, the rustic poet Hosea Biglow and his friends Parson Wilbur and Birdofredum Sawin, whose dialect provided much of the humor of *The Biglow Papers* (1848, 1867).

A southern tradition was growing at the same time. Its humor also relied heavily on dialect, but its violence and gusto made it markedly different from the northern brand of comedy. The forerunner of the southern line was Augustus Baldwin Longstreet, whose *Georgia Scenes* (1835) tells of shooting matches, horse swaps, fox hunts, and gander pullings. Longstreet's stress on authenticity set the tone for his followers. William Tappan Thompson's *Chronicles of Pineville* (1845) offers what he called "a few more interesting specimens of the genus Cracker." In what purports to be a political biography, Johnson J. Hooper's *Some Adventures of Capt. Simon Suggs* (1845) acquaints readers with a picaresque rogue who begins by stealing from his parents and moves on to stealing the collection box at a camp meeting. An even worse scoundrel is George W. Harris's Sut Lovingood, whose *Yarns* was published in 1867. Sut, a practical joker second to none, incarnated the irreverence, the brutality, and the concupiscence of southern humor. The zestful language of Harris's tales is that of the ne'er-do-well whose energy breaks all bonds, even those of language itself.

Racy dialect of the kind handled with such brilliance in the Lovingood yarns is a trademark of the southern stories, many of which originated as oral anecdotes. The lawyers, judges, and newspapermen who became the great southern humorists were deeply in touch with the tumultuous life around them, and they heard, and passed on, the folk tales and jokes of the Old Southwest. In a number of ways their writings were shaped by the conventions of oral storytelling: in a masculine concern with sporting and brawling, in the rapidity of narration, in the colorful language, in the use of the "frame" technique (having one narrator introduce another, who tells the story), in a closeness to American comic mythology. Many of these stories draw on the exaggerated exploits of our larger-than-life western heroes, the likes of Davy Crockett and Mike Fink. T. B. Thorpe's classic tale, "The Big Bear of Arkansas," embodies all these qualities of the comic tradition of the Old Southwest.

By the middle of the nineteenth century a different style of comedy was being popularized by the "literary comedians"—humorists who assumed the identity of the vital comic personalities they created. Thus, Charles Farrar Browne became internationally known as Artemus Ward; David Ross Locke wrote as Petroleum Vesuvius Nasby; Henry Wheeler Shaw was the famous Josh Billings; Robert H. Newell signed his work with the punning pseudonym Orpheus C. Kerr ("office seeker"); and Edgar Wilson Nye became plain Bill Nye. Their outrageous tales, naive letters, and aphoristic turns of speech all had precedents in our humor; as critic Walter Blair has said, "America by 1850 had discovered most of the things it was going to laugh at, and thereafter authors played variations on themes already announced." What *was* new with the literary comedians was the primarily verbal cast of their humor. Spelling had become sufficiently standardized and literacy sufficiently widespread for these "Phunny Phellows" to make comic capital out of mangled grammar, mashed words, and misused quotations, in their writings and also as lecturers—employing a deadpan platform style that prefigured the stand-up comedy of our own day.

The most remarkable of these professional humorists was Samuel Langhorne Clemens, the inimitable Mark Twain. Tutored by the literary comedians in the art of the comic lecture, indebted to the eastern humorists for their methods of characterization, and saturated in his youth with the humorous anecdotes of the Old Southwest, Twain absorbed all these species of American comedy into his own work until it came to articulate the very core of our comic experience. His first success, "The Celebrated Jumping Frog of Calaveras County" (1865), was praised as "the finest piece of humorous literature yet produced in America," and his masterpieces, *Tom Sawyer* (1876), *Life on the Mississippi* (1883), and *Huckleberry Finn* (1884), embrace the whole world of humor, from the frivolities of burlesque to the grim philosophical issues of black humor. Additionally, Twain relished dialect humor, and, like no American writer before him and only a few since, he exploited the riches of the American language to establish humor as a literary art.

Many writers of Twain's day realized the comic possibilities of dialect. The speech of southern Negroes was rendered in Joel Chandler Harris's tales of Uncle Remus, in Paul Laurence Dunbar's poetry, and in the short stories of Charles Chesnutt. Dialect writers whose stories focused on a particular region were called "local colorists." Bret Harte's *The Luck of Roaring Camp and Other Sketches* (1870) spoke for the Far West, Harriet Beecher Stowe's *Oldtown Folks* (1869) for New England, and Edward Eggleston's *The Hoosier Schoolmaster* (1871) for backwoods America. Dialect also became a comic device of burlesque skits, which often had ethnic overtones, and of such grass-roots philosophers as Finley Peter Dunne's Mr. Dooley, the Irish barkeep whose comments on national and international affairs delighted readers from the time of the Spanish-American War through World War I. Jewish immigrants of the early twentieth century peopled Montague Glass's books about Potash and Perlmutter, and Leo C. Rosten's stories about a night school for adults, *The Education of H*y*m*a*n K*a*p*l*a*n* (1937), also used dialect to humorous effect. However, dialect has gradually disappeared as a comic device in modern American humor.

Similarly, the humorous column that was a regular feature of most newspapers during the nineteenth and early twentieth centuries is less often encountered today. James M. Bailey wrote as the "Danbury News Man" after the Civil War; Eugene Field published his "Sharps and Flats" column in the *Chicago Daily News* until 1895; Franklin P. Adams, as "F.P.A.," did "The Conning Tower" (which appeared in several New York papers) for nearly thirty years. The most original of these humorists were George Ade, whose "Fables in Slang" helped fill his space in the *Chicago Record*, and Don Marquis, the New York columnist and creator of archy, the poetry-writing cockroach, and mehitabel, the cat. Currently, both Art Buchwald and Russell Baker continue to be prolific, syndicated, and highly popular.

Magazines have also helped mold the public taste in humorous writing. Most of the southwestern stories appeared originally in William Porter's *Spirit of the Times*, and the end of the nineteenth century brought several new humor periodicals, among them *Puck* and the first *Life*. Without question, however, the most important magazine for twentieth-century humor has been *The New Yorker*. Founded in 1925, with the legendary Harold Ross as editor, it soon became the flagship of a new kind of American comedy, witty, sophisticated, distinctly urban and urbane. It was, as the first issue announced, "not for the old lady in Dubuque"; its mascot, Eustace Tilley, wore top hat and tails, not a farmer's overalls.

At about the same time, the older line of rural humorists was culminating in Frank McKinney Hubbard, whose "Abe Martin" character had been amusing Americans since the turn of the century, and in Will Rogers, the beloved Oklahoma cowboy of the 1920s and '30s. The newer funmaker was exemplified by *The New Yorker*'s E. B. White, whose polished, graceful style made a flexible medium for his sharp wit. Still, the urbanite White, in collections of essays like *Quo Vadimus? or, The Case for the Bicycle* (1939) and *One Man's Meat* (1942), yearned for the peace of a simpler life. His image of the little man caught in the complexities of modern living was taken up by other writers of the *New Yorker* school, like Robert Benchley, S. J. Perelman, and, most successfully, James Thurber. Thurber's "The Secret Life of Walter Mitty," about a timid man forced by a domineering wife to retreat into his daydreams, has become a classic in our comic literature. Dorothy Parker and Ring Lardner also achieved wide reputations with their seriocomic portrayals of contemporary little minds—the kind of mentality H. L. Mencken lambasted in his attacks on the "booboisie."

The motif of the little soul remains strong in our humor; it is portrayed in the popular comedy routines of Woody Allen and in the light verse of Judith Viorst. But since World War II humor in the

United States has undergone another major change: now its predominant mood is dark. Our literature has always shown strains of black humor, which asks us to laugh at what is essentially unfunny, at the grotesque and the painful. In the nineteenth century, Edgar Allan Poe tinged his horror tales with humor, and Ambrose Bierce wrote a grisly satire about boiled babies; many of the stories of Nathaniel Hawthorne and Herman Melville are stamped with an absurd humor. More recently, Nathanael West's short novels *Miss Lonelyhearts* (1933) and *The Day of the Locust* (1939) developed the comic potential of the pathos and terror in modern life. By the 1950s and '60s morbid jesting had become the characteristic stance of our comic writers.

The tag "black humor" has been applied to the works of a wide group of contemporary novelists, including John Hawkes, Kurt Vonnegut, Jr., James Purdy, J. P. Donleavy, Thomas Pynchon, Donald Barthelme, Vladimir Nabokov, William Burroughs, Thomas Berger, and Joseph Heller. Despite their different styles, generally these writers question traditional values and beliefs, and generally their humor is parodic, linked to older forms. They write not so much novels as imitations of novels and other literary forms; thus, John Barth refers back to one of the first comic works written in America with his own *Sot-Weed Factor* (1967).

This is not to say that twentieth-century comedy no longer relies on folk humor. On the contrary, the violence of frontier comedy, with its pain and brutality, continues to appeal to contemporary writers. Eudora Welty's first novel, *The Robber Bridegroom* (1942), tells of incredibly long fistfights, of Indians and outlaws, even of Mike Fink, the tall-tale hero. The grotesque characterizations so typical of the southwestern tales reappear in Erskine Caldwell's *Tobacco Road* (1932) and in the brilliant fiction of Flannery O'Connor. Nobel Prize winner William Faulkner also makes use of grotesque folk comedy; *As I Lay Dying* (1930) is a comic treatment of death and depravity in backwoods America, and *Sanctuary* (1931), one of his most popular works, mingles comedy with a tale of rape and murder. Many of Faulkner's themes and characters are borrowed from our comic lore; *The Mansion* (1959), for example, is yet another ribald account of tricksters tricked.

Nor has ethnic humor, long a major strain in our comic tradition, lost its importance. Jewish novelists have combined the exaggerations of frontier comedy with the self-mocking humor of their East European ancestors. The schlemiel, or antihero, appears in various guises: as the sexually obsessed Alexander Portnoy, whose long lament to his analyst constitutes the substance of Philip Roth's best-selling *Portnoy's Complaint* (1969); as the scholar and would-be lover in Saul Bellow's *Herzog* (1964) and the aspiring academic in Bernard Malamud's *A New Life* (1961); as Bruce J. Friedman's inept suburbanite in *Stern* (1962). Antiheroes are also central in the comic fiction of many black writers.

The young hero of Ralph Ellison's *Invisible Man* (1952) is so antiheroic that he is in fact invisible in the eyes of white society. In the poetry of Langston Hughes and the novels of Claude McKay, *Home to Harlem* (1928), *Banjo* (1929), and *Banana Bottom* (1933), we frequently find a comic celebration of black life styles. In the poetry of Don Lee, in the fiction of Richard Wright, in the plays of Douglas Turner Ward, humor often blends with social protest, as it does in the novels and essays of James Baldwin. Baldwin's most recent book, *The Devil Finds Work* (1976), analyzes the way American films distort reality, but it deals largely with what Baldwin calls "the black American experience." Indeed, as long as American comedy and satire continue to reflect American culture, ethnic concerns will figure prominently in our literature.

Suggested Topics for Writing and Discussion

The following topics indicate areas in American humor that students may want to explore further or write about. Many of the questions can be answered by using only this sourcebook; others require more extensive research. The instructor should be consulted for help in choosing an appropriate subject, either from this list or from a topic suggested by the questions accompanying each selection.

1. This text has focused on the three major figures in American humor: the wise fool, the storyteller, and the little soul. You might investigate one of these types in greater detail by studying a writer or group of writers whose work you particularly enjoyed. You might want to learn more about a specific character, like Davy Crockett or Mike Fink. Or you could discuss other appearances of each figure. What television comedians can you name, for example, who have assumed the role of the little soul?

2. Write an essay comparing the three major types of comic figure. Do they have more similarities than differences? Explain. Describe other character types used by our comedians. How are they related to the figures discussed in this text? Which types are becoming more popular? Less popular?

3. Invent a modern wise-fool persona, carefully selecting such details as occupation, education, social status, and political concerns. Will your grass-roots philosopher speak in dialect? Have a sidekick? In what ways will this character be stupid? Shrewd?

4. Invent a little-soul character. What kinds of problems will concern the little soul who is a man? A woman? Why will your sketch probably take place in the city or the suburbs, rather than on a farm?

5. Review the selection by Constance Rourke on tall-tale humor. How has America changed since the birth of the tall tale? In what ways is it the same? How does Kurt Vonnegut, Jr., parody the tall tale in "Tom Edison's Shaggy Dog"? Write a contemporary tall tale, perhaps about an astronaut or a sports hero. Or use the form, as Vonnegut does, to satirize certain traits in the American character.

6. Many comic works, like the Vonnegut story, are parodies. Can every

creative work be parodied? Explain. Try writing a burlesque of a favorite TV show, book, or film.

7. Perhaps using Ambrose Bierce's "Devil's Definitions" as a model, try writing your own comic definitions. How do they reflect your biases?

8. Explain why American humor has generally been neglected by literary critics. As a starting point, read Samuel Johnson's "The Difficulty of Defining Comedy" (reprinted in Paul Lauter's *Theories of Comedy*). How does this essay by an eighteenth-century Englishman apply to comedy in the United States?

9. Study the humor of a particular ethnic group. What insights do you gain from a book like Theodor Reik's *Jewish Wit* (1962)? How has the humor of minority groups shaped American humor in general?

10. Analyze the role of bigotry in our humor. Do you think humor has served to unite us as a people or to divide us? Consider especially the nature of such popular TV shows as "All in the Family." Is our attitude toward the "lovable bigot" changing? How?

11. Women have been another favorite subject of American humor. Give examples and explain. Discuss how this kind of humor, too—or our attitude toward it—may be changing.

12. America has produced few well-known female writers of humor. Explain why you think this is so. Or choose one, such as Dorothy Parker or Nora Ephron, and explore her work in that light. Is it different in significant ways from humor written by men? Describe the comedy produced by the women's liberation movement.

13. The humor in this book covers a wide variety of comic styles. Compare and contrast several of these styles, illustrating them by references to particular works, or compare the styles of two different humorists.

14. What is meant by "low comedy"? What are its most common techniques? How significant is it in America? Explain.

15. Discuss the "higher humor" in American letters. You might refer particularly to the poetry of Walt Whitman or Emily Dickinson, to Henry David Thoreau's *Walden*, or to Ralph Waldo Emerson's essay "The Comic." What is the relationship between "higher humor" and American transcendentalism?

16. In the view of some critics, Edgar Allan Poe's horror stories—"The Fall of the House of Usher," "The Pit and the Pendulum," and others—are burlesques. Explain why you agree or disagree. What, if anything, do these stories have in common with Poe's "Diddling" piece, reprinted here?

17. Discuss the art of stand-up comedy or your favorite stand-up comedian. How appropriate is the term "stand-up comedy"? What themes and techniques characterize this brand of comedy?

18. Read Stanley Hoig's *The Humor of the American Cowboy* as the beginning of a study on western humor. Describe the characters, situations, and artistic devices typically used by western comedians. Review the sample of Will Rogers's humor reprinted here, and explain why he is often referred to as "the cowboy philosopher."

19. Silent-film comedy has been compared to the theater of the English Renaissance. In what ways is this true? Who were the comic geniuses of silent film, and what characteristics marked their art? As a start, reread the article here by James Agee, and then read Hugh Kenner's "The Man of Sense as Buster Keaton," in his book *The Counterfeiters* (1968).

20. America has traditionally been a puritanical country, and yet our humor has recently been saturated with scatology. Why might this be described as a kind of "inverted puritanism"? Refer especially to the work of Lenny Bruce. What do critics mean when they call Bruce a "shaman"? For background, see Albert Goldman and Lawrence Schiller, *Ladies and Gentlemen, Lenny Bruce!* (1974), and listen to some of Bruce's recordings. .

21. Investigate nonsense verse like that of Ogden Nash. Try writing some of your own, remembering that good nonsense always relies on a basis of sense.

22. Make a study of shaggy-dog stories like the one by Kurt Vonnegut, Jr., reprinted here. How do you account for their popularity? Be sure to consult Eric Partridge's *The Shaggy Dog Story*.

23. Reread the introduction to Part 1, "The Comic American." How poignantly do you and your friends feel the cultural crisis it refers to? In what ways is your humor a response to that crisis?

24. What story in this book did you find the most humorous? Explain the techniques that make it funny. How are they different from devices used in other selections?

25. Review the direction American humor is taking and speculate on its future. Begin by reading some of the articles cited in the introduction to Part 5, "Theories and Criticism." Explain why you agree or disagree with what they say.

26. Show how contemporary humor continues to draw, in theme and technique, on the traditions of the past. One approach might be to compare a piece by an early humorist, perhaps Ben Franklin, with a modern work in the same form.

27. Examine the types of humor that appear in your daily newspaper (excluding the comic strips). If there is a regular humor column, describe it. Is there humor in features not meant to be primarily comic, like the advice-to-the-lovelorn column? How?

28. Write a paper on your favorite comic strip, analyzing the reasons you like it. Discuss both the verbal humor and the graphic humor,

explaining how they have developed or changed during the years you have been reading the strip. You might also compare your favorite with a similar strip.

29. Review the history of comic strips. Which have been the most popular? How do they reflect American culture? In what ways are they a particularly American form of humor? Is their popularity increasing or declining?

30. How funny are the funnies? Survey the kinds of comedy found in comic strips today, and compare their humor with that of other visual media.

31. Investigate the amount and kind of humor found in a specific literary genre, such as science fiction or detective fiction. What function does comedy have in the type of literature you are studying?

32. Write a paper on black humor. The novelist Bruce Jay Friedman, one of the originators of the term, claims that it is easier to define a corned-beef sandwich. Do you agree? Read one or two of the writers discussed in the selection by Ihab Hassan to support your conclusions.

33. Study the humor of the Broadway theater. You might want to concentrate on the comedies of a particularly successful playwright, such as Neil Simon. How has Broadway humor changed in recent years?

34. Do the same for humor in contemporary films. Are there many kinds of comedy in our films? Give examples. Can a high percentage of American films be considered comic? Discuss.

35. Study several outstanding comedians of radio, like George Burns and Gracie Allen, Edgar Bergen, or Ed Wynn. Listen to the original sound tracks (see the listing in Comedy on Records) and describe a typical show. How was this comedy uniquely suited to the medium of radio? What does it have in common with other types of American comedy?

36. Beginning with Leon Harris's *The Fine Art of Political Wit*, explore American political humor. You might study the speeches of particular leaders known for their wit, such as Abraham Lincoln, John F. Kennedy, or Adlai Stevenson.

37. Discuss the art and the influence of political cartoons in the United States. How do the caricatures of Thomas Nast (see p. 62) compare with those of a modern cartoonist, like Herblock? Show how this kind of humor has helped shape public opinion, as in the Watergate scandal, for instance.

38. What is meant by "comedy of manners"? How is this brand of comedy developed in the work of Edith Wharton, Henry James, or F. Scott Fitzgerald? Write an essay describing the comic strategies in

one of their novels, perhaps James's *The Ambassadors* or *The Portrait of a Lady* or Fitzgerald's *The Great Gatsby.*

39. Comedy traditionally deals with the efforts of individuals to survive and to create a new and better world. Investigate the themes of survival and creativity in American comedy. Why do so many comedies end with marriage? Why do comedies often involve disguise and trickery? How does comedy celebrate the creative power of art itself?

40. Read Nathanael West's *Miss Lonelyhearts* and comment on the notion that modern comic heroes seem more like tragic heroes. Be sure to define your terms carefully.

41. Investigate the child as a comic figure in American literature. Why is the child or childlike figure a popular guise for comedians? How has our attitude toward this figure changed? Compare, for instance, Booth Tarkington's *Penrod* with Robert Benchley's "Kiddie-Kar Travel."

42. Explain how American humor has exploited the resources of the American language. Describe the role dialect has played in our comic tradition. Why is humor often difficult to translate into another language?

43. Compare American humor with the humor of other cultures. You might begin by reviewing Louis Kronenberger's essay in this volume and the section on "American and Foreign Humor" in Jesse Bier's *The Rise and Fall of American Humor.* Explain why you agree or disagree with their conclusions.

44. Some critics claim that the best American humor is essentially satiric. What evidence is there to support such a position? Be sure to look up the origin of our national symbol, Uncle Sam.

45. Analyze humor from a psychological point of view. What is meant by a "sense of humor"? Your research could begin with Sigmund Freud's *Jokes and Their Relation to the Unconscious* and Arthur Koestler's *The Act of Creation.*

46. Is humor a form of escape literature? What writers included in this text would you classify as escapists? Explain.

47. Trace the history of theatrical burlesque, discussing its origin, development, and ultimate decline in the United States. Who were some of the prominent burlesque comedians? Describe their art.

48. Write a paper on the humor of the animated cartoon. How do you account for Walt Disney's great success? In what sense is Mickey Mouse a hero of popular culture?

49. Make a study of humor magazines, such as *Spirit of the Times,* the first *Life, The New Yorker, Mad,* and *National Lampoon.* Show how they have influenced the development of American humor, and compare their comic styles.

50. Write a paper explaining why *Huckleberry Finn* is considered a classic of American humor. What is the relationship between this novel and other nineteenth-century comic works? For additional insights, refer to Kenneth Lynn's *Mark Twain and Southwestern Humor.*
51. Describe the humor of TV quiz shows. How is it geared to the audience's feelings of aggression and superiority? Give examples. How typical is this of TV humor? Of humor in general?
52. Study the work of an outstanding critic of American humor, like Walter Blair. What key insights has Blair given us? Where do you agree or disagree with his views? (A checklist of Blair's writings is in the April 1975 issue of *Studies in American Humor.*)
53. Examine the "sick jokes" that are popular today. What are their common themes? Why are they so appealing? How have they become part of our comic literature?
54. Write an essay on one of the terms defined in the Glossary, illustrating it with examples from the selections you have read. Or write an essay distinguishing between "humor" and "comedy." In what ways are such distinctions useful? Dangerous?

Suggestions for Further Reading

The reading lists that follow cover only the more significant writings that explore or illustrate American humor. For reasons of space, many fine works have had to be omitted, but the aim has been to provide a basic bibliography rather than an exhaustive one. Works by the authors of selections appearing in the text will be found in the headnotes to the individual selections; the Background Reading and the History and Criticism sections here are limited to collections and full-length studies. The intent is for students to use these titles (many of which are available in paperback editions) as the starting point for more extensive reading reflecting their individual tastes. Additional bibliographic information, as well as excellent essays on humor, are to be found in the journals *Scholia Satyrica, Journal of Popular Culture, American Literature,* and, especially, *Studies in American Humor.*

Background Reading

Blistein, Elmer, *Comedy in Action* (1964).
Clark, John R., and Motto, Anna, eds., *Satire: That Blasted Art* (1973).
Cook, Albert, *The Dark Voyage and the Golden Mean* (1966).
Eastman, Max, *The Enjoyment of Laughter* (1936).
Elliott, Robert, *The Power of Satire: Magic, Ritual, Art* (1960); *The Satirist: His Temperament, Motive and Influence* (1963).
Feibleman, James K., *In Praise of Comedy: A Study in Its Theory and Practice* (1939).
Freud, Sigmund, *Jokes and Their Relation to the Unconscious* (1963).
Grotjahn, Martin, *Beyond Laughter* (1957).
Highet, Gilbert, *The Anatomy of Satire* (1962).
Hodgart, Matthew, *Satire* (1962).
Kernan, Alvin, *The Plot of Satire* (1965).
Koestler, Arthur, *The Act of Creation* (1964).
Lauter, Paul, ed., *Theories of Comedy* (1964). See especially "The Argument of Comedy" by Northrop Frye and "The Great Dramatic Forms: The Comic Rhythm" by Susanne K. Langer.
Leacock, Stephen Butler, *Humour and Humanity: An Introduction to the Study of Humour* (1937).
Levin, Harry, ed., *Veins of Humor* (1972).

Paulson, Ronald, *The Fictions of Satire* (1967).
——, ed., *Satire: Modern Essays in Criticism* (1971).
Potts, Leonard J., *Comedy* (1966).
Sypher, Wylie, ed., *Comedy* (1956). See especially "Laughter" by Henri Bergson and "An Essay on Comedy" by George Meredith.
Wisse, Ruth R., *The Schlemiel as Modern Hero* (1971).
Worcester, David, *The Art of Satire* (1940).

History and Criticism

Bier, Jesse, *The Rise and Fall of American Humor* (1968).
Blair, Walter, *Horse Sense in American Humor, from Benjamin Franklin to Ogden Nash* (1942); *Mark Twain and Huck Finn* (1960).
——, and Meine, F. J., *Half Horse, Half Alligator: The Growth of the Mike Fink Legend* (1956).
De Voto, Bernard, *Mark Twain's America* (1932).
Gill, Brendan, *Here at the New Yorker* (1975).
Glanz, Rudolf, *The Jew In Early American Wit and Graphic Humor* (1972).
Harris, Leon A., *The Fine Art of Political Wit* (1964).
Hauck, Richard Boyd, *A Cheerful Nihilism: Confidence and the Absurd in American Humorous Fiction* (1971).
Hoig, Stanley W., *The Humor of the American Cowboy* (1958).
Inge, M. Thomas, ed., *The Frontier Humorists: Critical Views* (1975).
Kittredge, George Lyman, *The Old Farmer and His Almanack* (1904).
Lynn, Kenneth, *Mark Twain and Southwestern Humor* (1972).
Miles, Elton, *Southwest Humorists* (1968).
Partridge, Eric, *The Shaggy Dog Story: Its Origin, Development and Nature* (1954).
Tandy, Jennette Reid, *Crackerbox Philosophers in American Humor and Satire* (1925).
Thorp, Willard, *American Humorists* (1964).
Tuttleton, James W., *The Novel of Manners in America* (1972).
Yates, Norris W., *William T. Porter and the Spirit of the Times: A Study of the Big Bear School of Humor* (1957); *The American Humorist: Conscience of the Twentieth Century* (1964).

Collections

Blair, Walter, ed., *Native American Humor* (1937).
Carlisle, Henry C., Jr., ed., *American Satire in Prose and Verse* (1962).
Cerf, Bennett, ed., *An Encyclopedia of Modern American Humor* (1954).
Clough, Ben C., ed., *The American Imagination at Work: Tall Tales and Folk Tales* (1947).
Cohen, Hennig, and Dillingham, W. B., eds., *Humor of the Old Southwest* (1964).
Hughes, Langston, ed., *The Book of Negro Humor* (1966).

Lynn, Kenneth S., ed., *The Comic Tradition in America: An Anthology of American Humor* (1968).
Meine, F. J., *Tall Tales of the Southwest* (1930).
Weber, Brom, ed., *Art of American Humor: An Anthology* (1970).
White, E. B., and White, Katherine S., eds., *Subtreasury of American Humor* (1941).
Wilt, Napier, *Some American Humorists* (1929).

A Sampling of American Humor

Allen, Steve, *Schmock-Schmock!* (1975).
Anderson, Sherwood, *Winesburg, Ohio* (1919); *The Triumph of the Egg* (1921).
Bailey, James M., *Life in Danbury* (1873).
Baldwin, James, *Another Country* (1961).
Baldwin, Joseph G., *Flush Times of Alabama and Mississippi* (1853).
Bangs, John Kendrick, *A House-Boat on the Styx* (1899); *The Idiot at Home* (1900).
Barth, John, *Giles Goat Boy or, The Revised New Syllabus* (1966); *The End of the Road* (1967); *The Sot-Weed Factor* (1967); *Lost in the Funhouse* (1968); *Chimera* (1972).
Bellow, Saul, *Dangling Man* (1944); *The Victim* (1947); *The Adventures of Augie March* (1953); *Seize the Day* (1956); *Henderson the Rain King* (1959); *Herzog* (1964); *Mosby's Memoirs and Other Stories* (1968); *Mr. Sammler's Planet* (1970).
Berger, Thomas, *Crazy in Berlin* (1958); *Reinhart in Love* (1962); *Little Big Man* (1964); *Vital Parts* (1970).
Bontemps, Arna, *God Sends Sunday* (1931).
Brackenridge, Hugh Henry, *Modern Chivalry: Containing the Adventures of Captain John Farrago and Teague O'Regan His Servant* (1792–1815).
Bruce, Lenny, *How to Talk Dirty and Influence People* (1965).
Burroughs, William, *Naked Lunch* (1962).
Cabell, James Branch, *The Cream of the Jest* (1917); *Jurgen* (1919); *The Silver Stallion: A Comedy of Redemption* (1926).
Cahan, Abraham, *The Rise of David Levinsky* (1917).
Caldwell, Erskine, *Tobacco Road* (1932).
Cheever, John, *The Wapshot Chronicle* (1957).
Cobb, Irvin S., *Speaking of Operations—* (1916).
Cohen, Leonard, *Beautiful Losers* (1966).
Coover, Robert, *The Universal Baseball Association, Inc., J. Henry Waugh, Prop.* (1968).
Crane, Stephen, *Whilomville Stories* (1900).
Crockett, David, *A Narrative of the Life of David Crockett* (1834); *An Account of Col. Crockett's Tour to the North and Down East* (1835).
Cullen, Countee, *Color* (1925); *On These I Stand* (1947).
Cummings, E. E., *Complete Poems 1913–1962* (1972).
Day, Clarence, *This Simian World* (1920); *God and My Father* (1932); *Life with Father* (1935).
Donleavy, J. P., *The Ginger Man* (1958).

Ellison, Ralph, *Invisible Man* (1952).
Ephron, Nora, *Crazy Salad: Some Things About Women* (1975).
Field, Eugene, *The Tribune Primer* (1882).
Field, Joseph M., *The Drama in Pokerville* (1847).
Fisher, Rudolph, *The Walls of Jericho* (1928).
Fitzgerald, F. Scott, *The Great Gatsby* (1925); *Tender Is the Night* (1934).
Ford, Corey, *You Can Always Tell a Fisherman* (1959).
Friedman, Bruce Jay, *Stern* (1962); *A Mother's Kisses* (1964).
Gaddis, William, *Recognitions* (1955).
Glass, Montague, *Potash and Perlmutter* (1910).
Golden, Harry, *Only in America* (1950).
Gregory, Dick, *From the Back of the Bus* (1962).
Haliburton, Thomas Chandler, *The Clockmaker, or, The Sayings and Doings of Samuel Slick, of Slickville* (1837–40).
Harte, Bret, *The Luck of Roaring Camp and Other Sketches* (1870).
Hawkes, John, *The Cannibal* (1949); *The Beetle Leg* (1951); *The Lime Twig* (1961); *Second Skin* (1964); *The Blood Oranges* (1971); *Death, Sleep, & the Traveler* (1974); *Travesty* (1976).
Hawthorne, Nathaniel, *The House of the Seven Gables* (1851).
Hooper, Johnson Jones, *Some Adventures of Capt. Simon Suggs, Late of the Tallapoosa Volunteers . . . by a Country Editor* (1845).
Hubbard, Frank McKinney, *Abe Martin's Almanack* (1907); *Abe Martin's Primer* (1914); *Comments of Abe Martin and His Neighbors* (1923).
Hurston, Zora Neale, *Jonah's Gourd Vine* (1934); *Men and Mules* (1935).
James, Henry, *The American* (1877); *The Europeans* (1878); *The Portrait of a Lady* (1881); *The Bostonians* (1886); *The Wings of the Dove* (1902); *The Ambassadors* (1903); *The Golden Bowl* (1904).
Kesey, Ken, *One Flew Over the Cuckoo's Nest* (1962).
Leacock, Stephen Butler, *Literary Lapses* (1913); *Essays and Literary Studies* (1916); *Last Leaves* (1945).
Lewis, Sinclair, *Main Street* (1920); *Babbitt* (1922); *Arrowsmith* (1925); *Elmer Gantry* (1927); *Dodsworth* (1929).
Loos, Anita, *Gentlemen Prefer Blondes* (1925); *But Gentlemen Marry Brunettes* (1928).
McCullers, Carson, *The Ballad of the Sad Café* (1951).
McKay, Claude, *Home to Harlem* (1928).
Mailer, Norman, *Why Are We in Vietnam?* (1967).
Mencken, H. L., *Prejudices* (1919–27).
Morris, Wright, *My Uncle Dudley* (1942); *The Field of Vision* (1956).
Nabokov, Vladimir, *Lolita* (1958); *Pale Fire* (1962); *Ada* (1969).
Nash, Ogden, *I Wouldn't Have Missed It: Selected Poems* (1972).
Newell, Robert H., *The Orpheus C. Kerr Papers* (1862–71).
Paulding, James, *The Lion of the West* (1830).
Percy, Walker, *The Moviegoer* (1961); *Love in the Ruins* (1971).
Purdy, James, *Malcolm* (1959).
Pynchon, Thomas, *V* (1963); *The Crying of Lot 49* (1966).
Reed, Ishmael, *The Free-lance Pallbearers* (1967); *Yellow Back Radio Broke-Down* (1969).

Robb, John S., *Streaks of Squatter Life, and Far-West Scenes* (1847).
Rosten, Leo, *The Education of H*y*m*a*n K*a*p*l*a*n* (1937).
Salinger, J. D., *The Catcher in the Rye* (1951); *Franny and Zooey* (1961).
Schuyler, George, *Black No More* (1931).
Shaw, Henry Wheeler, *Josh Billings, His Sayings* (1865).
Shillaber, B. P., *Life and Sayings of Mrs. Partington* (1854).
Simon, Neil, *The Comedy of Neil Simon* (1971).
Smith, Charles H., *Bill Arp, So-Called* (1866).
Smith, Sol, *Sol Smith's Theatrical Apprenticeship* (1845); *Theatrical Journey-Work* (1854).
Southern, Terry, *The Magic Christian* (1960).
Stevens, Wallace, *Harmonium* (1923).
Stowe, Harriet Beecher, *Oldtown Folks* (1869); *Sam Lawson's Oldtown Fireside Stories* (1872).
Sullivan, Frank, *A Pearl in Every Oyster* (1938); *The Night the Old Nostalgia Burned Down* (1953).
Taliaferro, H. E., *Fisher's River (North Carolina) Scenes and Characters* (1859).
Tarkington, Booth, *Penrod* (1914).
Tensas, Madison (pseud.), *Odd Leaves from the Life of a Louisiana Swamp Doctor* (1850).
Thompson, William Tappan, *Major Jones's Courtship* (1843); *Chronicles of Pineville* (1845); *Major Jones's Sketches of Travels* (1847).
Thoreau, Henry David, *Walden: or, Life in the Woods* (1854).
Thurman, Wallace, *The Blacker the Berry* (1929); *Infants of the Spring* (1932).
Trumbull, John, *M'Fingal* (1776).
Tyler, Royall, *The Contrast* (1787).
Updike, John, *Rabbit, Run* (1960); *Couples* (1968).
Ward, Douglas Turner, *Two Plays: Happy Ending and Day of Absence* (1971).
Welty, Eudora, *The Robber Bridegroom* (1942); *The Ponder Heart* (1954); *Losing Battles* (1970).
Whitcher, Frances M., *The Widow Bedott Papers* (1835).
Wright, Charles, *The Wig* (1966).

Caricatures and Cartoons

For background information about pictorial humor, the following sources may be consulted:

Becker, Stephen D., *Comic Art in America: A Social History of the Funnies, the Political Cartoons, Magazine Humor, Sporting Cartoons and Animated Cartoons* (1959).
Seldes, Gilbert, *The Seven Lively Arts* (1957).
Sheridan, Martin, *Comics and Their Creators*, rev. ed. (1944).
Waugh, Coulton, *The Comics* (1947).

A research project on a particular artist or style of cartoon humor might be suggested by this selected listing of primary sources:

Addams, Chas., *Monster Rally* (1950); *Nightcrawlers* (1957); *Dear Dead Days: A Family Album* (1959); *Black Maria* (1960).

Arno, Peter, *Peter Arno's Parade* (1929); *Peter Arno's Circus* (1931); *Peter Arno's Cartoon Review* (1941); *Peter Arno's Man in the Show* (1944); *Sizzling Platter* (1949); *Ladies & Gentlemen* (1951); *Hell of a Way to Run a Railroad* (1956).

Feiffer, Jules, *Sick, Sick, Sick* (1958); *Passionella, and Other Stories* (1959).

Herriman, George, *Krazy Kat* (1975).

Hockinson, Helen Elna, *The Ladies, God Bless 'em!* (1950); *When Were You Built?* (1951).

Kelly, Walt, *Pogo: Cartoons* (1951); *I Go Pogo* (1952); *Pogo Papers* (1953); *Uncle Pogo So-so Stories* (1953); *Pogo Stepmother Goose* (1954); *Pogo Sunday Brunch* (1959); *Ten Ever-lovin' Blue-eyed Years with Pogo* (1959); *Beau Pogo* (1960); *Pogo à la Sundae, Including Australia and the Two Egg Candidates* (1961).

Levine, David, *Literary Caricatures from the New York Review of Books* (1964).

Mad Magazine editors, *Howling Mad* (1974); *The Ideas of Mad* (1974); *Mad Marginals* (1974); *Questionable Mad* (1974); *Mad Frontier* (1975).

The New Yorker editors, *The New Yorker Album* (various editions); *The New Yorker Album of Sports and Games* (1958); *The New Yorker Cartoon with the Talk of the Town*, special edition for the Armed Forces (1945); *The New Yorker Twenty-fifth Anniversary Album, 1925–1950* (1951); *1942 New Yorker Album* (1941).

Saturday Evening Post editors, *Honey, I'm Home! A Collection of Cartoons from the Post* (1954); *Saturday Evening Post Cartoon Festival: Twenty-five Years of Post Cartoons* (1958).

Schulz, Charles M., *Teen-Ager Is Not a Disease* (1970); *You're the Greatest, Charlie Brown* (1971); *Don't Give Up, Charlie Brown* (1974); *You're on Your Own, Snoopy* (1974); *You're So Smart, Snoopy* (1974); *You've Got It Made, Snoopy* (1974); *Peanuts Jubilee* (1975); *Watch Out, Charlie Brown* (1975).

Steinberg, Saul, *The Art of Living* (1949); *The Passport* (1954); *The Labyrinth* (1960); *The Inspector* (1973).

Trudeau, Garry, *The Doonesbury Chronicles* (1975); *Wouldn't a Gremlin Have Been More Sensible?* (1975).

Filmography of the Classic Comedians

All films are available from the Macmillan Audio Brandon Co.

Charlie Chaplin   *Between Showers, Caught in a Cabaret, Getting Acquainted, Mabel's Married Life, Making a Living, The Masquerader, The New Janitor, The Property Man,* and *Tango Tangles* (1914); *His New Job* and *A Night Out* (1915); *Behind the Screen, The Count, The Fireman, The Floorwalker, One A.M., The Pawnshop, The Rink,* and *The Vagabond* (1916); *The Adventurer, The Cure, Easy Street,* and *The Immigrant* (1917); *Triple Trouble* (1918).

Buster Keaton   Feature-length films: *Our Hospitality* (1923); *The Navigator* and *Sherlock, Jr.* (1924); *Go West* and *Seven Chances* (1925); *Battling Butler* and *The General* (1926); *College* and *Steamboat Bill, Jr.* (1927). Short films, each approximately 22 minutes: *Convict 13, The High Sign, Neighbors, One Week,* and *The Scarecrow* (1920); *The Boat, The Goat, The Haunted House, The Paleface,* and *The Playhouse* (1921); *Balloonatics, The Blacksmith, Cops, Daydreams, The Electric House, The Frozen North,* and *My Wife's Relations* (1922).

Harry Langdon   Feature-length films: *The Strong Man* and *Tramp Tramp Tramp* (1926); *Long Pants* and *Three's a Crowd* (1927); *The Chaser* (1928); *Hallelujah, I'm a Bum* (1933). Short films: *The Sea Squawk* (1924); *Boobs in the Woods* and *His Marriage Wow* (1925); *Soldier Man* (1926).

Laurel and Hardy   *The Finishing Touch, The Second Hundred Years,* and *With Love and Hisses* (1927); *Leave Em Laughing, Putting Pants on Philip, Two Tars,* and *You're Darn Tootin* (1928); *Bacon Grabbers, Big Business, Double Whoopee, Men O'War, Perfect Day,* and *Wrong Again* (1929); *Below Zero, Brats,* and *Hog Wild* (1930); *Laughing Gravy* (1931); *The Music Box* and *Their First Mistake* (1932); *Busy Bodies, Dirty Work, Me and My Pal,* and *Twice Two* (1933); *The Fixer Uppers* (1935).

Mack Sennett Comedies   Each 20 minutes: *The Big Fibber, Bring Em Back Sober, Caliente Love, Courting Trouble, Daddy Knows Best, Don't Play Bridge with Your Wife, Dream Stuff, False Impressions, Hawkins and Watkins, Inc., Husband's Reunion, Jimmy's New Yacht, Knockout Kisses, The Loud Mouth, Meet the Senator, The Plumber and the Lady, Roadhouse Queen, See You Tonight, Sweet Cookie, Too Many Highballs,* and *A Wrestler's Bride.*

W. C. Fields   Each from 15 to 22 minutes: *Pool Sharks* (1915); *The Golf Specialist* (1930); *The Dentist* (1932); *The Barber Shop, The Fatal Glass of Beer,* and *The Pharmacist* (1933). About 60 minutes: *W. C. Fields Festival* (1933).

The Marx Brothers   About 30 minutes: *Marx Brothers Festival!* ("Pigskin Capers" scene from *Horse-Feathers*, "This Is War" from *Duck Soup*, and "The Incredible Jewel Robbery").

Robert Benchley   Each 10 minutes: *Crime Control, The Forgotten Man, How to Take a Vacation, Keeping in Shape, The Man's Angle, Nothing but Nerves, Trouble with Husbands, Waiting for Baby,* and *The Witness.*

For reference material on comic films, see:

Anobile, Richard J., ed., *A Fine Mess! Verbal and Visual Gems from the Crazy World of Laurel and Hardy* (1975).
Lahue, Kalton C., *World of Laughter: The Motion Picture Comedy Short* (1966).
McCaffrey, Donald, *The Golden Age of Sound Comedy* (1973).
Maltin, Leonard, *Movie Comedy Teams* (1974).
Mast, Gerald, *The Comic Mind* (1973).
Parish, Jones, *The Slapstick Queens* (1973).
Poague, Leland A., *The Cinema of Frank Capra: An Approach to Film Comedy* (1975).

Comedy on Records

Listed below are the names of prominent artists whose comedy is now available on records. Additional information about individual titles will be found in any of the standard record catalogs. A more complete annotated audio-videography appears in the fall 1975 issue of *American Humor: An Interdisciplinary Newsletter.*

Don Adams
Jim Aggie
Woody Allen
Don Ameche and Frances Langford as the Bickersons
Archie
Jim Backus
Edgar Bergen and Charlie McCarthy
Blondie and Dagwood
Bob and Ray
Foster Brook
Mel Brooks
Lenny Bruce
George Burns and Gracie Allen
George Carlin
Johnny Carson
Carol Channing
Cheech and Chong
Bill Cosby
Ossie Davis
W. C. Fields
Redd Foxx
Stan Freberg
David Frye
Gasoline Alley and Moon Mullins
Buddy Hackett

Billy Holliday
Don Imus
George Jessel
Arte Johnson
Laurel and Hardy
Tom Lehrer
Rich Little
Little Orphan Annie
Little Rascals
Moms Mabley
Dewey Pigmeat Markham.
Groucho Marx
National Lampoon
Bob Newhart
Mike Nichols and Elaine May
S. J. Perelman
Richard Pryor
Carl Reiner
Don Rickles
Steve Rossi
Lily Tomlin
Jackie Vernon
Slappy White
Flip Wilson
Jonathan Winters
Ed Wynn

Acknowledgments (continued from copyright page)

HARCOURT BRACE JOVANOVICH, INC., for "A Late Encounter with the Enemy," copyright, 1953, by Flannery O'Connor, reprinted from her volume, *A Good Man Is Hard to Find and Other Stories*, by permission of Harcourt Brace Jovanovich, Inc. For excerpts from *American Humor* by Constance Rourke, copyright, 1931, by Harcourt Brace Jovanovich, Inc., copyright, 1959, by Alice D. Fore, reprinted by permission of the publishers.

HARPER & ROW, INC., for "Dusk in Fierce Pajamas" from *Quo Vadimus?* by E. B. White, copyright 1934 by E. B. White; originally appeared in *The New Yorker* and reprinted by permission of Harper & Row, Publishers, Inc.

IHAB HASSAN for "Echoes of Dark Laughter: The Comic Sense in Contemporary American Fiction" by Ihab Hassan, copyright © 1964 by Ihab Hassan; a part of this essay originally appeared in *The American Scholar*, autumn 1964, and in *The Rising Generation* (February 1973).

HOLT, RINEHART AND WINSTON, INC., for "The Storyteller," from *Vaudeville* by Joe Laurie, Jr., copyright 1953 by Joe Laurie, Jr., reprinted by permission of Holt, Rinehart and Winston, Publishers.

LIBERTY LIBRARY CORPORATION for "Back in Line" by Robert Benchley, copyright 1930 by Liberty Weekly, Inc., reprinted by permission of Liberty Library Corporation.

LITTLE, BROWN AND COMPANY for "Laughter in the Basement" from *Without a Stitch in Time* by Peter De Vries, copyright 1953 by Peter De Vries, reprinted by permission of Little, Brown and Co.; originally published in *The New Yorker*.

THE NEW AMERICAN LIBRARY, INC., for "Choices" and "Money" from *It's Hard to Be Hip over Thirty and Other Tragedies of Married Life* by Judith Viorst, copyright © 1968 by Judith Viorst, reprinted by arrangement with The New American Library, Inc., New York, N.Y.

NEW DIRECTIONS PUBLISHING CORPORATION for "Miss Lonelyhearts, Help me, Help Me" from *Miss Lonelyhearts* by Nathanael West, copyright 1933 by Nathanael West, © 1960 by Laura Perelman, reprinted by permission of New Directions Publishing Corporation.

THE NEW YORK TIMES COMPANY for excerpts from *Letters from a Self-made Diplomat to His President*, Vol. 1, by Will Rogers, © 1926 by The New York Times Company, reprinted by permission. For "On Conning Ed" by Russell Baker, © 1975 by The New York Times Company, reprinted by permission.

HAROLD OBER ASSOCIATES, INC., for "Dear Dr. Butts" from *Simple Takes a Wife* by Langston Hughes, copyright 1953 by Langston Hughes, reprinted by permission of Harold Ober Associates Incorporated.

DAVID OSSMAN for "The Adventures of Mark Time" by David Ossman, as performed by The Firesign Theatre; from *The Firesign Theatre's Big Mystery Joke Book*, copyright © 1974 by Philip Austin, Peter Bergman, David Ossman, and Philip Proctor, published by Straight Arrow Books.

G. P. PUTNAM'S SONS for "Upping Prison Requirements," reprinted by permission of G. P. Putnam's Sons from *The Establishment Is Alive and Well in Washington* by Art Buchwald, copyright © 1968, 1969 by Art Buchwald.

RANDOM HOUSE, INC., for "Spring Bulletin," copyright © 1968 by Woody Allen, reprinted from *Getting Even*, by Woody Allen, by permission of Random House, Inc. For excerpts from "Spotted Horses," copyright 1931 and renewed 1959 by William Faulkner, copyright 1940 and renewed 1968 by Estelle Faulkner and Jill Faulkner Summers, condensed by permission of Random House, Inc., from *The Faulkner Reader*, by William Faulkner.

RUTGERS UNIVERSITY PRESS for "The Great American Joke" from *The Comic Imagination in America* by Louis D. Rubin, Jr., © 1973 by Rutgers University Press.

CHARLES SCRIBNER'S SONS for "Large Coffee," reprinted by permission of Charles Scribner's Sons from *First and Last* by Ring Lardner, copyright 1934 by Ellis A. Lardner.

SIMON & SCHUSTER, INC., for "Catch-22: The Great American Trap" from *Catch 22* by Joseph Heller, copyright © 1955, 1961, by Joseph Heller. For "Insert Flap 'A' and Throw Away" from *The Most of S. J. Perelman*, copyright © 1930, 1931, 1932, 1933, 1935, 1936, 1937, 1938, 1939, 1940, 1941, 1942, 1943, 1944, 1945, 1946, 1947, 1948, 1950, 1951, 1952, 1953, 1955, 1956, 1957, 1958, by S. J. Perelman. Both are reprinted by permission of Simon & Schuster, Inc.

HELEN THURBER for "The Day the Dam Broke," copr. © 1933, 1961 by James Thurber, from *My Life and Hard Times*, published by Harper & Row. For "The Unicorn in the Garden" and "The Shrike and the Chipmunks," copr. © 1940 by James Thurber, copr. © 1968 by Helen Thurber, from *Fables for Our Time*, published by Harper & Row. All three selections were originally printed in *The New Yorker*.

THE VIKING PRESS, INC., for "Groucho and Chico Make a Deal" from *A Night at the Opera*, screenplay by George S. Kaufman and Morrie Ryskind, story by James Kevin McGuinness, starring the Marx Brothers, © by MGM Corporation, renewed © 1962 by Metro-Goldwyn-Mayer, Inc. For "Unfortunate Coincidence," "Comment," "Experience," "Social Note," and "Resume" from *The Portable Dorothy Parker*, copyright 1926, copyright renewed 1954 by Dorothy Parker. For "Our Mrs. Parker" from *While Rome Burns* by Alexander Woollcott, copyright 1934 by Alexander Woollcott, copyright © renewed 1962 by Joseph P. Hennessey. All are reprinted by permission of The Viking Press, Inc.

WALKER AND COMPANY for "Peanuts: The Americanization of Augustine" from *The Comic-Stripped American* by Arthur Asa Berger, published by Walker & Company, Inc., New York, N.Y., © 1973 by Arthur Asa Berger.

A 6
B 7
C 8
D 9
E 0
F 1
G 2
H 3
I 4
J 5